INTERNATIONAL
DEVELOPMENT

Sara Miller McCune founded SAGE Publishing in 1965 to support the dissemination of usable knowledge and educate a global community. SAGE publishes more than 1000 journals and over 800 new books each year, spanning a wide range of subject areas. Our growing selection of library products includes archives, data, case studies and video. SAGE remains majority owned by our founder and after her lifetime will become owned by a charitable trust that secures the company's continued independence.

Los Angeles | London | New Delhi | Singapore | Washington DC | Melbourne

INTERNATIONAL DEVELOPMENT

A GLOBAL PERSPECTIVE ON THEORY AND PRACTICE

PAUL BATTERSBY
& RAVI K. ROY

Los Angeles | London | New Delhi
Singapore | Washington DC | Melbourne

Los Angeles | London | New Delhi
Singapore | Washington DC | Melbourne

SAGE Publications Ltd
1 Oliver's Yard
55 City Road
London EC1Y 1SP

SAGE Publications Inc.
2455 Teller Road
Thousand Oaks, California 91320

SAGE Publications India Pvt Ltd
B 1/I 1 Mohan Cooperative Industrial Area
Mathura Road
New Delhi 110 044

SAGE Publications Asia-Pacific Pte Ltd
3 Church Street
#10-04 Samsung Hub
Singapore 049483

Editor: Natalie Aguilera
Assistant editor: Delayna Spencer
Production editor: Katie Forsythe
Marketing manager: Sally Ransom
Cover design: Stephanie Guyaz
Typeset by: C&M Digitals (P) Ltd, Chennai, India
Printed and bound by CPI Group (UK) Ltd,
Croydon, CR0 4YY

First published 2017

Library of Congress Control Number: 2017930218

British Library Cataloguing in Publication data

A catalogue record for this book is available from
the British Library

ISBN 978-1-4462-6681-6
ISBN 978-1-4462-6682-3 (pbk)

At SAGE we take sustainability seriously. Most of our products are printed in the UK using FSC papers and boards.
When we print overseas we ensure sustainable papers are used as measured by the PREPS grading system.
We undertake an annual audit to monitor our sustainability.

TABLE OF CONTENTS

LIST OF TEXT BOXES

LIST OF FIGURES AND TABLES

FIGURE

TABLES

LIST OF ABBREVIATIONS

ADB	Asian Development Bank
AusAID	Australian Agency for International Development
BRICS	Brazil, Russia, India, China and South Africa
C4D	Communication for Development
CDM	Clean Development Mechanism
CDSC	Communication for Development and Social Change
CEDAW	Convention on the Elimination of All Forms of Discrimination Against Women
CER	Certified Emissions Reduction
CFCs	Chlorofluorocarbons
CITES	Convention on International Trade in Endangered Species of Wild Fauna and Flora
CLACS	Centre for Latin American and Caribbean Studies
COP	Conference of Parties
CSC	Communication for Social Change
CSDH	Commission on Social Determinants of Health
DBV	Development Bank of Vanuatu
GFC	Global Financial Crisis
GMO	Genetically Modified Organism
HACAP	Hairdressers and Cosmetologists Association of the Philippines
IAP2	International Association for Public Participation
ICRC	International Committee of the Red Cross
ICT4D	Information Communication Technologies for Development
IEA	International Energy Association
IFRC	International Federation of Red Cross and Red Crescent Societies
IGO	Intergovernmental Organization
ILO	International Labour Organization
IMF	International Monetary Fund
INGO	International Non-Governmental Organization
MARPOL	International Convention for the Prevention of Pollution from Ships
MDGs	Millennium Development Goals
MNC	Multinational Corporation
NBV	National Bank of Vanuatu
NGO	Non-Governmental Organization
NNGO	Northern NGO

OECD	Organisation for Economic Co-operation and Development
OFW	Overseas Filipino Workers
PAR	Participatory Action Research
POEA	Philippine Overseas Employment Agency
PPP	Purchasing Power Parity
PRA	Participatory Rural Appraisal
RRA	Rapid Rural Appraisal
SD	Sustainable Development
SDGs	Sustainable Development Goals
SNGO	Southern NGO
SRPD	Self-Reliant Participatory Development
SWAP	Sector-Wide Approach
TNC	Transnational Corporation
UNCTAD	United Nations Conference on Trade and Development
UNDP	United Nations Development Programme
UNESCO	United Nations Scientific and Cultural Organization
UNHRBA	United Nations Human Rights Based Approach
UNODC	United Nations Office of Drugs and Crime
WCI	Women's Candidacy Initiative
WHO	World Health Organization
WTO	World Trade Organization

ABOUT THE EDITORS AND CONTRIBUTORS

Richard P. Appelbaum is Distinguished Research Professor and former MacArthur Foundation Chair in Global and International Studies and Sociology at the University of California at Santa Barbara, where he was a co-founder of the Global & International Studies Program, and co-PI at the NSF-funded Center for Nanotechnology in Society. He has published extensively in the areas of emerging technologies, particularly in China; the globalization of business; and the sociology of work and labor. He is a Fellow of the American Association for the Advancement of Science (AAAS); chairs the Advisory Council of the Workers' Rights Consortium; and is a member of the Committee on Trademark Licensing in the Office of the President, University of California.

Paul Battersby is Associate Professor and Deputy Dean, Global and Language Studies, in the School of Global, Urban and Social Studies at the Royal Melbourne Institute of Technology (RMIT) University, in Melbourne, Australia. His publications and research interests span globalization, governance, border security, and the history of Australia's business engagement with Asia. He teaches in the areas of global risk and governance, security, global crime, Asian business practices, and international development.

Desmond Cahill is Professor of Intercultural Studies in the School of Global, Urban and Social Studies, RMIT University. He has been teaching and researching on cross-cultural and language issues as well as about multicultural, multifaith and diasporic societies for four decades. Since 9/11, his focus has been on religion, globalization and interreligious issues. He is Chair of Religions for Peace Australia and, in 2010, he was awarded the Medal of the Order of Australia for 'his services to intercultural education and to the interfaith movement'.

Louise Coventry is a PhD candidate in the School of Global, Urban and Social Studies, RMIT University. Her doctoral research explores the governance of civil society organizations in Cambodia. She currently lives in Ho Chi Minh City, Vietnam, and works as an organizational development consultant and facilitator with civil society organizations across South East Asia. She holds degrees in social work, psychology, and community services management (BA, BSW, MSocSci), and her research interests include participatory methodologies, community and capacity development, peacebuilding, and governance.

Arthur T. Denzau teaches at Utah State University and is Professor Emeritus at Claremont Graduate University. He has held previous teaching appointments at Virginia Tech, the University of Arizona, Washington University, and Sultan Qaboos

University in Oman. His primary research has been in the field of Public Choice Economics. He has been working to expand upon the New Economic Institutionalist work on Shared Mental Models that he and his colleague, Douglass C. North, began together over two decades ago.

Rebekah Farrell is a PhD candidate in the School of Global, Urban and Social Studies, RMIT University. Her research focuses on the legal accountability of pharmaceutical companies in conducting unethical clinical trials in developing countries. Rebekah is admitted to practise in the Supreme Court of Victoria and works as a policy lawyer. She has published in the area of international project-based learning, globalization, and authenticity in Asia.

Kent Goldsworthy teaches in the Masters of International Development and Bachelor of International Studies programmes in the School of Global, Urban and Social Studies, RMIT University. Kent is also a PhD candidate affiliated with the School's Centre for Global Research. His research interests are aligned to his engagement with ReThink Orphanages: Better Solutions for Children, a global network of NGOs, government departments, and researchers who aim to prevent the unnecessary institutionalization of children by shifting the way in which countries engage with aid and development. Prior to academia, Kent pursued a career in international education management.

Damian Grenfell is the Director of the Centre for Global Research and a Senior Lecturer in the Global Studies Discipline, RMIT University. He researches social change in the context of conflict, security, and peace and governance. A significant aspect of Grenfell's work focuses on gender in the post-conflict and post-colonial context.

Jose Roberto Guevara is Associate Professor and Director of the Master of International Development Program in the School of Global, Urban and Social Studies, RMIT University. He is an educator with extensive experience in adult, community and popular education, and participatory action research with a focus on education for sustainable development, environmental education, global citizenship education and development education, within the Asia and South Pacific regions. He was inducted into the International Adult and Continuing Education Hall of Fame in October 2012 for his contribution to adult learning in the Asia-Pacific region, and was recently awarded a CONFINTEA Research Scholarship by the UNESCO Institute for Lifelong Learning to conduct research on education and resilience.

Vandra Harris is Head of Global Studies in the School of Global, Urban and Social Studies, RMIT University, where she teaches in the Master of International Development course. Vandra's research focuses particularly on the interface between different actors in the development space, especially militaries, police and NGOs, as well as contact between local and international development actors. Prior to joining academia, Vandra spent over a decade working for local and international community development NGOs. She has also served on the boards of a range of NGOs and is a member of the International Development Ethics Association (IDEA) and a fellow of the Inter-University Seminar on Armed Forces and Society (IUSAFS).

Anil Hira is Professor of Political Science at Simon Fraser University. For the first part of his career, his research was focused on international trade and investment, and how Latin American and other countries in the South could move towards long-term economic development. His more recent research focuses on a triple bottom-line agenda, examining how to promote renewable energy and labour rights in the developing world. He has completed studies on wireless, biofuels, and wine industries, using comparative cases and international teams to reveal which policies were most effective in producing successful competitive global industries.

Elizabeth Kath is a Senior Lecturer with the School of Global, Urban and Social Studies, RMIT University, where she teaches International Studies. She is also an Honorary Research Fellow with the UN Global Compact Cities Programme and Co-Director of Global Reconciliation, a global network of partners around the world that focuses on researching and promoting 'reconciliation', or 'dialogue across difference'. Her research has included study of the Cuban public health system, her work with organizations in Porto Alegre and Rio de Janeiro seeking to improve health, wellbeing and social inclusion for favela communities, and an action research project that includes intercultural exchanges between Australia and Brazil, focusing on themes of sport, wellbeing and reconciliation.

Robert Klitgaard is Professor at Claremont Graduate University, where he formerly served as President. He was Lee Ka-shing Distinguished Chair Professor for two summers at the National University of Singapore; Dean and Ford Distinguished Professor of International Development and Security at the Pardee RAND Graduate School, the world's leading PhD programme in policy analysis; Lester Crown Professor of Economics at Yale School of Management; and an Associate Professor of Public Policy at the Harvard Kennedy School.

Paul Komesaroff is a physician, medical researcher and philosopher at Monash University in Melbourne, where he is Professor of Medicine. He is also Executive Director of the international NGO, Global Reconciliation. He is engaged in various research and action projects in reconciliation and ethics, which cover clinical practice, public health, global health and research ethics and span a range of topics, including the impact of new technologies on health and society, consent in research, the experience of illness, palliative care and end-of-life issues, complementary medicines, obesity, psychological effects of trauma, and cross-cultural teaching and learning.

Scott Leckie is an international human rights lawyer and the Founder and Director of Displacement Solutions, an organization dedicated to resolving cases of forced displacement throughout the world, in particular displacement caused by climate change and conflict. Over the past three decades, he has established several human rights organizations and institutions. He regularly advises a number of United Nations agencies on housing, land and property rights issues, and has worked on these questions in 82 countries.

Julian C.H. Lee is a Senior Lecturer in Global Studies, School of Global, Urban and Social Studies, RMIT University. He is also a member of the Executive Committee of the Centre for Global Research. He is trained in the discipline of anthropology and, using ethnographic methods, his research has focused on civil society, gender, sexuality and multiculturalism with an area focus on Malaysia. He has been an Economic and Social Research Council Postdoctoral Fellow at the University of Kent, and maintains an interest in public engagement through regular columns in non-academic periodicals.

Cirila P. Limpangog teaches and researches in the areas of gender and development, human rights, women's rights, culture, globalization and migration. She has intermittently taught at RMIT University, Victoria University and the University of Melbourne for more than ten years, and has worked in the international and community development sector for close to twenty years, including being GenderWise Program Manager in International Women's Development Agency. She is a recipient of the Endeavour Australia Cheong Kong Research Fellowship.

Debbi Long is a medical anthropologist, whose research interests focus around health systems and health equity. She has undertaken ethnographic research in Swaziland, Turkey and in the Australian public hospital system. Debbi has taught in departments of anthropology, medicine, nursing and in an Indigenous foundation programme. She is on the board of Possible Dreams International and Lentil As Anything, both NGOs working within a social justice and equity framework, and is the founder of the Health Anthropology network. She is currently with the Department of General Practice at Monash University, working on a project incorporating family violence expertise into medical and health education curriculum.

Jonathan Makuwira is Professor of Development Studies at Nelson Mandela Metropolitan University (NMMU), South Africa. Prior to joining NMMU, he was a Senior Lecturer in International Development at the Royal Melbourne Institute of Technology (RMIT) University. His academic career has seen him teach Peace Studies at the University of New England, and Comparative Indigenous Studies at Central Queensland University. He has worked for the Ministry of Education in Malawi as a Primary, Secondary and Teacher Educator before joining the Malawi Institute of Education and then the Council for NGOs in Malawi (CONGOMA).

Gregoire Nimbtik completed his doctoral thesis at RMIT University, where he examined the social dynamics of corruption in Vanuatu. He began his career in Vanuatu's public service as Deputy Director of the Vanuatu Comprehensive Reform Program (CRP). In July 2004, he was appointed as the Director of the Department of Strategic Policy, Planning and Aid coordination at the Ministry of Prime Minister. He holds a Masters of Development Administration from the Australian National University (ANU) and a Bachelor of Arts from the University of the South Pacific. He is now working as the Director of the Department of Strategic Policy, Planning and Aid coordination at the Ministry of Prime Minister in Vanuatu.

Lesley J. Pruitt is a Senior Lecturer in Politics and International Relations at Monash University. She is also a member of the Centre for Global Research. Lesley's research focuses on recognizing and enhancing youth participation in peacebuilding and promoting gender equity in peace processes. A Truman Scholar and Rotary Ambassadorial Scholar, Lesley received her Masters and PhD in Political Science and International

Studies from the University of Queensland. In 2012, she was Visiting Research Fellow at George Mason University's Peacekeeping Operations Policy Program in Washington, DC.

Ravi K. Roy is Director of the W. Edwards Deming Incubator for Public Affairs (WEDIPA) at Southern Utah University and Research Fellow in Public Affairs with the W. Edwards Deming Institute. Prior to these appointments, Roy served as Director of various postgraduate programmes including the MPA programmes at Southern Utah University and California State University, Northridge as well as the International Development programme at RMIT University. Roy was also Visiting Research Scholar at the Orfalea Center for Global and International Studies at the University of California, Santa Barbara from 2011–2015.

Supriya Singh is Professor, Sociology of Communications at the Graduate School of Business and Law, RMIT University. Her work focuses on how communication and money shape each other. She has researched this in the areas of banking, migration, the transnational family, gender and financial inclusion, and the user-centred design of information and communication technologies. Her current projects include an ethnographic study of the use of Bitcoin, money, gender and family violence, and the impact of bank closures on remittances from Australia to the Horn of Africa.

Marianne D. Sison is a Senior Lecturer and a former Deputy Dean (International) at the School of Media and Communication at RMIT University. Her research interests focus on the role of communication in advocating social change. Her multiple-perspective approach is applied in her research in global and cross-cultural public relations practice and education, cultural and organizational values, corporate social responsibility, diversity and inclusion, within the Asia-Pacific context. A graduate of the University of the Philippines and University of Florida, she received her PhD at RMIT University.

Alexander Snow has a background in and passion for using the arts as a vehicle for enabling youth-led social change. Alex holds a Bachelor of Performing Arts (BPA) and Master of Social Science International Development (MSS ID), and over the last six years, he has designed, delivered and evaluated community development projects, peer-to-peer workshops and youth-led social change events across Australia and South East Asia. Currently, Alex is a Senior Project Manager at the Foundation for Young Australians (FYA), where he oversees the design, delivery and evaluation of a range of programmes and projects that enable youth-led change across Australia.

Thunradee Taveekan lectures in the Department of Public Administration, Faculty of Management Sciences, at Prince of Songkla University, Thailand. A Thai government postgraduate scholarship recipient, she completed her PhD thesis in the School of Global, Urban and Social Studies, RMIT University, in which she examined how theories of policy network formation can be used to bridge state–civil society divides in local government in Thailand. Her research interests are public governance, collaborative governance, participatory governance, public participation, public policy and planning.

PREFACE

It is fitting that an edited volume covering the theory and practice of International Development is honouring the legacy of my dear friend and colleague, Douglass C. North. Doug's passing in November 2015 left those of us who knew him with a deep sadness. However, his work in the area of New Institutional Economics, and economic development in particular, lives on and will no doubt continue to inspire new research for many years to come.

By way of reference, I worked with Doug closely during the years I spent in the Economics Department at Washington University (St Louis). Over the course of our friendship, Doug and I would often engage in deep discussions over why human beings make the decisions they do. Doug was stuck by the fact that people often seemed to ignore empirical data and behaved in ways that rational choice perspectives did not seem to explain. Eventually, Doug and I began developing a paper emphasizing the joint importance of institutions and ideologies, which came to be conceptualized as Shared Mental Models (SMMs). When our draft on SMM was done, Doug remarked that we had stumbled onto something important. Meanwhile, unbeknownst to us, Doug was being considered for the [Bank of Sweden] Nobel Memorial Prize in the Economic Sciences for his earlier work on Clio-metrics. Even before his acceptance of the Nobel in 1993, Bruno Frey had insisted that we publish our SMM paper in his social science journal, *Kyklos*. Since that time, our work on SMMs that Doug initiated would inspire discussion across a variety of fields, garnering over 2,200 cites (over half of my overall career total of 4,300) so far. In recent years, it has gained increasing traction in the area of International Development and would even be featured in the World Bank's *World Development Report 2015*.

It is personally gratifying to see this edited volume released under the co-editorship of my friends Paul and Ravi. Indeed, Ravi and I having been working together over the last 15 years to expand upon the work that Doug and I began on SMMs years ago at 'Wash U'. The authors of the impressive chapters contained in this volume have applied the SMM framework in some innovative and interesting ways, ranging from governance to sustainability. In the pages of this volume, the reader is treated to a fascinating and wide-ranging exploration of the various dimensions of this important and engaging field.

Arthur T. Denzau

INTRODUCTION

1

GLOBALIZATION AND GLOBAL DEVELOPMENT PRACTICE

PAUL BATTERSBY AND RAVI K. ROY

INTRODUCTION

How can we create new models of practice that will help us to build a more just and peaceful global world? In a time of rapid and unpredictable change, how can we prevent communities from fracturing and societies from tearing themselves apart? How should we prioritize economic, social and cultural demands for resources and opportunities? Innovatively, this book explores responses to these questions by adopting practice-oriented and practitioner-first perspective. 'Development' remains a fiercely contested idea and yet development, as a professional endeavour, is dynamic and expanding in scope. Distinctively, this book conceives 'global development' holistically as something constituted by the myriad aspirations, social circumstances, happenings, and daily routines of people grappling with the consequences of globalization in localities across the globe. It does not presume a single model of practice; rather, it envisages interconnected fields of social action evidencing complementary, competing and contradictory priorities. This 'globality' we argue demands a new mindset – new 'mental models' – and a new set of 'global' thinking skills. Globalization is thus employed as the principal connecting idea, and framework for analysis and action, because it is sufficiently broad to capture the cross-sectoral and trans-disciplinary qualities of 'development practice'.

Modern development challenges are increasingly framed in global terms, with globalization cited as the imperative for intervention (Annan, 2000; Ki-moon, 2014). These challenges are multifaceted, multi-level and multi-sector, and hence today's development professional must assimilate to a lengthening list of issues and agendas that span multiple knowledge domains, regardless of organizational role or geographical location. Importantly, development practitioners are also agents of globalization as they are actors caught in a world of rapid and unpredictable change. As bearers of ideas and values, development workers can influence in subtle ways the private and public norms that govern the strategies and means by which organizational priorities are pursued. As humanitarian advocates, they play a part in defining, through practice and debate, international rules governing aid allocations, armed humanitarian interventions, the treatment of refugees, and the management of liberal globalization. As educators and mediators, they can shift the ways in which development work is perceived and approached to, in terms of 'best' or 'sustainable practice', include the voices of intended beneficiaries. This highly diverse field of social action both generates and diffuses global norms, pertaining to social and economic progress, justice, human rights and the rule of law. As the contributors to this collection make explicit, sensitivity to the normative context of practice is essential if development is to be sustainable, anywhere.

GLOBALIZATION AND DEVELOPMENT

Globalization is a multidimensional phenomenon that encompasses, writes Roland Robertson, the material 'compression of the world and the intensification of consciousness of the world as a whole' (1992: 8). Indeed, the increasing range and frequency of development interventions reflects as much the globalization of public concern for human welfare (subject to periodic 'compassion fatigue') as it does the proliferation of interventionist state, intergovernmental and non-state development actors. Conceived as a set of dynamic and interrelated processes of social, economic, technological and cultural change, globalization is most commonly associated with instantaneous communication, shrinking travel times to distant destinations, rising trade interconnectedness, footloose capital and global consumer markets. Globalization both accentuates the connections between peoples and states in the developed and the developing world and accelerates the global impact of local events from natural disasters to financial meltdowns. We are living in a world of intensifying 'disjuncture', where structured linear explanations of change are no longer adequate, if they ever were, because this multiplicity renders organized social action more complex, both in terms of the range of motivations, alternatives, and possible aberrant consequences that could arise from a single step (Appadurai, 1990, 1996). Few can escape or evade the implications of these transformations for thought and practice.

Development, in its contemporary sense, is conceived as something that is 'done to' people in need of improvement or benevolent assistance. Conventionally, development work is imagined to occur at the margins of globalization, where peoples are presumed to desire, but have not yet secured, the means to prosper in a market society. Indeed, popular notions of development crystallize around images of assistance rendered to those living in conditions of poverty, or in conflict zones, or to those affected by environmental catastrophe. Outcomes are demonstrably unequal, which leads critical scholars and practitioners to seek to 'empower' the voiceless, by exposing and then challenging existing global power structures. Prescriptions range from the wholesale reordering of global society through a resurgence of popular democratic politics, to the more incremental development of human capacities through education, economic opportunity. Post-colonial and feminist critiques of global order stress the dominance of Western and 'masculinist' discourses in the upper echelons of global (and still) largely male executive authority (Enloe, 1990, 2007). The unequal and resilient disposition of power and wealth in the global system, however, means that aspirations for universal justice remain largely unrealized.

A global approach enables us to navigate between the many different and distant grid reference points that define this terrain of contested development, from the power centres of the 'global North' to the remote edges of the 'global South'.[1] Global history brings to the foreground the long trajectories of change that shape present dispositions. The institutional and ideological foundations of official development were laid in the aftermath of the Second World War. The United Nations System, which includes the Bretton Woods Institutions, the World Bank, International Monetary Fund, General Agreement on Tariffs and Trade (GATT) (after 1994, the World Trade Organization or WTO), offered a blueprint for international order. 'Social progress and better standards of life' were bound conceptually to 'international peace and security' in the wording of the UN Charter, 1945. The authorship of this current phase of development as broad-ranging technical assistance to an 'underdeveloped' and decolonizing world is widely attributed to US President Harry S. Truman (Truman, 1949; Schafer et al., 2009: 5). Yet, Truman's prescriptions were a logical extension of aspirations shared by his predecessor, Franklin D. Roosevelt, whose last, if 'undelivered' address, stressed the urgent need for a new 'science of human relationships' to put an end to 'the doubts and the fears, the ignorance and the greed' that led to the cataclysm of war (Roosevelt, 1945).

The institutionalization of international development undoubtedly complemented the aims of US post-war foreign policy, which included the geographic and economic expansion in capitalist-oriented as opposed to socialist-style development. While the most senior positions within the United Nations have been held by professional diplomats from Africa, Asia and Latin America, northern dominance persists in the ways in which power is structured and exercised within the UN system, which includes the Bretton Woods Institutions, albeit with some recalibrations in the latter to accommodate the rise of the so-called BRICS economies (Brazil, Russia, India, China and South Africa).

Official interventions are planned with a mixture of social altruism and strategic and commercial self-interest. Foreign aid budgets are, after all, instruments of state foreign policy, justified to taxpayers as being vital to the pursuit of national interests abroad. At the intersections of policy and practice, however, individual agents of official development can accord a higher priority to their social role as opposed to their overarching organizational mission.

The development 'profession' accommodates policy and programme officials from the development 'establishment' – the United Nations, the World Bank and associated regional multilateral banks, and regional institutions such as the European Union, and government officials working for state-level institutions. Development assistance is widely perceived as a central function of governments and intergovernmental agencies. Yet, there are significant limits to the willingness of governments and intergovernmental

---

[1]These political-geographical terms appear with varying forms of capitalisation, as global North and global South or without any capitalization. The terms *global North* and *global South* are used throughout for consistency to distinguish between industrially developed and affluent societies, largely in Western Europe, North America and industrialized Asia, and developing societies in Asia and Africa.

organizations (IGOs) to fund global welfare gaps, and to listen and learn. The category 'development practitioner' thus necessarily encompasses those who work in and for the myriad non-governmental organizations (NGOs), orientated to development, humanitarian assistance or both, and which continue to grow in number. It is the non-state sector that has historically led the way in providing aid to people that governments choose to ignore or who are afflicted by natural and human-made disasters, especially conflict. Save the Children, Oxfam, CARE, World Vision, are global actors and frequently among the international 'first responders' when a humanitarian crisis erupts. The International Committee of the Red Cross (ICRC), which is neither a state nor a non-state actor but a hybrid global humanitarian entity, pre-dates the UN by nearly a century in providing humanitarian care to those caught up in the horror of war. Bridging the differences in organizational forms, norms and missions between state and non-state actors often requires careful diplomacy. Managing, or more precisely, negotiating assistance efforts where, in an ideal case, national government bodies, intergovernmental agencies and local communities seek a broad collaborative approach, is a complex task requiring sophisticated professional skills.

New generations of development workers grew up in newly independent countries created through successive waves of decolonization in Asia and Africa. Their professional training was informed by developmentalist ideas received through domestic or international educational experiences in an era where education and technical assistance formed the substance of human development programming. Working with international aid agencies, or starting local NGOs in cooperation with developed country donors, partners and benefactors, global South NGOs today vastly outnumber their Northern counterparts. The microfinance pioneer, the Grameen Bank, is one of the better-known southern development transnationals that applies principles of market finance to enable the disadvantaged. This expansive pattern of inclusion extends, at the micro-level, to the involvement of local community leaders recruited by the development establishment to help translate social development policies and multiply social gains from welfare spending. Movements for social and political change draw upon the skills, knowledge and networks of these new classes of professionals and leaders to bridge social divisions and mobilize campaigns to claim political rights from oppressive authoritarian regimes.

Development defined as justice sits uncomfortably alongside the security and commercial imperatives of major international donors of development assistance, the majority of which are nation-states. Discomfort is most acute where humanitarian values are overridden in the name of security or economic development cast as 'progress'. But the development profession does not escape criticism for self-interestedness and error. Aid workers can quickly find their presumed 'neutrality' challenged, by shifting political alliances or moving battlefronts in countries wracked by poly-sided armed conflicts. In working towards the social inclusion of culturally diverse peoples, practitioners can, unwittingly perhaps, find themselves complicit in policies of cultural assimilation. Then there are the more egregious exhibitions of wealth and privilege by the affluent international development professional, a bright shining new four-wheel drive for example, emblazoned with corporate logos, symbols of cultural and economic distance and a trigger for sometimes violent resentment among those resentful of their own relative and immediately apparent deprivation (Kapoor, 2013). Manifestly, development practice, at the point of contact between practitioner and intended beneficiary at least, is not simply a matter of politically neutral and routine programme or project implementation.

DEVELOPMENT AS PRACTICE

Development interventions encourage cooperation or provoke conflict depending upon the purposes of development agents, their attitudes towards intended beneficiaries, and the responses of those who either accept or reject external development agendas. Unravelling the tangled imperatives that guide policy, planning and the implementation of development projects and programmes is thus vitally important if there is to be meaningful dialogue between different communities of practice within the broad development field. Arthur T. Denzau and Douglass C. North's (1994) seminal piece on 'shared mental models' (SMM) offers a conceptual framework of analysis to help us assess different and often divergent conceptions of development practice. Drawing on their heuristic, we argue that development as social action is conceived and shaped by a person's models of social reality and the shared mental models of practitioners. This approach paves the way for critiques of linear notions of change that are framed by grand narratives of social progress. According to Denzau and North (ibid.: 4), mental models are shared cognitive frameworks (or beliefs systems) that groups of individuals possess and use to interpret the political and economic environment in which they operate. They also involve prescriptive lenses as to how that environment should be structured.

Not all mental models, however, are similarly accurate or equally valid. The behaviours of development actors are directly informed by what they 'believe' their interests to be in the first place. In other words, 'rational actions' stem from actors' beliefs about what will maximize their gains and minimize their losses. Denzau and North argue that 'the performance of economies is a consequence of the incentive structures put into place; that is, the institutional framework of the polity and economy' (ibid.: 27). 'Practice' as praxis is therefore interwoven with the subjectivities of practitioners which form and reform in varying degrees of tension with institutionalized frameworks of order and control.

Complexity confronts the development practitioner at many levels but many are ill equipped to decode and manage competing demands and conflicting points of view, or to reflect upon their possible misconceptions. Current development mental models are shaped and reinforced within narrowly developed organizational cultures. Consequently, the mental models many development actors hold may prevent them from seeing problems and issues as shared concerns with others outside their own organizations. Hence, cooperation is evaded or ignored because it does not serve their expected utility to seek-out cooperative solutions. Indeed, the various agencies and actors participating in the delivery of development-based aid services (whether they are government sponsors or NGOs), or the independent consultants who underwrite the grant proposals, appear to work in discrete silos in isolation of one another, proceeding on the basis of their own discrete interests and subjective interpretations of the world. That said, if organizations are to cooperate and learn to work in partnership with one another, it is essential that they adopt shared interpretations regarding common problems and challenges.

Can developmental institutions and practitioners learn from their mistakes? Only if learning is embedded as part of the skills set of any development practitioner, as part of the values and practice of every development organization and as part of the implementation and evaluation of every development programme or project. Denzau and North (ibid.) and others explore how shared learning resulting from communication over shared experiences can lead individuals to adopt shared interpretations of what happened and what should happen next. Indeed, research confirms that different players engaging in a common game, who may start out possessing different interpretations of the interactions they are facing, can end up developing similar interpretations as they continue to play and interact with one another for extended periods of time. Denzau and North assert, therefore, that ideas or cognitive constructions matter significantly in building cooperation through shared understandings and learning. Surely, then, learning through collaborative engagement is the ideal towards which all practice should converge.

This brings us inevitably to the consideration of differences between development cultures and between peoples from different cultural groups. Culture is, in simple terms, the accumulated and embodied knowledge of a social group, upon which social norms are based and adhered to in the interests of order, and which define group identity. Culture can be overt or it can be hidden, but countless studies of cultural practices suggest that cultures exist, however much they are socially constructed. Culture was once viewed as an obstacle to liberal modernization, something to be diluted and then drained away by the acquisitive individualism of competitive and merit-driven market economies (Rostow, 1971). However much constructed or imposed by hegemonic social groups, culture and identity matter in practice. The culture of a social group is as much a site of negotiation between identities, values and social practices as it is a space for the assertion of a singular community identity (James et al., 2012). Development practitioners will therefore tread warily in intercultural contexts where a hegemonic national culture presses down upon local communities that subscribe to a different set of values and practices.

Cooperation in the social development space therefore requires some accommodation between differing mental models, or imagined social realities. Consideration thus needs to be given to the intellectual thrust of professional practice theory which points in the direction of more participatory and inclusive modes of leadership. Critical reflection, openness to new ideas, creativity and above all the ability to listen and respond to evidence, are essential leadership and managerial qualities without which organizations struggle to learn. Participatory development approaches stress the need for all participants, local communities and international institutions, to participate in learning. To date, most participatory approaches have focused on technique rather than on the underlying reason for participation, namely the need for the traditional development establishment to learn and transform itself. While there is evidence of reflexive capacity in international bureaucracies, there is also much resistance to time-consuming deep engagement.

ORGANIZATION OF THE BOOK

Global development practice is, then, a synthesis of theoretical ideas about globalization and global change with the study of practicalities that foreground relationships between theory, place, policy and social action. Written from a practitioner standpoint, this book presents a roadmap for exploring the interconnections between different domains of knowledge and practice maps across the fields of public policy, economics and finance, governance, security, law, environment, gender, corporate responsibility, ethics and education and learning. Chapter 2 introduces readers to key actors and to innovations in approaches to development and provides an introductory survey of the structures, policies and roles of development actors with explanations of the language or terminology of official development polices. Arthur T. Denzau and Ravi K. Roy revisit the concept of mental models, tracing its influence on public policy over the past two decades.

Part I, 'Models of Governance', examines key theories and approaches that shape practices of governing, with examples from Vanuatu, Thailand, the Philippines and Timor Leste. Richard P. Appelbaum maps out the main economic mental models that have influenced development planning and contemporary development policy. Paul Battersby, Thunradee Taveekan and Gregoire Nimbtik review the course of democratization and the status of governance through the lens of social and political change in Vanuatu and Thailand. Cirila P. Limpangog, Lesley J. Pruitt and Julian C.H. Lee examine interrelationships between gender issues, socio-economic status, economic disadvantage, and patterns of socio-economic development, focusing on the role of women in particular in multiplying the benefits of development assistance. Damian Grenfell reviews the meaning and relevance of human-centred global security, 'human security' in discourses of development.

Part II, 'Models of Justice', moves discussion of holistic and context-sensitive development into the normative realms of ethics and law. The place of law in international development has tended to be seen primarily as a matter of human rights and humanitarian protection. Paul Battersby and Rebekah Farrell explain how and why many spheres of law are now directly relevant to development, from humanitarian and war law to trade agreements, corruption, transnational organized crime and international telecommunications. Vandra Harris draws attention to the invidious choices that often confront development workers in the field – particularly in conflict zones – providing ethical frameworks to help clarify and overcome stark moral choices. Desmond Cahill illustrates the connections between organized religion and global development practice, highlighting the place of faith-based entities in secular development agendas. Robert Klitgaard exposes the root causes of corruption and those patterns of social behaviour that have become synonymous with corruption as a transnational crime.

Part III, 'New Models of Practice', returns attention to development as constituted by differing models of action. Anil Hira assesses the meaning of sustainability as idealized within the global environmental movement, and as alternatively conceived by states and private corporations as 'economically responsible' socio-economic development. Jose Roberto Guevara, Kent Goldsworthy and Alexander Snow, building on the ideas of Paulo Freire and Robert Chambers, exemplify the embedded learning process, which they argue should be at the centre of all development practice. Learning for sustainability is a challenge that reaches beyond the development establishment and into the global social, political and economic spheres.

Sustainability, responsibility and effectiveness are today's development buzzwords but what do they mean in practice? As Louise Coventry details in her study of organizational change in Cambodian NGOs, sustainable practice in developing country contexts presents many challenges that are best addressed through cooperative frameworks of practical engagement. Social change can be frustratingly but also necessarily slow – if speed is to be measured according to Western principles of time and efficiency that is! The private sector has been excluded from much of the discourse on international development because it is widely seen to be part of the problem rather than part of the solution. In development studies, the dominant image of the private sector is that of a foreign-owned multinational corporation exploiting local populations for profits that are expropriated and repatriated to the global North. Yet, the global private sector contributes much to development and is a source of valuable technical and financial resources. Marianne D. Sison assesses the roles of corporate actors in communicating development priorities including the use of new communications technologies (ICT) to mobilize local social action for sustainable development. The traditional or conventional subjects of development assistance, being peoples at the margins of globalization, are learning how to make their voices heard. Capital and technology are opening up new avenues for wealth accumulation. As Supriya Singh explains, development finance means much more than overseas development assistance (ODA) or intergovernmental programme funding. Mobile technologies have enabled some at the 'bottom of the pyramid' to harness the power of 'mobile money' to manage micro-financial flows.

There are many approaches to sustainability. Viewing climate change through the lens of human rights law, Scott Leckie explains how legal innovation can address the far-reaching consequences of climate change. If law is more malleable and effective that hard-headed political realists permit, then what other steps can we take to shake established verities? How can health, for example, be redefined and health professionals prepared for a world of social, cultural and biological complexity? Debbi Long, Paul Komesaroff and Elizabeth Kath examine the ethical and cultural dimensions to public health in international development, reminding us that there is no single or universal mental model of *good* health. In the concluding section, Jonathan Makuwira assesses new directions in international development thought and practice since the beginning of the 'post-development turn' during the 1980s and 1990s. Writing from an African perspective on the evolution and the future of development theory, Makuwira questions the UN's post-2015 agenda and asks if global institutions have learned anything at all about the need to build global frameworks of development and governance from the ground up.

REFERENCES

Annan, K. (2000) *We the Peoples: The Role of the United Nations in the 21st Century*. New York: United Nations.

Appadurai, A. (1990) 'Disjuncture and Difference in the Global Cultural Economy', *Theory, Culture and Society*, 7: 295–310.

Appadurai, A. (1996) *Modernity at Large: Cultural Dimensions of Globalization*. Minneapolis, MN: University of Minnesota Press.

Charter of the United Nations, 26 June 1945. Available at: www.un.org/en/documents/charter/ (accessed 6 July 2012).

Denzau, A.T. and North, D.C. (1994) 'Shared Mental Models: Ideologies and Institutions', *Kyklos*, 47: 3–31.

Enloe, C. (1990) *Bananas, Beaches and Bases: Making Feminist Sense of International Politics*. Berkeley, CA: University of California Press.

Enloe, C. (2007) *Globalization and Militarism: Feminists Make the Link*. Lanham, MD: Rowman & Littlefield.

James, P., Nadarajah, Y., Haive, K. and Stead, V. (2012) *Sustainable Communities, Sustainable Development: Other Paths for Papua New Guinea*. Honolulu, HI: University of Hawai'i Press.

Kapoor, I. (2013) *Celebrity Humanitarianism: The Ideology of Global Charity*. Abingdon: Routledge.

Ki-moon, B. (2014) 'The Road to Dignity by 2030: Ending Poverty, Transforming All Lives and Protecting the Planet, Synthesis Report of the Secretary-General on the Post-2015 Sustainable Development Agenda', 4 December, UNGA A/69/700. Available at: www.un.org/ga/search/view_doc.asp?symbol=A/69/700&Lang=E (accessed 3 August 2015).

Robertson, R. (1992) *Globalization, Social Theory and Global Culture*. Thousand Oaks, CA: Sage.

Roosevelt, F.D. (1945) 'Undelivered Address Prepared for Jefferson Day', 13 April, The American Presidency Project. Available at: www.presidency.ucsb.edu/ws/?pid=16602 (accessed 3 June 2014).

Rostow, W.W. (1971) *Stages of Economic Growth: A Non-Communist Manifesto* (2nd edn). London: Cambridge University Press.

Schafer, J., Haslam, P.A. and Beaudet, P. (2009) 'Meaning, Measurement, and Morality in International Development', in P.A. Haslam, J. Schafer and P. Beaudet (eds), *Introduction to International Development: Approaches, Actors, and Issues*. Don Mills, Ontario: Oxford University Press, pp. 2–27.

Truman, H.S. (1949) 'Inaugural Address, January 20, 1949', Harry S. Truman Library and Museum. Available at: www.trumanlibrary.org/whistlestop/50yr_archive/inagural20jan1949.htm (accessed 7 January 2015).

United Nations Global Compact, DNV GL (2015) 'Transforming Business – Changing the World: The United Nations Global Compact'. Available at: www.unglobalcompact.org/docs/publications/ImpactUNGlobalCompact2015.pdf (accessed 1 September 2015).

2

SHARED MENTAL MODELS AND INTERNATIONAL DEVELOPMENT: SOME BRIEF REFLECTIONS

ARTHUR T. DENZAU AND RAVI K. ROY

INTRODUCTION

The seminal article written by Arthur T. Denzau and Douglass C. North (1994) entitled 'Shared Mental Models: Ideologies and Institutions', has been helping to reshape the discourse of International Development in modern times. At just over twenty-two years from its publication, this 1994 article appears very different from how it did in our previous reconsideration of this work almost a decade ago (see Denzau, North and Roy, 2007). At the time of our 2007 post-script, we noted almost 100 citations of the original 1994 Denzau and North article, spread across many fields. This citation count has risen to over 300 in comparable sources and, most impressively, Google Scholar now shows over 2,200 citations. Most notably, however, has been a recent spike in the number of citations within the international development field. In emphasizing the importance of Denzau and North's work (and that of others) on shared mental models in its *Development Report 2015*, the World Bank Group has helped recast the spotlight on the importance of ideas and causal beliefs in influencing the field of international development.

WHY ARE SHARED MENTAL MODELS IMPORTANT FOR INTERNATIONAL DEVELOPMENT SCHOLARSHIP AND PRACTICE?

For any international development initiative to be successful, governments, consultants, donors, investors and NGOs must cooperate in a coordinated effort. It is further essential that international development practitioners develop an accurate picture of the political, social and economic environments in which they operate. Additionally, these actors must be able to see issues and problems as they actually are so they can make accurate assessments of the appropriate development tools and processes needed to address them. It is often difficult for human beings, however, to comprehend the world as it actually is. Human beings attempt to make sense of the political, social and economic environments (as well as the events that occur within them) through cognitive filters or mental lenses, including pre-existing biases and beliefs, reflections from past experience, stereotypes and disciplinary lenses, to name a few. In a broader sense, these filters may be considered as sub-sets of 'mental models', which involve internal cognitive constructions of the way the world works, as suggested by Denzau and North (1994). Mental models involve 'causal beliefs' as well as the constructed meanings of 'information', 'data' and 'experience' that are gained by studying or interacting with phenomena in both academia and the real world.

Risk assessments, for example, employed in decision-making calculi related to international development projects are based on analyses of prior experience and empirical data. Often times, however, international development actors must contend with new or unfamiliar phenomena when working in continuously shifting social, political and economic environments. Indeed, development actors must contend with environments continuously being shaped and reshaped by 'ubiquitous novelty', meaning essential prior experience or empirical data is often not available. Uncertainty, rather than risk, therefore, tends to inform their strategies and behaviours in these instances. Indeed, as Denzau and North (ibid.: 3) argue, people often tend to operate 'upon the basis of myths, dogmas, ideologies and "half-baked" theories' when managing problems and assessing alternative solutions. This makes their ability to make advanced predictions regarding which strategies will work best, and which ones will not, extremely difficult. Where high levels of uncertainty exist, the transaction costs associated with higher levels of risk naturally increase. However, development actors can improve the odds associated with risk by deeply familiarizing themselves with the stable social, political and economic parameters that simultaneously shape the environments in which they operate. By doing so, they can develop an improved understanding of these stable parameters that can, in turn, help them build mental models to contend with the forces of uncertainty. The more accurate the mental models we develop to assess the world, the more useful they can be in helping reduce many of the costs associated with uncertainty.

International development actors – even those who tend to deride theoretical analysis – often rely on implicit mental models to help make causal inferences about what sorts of development policies, programmes and projects would reduce poverty, as well as create conditions that promote 'good' governance and secure human rights. According to V.S. Ramachandran (2004: 105), 'Our brains are essentially model-making machines. We need to construct useful, virtual reality simulations of the world that we can act on. Within the simulation, we need also to construct models of other people's minds ... we need to do this so that we can predict their behavior.'

Shared mental models involve internal cognitive constructions that are communicated and/or experienced inter-subjectively among groups of individuals. They also involve shared meanings and understandings, which are conveyed through common experiences, language, rhetorical discourse, symbols, analogies and material referents. Mental models can be verbal or non-verbal. This is because, as Michael Polanyi (2009: 4) famously noted, at times 'we can know more than we can tell'.

Well-known examples of broader forms of shared mental models may include, but are by no means limited to, academic disciplines, scientific and organizational paradigms, global religions, and other knowledge and belief systems. More specific forms of shared mental models may include specific academic theories or approaches, scientific methodologies, and religious doctrines associated with particular denominations. More extreme forms of shared mental models may include group think or cults.

In its *World Development Report 2015*, entitled *Mind, Society, and Behavior* (2014; hereafter cited as WB), the World Bank Group emphasized Denzau and North's (and that of others) work in explaining how Shared Mental Models influence the development-related investment decisions and strategies that state and non-state (i.e., INGOs) actors pursue. According to the WB Report (2014: 62–3):

> Mental models include categories, concepts, identities, prototypes, stereotypes, causal narratives, and worldviews. Without mental models of the world it would be impossible for people to make most decisions in daily life. And without *shared* mental models, it would be impossible in many cases for people to develop institutions, solve collective action problems, feel a sense of belonging and solidarity, or even understand one another ... [A]t a given moment, there are potentially thousands of details that could be observed, but we have limited powers of observation. Mental models affect where we direct our attention. Mental models provide us with default assumptions about the people we interact with and the situations we face. As a result, we may ignore information that violates our assumptions and automatically fill in missing information based on what our mental models suggest is likely to be true.

Consistently, Denzau and North (1994: 27) argue that: 'it is impossible to make sense out of the diverse performance of economies and polities if one confines one's behavioural assumptions to that of substantive rationality in which agents know what is in their self-interest and act accordingly'. Therefore, the behaviours of political and economic actors are directly undertaken in accordance with their mental models of what they believe will maximize their benefits and minimize their losses. Denzau and North (ibid.: 27) also assert that: 'the performance of economies is the consequence of incentive structures put into place; that is, the institutional framework of the polity and economy'. That said, our ability to conceive and implement successful development strategies and programmes depends upon acquiring the most accurate mental models possible of these dynamics.

Indeed, not all mental models provide us with equally accurate lenses of the 'actual' or 'real' political and economic world. In fact, the WB Report (2014: 62) emphasizes that 'there is immense variation in mental models across societies, including different perceptions of the way the world "works"'. Often times, international development actors possess and, therefore, operate on the basis of seriously flawed mental models. This limits their ability – in some cases, severely – to accurately comprehend, and consequently, assess the environments in which they operate. When development actors operate under distorted lenses of the world, they tend to misapprehend the problems they are seeking to address. The good news is that, according to the WB Report (ibid.), 'individuals can adapt their mental models, updating them when they learn that outcomes are inconsistent with expectations'.

LEARNING CAN AFFECT SHIFTS IN HEGEMONIC SHARED MENTAL MODELS

Mental model learning can occur at two distinct levels. The first level is known as 'parameter learning' and involves routine, incremental or minor adjustments and refinements to the actor's existing causal beliefs and understandings about the environment in which they operate. This is consistent with what is known as Bayesian learning (see Text Box 2.1). Bayesian learners are unlikely to make any significant reappraisals of their existing core beliefs about how the world works. Under Bayesian learning, any new knowledge that may be acquired through real world trial and error, scientific experimentation or newly acquired data is unlikely to inspire radically new directions of thinking, innovations or breakthroughs. Hence, Bayesian learners are never surprised. Rather, Bayesian learners are prone to take any new information that they may encounter and simply interpret it through the lens of their prior beliefs. Hence, any new learning that may occur tends to result in mere refinements of those pre-existing shared beliefs or causal ideas (or shared mental models).

Text Box 2.1   Bayesian Learning

Bayesian learning is rooted in the work of the eighteenth-century mathematician and reverend Thomas Bayes. The well-known Bayesian estimation theorem was elegantly presented in his seminal 1764 *Essay Towards Solving a Problem in the Doctrine of Chances.* In this essay, published posthumously, Bayes proposed that the assumptions that people make when estimating probabilities related to outcomes are based on prior beliefs, which can be updated as new evidence surfaces. A Bayesian learner, therefore, starts with a given set of ideas about the likelihood of the possible outcomes related to a particular scenario. One of the most vivid illustrations of Bayesian learning involves a fighter pilot attempting to estimate the number of airplanes that the enemy

(Continued)

(Continued)

may have deployed in a dogfight. Each fighter plane has a number painted on its tail and a commonly held prior belief tends to be that all tail numbers in a given air squadron are labelled consecutively, beginning with the number '1'. Suppose that the fighter pilot shoots down 100 enemy planes and, at the same time, observes that the highest tail number was 200, he might assume that he has successfully destroyed half of the enemy's air squadron (100 out of 200). It has been suggested that some nations in the Second World War manipulated their tail numbers (to start at say 50 rather 1) in order to deceive the enemy into believing that they had more planes in their squadron than they actually did.

The second level of learning is much more dramatic and involves what Sunil Rongala (2007: 29) refers to as a 'shattering of mental models'. Learning at this level involves a radical rethinking of one's existing core beliefs or world views. As noted in the 2014 World Bank report for 2015, the continuous failure of a person's given belief system to provide plausible explanations of ongoing events or solve a persistent problem may compel one to rethink or abandon his/her causal beliefs or mental models. When this happens, one is typically inspired to begin the search for alternative explanations that can, in turn, lead to the adoption of a new mental model. If this experience is shared by a large number of people, who, for example, share an academic discipline, professional field or scientific community, then we may witness the shattering of a shared mental model. This form of learning is consistent with paradigm shifts, scientific revolutions and historical watersheds.

When 'Shared Mental Models' was being written over twenty years ago, the intention of Denzau and North was to encourage international development actors to begin questioning the rigid assumptions underpinning the dominant neoclassical (a.k.a. neoliberal) economic approaches, which tended to be narrowly focused on market-liberalizations and free-trade policies. In its various forms and guises, neoliberalism essentially represented a 'new' slant on nineteenth-century classical liberalism that had long been the core of Western capitalist ideology. While recognizing that substantial differences may exist between, say, the US economy and that of France or many of the newly industrializing economies of Asia, they all nonetheless represent strands of a broader neoliberal shared mental model (Roy et al., 2007). Uniting all of these strands, however, was both the false assumption that actors behave exclusively to maximize their rational self-interests, as well as the implication that all actors somehow magically possess the same 'correct' (universally rational) mental models of the world in the first place. Such mental models, Denzau and North (1994) reasoned, possessed a dangerous axiomatic flaw that could keep actors from seeing the potential strengths offered by wider sets of alternative development strategies.

THE SHIFT IN HEGEMONIC SHARED MENTAL MODELS

It is encouraging that some of the more rigid assumptions and axioms underpinning the neoliberal shared mental model are now being reexamined by the international development community. As the World Bank Report states (WB, 2014: 63), policy can go wrong when the designers fail to understand peoples' mental models. For example, the Global

Financial Crisis of 2008–09 (GFC), which appeared to have been initiated in the 'liberalized' financial markets of neoliberalism's leading advocate, the USA, quickly spread like wildfire throughout the world's interconnected developed economies; yet, interestingly, a number of the relatively closed economies in parts of Africa appeared immune to the contagion. The global repercussions and stagnant growth that have followed in its wake have inspired many to raise serious questions about the neoliberal shared mental model and its underlying assumptions about how the world works. The belief that simply cutting the size of government, reducing deficit spending, privatizing SOEs (state-owned enterprises), liberalizing capital controls and trade barriers would automatically spur investment and economic growth and alleviate poverty is being challenged in the mainstream discourse. Indeed, the spectacular market failure that culminated in the 2008–09 recession has even inspired some to claim that this shared mental model has been 'shattered'. Even if this were true, however, it is less than clear what alternative shared mental model, if any, would replace it. The mental models of China's burgeoning industrial economy were considered; China's rapid economic growth was attributed to its adoption of a counter-Washington Consensus, East Asian state-led, command and control, *developmentalist*-oriented paradigm. The recent slowdown of China, and its various environmental and overcapacity problems, however, now reveal flaws in this would-be alternative. Presently, no substantial consensus appears to have been reached on an alternative model.

CONCLUSION: INTERNATIONAL DEVELOPMENT THEORY AND PRACTICE SMMs MUST REFLECT CONTEXT

Alas, it seems that any successful development initiative is contingent upon matching the 'correct' mental models to the specific problems in particular environmental contexts. There can be no one-size-fits-all strategy. Any successful development strategy must be tailored to the particular social, economic and political context in which it is being implemented. In the 1990s, for example, monetary policy currency boards – pegged directly to major currencies such as the US dollar and the Deutche mark – were instituted to stabilize domestic currencies in various developing countries, from Latin America to Eastern Europe. This strategy proved to be a disaster for Argentina and appeared to be a godsend for Estonia. Obviously, the two countries vary widely in the size of their domestic markets, production profiles, import/export ratios, business cycles, level of economic interaction with foreign major economies, integrity of their fiscal systems, exposure to global forces and so forth. These two distinct outcomes demonstrate that a monetary currency board strategy that may work in one context may not work in another. Possessing an accurate mental model, which takes into account the complex interactions shaped by highly specific contextual national and regional environments, therefore, is essential. Possessing an accurate understanding of the range of possible solutions and their potential costs, benefits, and risks as they occur in any specific environment is equally important.

Enlightened development practitioners and scholars understand the importance of developing 'the correct' mental models that can be used to view and comprehend a specific problem in a given context. Given this, it should come as little surprise that some of the most successful development strategies and programmes are designed and implemented in a manner that is interwoven within the context-specific cultural norms, daily routines and social practices of a given society. In the 1970s, for example, Thai politician Mechai Viravaidya implemented a campaign of family planning awareness, which involved the distribution of condoms (now called *mechais* in Thailand) wherever a crowd was gathered. This included, for example, traffic jams and movie theatres. The campaign ultimately led to the development of a restaurant chain that became known as 'Cabbages and Condoms', where prophylactics were provided at the end of every meal with the bill. This campaign greatly facilitated one of the most spectacular demographic shifts in East Asia. Indeed, the programme resulted in a drop of cumulative rural fertility from 7 per cent in 1974 to 1.7 per cent by 2006. The campaign's success largely reflects the adoptability of a development-based mental model to the norms and values of the cultural context in which it was being applied.

Questions for Discussion

1   How do your mental models of development and development practice differ from those of your colleagues or classmates? In what ways are they similar?
2   Why has concern for the cognitive or psychological dimensions of development practice become prominent at the global policy level?
3   By what criteria might we judge a mental model to be 'correct'?

FURTHER READING

Denzau, A.T., Roy, R.K. and Minassians, H.P. (2016) 'Learning to Cooperate: Applying Deming's "New Economics" and Denzau and North's "New Institutional Economics" to Improve Inter-organizational Systems Thinking and Performance', *Kyklos*, 69: 471–91.

Ostry, J.D., Loungani, L. and Furceri, D. (2016) 'Neoliberalism Oversold?', *Finance and Development*, June, pp. 38–9. Available at: www.imf.org/external/pubs/ft/fandd/2016/06/ostry.htm (accessed 29 July 2016).

Roy, R.K. and Willett, T.D. (2014) 'Market Volatility and the Risks of Global Integration', in M.B. Steger, P. Battersby and J.M. Siracusa, *The Sage Handbook of Globalization*. Thousand Oaks, CA: Sage, p. 1088.

World Bank (2014) *World Development Report 2015: Mind, Society, and Behavior*. Washington, DC: World Bank.

REFERENCES

Denzau, A.T. and North, D.C. (1994) 'Shared Mental Models: Ideologies and Institutions', *Kyklos*, 47: 3–31.

Denzau, A.T., North, D.C. and Roy, R.K. (2007) 'Shared Mental Models Post-Script', in R.K. Roy, A. Denzau and T. Willett (eds), *Neoliberalism: National and Regional Experiments with Global Ideas*. London: Routledge.

Polanyi, M. (2009/1996) *The Tacit Dimension* (reissue). Chicago, IL: University of Chicago Press.

Ramachandran, V.S. (2004) *A Brief Tour of the Human Consciousness: From Impostor Poodles to Purple Numbers.* New York: Pearson Education.

Rongala, S. (2007) 'Experiments with Neoliberalism India: Shattering of a Mental Model', in R.K. Roy, A.T. Denzau and T.D. Willett (eds), *Neoliberalism: National and Regional Experiments with Global Ideas.* London: Routledge, pp. 229–56.

Roy, R.K., Denzau, A.T. and Willett, T.D. (eds) (2007) *Neoliberalism: National and Regional Experiments with Global Ideas.* London: Routledge.

World Bank (2014) *World Development Report 2015: Mind, Society, and Behavior.* Washington, DC: World Bank.

PART I

MODELS OF GOVERNANCE

3

MENTAL MODELS OF ECONOMIC DEVELOPMENT

RICHARD P. APPELBAUM

INTRODUCTION

The *World Development Report 2015*, subtitled *Mind, Society, and Behavior*, is organized around the belief that 'paying attention to how humans think (the processes of mind) and how history and context shape thinking (the influence of society) can improve the design and implementation of development policies and interventions' (World Bank, 2014: 2). The *Report* draws on recent research (especially by Denzau and North, 1994) to identify several ways in which human decision-making all too often yields poor results, in the hope that development professionals can avoid the pitfalls that frequently plague development efforts. It further identifies three problematic ways of thinking, said to be universal: thinking automatically, rather than deliberatively; thinking socially, in being overly influenced by community social norms and values; and thinking with mental models, often derived from historical experiences and understandings that no longer prevail. The *Report* argues that all three ways of thinking afflict the subjects as well as the practitioners of development efforts. Rational, evidence-based decision-making by development recipients often succumbs to irrational elements – a major reason that development projects are said to fail. In this chapter, I focus on mental models, the 'categories, concepts, identities, proto-types, stereotypes, causal narratives, and worldviews' that 'help people make sense of the world' (World Bank, 2014: 62).[1] The *Report* argues that mental models persist, even in the face of countervailing evidence, in large part because of confirmation bias – 'the tendency to search for and use information that supports one's beliefs' (ibid.: 69).

---

[1] The *Report* (World Bank, 2014: 72, n. 1) attributes the concept of 'mental models' to Denzau and North (1994) and Ostrom (2005), noting the similarities with the concepts of 'schemas' and 'cognitive frames' (Markus, 1977; DiMaggio, 1997).

While the *Report* focuses primarily on identifying and overcoming the mental models that constrain development recipients, I will discuss the mental models that guide the practitioners – ways of thinking that underlie some of the major theories that have addressed the question of economic development. I do so because they provide the key macro-level frameworks that have guided development policy-makers, practitioners and activists in this field; yet, they reflect vastly differing assumptions about how societies are organized. Although all are rooted in their historical times and places, they have had considerable influence and much staying power, even as time and circumstances have changed. Development theorists are not immune from such difficulties, given the complexity and uncertainties of global economic relations.

John Maynard Keynes (2011 [1936]: 69–70), whose *General Theory* sought to show that theoretically guided state intervention could overcome the seeming unpredictability of economic cycles, nonetheless recognized that:

> human decisions affecting the future, whether personal or political or economic, cannot depend on strict mathematical expectation, since the basis for such calculations does not exist; and that it is our innate urge to activity which makes the wheels go round, our rational selves choosing between the alternatives as best as we are able, calculating where we can, but often falling back on motive or whim or sentiment or chance. (Chapter 12, part 7)

This chapter selects and examines some key, paradigmatic mental models that, to varying degrees, necessarily reflect the untestable motives, whims, sentiments or chance that shape selected development theories.

DEVELOPMENT ECONOMICS: FOUNDATIONAL MENTAL MODELS

Two foundational maps provided the basic templates that have since shaped development economics. Classical Smithian/Ricardian economics continues to inform mental maps originating in the global North, while Marxian heterodox economics shapes mental maps originating in the global South.

Smith and Ricardo: Comparative Advantage through Free Trade

Adam Smith's *Wealth of Nations*, published in 1776, provided the mental model for much modern economic theory. Drawing on various strands of then-current economic thought, Smith argued that rational economic decisions by buyers and sellers of labour, capital, goods and services – guided by what he regarded as enlightened self-interest – constituted an 'invisible hand' that results in the best possible outcomes for society as a whole:

> Every individual necessarily labors to render the annual revenue of the society as great as he can … He intends only his own gain, and he is in this, as in many other cases, led by an invisible hand to promote an end which was no part of his intention … By pursuing his own interest he frequently promotes that of the society more effectually than when he really intends to promote it. (Smith, 2009 [1776]: 319)

The role of government, in Smith's view, should be limited, although perhaps not as limited as champions of his view today might claim. Governments should provide for national defence and internal police protection against crime, universal education, legal enforcement of property and contractual rights, and roads, bridges, and other public infrastructure. But the economy should be left to itself, guided by the invisible hand, except when people engage in economic crimes such as fraud and theft. Unfettered trade between nations – achieved by removing tariffs and other barriers – would extend benefits both domestically and internationally. Smith argued that countries should trade products for which they enjoyed a *competitive* advantage: 'If a foreign country can supply us with a commodity cheaper than we ourselves can make it, better buy it of them with some part of the produce of our own industry, employed in a way in which we have some advantage' (ibid.: 320).

Smith's arguments in favour of free trade ran counter to the then-dominant mental model – mercantilism – which held that countries would be better off if they adopted policies maximizing exports while restricting imports through tariffs and other forms of government regulation. Mercantilism held that a favourable trade balance would increase a country's store of gold (the backing for foreign exchange), and thereby increase national wealth. Smith, on the contrary, argued that free trade was preferable because both countries would prosper as a consequence of competitive advantage. Mercantilism, moreover, could result in retaliatory tariffs and trade wars, thereby reducing benefit on all sides.

David Ricardo (2015 [1817]) elaborated Smith's notion of competitive advantage into the theory of *comparative* advantage. This theory – central to the mental model that underlies much of modern economics – begins with the question: Can trade be beneficial for two countries if both produce the same goods, but one country produces these goods more cheaply than the other? While Smith might have concluded that under free trade, the country with a cost advantage in all goods would put its rival higher-cost firms in the other country out of business, Ricardo argued that under certain circumstances both countries could benefit if each chose to specialize in a different product. The key to this comparative advantage, Ricardo argued, was the opportunity cost of producing a good: that is, what a country loses by choosing to produce one good over the other. For example, if the cost to England of shifting production from wine to cloth is less than the cost to Portugal of shifting production from cloth to wine, then England should export cloth and Portugal should export wine. Wages will rise in England's cloth industry, attractingworkers from its wine industry; wages will rise in Portugal's wine industry, attracting workers from its cloth industry. Eventually, assuming *ceteris paribus*, a two-industry economy in two countries, full employment and cost-free labour mobility (and these are major assumptions), England's cloth industry and Portugal's wine industry will both thrive; consumers and workers in both countries will be better off.

The mental model underlying the theory of comparative advantage has enormous implications for development theory, since it clearly implies that poor, less economically developed countries can still enjoy a comparative advantage when trading with more economically advanced (and technologically sophisticated) countries, provided they shift production into those goods where such an advantage exists. Free trade, in this view, holds the promise of raising wages and living standards in both countries.

Whether this is likely to be true in the real world – as opposed to the simplified mental model of a *laissez-faire* world in which firms allocate their resources in keeping with their comparative advantage – has been challenged by theories rooted in the mental model provided by Marx.

Karl Marx: Unequal Exchange, Comparative Disadvantage

Although Smith (2009: 237) recognized that 'productive labour' adds to the value of a commodity, he stopped short of concluding that human labour alone is the source of value in society. In Marx's view, the classical division of capitalist economies into land, labour and capital obscured the fact that land and capital are rendered productive only through labour power; they are not independent entities that somehow contribute value on their own. Marx provided a mental model – the labour theory of value – that re-centred workers as the source of productive value in capitalist economies. By upending the classical mental model (which Marx dismissed as ideological) and replacing it with one based on the central role of human labour, Marx sought to empower workers. Markets and trade are never free, Marx (2011 [1867]) argued, since they are organized to benefit capitalists rather than workers. The optimally beneficial exchange envisioned by the theory of comparative advantage, in fact, is one of unequal exchange.

At the micro-level, workers labour for a given number of hours, for which they are compensated in wages, yet the value of the goods and services they produce during those hours exceeds their compensation. The capitalist then appropriates this 'surplus value' (unpaid labour) as profit. In order to remain competitive, capitalists are under constant pressure to extract surplus value from their workers. They do so through various means: extending the length of the working day; lowering wages; and increasing productivity through technological upgrading. Marx argued that workers would resist surplus value extraction; indeed, his mental model was intended to provide workers with the knowledge that they were being exploited.

At the macro-level, Marx predicted that capitalists would be increasingly driven to globalize production in search of raw materials and cheap labour. The globalization of production, when combined with technological upgrading, would have systemic consequences for capitalism: it reduces the market for goods produced, since the downward pressure on wages meant that workers would lack the means to purchase the very goods they were producing. Marx anticipated the problem of over-production and under-consumption – central features of modern Keynesian economics – along with two likely solutions to this problem: the creation of an ever-increasing stream of seemingly new products (consumerism), and the search for new markets around the globe (globalization). Capitalism, Marx concluded, would become the first truly global economic system – one that eventually spreads into the pores of every country and region around the planet.

Just as the struggle for surplus value extraction results in unequal exchange between capitalist and worker, so, too, would globalization result in unequal exchange between nations: technologically advanced nations would use their greater economic, political and military power to enforce their interests on weaker ones. Marx's mental model of the emerging global economy provided very different markings than those of Smith and Ricardo: the pathways all pointed to exploitation, at home and abroad, rather than a comparative advantage under which all prospered.

Marx also predicted, with remarkable prescience, that the capitalist system – with its need for surplus value extraction as a condition for profit and hence survival – would lead firms to constantly engage in technological upgrading, to the point where workers became largely superfluous and the labour theory of value no longer applied:

> But to the degree that large industry develops, the creation of real wealth comes to depend less on labour time and on the amount of labour employed … but depends rather on the general state of science and on the progress of technology, or the application of this science to production … As soon as labour in the direct form has ceased to be the great well-spring of wealth, labour time ceases and must cease to be its measure … The *surplus labour of the mass* has ceased to be the condition for the development of general wealth. (Marx, 1993 [1857–58]: 705, emphasis in original)

Production outstrips consumption; economic crises worsen; profits decline; and the ideological foundations of a capitalist system that is based on increasingly superfluous wage labour become self-evident. According to Marx's mental model, the conditions for revolutionary transformation into a more egalitarian communist system are ripe.

Post-Colonial Mental Models: Encountering Development

The anthropologist Arturo Escobar (2012: 6) has argued that the mental model of 'development' emerged when 'Western experts and politicians started to see certain conditions in Asia, Africa, and Latin America as a problem – mostly what was perceived as poverty and backwardness.' The resulting 'development discourse' can be seen as a powerful set of mental models (what Escobar calls 'regimes of representation') that view non-European areas through the lens of European constructs, resulting in:

> an extremely efficient apparatus for producing knowledge about, and the exercise of power over, the Third World. This apparatus came into existence roughly in the period 1945 to 1955 and has not since ceased to produce new arrangements of knowledge and power, new practices, theories, strategies, and so on. In sum, it has successfully deployed a regime of government over the Third World, a 'space for "subject peoples"' that ensures certain control over it. (Ibid.: 9)

Escobar's notion of 'regimes of representation' provides a way of understanding mental models as discursive frameworks that shape understanding and action: 'Geared toward an understanding of the conceptual maps that are used to locate and chart Third World people's experience, they also reveal – even if indirectly at times – the categories with which people have to struggle' (ibid.: 10). The modern wave of struggles followed the Second World War, as anti-colonialist movements spread throughout Africa and Asia. The newly independent countries all faced the challenge of development, and two competing mental models – reflecting the competing geopolitical interests of the Cold War – emerged to meet the challenge.

On the Smithian/Ricardian side, the prevailing mental model divided the globe into three worlds: a 'First World' of developed capitalist industrial countries, led by the USA and Europe; a 'Second World' of nominally communist (in fact, state socialist) industrial countries, led by the Soviet Union, its East European satellite nations and China; and a 'Third World' of non-aligned, pre-industrial and often impoverished newly independent colonies.[2] A large industry of development specialists emerged to guide the Third World along the First World path, in an effort to blunt the appeal of the Second World approach. On the Marxist side, the mental models that emerged emphasized the role of transnational corporations (which had superseded colonial administration) as the source of unequal exchange, nationalist beliefs in the historic destiny of the previously colonized peoples, and Marxist theory (Betts, 2004; Bereketeab, 2016; White, 2014; Chamberlain, 2014; Rothermund, 2006).

Envisioning Modernization, along Western Lines

Escobar's (2012) encounter with development was concerned in large part with unmasking modernization theory, a mental model promising a pathway from what the theory's proponents saw as (non-Western) economic, cultural, social and political backwardness to the light of modern (Western) society. These ideas were bound up with US Cold War concerns over the appeal of communism and the national liberation movements that were sweeping poor countries in Latin America, Africa and Asia. Modernization theory was touted as providing pathways to modern democracy (Gilman, 2007).

The most influential book on modernization was a popular treatise directed to opinion leaders and policy-makers by the economist W.W. Rostow (1961). *The Stages of Economic Growth: A Non-Communist Manifesto* was – as its subtitle states – intended as a capitalist guide to development. Rostow's personal background helped shape his economic theories: his parents were Russian Jewish immigrants with socialist leanings, and Rostow hoped, through economics, to improve the lives of people in the emerging post-colonial world. But Rostow's work also reflected US Cold War interests, and his 'non-communist manifesto' caught John Kennedy's attention during the 1960 presidential campaign. When Kennedy took office, Rostow was initially appointed deputy national security advisor, then made chairman of the State Department's Policy Planning

---

[2]Different terms have been historically used to describe global regions that differ economically, politically and culturally. All such terms reflect underlying mental models; all have been contested. The term 'Third World' is usually attributed to a 1952 article by the French demographer Alfred Sauvy, who likened Third World exploitation to that of France's Third Estate (commoners) at the time of the French Revolution. One of the first uses of the terms First and Second World occurs in a review by Peter Worsley (1967) of Irving Louis Horowitz's (1966) *Three Worlds of Development: The Theory and Practice of International Stratification*. This tripartite categorization implies a hierarchical ranking of nations (first, second, third), and with the collapse of the Soviet Union it has become obsolete. The terms global North and South, currently in vogue, avoid being evaluative at the expense of accuracy, insofar as economically wealthy and politically powerful countries are found in both hemispheres – as are economically impoverished and politically weak countries. With that caveat, lacking for the moment a better alternative, I will use the North/South distinction.

Council, which was responsible for long-term US foreign policy. Rostow's ideas helped to shape the Kennedy Administration's development policies, particularly the Latin American Alliance for Progress, which was officially inaugurated in August 1961 at an inter-American conference at Punta del Este, Uruguay (Ish-Shalom, 2006).[3] After Kennedy's assassination in 1963, Rostow stayed on with the Johnson Administration, becoming a leading advocate for the War in Vietnam.

Text Box 3.1   The Stages of Growth

According to Rostow's mental model (1961, 1964), countries could be arrayed along a modernization continuum comprised of five stages, each with its own set of characteristics:

1 *Traditional:* This stage is pre-scientific (what Rostow termed 'pre-Newtonian'), characterized by a culture steeped in fatalism, primitive technology, the absence of mass education, lacking in democratic forms of governance (power tends to be clan-based and local, even when there are central authorities), and dependence on subsistence agriculture.

2 *Preconditions for take-off:* During this stage, 'modern' conditions emerge alongside more traditional ones. A scientific approach emerges, along with a weakening of fatalistic attitudes, resulting in the belief that economic transformations are possible. Modern technology is adopted in some sectors; education is adapted to foster modern economic activity; risk-taking entrepreneurs emerge. Political power becomes more centralized; the state fosters increased investment, and modern manufacturing appears.

3 *Take-off:* Rostow describes this stage as the 'great watershed': all the 'old blocks and resistance to steady growth are finally overcome ... [economic] growth becomes the normal condition' (Rostow, 1961: 7). Key to this stage is that net investment reaches 10 per cent of national income, which sustains rising per capita income and rapid growth in key manufacturing sectors. Modernizing elites, rather than traditional ones, are now in control.

4 *The drive to maturity:* Technology is in full bloom, adapted to the resource base (thereby reflecting the country's comparative advantage). Infrastructure (railroads and the like) and new industrial sectors are developed. Entrepreneurial capacity is increased, along with expertise in engineering. Democracy takes hold; economic growth becomes self-sustaining.

5 *The age of high mass-consumption:* With the achievement of technical maturity, the country can now turn from issues of production to those of consumption: the modern democratic welfare state, in which issues of inequality, income redistribution, and increased leisure time, and the consumption of goods beyond food, clothing and shelter take precedence.

Rostow's mental model was compelling, both because of its simplistic aeronautical metaphor and its conclusion that traditional societies, mired in poverty, could take off

---

[3]The proposal, although adopted, was not universally well received; Che Guevara, representing Cuba, was vocal in his opposition.

into self-sustained growth and enter a golden age of high mass-consumption if 'they' could become more like 'us'. In this way of thinking, 'underdeveloped' countries have largely themselves to blame for their plight: the institutions and cultural values of traditional societies are primarily responsible. Colonialism receives only a few pages in *Stages*, where it is sometimes described as indirectly contributing to 'take-off' by igniting nationalism and contributing to the emergence of an anti-colonial centralized state that would later champion development. The perspective that poor countries' problems might result, at least in part, from the role they play in a world economy – that they might also suffer from exploitation under colonial rule or unequal exchange relations with more advanced economies – does not play a significant role: the word 'exploitation' appears only in the context of making more beneficial use of resources, as in 'exploitation of growth potential' (Rostow, 1961: 179), and never in the context of ill treatment of one country by another (ibid.: 179). Countries are treated largely as independent entities; absent is a systemic analysis of how individual economies might be affected by their role in a globalized economy.

Rostow does allow, however, for the positive role that developed economies should play in helping underdeveloped ones accelerate down the runway to a successful take off: during the preconditions stage they can provide capital for investment, in the form of government loans, grants and private investment, to help achieve the desired ten per cent investment rate. The Alliance for Progress reflected Rostow's mental model, calling on Latin America to achieve full adult literacy, price stability, land reform, more equitable income distribution, democratization and an increase in per capita income. These goals were to be achieved, in part, with help from the USA in the form of foreign direct investment and foreign aid. The latter, however, often had strings attached, in part to assure Congressional critics that it was not merely a 'giveaway' programme – for example, requiring the use of US firms for aid-funded development projects. While the ultimate goal was to blunt the appeal of national liberation movements and promote stability, the Alliance's goals also reflected a mental model that coupled modernization with democracy.

Historians are divided over whether Kennedy was truly concerned with the peaceful promotion of democracy, thereby reversing the more interventionist policies of the Eisenhower Administration. In Latin America, the Alliance was widely viewed as a public relations effort intended to mask the drive for US firms to gain stronger control over Latin American economies (Ish-Shalom, 2006; Taffet, 2007). This perception gained traction as a result of the abortive Bay of Pigs invasion in 1961,[4] followed by the Cuban economic blockade and CIA efforts to topple Castro, support for military coups in Brazil and the Dominican Republic, and the US Army's Project Camelot, which enlisted anthropologists to report to US intelligence sources the causes (and emergence) of possible insurgencies among indigenous peoples in Colombia, Ecuador, Peru and Bolivia.

Rostow's formulation in *Stages* was consistent with the mental model that energized many social scientists at the time – a model that envisioned a global march towards such

---

[4] The invasion, by anti-Castro Cuban exiles, was intended to ignite a popular revolution that would – in theory, at least – topple the Castro Government. Kennedy, who inherited the plan from the Eisenhower Administration, never fully supported it, and refused to provide US military support for the exiles, who were quickly defeated.

values as reason, contractual rights and democracy. The most influential social scientist, outside of economics, to advance modernization theory was Talcott Parsons, a Harvard sociologist, whose ideas – and those of his colleagues and students – were critical in shaping the field (Gilman, 2007). Parsons (1951; Parsons et al., 1953) argued that individual behaviour could be arrayed along a number of 'pattern variables', binary choices that govern all social relations:

- *Particularism/universalism*: Narrow norms that favour specific relationships versus general norms that are impartially applied to everyone.
- *Affectivity/affective neutrality*: Emotions versus reason.
- *Diffuseness/specificity*: Broad, loosely defined obligations versus precisely defined ones.
- *Ascription/achievement*: Perceptions of who one is (based, for example, on race, ethnicity, caste, status) versus what one has accomplished.
- *Self/collectivity*: Self-interest versus the interest of the larger society.

Traditional societies, Parsons argued, are based on norms and values that emphasize particularism, affectivity, diffuseness, ascription and self; modern societies require norms and values that emphasize the opposite. Parsons (1966) later came to extend these ideas into an evolutionary theory of social change, whereby societies moved from primitive to modern, with the latter characterized by increasingly complex and interdependent forms of social organization (exemplified by the division of labour), a process of 'adaptive upgrading' that results in the increased ability of modern societies to adapt to changing circumstances. Parsons' theory was unilinear, in that it reflected a one-size-fits-all mental model, in which 'primitive' societies, if they can get their act together, will all eventually wind up looking a lot like the USA.

Modernization theory, the dominant social science paradigm in the 1950s and 1960s (Gilman, 2007), viewed the march to modernity as both desirable and likely (Black, 1977; Brown, 1969: 366). Modernization theory arguably has had its day. Yet, it lives on in mental models that guide economic development today, which – in keeping with modernization theory – assume that free trade, foreign assistance and foreign direct investment are key to economic success. To take one prominent example, the United Nations General Assembly in 2000 adopted the United Nations Millennium Declaration, a statement of principles whose Section III ('Development and Poverty Eradication') promised that:

> We will spare no effort to free our fellow men, women and children from the abject and dehumanizing conditions of extreme poverty, to which more than a billion of them are currently subjected. We are committed to making the right to development a reality for everyone and to freeing the entire human race from want. (UN, 2000)

A team of experts, led by Columbia University economist Jeffrey Sachs, was tasked with turning the declaration into a set of 'measurable, universally-agreed objectives for eradicating extreme poverty and hunger, preventing deadly but treatable disease, and expanding educational opportunities to all children, among other development imperatives' (UNDP, 2016d). The results, formally announced in 2005, were eight Millennium Development

Goals (MDGs), to be achieved over the next decade.[5] The eighth MDG, 'Develop a Global Partnership for Development', called on developed countries to increase their foreign aid contributions to 0.7 per cent of GDP, and to open up trade by placing fewer restrictions on their imports from developing countries.

In 2015, the UN issued a report on progress made under the MDGs, listing a number of gains that were made between 2000 and 2014. These included a two-thirds increase in spending on development assistance;[6] a four-fifths increase in duty-free imports from developing to developed countries; and declines by roughly half in the proportion of undernourished people, mortality rates for children under the age of five, maternal mortality rates and lack of access to improved sources of water. Gains were also reported for increases in primary school enrolments, and the fight against HIV/AIDs, malaria and tuberculosis (UN, 2015; UNDP, 2016b). But in terms of its most important object – global poverty alleviation – the results were mixed. While the report claimed that 'the global mobilization behind the Millennium Development Goals has produced the most successful anti-poverty movement in history' (UN, 2015: 3), inasmuch as 'the number of people living in extreme poverty has declined by more than half' (UNDP, 2016b), it also noted that 'the world's most populous countries, China and India, played a central role in the global reduction of poverty' (UN, 2015: 5).

Further progress was clearly needed, and so the MDGs have been replaced with seventeen Sustainable Development Goals (SDGs), to be achieved by 2030, intended to 'finish the job that the Millennium Development Goals started, and leave no one behind' (UNDP, 2016a). The seventeenth SDG – intended to 'revitalize the global partnership for sustainable development' – reflects the mental model that underlies the eighth MDG, reaffirming modernization theory's belief in free trade: 'promoting international trade, and helping developing countries increase their exports, is all part of achieving a universal rules-based and equitable trading system that is fair and open, and benefits all' (UNDP, 2016c). Even within the modernization framework, there remain vigorous debates over the relative efficacy of foreign aid vs. free trade (see, for example, Easterly, 2006, 2014; Moyo, 2010, 2011; Sachs, 2009, 2011).

ENVISIONING DEPENDENCY AND ITS CHALLENGES

Modernization theory, with its emphasis on individual nation-building along the Western model, was challenged by mental models that originated in the post-colonial countries. These models led to theories that located economic challenges not in their own 'primitive' institutions and cultures of poor countries, but rather in their relations of dependency with

---

[5]The eight MDGs were: eradicate extreme poverty and hunger; achieve universal primary education; promote gender equality and empower women; reduce child mortality; improve material health; combat HIV/AIDS, malaria, and other diseases; ensure environmental sustainability; and develop a global partnership for development.

[6]This still fell far short of the original goal of 0.7 per cent of GDP on the part of developed economies. In 2000, the average foreign aid contribution for OECD countries was only 0.22 per cent of GDP; by 2015, it had risen to only 0.29 per cent (UN, 2015: 62).

their former colonial masters or – in the case of Latin America – with the USA. Building in part on Marxist ideas, so-called 'dependency theories' accepted the importance of economic growth but emphasized unequal economic relations between poor and rich countries as the key to understanding the failure of development in the former. Dependency theories ranged from reformist to revolutionary, and we shall consider four that provided key mental models during the 1950s and 1960s: W. Arthur Lewis and the role of surplus labour; Raúl Prebisch and the Economic Commission for Latin America; Fernando Henrique Cardoso and dependent development; and Andre Gunder Frank's call for revolution.

W. Arthur Lewis was a St. Lucian-born economist, whose writings provide a bridge between the mental map of modernization theory and what came to be known as the dependency school. In 1954, Lewis published 'Development with Unlimited Supplies of Labour' (Lewis, 1954), an article that earned him the Nobel Prize and is widely credited with helping to launch the field of development economics (Ranis, 2004; Tignor, 2006). Lewis' mental model drew on classical economics, although modified to take into account what he regarded as significant differences that characterized the agricultural post-colonial economies. Classical economic theory held that under conditions of full employment, the competition for workers would result in rising wages. Lewis, who knew from personal experience the realities of more traditional (pre-capitalist) economies, argued that such economies are in fact comprised of two distinct economic sectors: an industrial capitalist sector, and a traditional, pre-capitalist sector comprised of peasants, servants, handicraft workers and others who live at near-subsistence levels. The traditional sector grows in numbers because of population increase and economic pressures that drive women into the workforce. It therefore provides a virtually unlimited supply of cheap labour for the nascent capitalist industrial sector. Lewis argued that wages in the industrial sector would remain stagnant, so long as there was a surplus labour supply. Eventually, if the capitalist sector grows – if output increases and high capital returns (the result of stagnant wages) are wisely reinvested – a turning point occurs: the dual economy transitions into a single economy, labour becomes scarce and wages rise.

Lewis recognized that this would not happen automatically, but rather required government policies that would enable the fledgling industrial sector to thrive – for example, import-substitution policies in which tariffs are enacted to protect infant industries. Such policies, and his preference for a more *dirigiste* developmental state, reflected a clear break with more classical economic theory. His ideas were initially put to the test in 1957, the year that Ghana achieved independence from the UK. Lewis moved to Ghana, where he became economic advisor to Prime Minister Kwame Nkrumah, who had led Ghana's successful anti-colonial struggle. Although he helped to draft Ghana's first Five-Year Plan (a state-led industrial policy, reminiscent of Soviet Five-Year Plans, that Lewis came to disavow), within two years he had returned to academia, disillusioned by Nkrumah's spending on political patronage projects and growing repression (Tignor, 2006, 2016).

Lewis' writings, as exemplified by his 450-page *The Theory of Economic Growth* (1955), are works in classical political economy. Unlike *laissez-faire* classical and neoclassical economics, however, Lewis placed strong emphasis on the role of government – balanced with private initiative – as key to economic development in the post-colonial world. His work contains elements of Marx as well as Smith, Ricardo and other classical economists; it draws on economics, politics, culture and social conditions.

While notions of unequal exchange between countries of unequal power are implicit in Lewis' mental model, the theories more directly associated with the dependency school foregrounded such unequal relations. Dependency theories share a number of things in common, including a systemic understanding of underdevelopment resulting from the domination by a 'centre' of a 'periphery'; identifying such domination in terms of unequal exchange relations; and recognizing that the emerging middle class in the underdeveloped economies is in large part dependent on external forces, and thus at best constrained in its ability to play a progressive role (Angotti, 1981).

Raúl Prebisch is credited with creating a mental model that emphasizes the importance of centre–periphery relations that result in unequal trade relations between economically powerful and weak countries. Prebisch, a classically trained Argentinian economist, came to reject classical economics' free market assumptions during the Great Depression, when he was strongly influenced by Keynesian ideas calling for greater state involvement in managing the economy (although he also rejected Keynes' exclusive focus on developed economies, along with his failure to address their adverse trade relations with less developed economies) (Caldentey and Vernengo, 2015). Prebisch became General Manager of Argentina's newly created Central Bank in 1935, and led the effort to create a regional trade area with Brazil, Uruguay and Paraguay. But following the 1943 Brazilian military coup, Prebisch lost his Central Bank position, and his increasing political marginalization (and eventually self-imposed exile) under the Perón Government (1946–52) led to service as a technical advisor to other Latin American countries. Prebisch's mental model expanded beyond Argentina to encompass the varying experiences of countries such as Mexico, Venezuela and Chile (Dosman, 2010).

In 1948, the United Nations established the Economic Commission for Latin America (ECLA),[7] and Prebisch was asked to write an introduction to its *Economic Survey of Latin America* for ECLA's Havana meeting the following year. 'The Economic Development of Latin America and its Principal Problems' (Prebisch, 1950) – subsequently referred to as the Havana Manifesto – advanced Prebisch's challenge to the theory of comparative advantage.[8] In its simplest terms, Prebisch argued that when economically underdeveloped countries (the periphery) specialize in exporting raw materials and agricultural products to economically developed countries (the centre), from which they import industrial products, they necessarily lose out. Exports from the periphery are cheap, particularly since the combination of technologically driven gains in productivity and what Prebisch (1959: 255) termed 'surplus manpower' depress wages in the export sector. At the same time, imports from the centre remain expensive, and sometimes increasingly so if the centre's export sector wage gains outstrip productivity increases. The terms of trade (the ratio of the value of a country's exports to that of its imports) strongly favour the centre, whose export prices remain high or increase while the periphery's export prices stagnate

---

[7]The Spanish acronym is CEPAL (Comisión Económica para America Latina y el Caribe); the Caribbean region was added in 1984.

[8]This has also been termed the Prebisch–Singer theory, since Hans Singer (refugee from Nazi Germany, student of Keynes and UN economist) had independently advanced the same argument as Prebisch, at roughly the same time. Apparently, the two were unaware of each other's work, and did not collaborate on the thesis.

or fall. Prebisch backed up his theory with evidence from a United Nations (1949) study, showing that the result is a transfer of wealth from the periphery to centre, causing a downward spiral for the former.

Despite additional evidence at the time in support of Prebisch's arguments,[9] his mental model was not well received by modernization theorists. On the other hand, his theory carried with it policy prescriptions that were as well received in Latin America as they were rejected by more mainstream US economists (Prebisch, 1959: 255–7).

Prebisch called for protecting infant industries against foreign competition through tariffs and other trade barriers. These ideas were hardly radical; in fact, they received support from the Kennedy Administration during the early years of the Alliance for Progress, which adopted the ECLA doctrine. Prebisch went on to head the UN Conference on Trade and Development (UNCTAD), conceived as a developing nation counterweight to the General Agreement on Tariffs and Trade (GATT), and was instrumental in the creation of the developing nations' Group of 77 (Dosman, 2010). But, by the 1970s, Prebisch had come to reject some of his earlier ideas.[10] In a 1971 report he wrote for the Inter-American Development Bank, he called for increased foreign aid and investment, a growth in trade, and an end to dependence on 'import substitution alone', since 'the fruit has been squeezed too hard by now for the flow of juice to be as plentiful as at first' (Dosman, 2010; Prebisch, 1971: 5).

Prebisch's changing mental model reflected changes in the world economy. Beginning in the 1960s, the economies of many East Asia countries began a decades-long growth spurt, with Hong Kong, Singapore, South Korea and Taiwan achieving annual growth rates exceeding seven per cent. Their success was in part attributed to economic policies that welcomed foreign investment: they were the targets of global supply chains for the manufacture and export of low-cost goods, providing foreign exchange that developmentally oriented states could invest in infrastructure and other growth-inducing projects.

The promise of export-oriented industrialization informed the mental model of Fernando Enrique Cardoso, a Brazilian sociologist who later served two terms as Brazil's President (1995–2003). Cardoso argued that under certain circumstances economic development was possible, even in a world economy shaped by unequal exchange. In 1969, Cardoso and the Chilean sociologist Enzo Faletto co-authored *Dependencia y Desarrollo en América Latina*, which was translated into English 10 years later (Cardoso and Faletto, 1979). *Dependency and Development in Latin America* had an outsized influence on thinking about dependency, particularly in the USA (Packenham, 1982). Cardoso argued that the *dependistas*, 'a term that makes me shudder' (1977: 8), had failed to take into account the concrete 'historical-structural' circumstances faced by dependent countries: 'the present situation cannot be understood without an analysis, however brief, of the historical situations that explain how Latin American nations fit into the world-system of

---

[9]'It seems fairly clear that over long and crucial times in the twentieth century the terms of trade have been declining for many peripheral areas. And the periods of primary materials boom were not sufficient to build up enough reserves for adverse periods' (Baer, 1962: 179).

[10]Prebisch, concerned with Perón's policies, had begun warning against excessive protectionism a decade earlier (Dosman, 2010).

power and the periphery of the international economy' (Cardoso and Faletto, 1979: 30). These are circumstances that make 'associated-dependent development' possible.[11] Cardoso (1977: 12–13) was especially critical of 'vulgar' (Marxist) theories that 'regarded imperialism and external economic conditioning as the substantive and omnipresent explanation of every social or ideological process that occurred'.

According to Cardoso's mental model, dependency was a function of social, economic and political relations that were both internal and external to a specific economy. The governments of developing countries were caught in a contradictory structural location – they served national interests while also serving as instruments of international capital. To understand how this played out required a concrete empirical analysis of the international and national conditions in a specific country such as Brazil. Under what circumstances is the national bourgeoisie truly *comprador*? Under what circumstances does it become developmental in a way that serves national (even if at the same time global capitalist) interests? Cardoso (ibid.: 16) emphasized the importance of analyzing the 'classes and groups which, in the struggle for control or for the reformulation of the existing order (through parties, movements, ideologies, the state, etc.) are making a given structure of domination historically viable or are transforming it'.

Cardoso acknowledges that his 'dependent-associated development' model does not apply universally to all peripheral countries: his is not a one-size-fits-all approach, dictated by some grand overarching theory. Although the different circumstances confronting peripheral economies, along with the greater technological, economic and political power of the centre, 'leave no doubt about the distinction between central and dependent economies … [there are] more dynamic forms of dependence than those characterizing enclave or quasi-colonial situations (even allowing greater degrees of maneuver to the national states and to the bourgeoisies locally associated to the state and the multinationals' (ibid.: 20).

In *Dependency and Development*, Cardoso and Faletto examine the developmental trajectories of Chile, Argentina, Brazil, Mexico, Bolivia, Puerto Rico and Cuba, identifying various developmental phases, the most recent of which involves the penetration of multinationals, whose supply chains render the relations between periphery and centre more interdependent then was previously the case (the relationship under colonialism, for example, was more of a one-sided dependency). Such interdependence does not imply equal relations between centre and periphery, since the latter remains highly constrained. It does, however, create a space for some degree of local autonomy. The formation of an industrial working class, for example, may result in labour militancy, as workers demand a share of the wealth they are producing. Under such circumstances, if labour movements and other marginalized groups are not repressed, class struggle may result in a developmental state, in which the benefits of economic growth are more widely shared.

Since the possibilities for dependent-associated development are contingent on a country's internal and external circumstances, Cardoso does not provide any universally clear pathways for development. On the contrary, his prognosis is generally pessimistic for many of the Latin American countries he reviews, at least in the short run: he does not see either the national bourgeoisie or the working class as revolutionary, although more 'episodic' uprisings may occur and bring short-term benefits. The best hope is for sustained

---

[11]Cardoso's phrase is often abbreviated to 'dependent development'.

economic growth, from which some of the benefits would trickle down to workers. For Brazil, patience is required: uneven development (along with increased inequality) is seen as a best case scenario (Cardoso, 1973a, 1973b; see also Myer, 1975).

Patience was not regarded as a virtue under Andre Gunder Frank's mental model for economic development in the periphery, which called for revolutionary action. Frank, a German-born economist whose family immigrated to the USA when Hitler came to power, was one of the most influential and controversial *dependistas*.[12]

Frank was the author of dozens of books and countless publications, the most important of which were translated into Spanish, earning him iconic status among young Latin American activists seeking revolutionary change (Bhattacharya, 2005). His most influential writings for dependency theory included his essay 'The Development of Underdevelopment' (Frank, 1966), the expanded argument in his book *Capitalism and Underdevelopment in Latin America* (Frank, 1967), and *Latin America: Underdevelopment or Revolution* (1969). As the title of the latter suggests, Frank came to the conclusion that the only solution for dependency was to delink the periphery from the centre (or satellite from metropole, Frank's preferred term in his earlier writings), as Cuba had done a decade earlier – something that could be achieved (as Cuba had done) through revolution.

In Frank's mental model, underdevelopment in Latin America resulted not from the region's supposed feudal past and *latifundista* landholdings, but rather stemmed from the region's role in a global capitalist system. In 'The Development of Underdevelopment', Frank described an economic system in which development in the metropole both requires and results in cascading underdevelopment throughout satellite economies, in which economic wealth flows ever upward, with some siphoned off by countries that serve both as metropole to those below them on the economic food chain, and as satellite to those above:

> a whole chain of constellation of metropoles and satellites relates all parts of the whole system from its metropolitan center in Europe or the United States to the farthest outpost in the Latin American countryside … When we examine the metropolis-satellite structure, we find that each of the satellites, including now underdeveloped Spain and Portugal, serves as an instrument to such capital or economic surplus out of its own satellites and to channel part of this surplus to the world metropolis of which all are satellites. Moreover, each national local metropolis serves to impose and maintain the monopolistic structure and exploitative relationship of this system … as long as it serves the interest of the metropoles which take advantage of this global, national, and local structure to promote their own development and the enrichment of their ruling classes. (Frank, 1966, reprinted in Corbridge, 2008: 227–8)

---

[12]Frank was a professor at the University of Chile during the Allende Government, which was violently overthrown in 1973 by the Chilean military with US CIA support. During the period of repression that followed, Frank penned several 'open letters' to his former University of Chicago economics professor, Milton Friedman, a leading free market theorist, in which Frank 'began by reminiscing about the genesis, during the mid-1950s, when I was your graduate student, of the "Chile programme" in the Department of Economics at the University of Chicago, in which you trained the so-called "Chicago boys," who now inspire and execute the economic policy of the military junta in Chile … I examined with you the consequences … political repression and torture, monopolization and sell-out to foreign capital, unemployment and starvation, declining health and increasing crime, all fostered by a calculated policy of political and *economic* genocide' (Frank, 1976: 880).

Frank further argued (in what he offered as a testable hypothesis) that contrary to pre-vailing economic theory, economic growth in the satellite is inversely related to the strength of its ties to the metropole: the weaker the relationship, the stronger the growth. Preliminary supporting evidence was to be found in growth spurts of Argentina, Brazil, Mexico and Chile, which occurred when their economic ties to the USA were weakened during two world wars and the Depression – growth spurts that ended, he argued, when the USA resumed economic growth and resumed strong trade relations with its Latin American satellites. He strongly rejected the moderate, import-substitution approach of Prebisch and his ECLA colleagues, as well as the doctrinaire approaches of Soviet-style communism (from which he excluded Cuba, which he regarded as a positive example).

Frank also came to believe that, by the 1970s, the global capitalist system was experi-encing crises of capital accumulation and declining profits, which led him to the conclu-sion that dependence 'has ended or is completing that cycle of its natural life, at least in the Latin America that gave it birth' (Frank, 1974: 89). In *Latin America: Underdevelopment or Revolution* (1969), he argues that Latin America must free itself from its metropole-satellite relations in a capitalist world economy if it hopes to throw off the shackles of underdevelopment. Trade and foreign investment only benefits a small middle class, buying their support while blunting the fact that conditions become worse for the large majority of people. Foreign investment 'progressively denationalizes Brazilian indus-try, misdirects Brazilian investment [and] integrates the weaker Brazilian economy increasingly with the stronger American one' (ibid.: 152). The final chapter of the book, 'Capitalist Underdevelopment or Socialist Revolution', makes it clear that Cuban-style socialism is the only alternative.

In one of his last major works, *ReOrient: Global Economy in the Asian Age*, Frank (1998) sought to overturn what he had come to see as a Eurocentric emphasis on the rise of a dominant West, by arguing that a Chinese-centred world-system long predated the European one, and that the West rose only when Asia declined because of self-inflicted limitations such as population pressures on limited resources (for an evaluation and cri-tique, see Arrighi, 1999).

ENVISIONING THE UNSTABLE UNITY OF THE WORLD-SYSTEM

Frank's theories served as a bridge to world-systems theory, an approach with which he later came to be identified. Immanuel Wallerstein is the name most strongly associated with world-systems theory: he created its foundational mental model, its intellectual centre at the State University of New York at Binghamton, its leading journal (*Review*), and the Political Economy of the World-System (PEWS) section of the American Sociological Association.[13] Wallerstein is also the most prolific writer on the theory, whose works range from historical analyses of modern capitalism to epistemological reflections on the emergence and consequences of disciplinary boundaries. Like the dependency theories it

---

[13]PEWS also sponsors the online *Journal of World-Systems Research*. (Available at: http://jwsr.pitt.edu/ojs/index.php/jwsr (accessed 27 February 2017).

draws upon, world-systems theory seeks to be interdisciplinary, drawing on economics, sociology, political science and, most recently, environmental science.

Wallerstein began his scholarly career as an Africanist, doing his doctoral research in West Africa (today, Ghana and Côte d'Ivoire) as the region was fighting for independence from British and French colonialism. For a decade and a half, his publications focused on post-colonial Africa, where one of his key influences was Frantz Fanon, whose writings on the Algerian national liberation movement and the struggles (and voices) of the disenfranchised contributed to Wallerstein's focus on the possibilities of resistance to the modern world-system (Wallerstein, 2000).[14] He was also heavily influenced by the French *Annales* school, particularly the work of Fernand Braudel (for whom Wallerstein's SUNY-Binghamton centre was named), with its emphasis on understanding long-term trends in history (Braudel's *longue durée*) and the importance of rural populations as a source of surplus labour (although unlike W. Arthur Lewis, Wallerstein rejected the assumption that proper government planning and import controls could solve the surplus labour problem).

Drawing selectively on Marx and dependency theory, Wallerstein argued that capitalism had to be understood as a world-system – that the economic misfortunes of individual countries could not be resolved without a change of the world-system as a whole. By 'world-system',[15] Wallerstein meant a social system that encompassed multiple polities:

> one that has boundaries, structures, member groups, rules of legitimation, and coherence. Its life is made up of the conflicting forces which hold it together by tension, and tear it apart as each group seeks eternally to remold it to its advantage. It has the characteristics of an organism, in that is has a life-span over which its characteristics change in some respects and remain stable in others ... Life within it is largely self-contained, and the dynamics of its development are largely internal. (Wallerstein, 1974, quote from 2011 reprint: 347)

World-systems range from prehistoric (and pre-capitalist) 'mini-systems'[16] to the modern capitalist world-system that has (as Marx predicted) come to penetrate the entire planet. From dependency theory, Wallerstein extended the relational concepts of core and periphery by adding that of semiperiphery – a global group of nations that extracted

---

[14]Wallerstein played a key role in the US publication of Fanon's best-known work, *The Wretched of the Earth* (Goldfrank, 2000: 157).

[15]The hyphen in world-system is intended to show that the system is not necessarily global in extent (which Wallerstein argues would be implied absent the hyphen), but refers to whatever spatial unit makes sense in historical context.

[16]Wallerstein argued that mini-systems – economically interlinked tribal economies – have been largely absorbed into capitalist economies; anthropologists therefore erred in treating them as separate from the modern world-system. While Wallerstein devoted his attention to the modern capitalist world-system, other world-systems theorists have examined much smaller pre-modern mini-systems as well as world-systems 'from the stone age to the present' (Chase-Dunn and Lerro, 2013). See also Chase-Dunn and Anderson (2005), Chase-Dunn and Mann (1998), Chase-Dunn and Hall (1991).

surplus from peripheral nations while yielding surplus to core nations.[17] The semiperiphery offered the promise of upward mobility within the world-system and thereby providing a degree of system stability. Contrary to dependency theorists, however, Wallerstein rejected the notion that development was possible through such national strategies as import substitution (or, for that matter, completely disconnecting from the world-capitalist system through revolution): it is the system itself that must be changed.

According to Wallerstein's mental model, two principal types of world-systems have existed in recent centuries: world-empires and world-economies. While both involve the interaction of different cultures or polities, world-empires are unified politically under a single administrative structure, while world-economies are unified economically through trade and a division of labour. World-empires were a dominant form of world-system in the past; world-economies dominate today. Neither is stable: world-empires come and go, and world-economies are characterized by struggles for dominance by core countries. Wallerstein introduced the notion of 'commodity chain' as a way of emphasizing the centrality of core-periphery relations in the capitalist world-economy:

> take an ultimate consumable item and trace back the set of inputs that culminated in this item, including prior transformations, the raw materials, the transportation mechanisms, the labor input into each of the material processes, the food inputs into the labor. This linked set of processes we call a commodity chain. (Wallerstein and Hopkins, 1977: 128)[18]

Within commodity chains, there are core and peripheral labour processes, which change over time. Manufacturing, for example, may have been a core, capital-intensive process (given the technology of the time) in the textile industry centuries ago, enabling Britain to rise to core status in the world-economy. Today, however, it has been relegated to peripheral status, involving low-wage labour in peripheral countries.

Within the world-economy, the struggle for dominance reflects the interests and strength of the leading capitalists in competing core nations, and, importantly, the ability

---

[17] Among dependency theorists, Wallerstein drew on Samir Amin's (1974, 1976) ideas about peripheral capitalism; Fernando Enrique Cardoso's notion of associated dependent development; Emmanuel Arghiri's (1972) emphasis on unequal exchange (which includes critique of Lewis and Prebisch); and Andre Gunder Frank's ideas about satellitization – the chain of metropole-satellite dependency relations, previously discussed. Other influences included the economic historian Karl Polanyi, from whom Wallerstein derived his three principal types of world-systems (mini-systems, world-empires and world-economies), and the political economist Joseph Schumpeter, who emphasized the disruptive effects of business cycles (see Goldfrank, 2000, for a complete discussion).

[18] The notion of a commodity chain has been most fully developed by the sociologist Gary Gereffi and his colleagues (see: https://globalvaluechains.org/). Three decades ago, Wallerstein and Hopkin's conceptualization was radical in calling for focusing on cross-border economic flows as a way of understanding the inequalities built into core–periphery relations – an understanding that is absent from today's seemingly parallel notion of global supply chains, which is focused instead on enhancing economic efficiency in cross-border business operations. For a discussion of the ways in which twenty-first-century global supply chains affect workers, see Appelbaum and Lichtenstein (2016).

of their respective state structures to create conditions favourable to success.[19] Nationally, this can take such form as product protection (for example, through government-issued patents), state spending on infrastructure and other economic investments, and state spending through purchases or subsidies in key industries. Globally, dominance may be sought by championing open markets ('free trade'), under which the strongest core state is most likely to be competitive.

States thus play a key role in Wallerstein's framework, since they can propel a core state to hegemonic status in the world-economy.[20] In the capitalist world-economy, periods of hegemonic dominance – characterized by relative system stability – alternate with transitional periods that are characterized by system instability. In Wallerstein's analysis, the Dutch were hegemonic in terms of trade and finance in the seventeenth century, the British in the nineteenth and the USA in the twentieth; transitional periods were plagued by world wars and financial chaos.[21] The transition from Dutch to British hegemony was marked by the industrial revolution, which initiated the shift from agriculture to industry as the basis for capitalism; the transition from British to US hegemony by the globalization of the world-economy, and the emergence of socialist alternatives (which, in Wallerstein's view, became a part of the capitalist world-economy that they challenged). The rise and fall of hegemonic powers can in part be tracked – and perhaps predicted – by long waves of expansion and contraction in the global economy, some waves a half-century or so in length, some longer (so-called Kondratieff waves, named after the Soviet economist who first identified them in the 1930s).[22] Hegemonic expansion has been limited historically by the key system contradictions identified by Marx, previously discussed: overproduction relative to the consumption ability of workers whose earnings are systematically kept low by the pressures of interstate capitalist competition. As Marx had recognized more than a century and a half earlier, the solutions to this problem – technological change and the offshoring of production – only serve to worsen it.

In Wallerstein's mental model (2001: 87), the world-economy today is 'in the period immediately preceding a bifurcation. The present historical system is in fact in

---

[19]In contrast to Wallerstein's formulation of world-systems theory, William Robinson's theory of global capitalism (2004, 2007, 2014) argues that in its current phase, the global capitalist-system is increasingly characterized by a globalized production and financial system, a transnational capitalist class, a transnational state and a rising global police state; individual state actors are replaced by a global class of actors with limited or no state loyalties.

[20]Hegemony involves political, economic, cultural and – if necessary – military dominance. The notion of hegemony was most fully developed by the Italian Marxist theorist Antonio Gramsci, who advanced the notion that hegemony also involves cultural dominance and hence some degree of 'rule by consent'. Gramsci developed these ideas while in prison from 1926 and 1935 (for selections from his *Prison Notebooks*, see Gramsci, 2015).

[21]Giovanni Arrighi and Beverly Silver (1999) aptly described periods of hegemonic dominance as characterized by 'governance' and transitional periods as 'chaos,' noting that 'the life-cycles of the regimes of accumulation [and therefore hegemonic dominance] have become shorter' (Arrighi, 2010: 377).

[22]For an effort to empirically link Kondratieff waves with leading economic sectors and hegemonic shifts from the fifteenth through the twentieth centuries, see Boswell and Chase-Dunn, 2000).

terminal crisis. The issue before us is what will replace it. This will be the central political debate of the next twenty-five to fifty years.' This 'terminal crisis' results from the fact that, on a global scale, the costs of production will outstrip the revenues that they can bring, reducing profits to a point where the capitalist system is no longer viable. Wallerstein sees production costs as rising for three reasons. First, remuneration costs increase, as employees – from factory workers to managers and professionals – demand their fair share. While offshoring production is one strategy to reduce these costs, it also results in the higher transaction costs associated with sustaining global supply chains, while further reducing the purchasing power required to consume the goods produced. Second, Wallerstein argues that the costs of economic inputs are also rising, the result of growing demand for increasingly scarce raw materials, the environmental costs associated with raw material extraction and waste disposal,[23] and the costs of providing the roads, transport and other infrastructure required to produce and distribute goods on a global scale. These costs are either born by businesses (thereby cutting into profits), or externalized to governments, which then contributes to the third source of rising production costs: taxation. Modern states must not only pay for such things as infrastructure, internal and external security, and environmental cleanup, but also are expected by their citizens to provide universal education, health benefits, and lifetime income guarantees in the form of unemployment compensation and retirement income. Businesses resist paying rising taxes, which either shifts the burden to citizens, or results in declining public services, as state power declines (Wallerstein, 2004, chapter 5; see also Wallerstein, 2001, chapter 5).

Over the coming decade or so, Wallerstein envisions further decline in US hegemony, with probable (if uncertain) outcomes, including the disappearance of the dollar as the dominant currency, replaced by a multicurrency system; the growing power of China, Japan and South Korea, particularly if historic differences between the three countries can be overcome; and the emergence of South America as an economic power no longer dependent on the USA (Wallerstein, 2016). In the short term, Wallerstein calls for 'actions that minimize the pain' of the billions who are marginalized by the global capitalist system. But such actions in no way address the system itself, which as it approaches its 'terminal crisis', is up for grabs:

> In the middle-run (that is, the next 20–40 years), the debate is fundamental and total. There is no compromise. One side or the other will win. I call this the battle between the spirit of Davos and the spirit of Porto Alegre.[24] The spirit of Davos calls for a new non-capitalist system that retains its worst features – hierarchy, exploitation, and polarization.

---

[23]Wallerstein (2001: 85) views ecological degradation as 'a central locus of this debate' (over what will replace the current system).

[24]Davos refers to the World Economic Forum, an annual meeting in Davos, Switzerland, of 'the foremost political, business and other leaders of society to shape global, regional and industry agendas' (https://www.weforum.org/about/world-economic-forum). 'Porto Alegre' refers to the World Social Forum, created in 2001, as an anti-capitalist, anti-globalization alternative to the World Economic Forum; its annual meetings are comprised of 'people from groups in civil society, organizations and social movements who want to build a sustainable and inclusive world, where every person and every people has its place and can make its voice heard' (https://fsm2016.org/en/) under the slogan 'Another world is possible'.

They could well install a world-system that is worse than our present one. The spirit of Porto Alegre seeks a system that is relatively democratic and relatively egalitarian … We do not know who will win in this struggle. What we do know is that, in a chaotic world, every nano-action at every nano-moment on every nano-issue affects the outcome (Wallerstein, 2014: 171).

CONCLUSION: RE-ENCOUNTERING DEVELOPMENT

The *World Development Report 2015* argues that 'economic and political forces influence mental models', which in turn 'can have an independent influence on development by shaping attention, perception, interpretation, and the associations that automatically come to mind' (World Bank, 2014: 72). The *Report* offers numerous suggestions for understanding how the mental models that presumably blind the recipients of aid can thwart effective policy-making, and how such obstacles can be overcome. In this chapter, I have sought to reverse the lens, focusing instead on the mental models that guide the policy-makers themselves. While the *Report* correctly challenges the rational-choice mental model of the 'standard economic theory' that provides 'the analytical foundations of public policy' (ibid.: 29), it fails to address the ways in which the leading theories are themselves subject to largely unchallenged assumptions. Despite an epistemological commitment to evidence-based theorizing, social scientists are hardly immune to confirmation bias. Theories can have a long shelf life, even after the circumstances that gave rise to them have radically changed.

Modernization theories gained traction in the second half of the twentieth century, a time when the Cold War struggle for the hearts and minds (not to mention wealth) of newly independent nations gave rise, in the global North, to the mental model called 'development', along with an industry of practitioners schooled in its associated theories. This mental model included a belief in the inevitability of progress, so long as the benevolent hands of well-schooled practitioners guided the benighted citizens of poor countries. Progress, in turn, was understood as moving towards the economic, social and cultural practices of the most economically advanced capitalist countries. This mental model continues to hold sway over much development thinking.

In the global South, such ideas were strongly resisted. The experience of scholars living under the less beneficent side of global capitalist relations resulted in a very different mental map – one that emphasized a vicious downward spiral of dependency and exploitation, resulting from the vastly unequal economic and power relations between the global North and South. Although dependency theory reversed the valences of modernization theory – the principal evils were to be found in the exploitative practices of the global North, rather than the failings of the global South – the notions of economic progress remained largely unchallenged. Modernization theory's end point – the 'age of high mass consumption' – remained a worthy goal for the *dependistas*, provided the fruits of progress were equitably shared under democratic socialist principles. Yet, dependency theorists, as we have seen, varied in their understanding of the possibilities for economic development in the global South.

World-system theory rethinks and builds upon dependency theory, reframing dependency's mental map historically and geographically, in light of the fact that globalization has now resulted in a true world-economy. The theory addresses the role of states within such an economy, arguing for the inevitability of hegemonic shifts, while taking into account what it sees as the impending limits to the world-system itself – limits that stem both from the internal logic of the global capitalism, as well as growing ecological constraints on future growth. The inevitability of progress, however defined, is clearly not a central assumption of world-system theory's mental model. The mental model that emphasizes the centrality of the capitalist world-system predicts eventual system collapse – and the need to replace it with something different.

In the social sciences, theories can never be subject to the same canons of evidence that, at least ideally, characterize the natural sciences. Distilling the complexities of history, or of a world-economy, into propositions that are capable of indisputable empirical verification remains an elusive goal. Some degree of confirmation bias will always afflict the mental models underling social science theorizing. Although any acceptable theory must be consonant with the observed evidence, the beauty of a particular theory will always be, at least in part, in the eyes of the beholder. Yet, all theories are not equal: some will stand the test of time better than others. The world is in the midst of seismic economic, political and ecological shifts that will surely test the staying power of the theories we have reviewed – and, most likely, others that will challenge them.

Questions for Discussion

1   Why does modernization theory remain an influential mental model of development?
2   Is development simply a matter of good economic management?
3   If all mental models are to some extent biased, how can development practitioners reconcile differences and act in concert to achieve development goals?

📖 FURTHER READING

Arrighi, G. (2010) *The Long Twentieth Century: Money, Power and the Origins of Our Times*. London: Verso.
Piketty, T. (2014) *Capital in the Twenty-First Century* (Arthur Goldhammer trans.). Cambridge, MA: Harvard University Press.
Stiglitz, J., Sen, A. and Fitoussi, J.-P. (2010) *Mismeasuring Our Lives: Why GDP Doesn't Add Up*. New York: The New Press.

REFERENCES

Amin, S. (1974) *Accumulation on a World Scale*. New York and London: Monthly Review Press.
Amin, S. (1976) *An Essay on the Social Formations of Peripheral Capitalism*. New York and London: Monthly Review Press.

Angotti, T. (1981) 'The Political Implications of Dependency Theory', *Latin American Perspectives Dependency and Marxism*, 8(3–4): 124–37.

Appelbaum, R.P. and Lichtenstein, N. (eds) (2016) *Achieving Workers' Rights in the Global Economy*. Ithaca, NY: Cornell University Press.

Arghiri, E. (1972) *Unequal Exchange: A Study of the Imperialism of Trade*. New York and London: Monthly Review Press.

Arrighi, G. (1999) 'The World According to Andre Gunder Frank', *Review*, 22(3): 327–54.

Arrighi, G. (2010) *The Long Twentieth Century: Money, Power and the Origins of Our Times*. London: Verso.

Arrighi, G. and Silver, B. (1999) *Chaos and Governance in the Modern World System*. Minneapolis, MN: University of Minnesota Press.

Baer, W. (1962) 'The Economics of Prebisch and ECLA', *Economic Development and Cultural Change*, 10(2): 169–82.

Bereketeab, R. (ed.) (2016) *Self-Determination and Secession in Africa: The Post-Colonial State*. New York: Routledge.

Betts, R.F. (2004) *Decolonization: The Making of the Contemporary World* (2nd edn). New York: Routledge.

Bhattacharya, S. (2005) 'Andre Gunder Frank, 1929–2005: The Scholar Gypsy', *Economic and Political Weekly*, 40(19): 1946–7.

Black, J.K. (1977) 'Development and Modernization Theory: A Critical Review', *CrossCurrents*, 27(1): 41–56.

Boswell, T. and Chase-Dunn, C. (2000) *The Spiral of Capitalism and Socialism: Toward Global Democracy*. Boulder, CO: Lynn Reiner.

Brown, B. (1969) 'The French Experience of Modernization', *World Politics*, 21(3): 366–91.

Caldentey, P.E. and Vernengo, M. (2015) 'Reading Keynes in Buenos Aires: Prebisch and the Dynamics of Capitalism', *Cambridge Journal of Economics* (November): doi: 10.1093/cje/bev074

Cardoso, F.E. and Faletto, E. (1979) *Dependency and Development in Latin America*. Berkeley, CA: University of California Press.

Cardoso, F.H. (1973a) 'Associated-Dependent Development: Theoretical and Practical Implications', in A. Stepan (ed.), *Authoritarian Brazil: Origins, Policies, and Future*. New Haven, CT: Yale University Press, pp. 142–76.

Cardoso, F.H. (1973b) 'Imperialism and Dependency in Latin America', in F. Bonilla and R. Girling (eds), *Structures of Dependency*. Redwood, CA: Stanford University Press, pp. 7–16.

Cardoso, F.H. (1977) 'The Consumption of Dependency Theory in the United States', *Latin American Research Review*, 12(3): 7–24.

Chamberlain, M.E. (2014) *Longman Companion to European Colonization in the Twentieth Century*. New York: Routledge.

Chase-Dunn, C. and Anderson, E.N. (eds) (2005) *The Historical Evolution of World-Systems*. Basingstoke: Palgrave Macmillan.

Chase-Dunn, C. and Hall, T.D. (1991) *Core/Periphery Relations in Precapitalist Worlds*. Boulder, CO: Westview Press.

Chase-Dunn, C. and Lerro, B. (2013) *Social Change: Globalization from the Stone Age to the Present*. Boulder, CO: Paradigm Publishers.

Chase-Dunn, C. and Mann, K.M. (1998) *The Wintu and Their Neighbors: A Very Small World-System in Northern California*. Tucson, AZ: University of Arizona Press.

Corbridge, S. (ed.) (2008) *Development: Critical Concepts in the Social Sciences. Vol. 1: Doctrines of Development*. New York: Routledge.

Denzau, A.T. and North, D.C. (1994) 'Shared Mental Models: Ideologies and Institutions', *Kyklos*, 47(1): 3–31.

DiMaggio, P. (1997) 'Culture and Cognition', *Annual Review of Sociology*, 23(1): 263–87.

Dosman, E.J. (2010) *The Life and Times of Raúl Prebisch, 1901–1986*. Montreal: McGill-Queen's University Press.

Easterly, W. (2006) *The White Man's Burden: Why the West's Efforts to Aid the Rest Have Done so Much Ill and so Little Good*. New York: Penguin Press.

Easterly, W. (2014) *The Tyranny of Experts: Economists, Dictators, and the Forgotten Rights of the Poor*. New York: Basic Books.

Escobar, A. (2012) *Encountering Development: The Making and Unmaking of the Third World*. Princeton, NJ: Princeton University Press.

Frank, A.G. (1966) 'The Development of Underdevelopment', *Monthly Review*, 18(4): 27–37.

Frank, A.G. (1967) *Capitalism and Underdevelopment in Latin America*. New York: Monthly Review Press.

Frank, A.G. (1969) *Latin America: Underdevelopment or Revolution*. New York: Monthly Review Press.

Frank, A.G. (1974) 'Dependence is Dead, Long Live Dependence and the Class Struggle: An Answer to Critics', *Latin American Perspectives*, 1(1): 87–106.

Frank, A.G. (1998) *ReOrient: Global Economy in the Asian Age*. Berkeley, CA: University of California Press.

Gilman, N. (2007) *Mandarins of the Future: Modernization Theory in Cold War America*. Baltimore, MD: Johns Hopkins University Press.

Goldfrank, W.L. (2000) 'Paradigm Regained? The Rules of Wallerstein's World-System Method', *Journal of World-Systems Research*, 6(2): 150–95. Available at: http://jwsr.pitt.edu/ojs/index.php/jwsr/article/view/223.

Gramsci, A. (2015) *Selections from the Prison Notebooks*. Amazon Digital Services LLC.

Horowitz, I.L. (1966) *Three Worlds of Development: The Theory and Practice of International Stratification*. New York: Oxford University Press.

Ish-Shalom, P. (2006) 'Theory Gets Real, and the Case for a Normative Ethic: Rostow, Modernization Theory, and the Alliance for Progress', *International Studies Quarterly*, 50: 287–311.

Keynes, J.M. (2011) (orig. 1936) *The General Theory of Employment, Interest, and Money*. CreateSpace Independent Publishing Platform.

Lewis, W.A. (1954) 'Development with Unlimited Supplies of Labour', *The Manchester School*, 22(2): 129–91.

Lewis, W.A. (1955) *The Theory of Economic Growth*. London: George Allen & Unwin, Ltd.

Markus, H. (1977) 'Self-Schemata and Processing Information about the Self', *Journal of Personality and Social Psychology*, 35(2): 63–78.

Marx, K. (1993) (orig. 1857–58) *Grundrisse: Foundations of the Critique of Political Economy.* London: Penguin Classics.

Marx, K. (2011) (orig. 1867) *Capital, Volume One.* New York: Dover Publications.

Moyo, D. (2010) *Dead Aid: Why Aid is not Working and How There is a Better Way for Africa.* New York: Farrar, Straus and Giroux.

Moyo, D. (2011) 'Aid Ironies: A Response to Jeffrey Sachs', *The Huffington Post* (25 May). Available at: www.huffingtonpost.com/dambisa-moyo/aid-ironies-a-respo nse-to_b_207772.html.

Myer, J. (1975) 'A Crown of Thorns: Cardoso and Counter-Revolution', *Latin American Perspectives,* 2(1): 33–48.

Ostrom, E. (2005) *Understanding Institutional Diversity.* Princeton, NJ: Princeton University Press.

Packenham, R.A. (1982) 'Plus ca Change …: The English Edition of Cardoso and Faletto's *Dependencia y Desarrollo en America Latina*', *Latin American Research Review,* 17(1): 131–51.

Parsons, T. (1951) *The Social System.* Glencoe, IL: Free Press.

Parsons, T. (1966) *Societies: Evolutionary and Comparative Perspectives.* Englewood Cliffs, NJ: Prentice-Hall.

Parsons, T., Bales, R. F. and Shils, E. (1953) *Working Papers on the Theory of Action.* Glencoe, IL: Free Press.

Prebisch, R. (1950) 'The Economic Development of Latin America and its Principal Problems', Introduction to the *Economic Survey of Latin America.* UN ECLA, Department of Economic Affairs, Lake Success, NY.

Prebisch, R. (1959) 'Commercial Policy in the Underdeveloped Countries', *American Economic Review, Papers and Proceedings of the Seventy-First Annual Meeting of the American Economic Association* (May): 251–73.

Prebisch, R. (1971) 'Change and Development: Latin America's Great Task', UN Economic Commission for Latin America (March).

Ranis, G. (2004) 'Arthur Lewis's Contribution to Development Thinking and Policy', *The Manchester School,* 72(6): 712–23.

Ricardo, D. (2015) (orig. 1817) *On the Principles of Political Economy, and Taxation.* Cambridge: Cambridge University Press.

Robinson, W.I. (2004) *A Theory of Global Capitalism: Production, Class, and State in a Transnational World.* Baltimore, MD: Johns Hopkins University Press.

Robinson, W.I. (2007) *Global Capitalism: Its Fall and Rise in the Twentieth Century.* New York City: W.W. Norton & Company.

Robinson, W.I. (2014) *Global Capitalism and the Crisis of Humanity.* Cambridge: Cambridge University Press.

Rostow, W.W. (1961) *The Stages of Economic Growth: A Non-Conformist Manifest.* Cambridge: Cambridge University Press.

Rostow, W.W. (1964) 'The Takeoff into Self-Sustained Growth', in A. and E. Etzioni (eds), *Social Change.* NY: Basic Books, pp. 275–90.

Rothermund, D. (2006) *The Routledge Companion to Decolonization.* New York: Routledge.

Sachs, J. (2009) 'Aid Ironies', *The Huffington Post* (24 June). Available at: www.huffing tonpost.com/jeffrey-sachs/aid-ironies_b_207181.html.

Sachs, J. (2011) 'Moyo's Confused Attack on Aid to Africa', *The Huffington Post* (25 May). Available at: www.huffingtonpost.com/jeffrey-sachs/moyos-confused-attack-on_b_208222.html.

Sauvy, A. (1952) 'Trois Mondes, Une Planete', *L'Observateur*, 14 August, 118, p. 14.

Smith, A. (2009) (orig. 1776) *An Inquiry into the Nature and Causes of the Wealth of Nations*, Book 4, Chapter 2. Thrifty Books. Available at the Project Gutenberg EBook: www.gutenberg.org/files/3300/3300-h/3300-h.htm.

Taffet, J. (2007) *Foreign Aid as Foreign Policy: The Alliance for Progress in Latin America.* New York: Routledge.

Tignor, R.L. (2006) *W. Arthur Lewis and the Birth of Development Economics.* Princeton, NJ, and Oxford: Princeton University Press.

Tignor, R.L. (2016) 'The lessons Ghana Learned from Kwame Nkrumah's Fallout with his Economic Adviser', *Quartz Africa* (March 16). Available at: http://qz.com/632155/the-lessons-ghana-learned-from-kwame-nkrumahs-fallout-with-his-economic-adviser/.

UN (1949) *Relative Prices of Imports and Exports of Under-Developed Countries.* UN Department of Economic Affairs (December), Lake Success, NY.

UN (2000) 'Resolution Adopted by the General Assembly, 55/1: United Nations Millennium Declaration' (18 September). Available at: www.un.org/millennium/declaration/ares552e.pdf.

UN (2015) *The Millennium Development Goals Report, 2015.* United Nations. Available at: www.undp.org/content/dam/undp/library/MDG/english/UNDP_MDG_Report_2015.pdf.

UNDP (2016a) 'A New Sustainable Development Agenda', United Nations Development Programme. Available at: www.undp.org/content/undp/en/home/sdgoverview.html.

UNDP (2016b) 'Millennium Development Goals', United Nations Development Programme. Available at: www.undp.org/content/undp/en/home/sdgoverview/mdg_goals.html.

UNDP (2016c) 'Goal 17: Partnerships for the Goals', Sustainable Development Goals, United Nations Development Programme. Available at: www.undp.org/content/undp/en/home/sdgoverview/post-2015-development-agenda/goal-17.html.

UNDP (2016d) 'A New Sustainable Development Agenda', Sustainable Development Goals, United Nations Development Programme. Available at: www.tl.undp.org/content/timor_leste/en/home/mdgoverview.html.

Wallerstein, I. (1974) *The Modern World-System I: Capitalist Agriculture and the Origins of the European World-Economy in the Sixteenth Century.* New York and London: Academic Press (reprinted by University of California Press, 2011).

Wallerstein, I. (1980) *The Modern World-System II: Mercantilism and the Consolidation of the European World Economy, 1600–1750.* New York and London: Academic Press (reprinted by University of California Press, 2011).

Wallerstein, I. (1989) *The Modern World-System III: The Second Era of Great Expansion of the Capitalist World-Economy.* New York and London: Academic Press (reprinted by University of California Press, 2011).

Wallerstein, I. (2000) *The Essential Wallerstein.* New York: The New Press.

Wallerstein, I. (2001) *The End of the World as We Know It: Social Science for the Twenty-First Century.* Minneapolis, MN: University of Minnesota Press.

Wallerstein, I. (2004) *World-Systems Analysis: An Introduction*. Durham, NC: Duke University Press.

Wallerstein, I. (2014) 'Antisystemic Movements: Yesterday and Today', *Journal of World-Systems Research*, 20(2) (summer/fall): 158–72. Available at: http://jwsr.pitt.edu/ojs/index.php/jwsr/article/view/593.

Wallerstein, I. (2016) 'The Increasingly Unstable United States', I. Wallerstein, *Commentaries*, 426 (June 1). Available at: http://iwallerstein.com/the-increasingly-unstable-united-states/.

Wallerstein, I. and Hopkins, T.K. (1977) 'Patterns of Development of the Modern World System', *Review*, 1(2): 111–45.

Weiner, M. (ed.). (1964) *Modernization: The Dynamics of Growth*. New York: Basic Books.

White, N. (2014) *Decolonization: The British Experience Since 1945*. New York: Routledge.

World Bank (2014) *World Development Report 2015: Mind, Society, and Behavior*. Washington, DC: The World Bank Group. Available at: www.worldbank.org/en/publication/wdr2015.

Worsley, P.M. (1967) 'Review of Horowitz', *Political Science Quarterly*, 82(1): 155–6.

4
GOVERNANCE, POWER AND PARTICIPATION

PAUL BATTERSBY, THUNRADEE TAVEEKAN AND GREGOIRE NIMBTIK

INTRODUCTION

Governance is widely interpreted to mean the art and practice of governing well, with the conceptual complication that governance can be 'bad' when agreed norms are ignored by those in power. The term is ubiquitous in the lexicon of development and is closely associated with models of democracy, participation and consensus. Governance has been described in the field of international relations as governing 'without government', but in practice government and governance at the national and global levels are two sides of the same coin (Rosenau, 1992: 2). Government, in its simplest sense, involves the direction of public affairs through formal executive and bureaucratic processes, where direct popular participation is limited to periodic voting conducted within widely varying limits or bandwidths of political choice. Governance, in the ideal, accommodates a greater degree of informality in the making of collective choices, and where decisions reflect a general consensus derived from multiple sources of legitimate authority and through a variety of direct and indirect means (Stevenson and Dryzek, 2014; Weiss, 2013; Dryzek, 2010; Held, 2010; Whitman, 2005; Commission on Global Governance, 1996). Yet, not everyone can be persuaded to happily accept rules made in their name.

This chapter reviews the adoption and adaptation of imported models of governance in two developing countries.[1] The first outlines incongruities and potential complementarities between Western and indigenous ideas of political authority in the Pacific Island state of Vanuatu. The second explains the limits to grassroots political

---

[1]Designated as such by Australia's Department of Foreign Affairs and Trade, at: https://dfat.gov.au/about-us/publications/Documents/list-developing-countries.pdf (accessed 3 March 2016).

participation in Thailand's rural Northeast. Both highlight why deep contextual knowledge is essential for development practitioners planning governance interventions in complex social settings.

REPERTOIRES OF GOVERNANCE

There is no single agreed definition of governance. Instead, there is a diverse range of cognate terms differentiated by prefix, which are distinct but where there is substantial overlap (see Table 4.1). Then there is the notion of 'good enough governance', where the quest for the perfect universal model is abandoned in search of workable accommodations, or compromises, in recognition that what applies in one context is not necessarily appropriate to another (Grindle, 2005). This is the 'best-fit' approach of 'second generation governance' (Carothers and de Gramont, 2011: 11, 18), in which technocratic schemes are adapted to correspond with realities on the ground in such a way that existing social institutions, and established modes of operation, are acknowledged and accommodated, not dismissed and ridden over roughshod (ibid.: 11; Duncan, 2011; IDS, 2010; Rodrik, 2008; Tuimaleali'ifano, 2006).

The phrase 'good enough' presupposes a universal ideal, which in turn implies that practices which do not accord with this ideal must be judged as 'second best' (Rodrik, 2008). From a World Bank perspective, this ideal encompasses the 'rule of law', 'control of corruption', 'accountability', 'political stability' and 'voice', where the latter accommodates

Table 4.1   A Typology of Governance Terms

Forms of Governance	Salient Principles
Global governance	Order, power, security, cooperation, regulation, compliance, legal rights, obligations, the rule of law
Democratic governance	Public accountability, electoral and multi-party democracy, negotiation, consensus, pluralism, global justice, human rights, public interest
Network governance	Collaboration, cooperation, coordination, social networks and social capital
Deliberative governance	Deliberation, negotiation, consensus, multiplicity, polyvocalism, community
Multi-stakeholder governance	Consultation, cooperation, coordination, voice, community, compliance
Corporate governance	Legal compliance, financial viability, social and environmental responsibility, transparency and accountability
Cosmopolitan governance	Responsiveness, social justice, democracy, rights, public interest and public accountability
Environmental governance	Sustainability, complexity, adaptiveness, stewardship, stakeholders, community

Note: Many other principles are common to all, for example freedom, which is implicit in the notion of rights and obligations and intrinsic to accepted notions of consultation and deliberation (Weiss, 2013; Dryzek, 2010; Bevir, 2009; Sørensen and Torfing, 2008; Rhodes, 1997, 2006, 2012; Held, 2010; Whitman, 2005).

collective forms of participation in governmental decision-making, with electoral democracy clearly the preferred model (World Bank, *c.* 2016; Kaufmann et al., 2010; Kaufmann et al., 2007). This is a didactic approach, based on a presumed universality of the Western experience of democratization, but one that is nonetheless amenable to measurement and measured policy intervention. It echoes the aggregative definition advanced by the Commission on Global Governance, for which governance is 'the sum of the many ways individuals and institutions, public and private, manage their common affairs' (1996: 2). The Commission's definition encapsulates multidimensional and multi-level interactions, but while there is acknowledgement of a society's right to shape institutional agendas, the guiding concern is with 'compliance' and 'enforcement', or, in other words, with the exercise of executive power (ibid.: 2). At the global level, executive decision-making is the norm, and any idea of participation by the world's 7.2 billion people in this global executive governance necessarily dissolves into metaphor (Joseph, 2012; Held, 2010; Sen, 1999; Rosenau, 1992).

We can look to formal governmental organizations, their rules and practices, as the means whereby decisions are made, policies framed and implemented, rules and laws defined and enforced, as only one side of the governance equation. Outside the exclusive sphere of governmental interactions, governance happens and governance relations form within and between a myriad of social groups. Much recent thinking, be this focused on the global or the local level, emphasises this social dimension to governance (Dryzek, 2010; Carothers and de Gramont, 2011; Bevir, 2009; Ansell, 2000). Alternatives to top-down or didactic models of decision-making commonly invoke faith in the capacity of rational publics to overcome the power and interest of the Pretorian few. For Jim Whitman, writing in deliberative mode, 'governance is a social function centred on the making of collective choices regarding matters of common concern to the members of human groups', involving both 'command' processes but, crucially, 'public and private deliberation' (2005: 16–17). Hayley Stevenson and John Dryzek are concerned with the invention of 'polyvocal' governance spaces, where the voices of multiple 'mini-publics' are heard within 'mini-lateral' processes or 'deliberative minilateralism' (2014: 187–92). Whitman, Stevenson and Dryzek privilege dialogue and inclusion, or what might be thought of as the institutionalization of democratic norms by communicative means, paralleling models of 'democratic network governance' advanced by progressive scholars in the fields of public administration and public policy and applied to the analysis of governance arrangements at national and local levels (Sørensen and Torfing, 2008: 27).

Formal democratic and public institutions are not prerequisite to *effective* governance. The challenge for development practitioners when confronted with alternative models of social and political organization is not to interpret the overwhelming presence of customary practice as a deficiency in need of urgent correction (Msukwa and Taylor, 2011; Carothers and de Gramont, 2011). As is argued by the Institute of Development Studies (IDS), 'informal institutions and personalized relationships are usually seen as governance problems, but the research suggests that they could also be part of the solution' (2010: 2).

This emphasis on the social dimension necessarily brings the notion of civil society into frame, which, like Westminster-style democracy, is problematic when applied outside the societies to which the concept and its cognates are indigenous. This is not to argue that institutions of social trust and mutual obligation or reciprocity, upon which legitimate systems of governance depend, flourish only in democratic societies. Civil society is a concept derived from Western philosophy that, in its current usage, presupposes a universal human capacity to organise, at a level below and increasingly above the state, for reasons of shared social or political interest – or both. The word is ingrained in the governmentality of development as a synonym for normative agency and confers a significant burden of expectations on a broad range of non-governmental, not-for-profit and civic entities (Spini, 2011; Edwards, 2014; Joseph, 2012). For Robert Putnam (1993), the existence of civil society is a prerequisite to democratization and a dynamic civic sphere essential for popular engagement with democratic processes. Social capital can be thought of as the substance of civil society, being the quality of human relations that draw people together beyond kinship or family units, facilitating the formation of public or civic groups, or 'mini-publics' (after Stevenson and Dryzek, 2014; Putnam, 1993; Putnam and Goss, 2004; Coleman, 1988). Pierre Bourdieu defines social capital as: 'the aggregate of the actual or potential resources which are linked to possession of a durable network of more or less institutionalized relationships of mutual acquaintance and recognition' (1977: 51). Using more instrumental terms, Putnam identifies the same as being the: 'trust, norms and networks that can improve the efficiency of society by facilitating coordinated actions' (1993: 167) and as 'dense networks of social interaction' (ibid., 2001: 21; Putnam and Goss, 2004). Mobilized social or civic networks can serve an instrumental and a deliberative purpose in sourcing opinions and ideas useful to decision-making (Lidskog, 2000). Still, it is important to remember that social capital formation does not occur in politically neutral settings, beyond the scope of formal and informal structures of power.

Rhodes (2006: 426) defines a policy network as a: 'set of formal and informal institutional linkages between governmental and other actors structured around shared interests in public policy making and implementation'. Much hinges, however, upon the degree to which communication within policy networks is horizontal (or genuinely two-way). Where governmental decision-making is highly centralized and relations of political authority vertical, the scope for inclusiveness is heavily restricted. Yet, if social trust is deep, logically, there is scope for new deliberative processes to form, or for customary processes to evolve in directions that speak to contemporary ideas of justice and democracy, and which articulate ideas in forms that are audible to local publics (Edwards, 2014; Putnam, 1993; Nimbtik, 2016; Taveekan, 2013).

Governance interventions have long been interpreted by proposed beneficiaries as an external imposition, be this by the state or an international development aid organization (Msukwa and Taylor, 2011: 62–3). Even where interventions are conceived according to more contextually responsive models of practice, pre-scripted approaches can produce a contrary effect. For some, like Nobel Laureate Douglass North and colleagues, 'exporting good economic institutions is as hopeless as exporting democracy' (North et al., 2008: 3). Property rights, for example, are considered the bedrock of a liberal democratic society, and the norm to which all societies ought to conform (De Soto, 2001). And, yet, the ideal of individual or private property is alien to many parts of the world where its introduction has caused serious social disruption. Where the rule of law runs parallel, and often second to customary practice, and where political power depends substantially upon kinship and patronage ties, government and governmental bureaucracies are vulnerable to capture by powerful groups (Felson, 2011; Buchan and Hill, 2014; Graycar and Prenzler, 2013; Kaufmann et al., 2007, 2010; Cain and Jowitt, 2004; Ackerman, 1999). As Carothers and de Gramont write, international development aid agencies stand accused of: 'exporting precooked and inappropriate institutional blueprints as well as failing to take into account local political realities and resistance to reform' (2011: 4). This brings us to the recent experience with democracy and governance in Vanuatu and Thailand.

GOVERNANCE, *KASTOM*[2] AND CORRUPTION IN VANUATU

Situated in the South Pacific, the Republic of Vanuatu is an archipelagic nation home to over one-quarter of a million people. The islands and their diverse peoples were aggregated into an Anglo-French Condominium in 1904 and granted independent statehood in 1980. With a per capita GDP (PPP) of just over US$3,000, the country ranks well down on global indicators of economic development. Poverty is widespread and income and gender inequality is pronounced (World Bank, 2014; UNDP, 2015).

The country adopted a Westminster-style system of responsible government but, as with other South Pacific post-colonial states, democratic modes of government and governance were introduced without regard for the commensurability between democratic principles and local social and political norms (Larmour, 2002, 2008, 2012). Under these conditions, democratization is constrained, even in the procedural sense, because many, indeed the majority, are excluded or included according to education, gender, kinship associations, social status and political connections. This is compounded by the diverse nature of customary authority systems that work to a different logic to that presupposed in Vanuatu's Constitution (Nimbtik, 2016). Fundamental to the liberal democratic model, public accountability is more difficult to operationalize in archipelagic states, like Vanuatu, where islands are dispersed and people are divided on the basis of language, religion, and tradition. The bridging of linguistic and conceptual gaps between imported notions of the public good and indigenous ideas about the exercise of power were simply not part of the state-building agenda (Huffer, 2005; Larmour, 2008).

The conservatism of *jifly* institutions frustrates many ni-Vanuatu who, for religious reasons, have moved away from their ancestral villages. Moreover, the introduction of Christianity cannot be dismissed or rejected as a straightforward colonial intrusion, not least because missionary advocacy proved empowering to Vanuatu women. For those brought up within Catholic or Protestant communities, involvement in women's civic organizations and women's political activism in pursuit of independence provided a sense of social purpose beyond the family (Jolly, 1997; Douglas, 2002). *Kastom* authority is overwhelmingly patriarchal and traditional village societies are hierarchically structured.

---

[2]Used here to denote systems of beliefs and values grounded in local lore. There is no fixed *kastom* system in Vanuatu, where the nature of tradition remains controversial and contested. The word *kastom* is used interchangeably with custom here to denote practices and expectations regarded as indigenous to Vanuatu, which, as best as can be judged, have their origins in pre-colonial era island societies.

However, this does not invalidate *kastom* as a basis for negotiation about the most appropriate forms of governance for a community or the nation as a whole. Institutions of reciprocity require that people within defined social groups support each other and share benefits as these accrue. A traditional or customary leader's interest is thus, in principle, entwined with their family and community to the extent that distinctions between leaders and their social group, their immediate family and extended kinship group especially, are difficult to sustain in any formal legal or bureaucratic sense. In Vanuatu, the only goods that approximate to public goods at a local community level are communal roads, land, beaches, coastal waters and rivers, which are held under common stewardship according to local customary law, or *kastom*. A *kastom jif* can legitimately exercise their authority to temporarily restrict access to food resources to, for instance, allow fish stocks to replenish, thereby providing a measure of food and ecological security to their people. When people transgress these rules they are sanctioned under *kastom* rather than state law. Viewed sympathetically, customary rules and practices provide the normative sources of authority in Vanuatu that have not yet lost their moral force, despite the impacts of colonialism and contemporary globalization (Nimbtik, 2016; Zorn, 2010; Kaufman, 1974).

Kastom authority was displaced by the political and bureaucratic structures of the newly formed Vanuatu state, but not erased. In practice, Vanuatu politicians are elected and governments formed through the mobilisation of family connections and local power-bases built and maintained with the promise of a share in government largesse. The point here is not that the modern state is an inappropriate imposition or that the abuse of political power is somehow to be accepted. Rather, there is a lingering conceptual gap between traditional or customary notions of authority and the legal rational principles that underpin the modern nation-state ideal. To this confused cultural layering must be added the parallel chiefly[3] systems introduced by the Christian churches to further erode popular attachment to *kastom*. This does not mean that a common coherent accountability mechanism that connects village and state is impossible, but rather, that the starting points for the creation of such a mechanism, or more to the point, mechanisms, have to be conceived in terms that correspond with customary norms (AusAid, 2005). In Vanuatu, however, the notion of 'good enough governance' comes sharply up against the now deeply entrenched *problématique* of corruption.

Maladministration of public finances has had a deleterious effect upon Vanuatu's economy and the legitimacy of the state. In the late 1990s, Vanuatu implemented austerity measures under the Asian Development Bank (ADB)-sponsored, and designed, 'Comprehensive Reform Program' (Saldanha, 2004: 30; Duncan and Nakagawa, n.d.). Policy intervention occurred in a context of deteriorating domestic economic conditions accentuated by scandals associated with the misappropriation of public finances, in particular those vested in the Development Bank of Vanuatu (DBV) (Vanuatu Ombudsman, 1999). Irregularities in the awarding of government contracts, concessions and the privatization of public assets reached epidemic proportions, and, despite the CRP, such irregularities persist (Makin, 2014; Joshua, 2014; ADB, 2002). Tackling corruption was regarded as essential to ensuring the long-term sustainability of government finances and

---

[3]To distinguish this form of authority from that of the *kastom jif*.

the country's economy and, yet, despite concerted international pressure, and the adoption of national action plans, the underlying sources of corrupt behaviour went unaddressed (Nimbtik, 2016).

The use of public office for private financial gain is accepted as corrupt, in a formal legal sense, by the 178 states parties to the *United Nations Convention Against Corruption*, of which Vanuatu is one (UNODC, 2004). Yet, in the official creole language of Vanuatu, Bislama, there is no distinguishable local synonym for the term corruption. Even though the English word 'corruption' is now incorporated into everyday speech, its English lan-guage meaning does not so easily translate. This is to say nothing of the difficulty in establishing the kinds of national accountability and integrity mechanisms envisaged by the UN Convention's framers.

As with the issue of corruption, a significant part of the challenge to effective gov-ernance in Vanuatu is the identification of a linguistic basis for accountable govern-ment. Major improvements in financial governance have occurred not through the better enforcement of law but through the adoption of micro-credit schemes that employ tradi-tional economic ideas. The National Bank of Vanuatu (NBV), which took control of the DBV's micro-credit schemes, adopted traditional economic ideas into its financial literacy programmes to engage communities in practices of effective financial management based upon indigenous notions of savings, interest and loans. Pigs and pig tusks, shell money and necklaces, mats made from grass and pandanus leaves, and edible tubers like yams and taro, are traditional currencies in almost all the islands of Vanuatu, and the exchange systems in which they are used include institutions of credit commensurate with modern banking (Nimbtik, 2016; Regenvanu, 2009; Huffman, 1996). This initiative suggests how international norms might be assimilated into traditional institutions through the use of a common language and mutually comprehensible mediums of exchange, to facilitate negotiation, learning and cooperative adaptation (Nimbtik, 2016).

Can this approach be translated into the political sphere? Pointing to examples from the Solomon Islands, Scales (2005: 146) argues that home-grown informal systems of governance, because they are contextually appropriate, are a more durable basis for deliberative democracy. The same is possible in Vanuatu. One institution that has the potential to create possibilities for weaving a new fabric of direct state-society engage-ment is the *nakamal*, or the *nasara*, which are formal gatherings similar in function and principle across Vanuatu (Forsyth, 2009). The *nakamal* serves as a communal meeting place for ceremonial activities and rituals such as circumcisions and pig killing, as a venue for kava drinking, a space for the public discussion of communal issues, and for the resolution of intra- and inter-communal conflicts (Kernot and Sakita, 2008). There are variations, of course. On some islands, *nakamal* and *nasara* denote different levels of functional gathering. In Malekula, for instance, a *nasara* can serve as a higher court. In all circumstances, however, *kastom jifs* are the decisive source of authority (Walker and Garu, 2009; Nimbtik, 2016).

Anthropologists debate the extent to which such gatherings are consultative and consensus-driven or vehicles for the exercise of autocratic *jifly* power (Forsyth, 2009; Allen, 1981; Lindstrom, 1990). Even if the circle of consent is tightly constrained, there is evidence of women's direct involvement in decision-making, on the islands of Pentecost and Big Bay in Santo for example (Thomas, 2013; Rodman, 1977; Deacon, 1934).

To dismiss *kastom* authority as an ideological preserve of a hidebound *jifly* elite, therefore, risks missing the possibility that it could also be an agent of social change, provided that people of all genders are permitted a constructive role in the reinterpretation of the collective past (Jolly, 1997). If *kastom* is amenable to 'reform', then customary spaces are appropriate places to initiate or precipitate evolutionary processes, to, for example, challenge kastom *jifs* who appeal to tradition to impede the social and political advancement of women (Douglas, 2002).

A critical link between *kastom* authority at the communal level and the state is the Malvatumauri[4] National Council of Chiefs. The Council has the capacity to broker dialogue between traditional leaders and modern state institutions, and provide an effective means for the resolution of social divisions across the archipelago (AusAID, 2005, 2010). A constitutional entity incorporated into the state as an arm of the bureaucracy, the Council's democratic potential remains unrealized. As an institution where electoral participation and membership is open only to hereditary *kastom jifs*, its representativeness remains in question. It is, nonetheless, arguably the best placed institution to lead the search for a more effective model of governance, based upon a differently conceived social contract that resonates with the experiences and expectations of ni-Vanuatu (Nimbtik, 2016).

CIVIC NETWORKS AND STATE POWER IN THAILAND

The historical trajectories of Vanuatu and Thailand are vastly different. Still, the Thai experience of state-building and parliamentary rule offers some salient lessons for the world's newer democracies. A country of 67 million people, Thailand was the only South East Asian state never to be formally colonized. The country climbed rapidly up the development ladder on the back of an industrial boom in the 1980s and, despite the 1997 Asian financial crisis and periodic political crises, poverty rates have continued a downward trend while health and literacy have steadily climbed. Inequality, however, is high and increasing, and this economic fact draws attention to the persistence of less easily quantifiable forms of inequality that have an enduring and deadening effect on governance (World Bank, 2014; UNDP, 2015; Yang and Callahan, 2007; Yang, 2005).

The modern Thai state was conceived and constructed by its royal elite well before the idea of the Thai nation was invented and popularised. With the switch from absolute monarchy to parliamentary democracy in 1932, the kingdom's civilian bureaucracy and military reinvented Thai tradition to preserve an elite-orientated system with the monarch at its apex that has survived more than eight decades of constitutional experimentation. Thailand's political cycle veers between parliamentary rule and direct military control, with the military claiming a prerogative to intervene in politics to restore peace and order by means of coup d'état. This state of internal affairs inhibits the maturation of electoral politics and stunts the growth of participatory modes of governance.

The notion of a sovereign public, and of public service, is alien to Thailand's heavily bureaucratic system, in which government officials are still regarded as 'servants of

---

[4]A composite name, incorporating the indigenous words *mal* (chief), *vatu* (stones or islands) and *mauri* (organic living things) (Bolton, 1999; Lindstrom, 1997: 217).

the king' (*kharachakan*), not 'public' servants as is the norm in Western democracies. Functional models of state organization, adopted before the institution of parliamentary rule to appease Western colonial powers, created highly centralized ministries which were primarily vehicles for the administration of the royal prerogative and subsequently sources of political and commercial patronage. The historical imprint of this devolved autocracy is evident at the provincial and municipal levels where government officials continue to administrate in the interests of state and monarchy. Centrally appointed provincial governors and the provincial offices of central government departments, especially those responsible for agriculture, forestry and waterways, exercise a decisive influence in local government (Baker and Phongpaichit, 2005). This is the authoritarian core of a paternalistic Thai polity, in which democratic norms are accommodated within strictly controlled limits (Phatharathananunth, 2007; Chaloemtiarana, 2007).

With the entry of international NGOs into Thailand during the 1970s, the term 'civil society' has gradually filtered into Thai political discourse, where it is translated as *prachasangkhom*, '*pracha*' meaning 'civic' and '*sangkhom*' meaning society (Phatharathananunth, 2007). Contrary to the prescriptions of international donors, the state is not interested in taking advantage of the rapid emergence of autonomous civic organizations, including a significant number of Thai NGOs, to forge partnerships for development. Indeed, the state is mistrustful and quite hostile towards civil society. Empowered public deliberations, be these mass protests in the streets of the capital, Bangkok, or social media activism, are most potent when parliament temporarily assumes the ascendancy or when the military is highly factionalized. When the military assumes the ascendancy, as occurred in the coups of 2006 and 2014, the scope of public action is heavily circumscribed and effective popular opposition to the state is curtailed by draconian and often violent means (Taveekan, 2013).

Governance, the word and the idea, is another recent addition to Thai public policy discourse, and is strongly associated with the World Bank's good governance agenda of the 1990s (Baker and Phongpaichit, 2005; Phongpaichit and Baker, 1999). The term acquired prominence in Thailand after the 1997 Asian financial crisis, in which Thailand was pivotal, and where the country's economic malaise was causally linked to the issue of poor financial regulation. In return for international assistance, Thailand was forced to adopt austerity and to accept strict IMF and ADB conditions, which included the opening up of the economy to foreign investment and other market-friendly policies consistent with the Washington Consensus (Baker and Phongpaichit, 2005). Political decentralization was also part of the reform blueprint, complementing a process of major political reform precipitated by a political crisis marked by a military coup d'état in September 1991 and the violent suppression of pro-democracy street protests by the military in May 1992.

Intended to increase the scope of popular participation in the affairs of state, at a national and local level, the 1997 Constitution was drafted in a nation-wide process of consultation.[5] It was accompanied by Thailand's 8th National Economic and Social Development Plan (1997–2001), in which development was defined, in a paradigmatic shift, as a people-centred process. The Plan emphasized empowerment through

---

[5]Thai lawmakers, civilian and military, between them authored 19 constitutions over the period 1932 to 2014.

the enlargement of public participation in local decision-making, which it was claimed would lead to greater transparency in local government affairs. The Tambon[6] Council and Tambon Administration Authority Act of 1994 created new elected administrative bodies that were supposed to devolve decision-making power and decentralize govern-ance (*Royal Thai Government Gazette*, 1999; Wongreedee and Mahakanjana, 2011). There were high expectations that this reform would improve access to government services and, most importantly, promote democracy at the local level by restraining the power of state-appointed officials. However, Tambon Administrative Organizations (TAOs) were quickly captured by local business elites. Still, in communities where social networks of mutual assistance had become institutionalized, significant strides were made in refash-ioning local politics to loosen up structures of state power through popular mobilisation (Chardchawarn, 2010; Phongpaichit and Baker, 2000).

Text Box: 4.1   Case Study: Bridging State and Civil Society in Khao Khok, Northeast Thailand

Mutual dependence between local government and civil society groups is a nec-essary condition for the development and the maintenance of civic 'governance networks' in Khao Khok, a community comprising 15 villages and numbering 2,274 households, in the northeastern province of Buriram, situated on the border between Thailand and Cambodia. The recent history of local government politics here evidences the democratic potential of well-organized autonomous social networks, formed to address community governance concerns. The first such civic entity, the community forest conservation group, was initiated by a female com-munity leader with sufficient social status and social capital to build an effective civic network. As she recalls:

> Initially, I lived my everyday life as the teacher's housewife. But I do love to gather with others, so I joined the community female working group and later I became the leader of the group. Amm ... The changing point of my interest and concern is an increase of illegal logging by some business companies and deforestation for farmland took place. I noticed that our community forest was decreasing dramatically. I thought, I need to do something before getting late. Fortunately, I had got the funding from NGO to set the community forum to raise the com-munity problem and then the community forest was set as the first priority. We decided to set the civil society group to work along and I was elected to be its head. (Quoted in Taveekan, 2013: 96)

These achievements highlight the important developmental role played by people, not drawn from among an educated elite, who possess local or deep contextual knowledge and can exercise transformative leadership. This leader's experiences also

(Continued)

---

[6] *Tambon* being a Thai word used to denote an administrative sub-district, comprising an aggregation of villages.

(Continued)

further exemplify the multiplier effect attributed to women's agency in development by development economists, for example Amartya Sen (1999). Her social status was elevated by external recognition and support from the Thai corporate sector, and from Thai development NGOs. The Khao Khok forest conservation group then won the Petroleum Authority of Thailand (PTT) 6th Green Global Award in 2004. The community forest was then selected as the pilot for PTT's forest guardian and sustainable community project. As the group's leader, she became the primary intermediary with provincial officials and central government agencies, the Department of Forestry in particular. Sponsorship from national non-government organizations and academic institutions helped her to foster a connection between community and state, to for example assess the potential for participatory local environmental management to improve the livelihoods of people in rural areas. She became central to local processes of knowledge-sharing and decision-making, which together translate into significant informal authority (Taveekan, 2013). Her newfound status brought with it an office building, which also serves as a civic training centre, a staffing allowance and office equipment, including a computer, desks, tables and chairs. These are significant resources in a rural community; however, being capable, outspoken and effective brings not just added responsibility but also suspicions of a conflict of interest, not least because the new PTT-sponsored facility was built in the grounds of her home.

There are hard social realities to be navigated and accommodated in Khao Khok. The foundations of civic mindedness are shallow and thus appeals to community spirit are on their own insufficient to ensure the sustainability of any community initiative. The forest conservation group and other related community projects rely heavily upon this leader's kinship networks. This is understandable in a society where authority hinges upon the strength of a person's entourage, their connections, and their access to human and financial resources. Money flows from the state into the community group from a number of environmental projects. For these reasons, this civil society network is governed by a committee which permits a degree of accountability and transparency, but again, the committee is comprised of members of the leader's kinship network. Alert to the criticisms and the dangers that they pose to her legitimacy, she asserts:

> Sincerely, I do not want to be seen as the mercenary person and I do not like others gossiping about me, that I take advantage of my leader position. So, we always use group meetings to find solutions to problems or before implementing new activities. I believe that the committee and its members can check my performance from that. Accountability is essential when money is involved. (Quoted in Taveekan, 2013: 98)

The Khao Kok community is no exception to the traditional style of leadership and administration that is so pervasive in Thailand. The crucial difference is the political influence of this grassroots civil society network. Its affiliative capacity has enabled it to mobilize against the power of local business interests and to enter the political arena. In the 2007 TAO election, a new Tambon president was chosen from outside the local political-business elite. An ex-school teacher, this person secured decisive support for his electoral campaign from local civil society groups, which were rewarded with executive positions and financial assistance. The forest conservation group's influential female leader won election to the Tambon Council from where she was able to campaign in support of her preferred candidate for the position of headman in her home village. The community forestry group gained influence through a deliberate strategy to engage the state through the policy process and also the political process (Taveekan, 2013).

Collaborative governance, according to Ansell and Gash, is an 'arrangement where ... public agencies directly engage non-state stakeholders in a collective decision making process that ... aims to make or implement public policy or manage public programs or assets' (Ansell and Gash, 2007: 544). The fragmentation of political power among wider circles of actors allowed the conservation group to reap the benefits of engaging with government officials. In diminishing elite control through a new type of TAO president, who was neither a business person nor part of the local political elite, more opportunities were created for the civic sector to build influential networks. Through this action, the hegemony enjoyed by local business power-brokers was destabilized, with immediate benefits for community projects like the community forest (Taveekan, 2013).

In one sense, governance in Khao Khok was rendered more democratic, and local governance made more accountable beyond formal electoral processes and controlled formal public consultation. However, even though the civil society groups increased their access to the machinery of state, there is still limited room to exercise their power in the policy-making process. Civil society group members have been viewed as a human resource to be co-opted by the state to legitimate state project implementation. The power to act, even when enjoying substantial influence within the TAO, is also constrained by fiscal realities. The forest conservation group and others annually receive financial support from local government but they are not able to exercise discretion on how this is spent, which remains the prerogative of the Ministry of the Interior and the government of the day (Taveekan, 2013).

CONCLUSION

There is no simple governance formula or prescription that is applicable to all societies, and there is no simple means to negotiate or enforce national or local compliance with the global good governance script. Neither is there any guarantee that formal steps towards greater public participation in government will yield greater democratic returns. This is not to argue that every context of governance is unique, but rather that development trajectories are not linear and that linear models of modernization are inadequate guides to development practice. The idea that local traditions must be neutralized or swept aside in the interests of economic modernization can be challenged on many grounds. Not least in the translation of modernizing ideas, customary practices and local languages of governance have an important mediating role in countries where the impacts of globalization have not dissolved their normative power. Yet, as is evident in Thailand, what is conceived as tradition in a popular sense can be reinvented as ideology and sustained by the exercise of state power through law. Where changes to governance arrangements are sought, liberal models of authority and the proper role of government have to be rendered commensurate with prevailing power structures and societal expectations. In a highly generalized sense, the effectiveness of interventions to reform government and governance hinge upon the acceptance of change by those in power, and, indeed, their acceptance of their possible displacement – otherwise, there will be societal chaos. Viewed in this light, governance in practice might also be understood as pragmatic compromise and the restraint of arbitrary and reactionary power as much as the empowerment of peoples to assume control of their collective fates.

Questions for Discussion

1　To what extent should development practitioners accommodate local social norms when making development plans?
2　What is meant by the term 'tradition'? What are your traditions? From where are these derived and are they still relevant to your life at this moment?
3　Is it practical to include every person and every civic group in governance deliberations? Are there limits to inclusiveness?

📖 FURTHER READING

Carothers, T. and de Gramont, D. (2011) *Aiding Governance in Developing Countries: Progress Amid Uncertainties*. Washington, DC: Carnegie Endowment for International Peace.

Dryzek, J. (2010) *Foundations and Frontiers of Deliberative Governance*. Oxford: Oxford University Press.

Larmour, P. (2012) *Interpreting Corruption: Culture and Politics in the Pacific Islands*. Honolulu, HA: University of Hawaii Press.

REFERENCES

Ackerman, S.R. (1999) *Corruption and Government: Causes, Consequences, and Reform*. Cambridge: Cambridge University Press.

Allen, M. (1981) *Vanuatu: Politics, Economics, and Ritual in Island Melanesia*. Sydney: Academic Press of Australia.

Ansell, C. (2000) 'The Networked Polity: Regional Development in Western Europe', *Governance*, 13(2): 279–91.

Ansell, C. and Gash, A. (2007) 'Collaborative Governance in Theory and Practice', *Journal of Public Administration Research and Theory*, 18(4): 543–71.

Asian Development Bank (ADB) (2002) *Program Completion Report on the Comprehensive Reform Program (Loan 1624-Van) [SF] to the Republic of Vanuatu*. Manila: Asian Development Bank.

AusAID (2005) *Kastom Governance is for Everyone: Activities and Impacts of the Vanuatu Kastom Kavenens Partnership 2005–2012*. Port Vila: AusAID.

AusAID (2010) *Vanuatu Kastom Governance Partnership*. Port Vila: AusAID.

Baker, C. and Phongpaichit, P. (2005) *A History of Thailand*. Cambridge: Cambridge University Press.

Bevir, M. (2009) *Key Concepts in Governance*. London: Sage.

Bolton, L. (1999) 'Chief Willie Bangmatur Maldo and the Incorporation of Chiefs into the Vanuatu State', State Society and Governance in Melanesia, Discussion Paper 99/2, No. 2.

Bourdieu, P. (1977) *Outline of the Theory of Practice*. Cambridge: Cambridge University Press.

Buchan, B. and Hill, L. (2014) *An Intellectual History of Political Corruption*. New York: Palgrave Macmillan.

Cain, T.N. and Jowitt, A. (2004), *National Integrity systems: Transparency International Country Report, Vanuatu 2004*. Available at: http://transparency.org.au/wp-content/uploads/2012/08/vanuatu.pdf (accessed June 3, 2014).

Carothers, T. and de Gramont, D. (2011) *Aiding Governance in Developing Countries: Progress Amid Uncertainties*. Washington, DC: Carnegie Endowment for International Peace.

Chaloemtiarana, T. (2007) *Thailand: The Politics of Despotic Paternalism*. Ithaca, NY: Cornell University Press.

Chardchawarn, S. (2010) *Local Governance in Thailand: The Politics of Decentralization and the Roles of Bureaucrats, Politicians, and the People*. Chiba, Japan: Institute of Developing Economies.

Coleman, J.S. (1988) 'Social Capital in Creation of Human Capital', *American Journal of Sociology*, 94: 95–121.

Commission on Global Governance (1996) *Our Global Neighborhood: The Report of the Commission on Global Governance*. Oxford: Oxford University Press.

De Soto, H. (2001) *The Mystery of Capital: Why Capitalism Triumphs in the West and Fails Everywhere Else*. London: Black Swan.

Deacon, B. (1934) *Malekula: A Vanishing People of the New Hebrides*. London: George Routledge & Sons.

Douglas, B. (2002) 'Christian Citizens: Women and Negotiations of Modernity in Vanuatu', *The Contemporary Pacific*, 14(1): 1–38.

Dryzek, J. (2010) *Foundations and Frontiers of Deliberative Governance*. Oxford: Oxford University Press.

Dryzek, J. and Stevenson, H. (2014) *Democratizing Global Climate Governance*. Cambridge: Cambridge University Press.

Duncan, R. (2011) 'Governance Reform in the Public Sector in Pacific Island Countries: Understanding How Culture Matters', in R. Duncan (ed.), *The Political Economy of Economic Reform in the Pacific*. Manila: Asian Development Bank, pp. 139–62.

Duncan, R. and Nakagawa, H. (n.d.) 'Obstacles to Economic Growth in Six Pacific Island Countries', World Bank. Available at: http://siteresources.worldbank.org/INTDEBTDEPT/Resources/468980-1206974166266/4833916-1206989877225/DuncanNakagawaObstacles.pdf (accessed 8 July 2015).

Edward, H. (2001) *Ombudsman of Vanuatu Digest of Public Reports 1996–2000*. University of the South Pacific, Suva: United Nations Development Program Governance and Accountability Project.

Edwards, M. (2014) *Civil Society*, 3rd edn. Cambridge: Polity.

Felson, M. (2011) 'Corruption and the Broad Sweep of History', in A. Graycar and R.G. Smith (eds), *Handbook of Global Research and Practice in Corruption*. Cheltenham: Edward Elgar, pp. 12–17.

Forsyth, M. (2009) *A Bird that Flies with Two Wings: Kastom and Justice Systems in Vanuatu*. Canberra: ANU Press.

Graycar, A., and Prenzler, T. (2013) *Understanding and Preventing Corruption*. Basingstoke: Palgrave Macmillan.

Grindle, M.S. (2005) 'Good Enough Governance Revisited: A Report for DFID with Reference to the Governance Target Strategy Paper, 2001'. London: Overseas Development Institute. Available at: www.odi.org/sites/odi.org.uk/files/odi-assets/events-documents/1281.pdf (accessed 4 June 4 2010).

Held, D. (2010) *Cosmopolitanism: Ideals and Realities*. Cambridge: Polity Press.

Huffer, E. (2005) 'Governance, Corruption and Ethics in the Pacific', *Contemporary Pacific*, 17(1): 118–40.

Huffman, K. (1996) 'Trading, Cultural Exchange and Copyright: Important Aspects of Vanuatu Arts', in J. Bonnemaison, K. Huffman, D. Tryon and C. Kaufmann (eds), *Arts of Vanuatu*. Honolulu: University of Hawai'i Press, pp. 182–94.

Institute of Development Studies (IDS) (2010) *An Upside Down View of Governance*. Brighton: Institute of Development Studies.

Jolly, M. (1997) 'Women-Nation-State in Vanuatu: Women as Sign and Subject in the Discourse of Kastom, Modernity and Christianity', in T. Otto and N. Thomas (eds), *Narratives of Nation in the South Pacific*. Amsterdam: Harwood Academic Publishers, pp. 141–72.

Joseph, J. (2012) *The Social in the Global: Social Theory, Governmentality and Global Politics*. Cambridge: Cambridge University Press.

Joshua, J. (2014) 'Airport Concession Company Not Registered: VIPA'. *Vanuatu Daily Post*, 2 August. Available at: http://dailypost.vu/news/airport-concession-company-not-registered-vipa/article_87dca5ed-404e-5108-a54e-8ee558037682.html (accessed 29 February 2016).

Kaufman, R. (1974) 'The Patron–Client Concept and Macro-Prospects and Problems', *Comparative Studies in Society and History*, 16(3): 284–308.

Kaufmann, D., Kraay, A. and Mastruzzi, M. (2007) 'The Worldwide Governance Indicators Project: Answering the Critics'. Available at: http://siteresources.worldbank.org/INTWBIGOVANTCOR/Resources/1740479-1149112210081/2604389-1167941884942/Answering_Critics.pdf (accessed 23 June 2012).

Kaufmann, D., Kraay, A. and Mastruzzi, M. (2010) *The Worldwide Governance Indicators: Methodology and Analytical Issues*. Washington, DC: World Bank Development Research Group Macroeconomics and Growth Team.

Kernot, S. and Sakita, L. (2008) *The Role of Chiefs in Peacebuilding in Port Vila*. Discussion Paper 2008/4. Canberra, ACT: ANU Research School of Pacific and Asian Studies, State, Society and Governance in Melanesia Program.

Larmour, P. (2002) 'Westminster Constitutions in the South Pacific: A "Policy Transfer" Approach', *Asian Journal of Political Science*, 10(1): 39–54.

Larmour, P. (2008) 'Corruption and the Concept of Culture: Evidence from the Pacific Islands', *Crime and Law Social Change*, 49(3): 225–39.

Larmour, P. (2012) *Interpreting Corruption: Culture and Politics in the Pacific Islands.* Honolulu, HA: University of Hawaii Press.

Lidskog, R. (2000) 'Scientific Evidence or Lay People's Experience? On Risk and Trust with Regard to Modern Environmental Threats', in M.J. Cohen (ed.), *Risk in the Modern Age: Social Theory, Science and Environmental Decision-Making.* New York: St. Martin's Press, pp. 196–224.

Lindstrom, L. (1990) 'Straight Talk on Tanna', in K.A. Watson-Gegeo and G.M. White (eds), *Disentangling: Conflict Discourse in Pacific Societies.* Stanford, CA: Stanford University Press, pp. 373–411.

Makin, B. (2014) 'Airport Rights and Profits Given Away', *Vanuatu Daily Post*, 5 June. Available at: http://dailypost.vu/airport-rights-and-profits-given-away/article_aeafc 04e-a840-5a79-9c5f-f4d080744e74.html (accessed 3 January 2016).

Msukwa, C.A.P.S. and Taylor, D. (2011) 'Why Can't Development be Managed More Like a Funeral? Challenging Participatory Practices', *Development in Practice*, 21(1): 59–72, doi:10.1080/09614524.2011.530244.

Nimbtik, G. (2016) '"Worlds in Collision": An Inquiry into the Sources of Corruption in Vanuatu Government and Society'. PhD thesis, RMIT University, Melbourne.

North, D., Acemoglu, D., Fukuyama, F. and Rodrik, D. (2008) *Governance, Growth, and Development Decision-Making.* Washington, DC: IBRD/World Bank.

Phatharathananunth, S. (2007) *Civil Society and Democratization: Social Movements in Northeast Thailand.* Copenhagen: Nordic Institute of Asian Studies.

Phongpaichit, P. and Baker, C. (1999) 'The Political Economy of the Thai Crisis', *Journal of the Asia Pacific Economy*, 4(1): 193–208.

Phongpaichit, P. and Baker, C. (2000) 'Chao Sua, Chao Pho, Chao Thi: Lords of Thailand's Transition', in R. McVey (ed.), *Money and Power in Provincial Thailand.* Singapore: ISEAS; and Chiang Mai: Silkworm, pp. 30–52.

Putnam, R.D. (1993) *Making Democracy Work: Civic Traditions in Modern Italy.* Princeton, NJ: Princeton University Press.

Putnam, R.D. (2001) *Bowling Alone: The Collapse and Revival of American Community.* New York: Simon and Schuster.

Putnam, R.D. and Goss, K.A. (2004) 'Introduction', in R.D. Putnam (ed.), *Democracies in Flux: The Evolution of Social Capital in Contemporary Society.* Oxford: Oxford University Press, pp. 3–20.

Regenvanu, R. (2009) 'The Traditional Economy as the Source of Resilience in Melanesia'. Paper presented to the Lowy Institute Conference, Pacific Islands and the World: The Global Economic Crisis, Brisbane, 3 August. Available at: www. aidwatch.org.au/sites/aidwatch.org.au/files/Ralph-Brisbane2009LowyInstitute.pdf (accessed 5 June 2014).

Rhodes, R.A.W. (1997) *Understanding Governance: Policy Networks, Governance, Reflexivity, and Accountability.* Buckingham/Philadelphia, PA: Open University Press.

Rhodes, R.A.W. (2006) 'Policy Network Analysis', in M. Moran, M. Rein and R. Goodin (eds), *The Oxford Handbook of Public Policy.* Oxford: Oxford University Press, pp. 425–47.

Rhodes, R.A.W. (2012) 'Waves of Governance', in D. Levi-Faur (ed.), *The Oxford Handbook of Governance.* Oxford: Oxford University Press, pp. 33–48.

Rodman, W.L. (1977) 'Big Men and Middlemen: The Politics of law in Longana', *American Ethnologist*, 4(3): 525–37.

Rodrik, D. (2008) 'Second Best Institutions', *American Economic Review: Papers and Proceedings*, 98(2): 100–4. Available at: http://drodrik.scholar.harvard.edu/files/dani-rodrik/files/second-best-institutions.pdf (accessed 5 November 2015).

Rosenau, J.N. (1992) 'Governance, Order, and Change in World Politics', in J.N. Rosenau and E. Czempiel (eds), *Governance without Government*. Cambridge: Cambridge University Press, pp. 1–29.

Royal Thai Government Gazette (1999) *Tambon (Sub-District) Council and Tambon Administration Organisation Act of 1994*. Bangkok: Se-ed.

Saldanha, C. (2004) 'Strategies for Good Governance in the Pacific', *Asian-Pacific Economic Literature*, 18(2): 30–43.

Scales, I.A. (2005) 'State and Local Governance in Solomon Islands: Building on Existing Strength', *Pacific Economic Bulletin*, 20(2): 140–8.

Sen, A. (1999) *Development as Freedom*. Oxford: Oxford University Press.

Sørensen, E. and Torfing, J. (2008) 'Theoretical Approaches to Governance Network Dynamics', in E. Sørensen and J. Torfing (eds), *Theories of Democratic Network Governance*. London: Macmillan, pp. 25–42.

Spini, D. (2011) 'Civil Society and the Democratisation of Global Public Space', in D. Armstrong, V. Bello and J. Gilson (eds), *Civil Society and International Governance: The Role of the Nation State*. Abingdon: Routledge, pp. 15–30.

Stevenson, H. and Dryzek, J.S. (2014) *Democratizing Global Climate Governance*. Cambridge: Cambridge University Press.

Taveekan, T. (2013) 'Bridging State and Civil Society at the "Grassroots": Network, Collaboration and Local Governance in Two Rural Thai Communities'. PhD thesis, RMIT University, Melbourne.

Thomas, A.K. (2013) 'Empowering Ni-Vanuatu Women: Amplifying Wantok Authority and Achieving Fair Market Access'. PhD thesis, University of Waikato.

Tuimaleali'ifano, M. (2006) 'Matai Titles and Modern Corruption in Samoa: Costs, Expectations and Consequences for Families and Society', in S. Firth (ed.), *Globalisation and Governance in the Pacific Islands*. Canberra: ANU E Press, pp. 362–74.

United Nations Development Programme (UNDP) (2015) *Human Development Report, 2015: Work for Human Development – Thailand* (Web Version). Available at: http://hdr.undp.org/en/countries/profiles/THA (accessed 4 April 2016).

United Nations Office on Drugs and Crime (UNODC) (2004) *United Nations Convention Against Corruption*. New York: United Nations.

Vanuatu Ombudsman (1999) *Public Report on the Maladministration and Political Interference in the Granting of Loans by the Development Bank of Vanuatu*. Port Vila: Office of the Ombudsman.

Walker, P. and Garu, S. (2009) 'A Few More Arrows: Strengthening Mediative Capacity in Vanuatu', in D. Bagshaw and E. Porter (eds), *Mediation in the Asia-Pacific Region: Transforming Conflicts and Building Peace*. London: Routledge, pp. 94–110.

Weiss, T. (2013) *Global Governance: Why? What? Whither?* Cambridge: Polity.

Whitman, J. (2005) *The Limits of Global Governance*. London: Routledge.

Wongreedee, A. and C. Mahakanjana (2011) 'Decentralization and Local Governance in Thailand', in E. Berman (ed.), *Public Administration in Southeast Asia: Thailand, Philippines, Malaysia, Hong Kong and Macao*. Boca Raton, FL: CRC Press, pp. 54–77.

World Bank (2014) 'World Development Indicators: Size of the Economy'. Available at: http://wdi.worldbank.org/table/1.1 (accessed 4 April 2016).

World Bank (*c*. 2016) 'Worldwide Governance Indicators'. Available at: http://info. worldbank.org/governance/wgi/index.aspx#home (accessed 4 February 2016).

Yang, K. (2005) 'Public Administrators' Trust in Citizens: A Missing Link in Citizen Involvement Efforts', *Public Administration Review*, 65(3): 273–85.

Yang, K. and Callahan, K. (2007) 'Citizen Involvement Efforts and Bureaucratic Responsiveness: Participatory Values, Stakeholder Pressures, and Administrative Practicality', *Public Administration Review*, 67(2): 249–64.

Zorn, J.G. (2010) 'Custom Then and Now: The Changing Melanesian Family', in A.M. Jowwit and T.N. Cain (eds), *Passage of Change: Law, Society and Governance in the Pacific*. Canberra: ANU E-Press, pp. 95–123.

5

GLOBALIZATION, GENDER AND DEVELOPMENT

CIRILA P. LIMPANGOG, LESLEY J. PRUITT AND JULIAN C.H. LEE

INTRODUCTION

The array of issues to be explored in an examination of the intersections between globalization, gender and development are many, and this brief chapter will not seek to map them all. Readers interested in a more sustained treatment might consider consulting works such as those by Momsen (2010), Visvanathan et al. (2011), Jackson and Pearson (1998) and Østergaard (1992). Rather, this chapter pursues an introductory discussion that revolves around seeking to first consider an examination of systematic issues relating to the impact of gender in a major global event and two case studies that describe different responses to the marginalization of women in Malaysia and transgender women in the Philippines.

The approach that we have taken in this chapter – to examine one very large-scale event, and then to examine two local-level case studies – is affirmed by Boulton et al. (2015) who, in their discussion of development, argue that among the things we must consider in understanding a given context or issue, is that we 'look back', 'look up and around' and 'look down' (Boulton et al., 2015: 196–7). By looking back, they refer to the importance of history, by looking up and around, they refer to the importance of considering the large-scale forces at play, and by looking down, they refer to the importance of the specific elements and individuals who act in local circumstances. 'This approach,' Boulton et al. note, 'sensitizes people to the particular as well as the general, to the small as well as the global' (ibid.: 198), which they believe is important in the field of development. In the course of taking this approach, we contend that gender is embedded in various planes – global, transnational and local, and that being alert to issues of gender enables a nuanced understanding of advantage and disadvantage, access and exclusion, and representation and marginalization of people on the basis of their gender.

This chapter thus undertakes its exploration of globalization, gender and development by first examining the global financial crisis, the causes and impacts of which are critically examined in terms of their gendered aspects. As economic development is usually central to how development and 'progress' is imagined, the global financial crisis (GFC) throws light on to the economic life of society and the globe, which is modulated by issues of gender. From there, we examine in finer-grain detail how women's rights activists in Malaysia have understood the relative disadvantage of women in Malaysia and sought to respond to it in the political sphere. By examining the Women's Candidacy Initiative, we show how women in Malaysia have sought their political empowerment. This up-close perspective is then turned towards the way a social group that is often overlooked in both development and gendered analysis – transgender women – is impacted by global processes. The examination of trans women in the Philippines demonstrates how globalization can also afford opportunities for segments of populations to achieve social, political and economic empowerment.

THE NEED FOR A GENDER PERSPECTIVE

All over the world, women commonly occupy positions of formal and informal disadvantage relative to men. The causes of this have been explored from diverse perspectives (e.g., Ortner, 1974; Lerner, 1986; Lee, 2011a: 27–69), with diverse conclusions, but it is also now axiomatic that successful development requires the inclusion of women and the integration of their concerns throughout the development process. This was officially recognized in the Millennium Development Goal to 'promote gender equality and empower women', and is now recognized in the Sustainable Development Goal to 'achieve gender equality and empower all women and girls'. An indicator for success here is the increasing numbers of girls in education at all levels, and improved proportions of seats held by women in national parliaments (UN, 2011).

At the same time, it must be recognized that few countries are led by women. Until mid-2016, German Chancellor Angela Merkel was the only female leader in the G8, the group representing the world's richest countries. However, since Theresa May became the UK's Prime Minister in July 2016, now 25 per cent or 2 out of 8 leaders of G8 countries are women. Similarly, women are significantly underrepresented in finance – only 25 women currently lead Fortune 500 companies. Meanwhile, women are disproportionately overrepresented among people living in poverty. This has led to what some scholars call the 'feminization of poverty', which is often linked to globalization (Chant, 2007; Sassen, 2007), as states have cut social services that disproportionately helped women and implemented policies through which the labour of women, especially women in the global South, is 'made cheap' for global corporations (Enloe, 2007).

Gender norms also significantly influence economic outcomes, in terms of women's participation and divisions of labour. Globally, women are disproportionately represented in the domestic sphere, both as unpaid mothers and carers and paid workers in reproductive services and provision of care. In this sense, economic – as well as social and political – institutions produce and reproduce gender inequalities. Expectations about gender roles impact on the ability of women to exercise influence in the public sphere – as will be exemplified in the case study from Malaysia below. Feminists have challenged claims of innate or natural differences by highlighting the social origins of gendered norms, which are constructed and hence malleable.

Processes of globalization have had significant impacts on gender relations that are sometimes contradictory and complex (Chinkin, 2000). Economic globalization has weakened governmental decision-making power around economic and labour policies, as states, in (ostensible) pursuit of national economic development, have often not asserted workers' rights where this impacts upon investment incentives and global profits, to the detriment of gender equality (ibid.). At the same time, however, globalization has arguably opened up some potential for transforming gendered relations or advancing gender equality (Harrington, 1992: 66).

As explored in the case study from the Philippines below, women have gained employment opportunities that can afford independence and allow them to assert their agency (Chinkin, 2000). Human rights concerns, that include attention to women's rights, have gained global force, including legal norms that prohibit sex discrimination and uphold women's equality through international standards – such as the Convention on the Elimination of All Forms of Discrimination Against Women (CEDAW) (ibid.). Finally, information and communications technology have offered prospects for women's transnational organizing, although there are concerns that this is often created and based in the North while targeting those in the South, and engenders a digital divide between those who have access and those who do not (ibid.).

Women's empowerment has been noted in the field of gender and development as a key objective for many women's groups around the world (Cornwall et al., 2007; Parpart et al., 2003). 'Empowerment' refers to the ability of groups and individuals to resist unjust power relations that exist between and among genders, across various spheres of control, such as family, community, the state and transnational relations. It is a process that involves changing individual and collective consciousness, and being able to progress from ideas to action, as illustrated in Black American women's struggle for equality in a once predominantly White, male-centric society (Collins, 2002). In the global South, empowerment has been observed in women's movements that have sought to redefine development visions for themselves that are otherwise defined for them by those in privileged positions in their country and by the West (Sen and Grown, 1988).

Agency and activism are central in the empowerment process (Collins, 2002: 273–90). Importantly, redistributing power and privilege requires the cooperation of those commonly depicted as perpetrators, i.e. men, within both the private and public domains. Still, deep-seated and institutionalized domination of women in some contexts cannot be easily dismantled by attempting to improve people's individual agency alone.

A gendered analysis needs, of course, to understand the nature of gender and thus a clear understanding of key terms including 'gender', 'sex' and 'sexuality' is important. While often confused with the term 'sex', 'gender' has a distinct meaning. According to the World Health Organization (WHO), '"Sex" refers to the *biological and physiological* characteristics that *define* men and women,' while '"[g]ender" refers to the *socially constructed* roles, behaviors, activities, and attributes that a given society *considers appropriate* for men and women' (WHO, 2015). Gender categories include things like 'masculine' and 'feminine', while sex categories include 'male' and 'female' (ibid.). Gender aspects may differ quite a lot between different societies, but aspects of sex generally do not (ibid.). Gender characteristics are culturally ascribed understandings of what it means to be masculine or feminine. It is as a result of cultural understandings of gender that gender norms and roles come to be understood, such as when in Saudi Arabia women cannot drive cars, while men are allowed to; in most places, men do less housework than women; and in the USA and most other countries, men earn significantly more money for similar work than women (ibid.).

Although the WHO definitions for 'gender' and 'sex' are commonly used in international policy and practice, these terms have been contested, politicized and altered by scholars and activists (see Lee, 2011a: 7–26). Many feminist scholars have problematized the distinction between the two terms, arguing that sex can also be at least partially socially constructed, and that focusing on these differentiations ignores differences between and among women and men. Many also take issue with how gender discrimination is often based on upholding 'natural sexual differences'.

Many scholars agree that gender is not innate; rather, it is something that happens (and must be made to happen) through particular performances (Connell, 2002: 14; Butler, 1988). As Connell explains, society sends dominant messages to boys and girls based on a 'gender order', teaching boys to be competitive, hard, tough and dominant, while girls are taught to be desirable (2002: 14). Gender norms are thus an important component of ordering contemporary societies in hierarchical ways, with characteristics seen as masculine being valued over those seen as feminine (Ortner, 1974; Tickner, 2001).

Individuals are expected to display behaviours associated with the gender deemed 'socially appropriate' for them. In this sense, particular types of gendered performance dominate within a culture and are seen to be the 'ideal' standard (Connell, 1987). Connell explores this through 'hegemonic masculinity', which she explains to be the dominant ideal of masculinity in the gender hierarchy (Connell, 1995, 2002). Likewise, hegemonic masculinity can marginalize other types of masculinities and femininities, though they can also challenge hegemonic masculinity. Connell says most men get what she calls the 'patriarchal dividend', although she notes that, depending on one's location in the present social order, he may receive more, less or none. Furthermore, it should be noted that the ways this cultural dividend is made manifest will vary greatly depending on the culture of the society in question. However, in any case, it is not only women who may be oppressed by existing gender hierarchies but also men who perform non-hegemonic types of masculinity, such as gay men in many Western contexts.

In a similar vein, although this is incrementally changing, transgender women and men are considered anomalous in the gender binary and within the feminine and masculine hierarchies, as they cannot be easily accommodated in existing assumptions about feminine or masculine genders. This leads us to the final term to be considered, which is 'sexuality'. Sexuality, like gender, is a term that accommodates a considerable array of aspects of the human condition, including both sexual orientation and gender identity. The WHO provides the following encompassing definition:

Sexuality is a central aspect of being human throughout life and encompasses sex, gender identities and roles, sexual orientation, eroticism, pleasure, intimacy and reproduction. Sexuality is experienced and expressed in thoughts, fantasies, desires, beliefs, attitudes, values, behaviours, practices, roles and relationships. While sexuality can include all of these dimensions, not all of them are always experienced or expressed. Sexuality is influenced by the interaction of biological, psychological, social, economic, political, cultural, ethnical, legal, historical, religious and spiritual factors. (WHO, 2006)

What the above definition points to is the extent to which elements of the human condition are affected by fact that we are gendered and sexed entities, and therefore also, how complex are the likely array of elements that need to be considered in specific circumstances, given the importance of culture and history (to name but two factors) in influencing the lived realities of people.

In the following section, we consider how a gendered analysis advances our understanding of the GFC. We then move on to exploring how a group of women have sought increased political representation in Malaysia, a country that is overtly seeking to acquire 'developed nation status'. In Malaysia, the Women's Candidacy Initiative (WCI) has diagnosed the causes of the poor responsiveness to women's issues by Malaysia's parliament, which were systemic impediments to women's participation in political and electoral processes, leading in turn to a lack of representation in parliament. And finally, we reflect on the ways in which gender diversity has been addressed in the Philippines, a country likewise seeking to move from the category of 'developing nation'. There, as elsewhere, those who possess non-hegemonic gender identities are especially likely to suffer social and political marginalization as well as economic deprivation, and this should be a concern for those seeking to eliminate such disparities. Here, again, political participation is revealed as an important means of empowerment and as a means to raise the consciousness of gender issues. Together, the discussions below seek to draw out important common threads relating to the intersection between globalization, gender and development from diverse contexts and to demonstrate the utility of a gendered lens.

APPLYING A GENDERED LENS TO THE GFC

Many economists considered the GFC the worst financial crisis to hit since the Great Depression last century. Originating in US financial markets, the GFC led to marked economic slowdowns for most developing countries, as it impacted their financial markets and growth prospects (Cali et al., 2008). Overall, the GFC's impacts differed for people within and between countries. Applying a gendered analysis can help to understand and account for how people experienced the GFC differently or had different roles to play in it.

In conducting gendered analyses of the GFC, several have argued that the dominance of men, masculinity and macho behaviours in the financial sphere were a significant contributing factor to the GFC (Kristof, 2009; Morris, 2009; Lagarde, 2010). While most analysts agree that several complicating factors contributed to the origin of the GFC and the outcomes that followed, speculation emerged around whether the crisis could have been caused, to some degree at least enabled, 'by masculinity run amuck' (Nelson, 2012: 2).

At the World Economic Forum in Davos, some questioned whether the crisis would have occurred, or taken on the same proportions, if Lehman Brothers instead had been Lehman Sisters; others suggested that the preferred bank would be Lehman Brothers *and* Sisters (Kristof, 2009). People started to wonder whether 'having more women in leadership positions in finance and its regulation' would 'naturally lead to a kinder, gentler, and tidier economy?' (Nelson, 2012: 2). In Iceland, high-profile male banking leaders were replaced by women in the hopes of creating a 'new culture' (ibid.).

Wall Street remains among the most male-dominated business arenas, which some maintain leads to suboptimal decision-making (Kristof, 2009). Just as in financial decision-making, women also represent a tiny proportion of the main decision-makers in the public institutions faced with addressing the crisis – at the time, women made up 5 per cent of the main decision-makers at the European Central Bank (which also had a male chair), and at the International Monetary Fund (IMF) on its Board of Directors, women held 4.5 per cent of seats, although now a woman is managing director (Pearson and Elson, 2015: 4).

Just as the causes and responses to the GFC can be understood as gendered, research has suggested that the impacts of the GFC were gendered, disproportionately impacting women, particularly those from minority ethnic communities within their respective countries (ibid.: 16). Furthermore, austerity measures in response to the GFC have disproportionately impacted women around the world, and cuts to things like free school meals, early childhood education, and disability services have added to the unpaid care work women tend to shoulder within households, as they take on a disproportionate load of both paid and unpaid care activities (UN Women, 2014: 5; Pearson and Elson, 2015: 19). Likewise, women face acute impacts from such cuts, given they make up a significant proportion of social service workers, are over-represented in insecure jobs, have smaller savings and fewer assets (UN Women, 2014: 5).

While acknowledging that this lack of women's representation in decision-making is important, some feminist scholars have argued that the insertion of women into decision-making roles at large banks could not in itself necessarily prevent such a crisis from recurring (Bedford and Rai, 2010). Instead, they argue, systemic changes to bank regulation are also crucial, as are changes to the structures that underlie society in business, such as the way production and reproduction relate to finance (Pearson and Elson, 2015: 11). In short, they propose that further complex, comprehensive changes are required.

Feminist economists have offered insights, suggesting new, alternative economic arrangements. For example, Nelson suggests that, while there is a gendered angle to be taken on the GFC, it is important to refute the oversimplified idea that it is merely about the natural 'differences' women and men 'bring' to their jobs (2012: 2). Instead, we need to look carefully and think deeply to get a clearer picture of gender and the GFC. While some would call on evidence that men are less risk-averse than women, more prone to overconfidence, more competitive, less sensitive to losses, and more short-term-oriented than women, few mention how such differences may relate to socialization – instead, evolutionary and biological explanations to these appear to be in fashion (ibid.: 4). A meta-analysis of existing studies indicates that where differences in adult women and men's behaviour are found, they are usually very small (ibid.: 5). Furthermore, neither traits stereotypically associated with femininity nor those stereotypically associated with masculinity are themselves adequate for making up a competent and wise financial leader (ibid.: 16).

These ideas might then cause some hesitancy in insisting that a greater inclusion of women in processes will result in improvements. However, none of these detract from arguments that women ought to be far better represented in many fields – including economic and political fields – than they presently are. This is arguably especially so in the political sphere, where representation may result in improved recognition of and action on concerns that are faced by women and which men may not be sufficiently aware or invested in. To explore this, we turn now to our examination of the Women's Candidacy Initiative in Malaysia.

Text Box 5.1   Case Study: The Women's Candidacy Initiative

The spaces in which representational democracy unfolds are among the most quintessential and important public spheres, as it is within parliament that policies and laws that shape life choices are made and amended. In the context of this chapter, the critique of Malaysia's democratic spaces and processes by the Women's Candidacy Initiative (WCI) point towards the way that some women have sought to identify the causes of systemic problems and have sought to improve women's access to political processes.

WCI was formed in the lead up to the 1999 General Elections in Malaysia. An important context to these elections was a groundswell of popular discontent and civil society activism, which arose in the wake of the Asian Financial Crisis, which like the Global Financial Crisis described above, had far-reaching economic impacts.

Malaysian activists recognize the importance of political engagement in order to advance their respective agendas (Lee et al., 2010). This is well illustrated by the efforts of women's groups in Malaysia to secure critical amendments to laws relating to violence against women. Beginning in 1984, these efforts led a decade later to a still unsatisfactory Domestic Violence Act – in which, lamentably, marital rape was not recognized as violence.

Poor representation of women in parliament is a major factor for these frustrations. In 1999, only 10.4 per cent of parliamentarians were women (Lee, 2011b). The reasons behind the low numbers are diverse. In their publication *The Progress of Malaysian Women Since Independence 1957–2000*, the Ministry of Women and Family Development (2003) pointed to some of these impediments, including cultural factors, the prioritizing of domestic roles, and socialization into roles as followers of men, and values relating to their ethnic group (Rashila and Saliha, 2009). Malaysia's ethnic politics is also a key issue because, as Malaysian sociologist Cecilia Ng has pointed out, women's political activities are likely to be orientated towards ethnic rather than gender-related issues (Ng, 1999: 180). And being thus framed in ethnic terms, religious discourses become salient, particularly for those of the majority Malay ethnic group, for whom Islam is central. And in the Malaysian context, religiously framed discourses regularly suggest that women should not hold leadership positions in ordinary circumstances, a notion which carries weight but which is by no means uncontested (Lee, 2011b: 21).

In this context, members of WCI sought to address one of the causes that they saw as leading to women's political voices being marginalized in a country where politics is dominated by the United Malays Nationalist Organization (UMNO), the largest political party and principal in the ruling Barisan National, a coalition of parties that has monopolized government since Malaysia's independence from Britain in 1957. WCI mobilized support for an independent female candidate to contest a federal parliamentary seat in the 1999 elections – a candidate who would explicitly run on a women's rights agenda. The WCI campaign sought not only to win the seat of Selayang which they contested, but through engagement with the media to raise public consciousness about the electoral and political processes that worked to preclude women from political life.

WCI's critique of the political processes in Malaysia included pointing out that electoral deposits for contestants are among the highest in the world. A Federal Parliament candidate's deposit is RM15,000 (US$3,850), which a contestant would lose if she did not receive enough votes or if her campaign materials were deemed to be inadequately cleared from public spaces after the elections. These deposits were regarded by WCI as exorbitant, especially in view of the fact that elsewhere in the world such deposits either do not exist (for example, in Ireland) or are very modest (for example, in Australia, where it is less than US$200). Further, WCI pointed out that women tend to earn much less than men, making participation difficult, especially for independent candidates who are without the financial support of large parties and are disadvantaged by features of Malaysia's electoral system (see Lee, 2007). Within major parties, the WCI cited impediments to women's participation that included a masculine culture, non-transparent nomination systems and, if appointed to contest a seat, regularly being placed in contests that were difficult or impossible to win. Furthermore, being beholden to a party line that can diminish the importance of women's issues was a further cause of dissatisfaction with seeking political engagement through existing major parties.

In this context, WCI's campaign in 1999 sought to be both critical and transformative, to provide a model for future participation by women in the electoral process. A key member of WCI, and its candidate for Selayang in 1999, was Toni Kasim. In 2008, she described the thinking behind the WCI's modus operandi for women's inclusion during the 1999 election campaign:

> Because women often have multiple duties at home and work, we were flexible with letting people contribute time when they were able to. We weren't hardnosed about it like other political parties who demanded that you gave 150 per cent. And we only got people to do things they were comfortable doing. We didn't make anyone climb poles [to hang flags]. Some women just felt they could run the office or even just clean it, because that was what they knew how to do. One woman just wanted to give people massages when they needed one because that was what she knew how to do. We gave people the space to contribute in the way they wanted. And in the evening we sat in a circle to talk about how the day went. Of course, the PAS [Parti Islam SeMalaysia, Malaysian Islamic Party] guys told us not to do all this touchy-feely stuff, but we were running a different kind of campaign to the ones they were used to.[1]

Although WCI was unsuccessful in contesting Selayang, defeat was by a very slim margin in what was regarded by the incumbent as a safe seat. Their campaign provoked

(Continued)

---

[1]Interview with Julian Lee, 5 March 2008.

(Continued)

discussion of women's engagement in politics and helped put women's issues of the agendas of major political parties (Martinez, 2004: 91).

In 2008, the WCI resurfaced to contest the general elections of that year. Despite lifting the profile of women's issues, the WCI sought redress for numerous ongoing issues relating to the rights of women and attitudes towards women. The prevalence of sexism in parliament is illustrated by a comment from former Minister for Works, Samy Vellu, who, in parliament stated that: 'Toilets are like new brides after they are completed. After some time, they get a bit spoiled. Even if you do not use them frequently, you need someone to clean them every 25 minutes' (cited in Amir, 2007: 50). Such comments are common in parliament, making it a hostile space for women.

The WCI's prime candidate, Toni Kasim, was forced to withdraw from the campaign for health reasons. The remaining members of the WCI, of which one of the present authors (Lee) was a member, thus shifted tactics. What came to pass was a theatrical voter-education campaign that revolved around an ethnically indistinct character called Mak Bedah (Lee, 2013). Mak Bedah would find high-profile political candidates and publicly corner them and force them to state on record their views about an array of gender issues in Malaysia. In this way, Mak Bedah could serve as a model for other voters who ought to demand of their representatives their views on matters of importance on which they can then base their vote on election day.

This media-orientated strategy was successful in garnering a great deal of media coverage, including featuring on *Al Jazeera* and the front page of a magazine pullout from Malaysia's foremost financial newspaper *The Edge*. It also placed on record the views and reactions of an array of candidates, some of whom responded very warmly, some of whom responded less warmly. When approached by Mak Bedah, Samy Vellu, who had been receiving flak for comments he had made, including (but sadly not limited to) his 'toilets are like brides' comment, shouted: 'Go away! I don't want to talk to you. You all can say what you want!' (Mahendran, 2008).

We can see, through the example of the WCI, that gains can be made in awareness-raising by reimagining political engagement, and by making this accessible to those beyond a political elite. Imagination was required to break with common moulds for political participation and to develop the means of participation without the resources of large political parties and to formulate a gender-based critique of systemic issues that lead to the marginalization of women in the public sphere. The WCI thus sought to raise public consciousness by undertaking two very different forms of engagement with the political process – a process likewise deemed important for gender non-conforming women in the Philippines.

Text Box 5.2   Case Study: Classing and Gendering Filipino Trans Women

In the Philippines, there is no local equivalent for 'transgender woman', abbreviated as 'trans woman'. The closest would be *bakla* (gay), with a pronoun 'he' used in the larger society. That is so, even though a significant segment of the *bakla* society behaves in this manner – acts, talks, dresses in a feminine way; adopts a female name; works in the highly feminised sectors; and some have even gotten married and adopted or acted as surrogates for children, in some ways reconstituting the practice of the traditional family, in a context where same-sex marriage is not (yet) legal. While sex reassignment surgery has become gradually available, it remains beyond the reach of many of those who desire it, and many insist that it is not a prerequisite to their re-identification as female. Specifically, a transsexual may be a trans woman but the reverse is not necessarily true. Thus, it can be defined that a trans woman is one who was assigned as male by birth because of sexual organs, but who identifies as a woman. That identity is felt and lived in the life of the person, regardless of lingering familial and social stigma against them.

As a sector and, in particular, a workforce sector, there has been a widespread acceptance of *bakla* long before 'transgender' became part of the local lexicon. Tan (2001) emphasizes that the *parlorista bakla* (literally, beauty-parlour working gay) community constitutes the biggest, most organized sector of transgender women. The *parloristabakla* regularly participates in certain aspects of the entertainment industry, especially in beauty pageants and Santacruzans (a Roman Catholic commemoration of the Christianization of Spain, which colonized the Philippines for 300 years), as well as in specially created neighbourhood associations. Economic participation of the *parloristabakla* extends to domestic work, market vending and a range of hospitality work – from serving beer, stage performing, to servicing the sexual needs of some male clients in the urban districts of Manila (ibid.:120–1). This work takes place across the country, in varying degrees.

The *parlorista* holds the biggest and most organized trans woman group – thanks to the *barangay* (village)-level beauty pageants and routinized Miss Gay competition in almost all major cities and their co-national's support of such entertainment-packed events. Equally due to support from the Hairdressers and Cosmetologists Association of the Philippines (HACAP), which is composed of at least 15,000 trans women (although they also have women members), the *parlorista bakla* is a significant economic force. Despite their high levels of education, a recent study shows that trans women experience unemployment more often than other people of their age (Winter et al., 2007). While 'parlorista' is often referred to as the low-income *bakla,* who is also perceived by society as dirty and loud in speech (thanks to gay slang), they are, in reality, diverse in class status. Some beauty parlour owners have built an empire of franchises in their names, while others have held on to their single-shop business but have created loyal clientele through the years.

Aside from the beauty and fashion, and hospitality industries, trans women are also highly visible in the local and Japan-bound entertainment industry. These are highly gendered work categories. While, at times, the term 'Japayuki' is used as a euphemism for prostituted women, and the latter is again appropriated by society as a dirty job, the *parloristabakla* vary in their demeanour when they interact with one another, and this is modified when they negotiate with their family members and co-workers. For the transgender community, the use of *bakla* language is an assertion of their gendered subculture.

Aside from income and education, decorum is implicit in the middle-class category of women in the Philippines. Class and femininity are very much linked to the Madonna image, which is central in their Catholic socialization. The *bakla* may then be situated in the fringe when compared to the well-mannered and productive Filipino women, an image that is at times more illusory than real. What the above indicates among the things that this discussion of Filipino trans women seeks to highlight, is that in contexts where livelihood and wellbeing improvements are sought for women, that the category of 'woman' or 'female' has many sub-categories which can be subjected to diverse

(Continued)

(Continued)

further forms of marginalization. Addressing the needs of diverse categories of women requires a sound understanding of the contexts of their lives.

With the creation of the Philippine Overseas Employment Agency (POEA) in 1982 and preceding national directives of then-dictator Ferdinand Marcos, the country became the first in the world to officially and directly broker the deployment of its human capital to industrializing zones, especially the Middle East, South East and East Asia, the USA and Canada, Northern and Western Europe, as well as the Pacific and many parts of Africa. Clearly, the POEA has been instrumental in the burgeoning of the *parlorista bakla* as entertainers in Japan, an important means for their upward economic mobility in a context where the trans woman is pigeonholed to certain professional identities, although this has been rapidly changing. Like other Overseas Filipino Workers (OFWs), the *parloristas* sent home remittances and, in many cases, are the main breadwinners in their families. Thus, *parloristas* were often responsible for sending their younger siblings and extended family to school.

The family remains the most important and enduring institution for Filipinos (Asis, 1994: 16), and being able to provide financial support as well as care support are important features of this respectability. Yet, such social and family status does not grant the trans woman the equivalency of Filipino woman. Still, there is greater awareness to their inclusion to the women category with the Philippine Commission of Women's recent move to integrate trans women in its strategic plan (Philippine Commission on Women, 2014).

The emerging 'purple collar labour', a term coined by David (2015) to refer to trans women's significant segregation in the thriving business outsourcing operations (BPO), highlights their affective labour. In call centres, trans women use their female voice and female name if they are talking to male clients in order to induce them to buy, and they revert back to their male identity when the customer is a woman. Thus, by concealing their identity, it becomes a new form of transnational commodification of women, but in a way that also increases the trans woman's social status. Not only do they receive a better than average income, but the virtual nature of their work enables them to manipulate their gender identities, to their advantage (ibid.: 16–17). The BPO is one important sector where lesbians, gays and transgendered people can feel secure in their identities, and like the earlier job niches, the *parlorista* and the *Japayuki*, their growing numbers at times translate to economic power. Since call centre agents are expected to speak English proficiently, and handle transactions with the highest standards of etiquette, this purple collar labour is likewise providing trans women the validation they may seek as de facto Filipino women. Although their affective labour is commodified and effectively translates to profit, it also provides space for trans power to be enacted. It likewise produces a revised status in which, like *parlorista* and *Japayuki* workers, these trans women sit within a sector that is open to gender diversity, but also enables them to inhabit a restrained character that is akin to traditional Filipino femininity. The BPO becomes then a space where gender and class discrimination are dismantled, but new forms of structural discriminations are formed.

The case of the WCI demonstrates that endeavours emanating from the grassroots can emerge and posit thoughtful alternatives. However, it is also sometimes the case that bottom-up approaches are not enough for the gains to be sustained. Structural changes are often needed, as for instance through sensitizing the BPO against the undue commodification of the affective labour of trans women in the transnational space. For the WCI, wider structural hurdles to independent participation in elections in Malaysia need to be overcome. Yet, it is obvious that the advocacy of the WCI in Malaysia, and in the Philippines of the *parlorista bakla* associations, and the human rights-focused organizations within the various transgender communities, have challenged the status quo and raised consciousness of critical issues in the areas of gender and sexuality in the political and social domains.

CONCLUSION

In our above discussions, several key themes emerge that are important considerations in any examination of globalization, gender and development. Among these is that gender is one key dimension that consistently impacts on advantage and disadvantage, access and exclusion, and representation and marginalization. There is no doubt that there is an array of other aspects of a person which have significant impact, but gender is a foremost trait which intersects with them and an important one to address when seeking to ameliorate inequalities. Because greater gender equity has been recognized as a facilitator of wider socio-economic development, the grounds for pursuing it are great. However, irrespective of its economic impacts on development, gender equity it is a worthy pursuit. Indeed, we should problematize simplistic notions that events such as the GFC might have been avoided with more women in the financial sector.

Conceiving of the ways in which such gender disparities might be addressed requires an understanding of both local and global dynamics, as our discussions of the GFC and WCI indicate. Meanwhile, attention is also needed to consider the ways in which attempts to mainstream gender consciousness could inadvertently overlook the needs of gender non-conforming persons, as demonstrated by the case study from the Philippines. The Filipino and Malaysian case studies demonstrate the need and capacity of all women (including trans women) to diagnose problems and then self-organize to undertake actions that seek to address them. Nowhere has gender equity been achieved; it is everywhere a work in progress. But how that work is undertaken necessarily unfolds in global and local contexts simultaneously.

Questions for Discussion

1 What different mental models of gender are raised in this chapter?
2 In what ways might global governance be different/better if more women held positions of decision-making power?
3 How possible is it for people to self-organize to challenge entrenched structures of power 'from below'?

📖 FURTHER READING

Briones, L. (2013) *Empowering Migrant Women: Why Agency and Rights are Not Enough.* Aldershot: Ashgate Publishing, Ltd.

Lee, J.C.H. (2011a) *Policing Sexuality: Sex, Society, and the State.* London: Zed Books.

Lerner, G. (1986) *The Creation of Patriarchy.* Oxford: Oxford University Press.

REFERENCES

Amir, M. (2007) *Malaysian Politicians Say the Darndest Things, Vol. 1.* Kuala Lumpur: Matahari Books.

Asis, M.M. (1994) 'Family Ties in a World Without Borders', *Philippine Sociological Review*, 42(1): 16–26.

Bedford, K. and Rai, S.M. (2010) 'Feminists Theorize International Political Economy', *Signs*, 36(1): 1–18.

Boulton, J.G., Allen, A. and Bowman, C. (2015) *Embracing Complexity: Strategic Perspectives for an Age of Turbulence.* Oxford: Oxford University Press.

Butler, J. (1988) 'Performative Acts and Gender Constitution: An Essay in Phenomenology and Feminist Theory', *Theatre Journal*, 40(4): 519–31.

Cali, M., Massa, I. and te Velde, D.W. (2008) 'The Global Financial Crisis: Financial Flows to Developing Countries Set to Fall by One Quarter', Overseas Development Institute. Available at: www.odi.org/publications/2523-global-financial-crisis-financial-flows-developing-countries-set-fall-one-quarter (accessed 15 June 2015).

Chant, S.H. (2007) *Gender, Generation and Poverty: Exploring the Feminisation of Poverty in Africa, Asia and Latin America.* Cheltenham: Edward Elgar Publishing.

Chinkin, C. (2000) 'Gender and Globalization', *UN Chronicle*, 39(2): 69–70. Available at: https://www.questia.com/magazine/1G1-66579870/gender-and-globalization (accessed 8 April 2015).

Collins, P.H. (2002) *Black Feminist Thought: Knowledge, Consciousness, and the Politics of Empowerment.* London: Routledge.

Connell, R. (1987) *Gender and Power: Society, the Person and Sexual Politics.* Oxford: Polity.

Connell, R. (1995) *Masculinities.* St. Leonards: Allen and Unwin.

Connell, R.W. (2002) *Gender: Polity Short Introductions.* Cambridge: Polity Press.

Cornwall, A., Harrison, E. and Whitehead, A. (2007) *Feminisms in Development: Contradictions, Contestations and Challenges.* London: Zed Books.

David, E. (2015) 'Purple-Collar Labor Transgender Workers and Queer Value at Global Call Centers in the Philippines', *Gender and Society*, 29(2): 169–94.

Enloe, C. (2007) *Globalization and Militarism: Feminists Make the Link.* Lanham, MD: Rowman & Littlefield Publishers.

Harrington, M. (1992) 'What Exactly is Wrong with the Liberal State as an Agent of Change?', in V.S. Peterson (ed.), *Gendered States: Feminist (Re)Visions of International Relations Theory.* Boulder, CO, and London: Lynne Rienner Publishers, pp. 65–82.

Jackson, C. and Pearson, R. (1998) *Feminist Visions of Development: Gender, Analysis and Policy.* London: Routledge.

Kristof, N.D. (2009) 'Mistresses of the Universe', *New York Times.* Available at: www.nytimes.com/2009/02/08/opinion/08kristof.html?_r=0. (accessed 8 April 2015).

Lagarde, C. (2010) 'Women, Power and the Challenge of the Financial Crisis', *International Herald Tribune*, Op-Ed. Available at: www.nytimes.com/2010/05/11/opinion/11iht-edlagarde.html. (accessed 8 April 2015).

Lee, J.C.H. (2007) 'Barisan Nasional Political Dominance and the General Elections of 2004 in Malaysia', *Südostasien Aktuell – Journal of Current Southeast Asian Affairs*, 2: 39–66.

Lee, J.C.H. (2011a) *Policing Sexuality: Sex, Society, and the State*. London: Zed Books.

Lee, J.C.H. (2011b) 'Shopping for a Real Candidate: Aunty Bedah and the Women's Candidacy Initiative in the 2008 Malaysian General Elections', in C. Derichs (ed.), *Women and Democracy in Asia: A Springboard for Democracy?* Berlin: LITVerlag, pp. 19–40.

Lee, J.C.H. (2013) 'The Supra-Ethnic Malaysian', in J. Linquist, J. Barker and E. Harms (eds), *Southeast Asian Figures of Modernity*. Honolulu, HI: University of Hawaii Press, pp. 183–5.

Lee, J.C.H., Wong, C.H., Wong, M. and Yeoh, S.G. (2010) 'Elections, Repertoires of Contention and Habitus in Four Civil Society Engagements in Malaysia's 2008 General Election', *Social Movement Studies*, 9(3): 293–309.

Lerner, G. (1986) *The Creation of Patriarchy*. Oxford: Oxford University Press.

Mahendran, B. (2008) 'Women Activists Manhandled by MIC Workers', *Malaysiakini*, 2 March. Available at: www.malaysiakini.com/news/79004 (accessed 2 June 2015).

Martinez, P. (2004) 'Complex Configurations: The Women's Agenda for Change and the Women's Candidacy Initiative', in M.L. Weiss and S. Hassan (eds), *Social Movements in Malaysia: From Moral Communities to NGOs*. London: RoutledgeCurzon, pp. 75–96.

Ministry of Women and Family Development (2003) *The Progress of Malaysian Women Since Independence 1957–2000*. Kuala Lumpar: Ministry of Women and Family Development.

Momsen, J. (2010) *Gender and Development* (2nd edn). London: Routledge.

Morris, N. (2009) 'Harriet Harman: "If Only it Had Been Lehman Sisters"', *Independent*. Available at: www.independent.co.uk/news/uk/home-news/harriet-harman-if-only-it-had-been-lehman-sisters-1766932.html (accessed 8 April 2015).

Nelson, J.A. (2012) 'Would Women Leaders Have Prevented the Global Financial Crisis? Implications for Teaching about Gender, Behavior, and Economics', Global Development and Environment Institute, Working Paper No. 11–03. Available at: www.ase.tufts.edu/gdae/pubs/wp/11-03nelsonwomenleaders.pdf (accessed 8 April 2015).

Ng, C. (1999) *Positioning Women in Malaysia: Class and Gender in an Industrializing State*. London: Macmillan.

Ortner, S.B. (1974) 'Is Female to Male as Nature is to Culture?', in M.Z. Rosaldo and L. Lapmphere (eds), *Woman, Culture, and Society*. Stanford, CA: Standford University Press, pp. 67–87.

Østergaard, L. (1992) *Gender and Development: A Practical Guide*. London: Routledge.

Parpart, J.L., Rai, S.M. and Staudt, K.A. (2003) *Rethinking Empowerment: Gender and Development in a Global/Local World*. London: Routledge.

Pearson, R. and Elson, D. (2015) 'Transcending the Impact of the Financial Crisis in the United Kingdom: Towards Plan F – A Feminist Economic Strategy', *Feminist Review*, 109(1): 8–30.

Philippine Commission on Women (2014) *Women's Empowerment, Development, and Gender Equality Plan 2013–2016*. Available at: http://pcw.gov.ph/sites/default/files/documents/resources/womens_edge_plan.pdf. (accessed 9 May 2016).

Rashila, R. and Saliha, H. (2009) 'Women and Political Development in Malaysia: New Millennium, New Politics', in A. Jamilah (ed.), *Readings on Women and Development in Malaysia, A Sequel: Tracing Four Decades of Change*. Petaling Jaya: MPH Publishing, pp. 71–99.

Sassen, S. (2007) 'Countergeographies of Globalization: The Feminization of Survival', in L. Lucas (ed.), *Unpacking Globalization: Markets, Gender, and Work*. Lanham, MD: Lexington Books, pp. 21–34.

Sen, G. and Grown, C. (1988) *Development Crises and Alternative Visions: Third World Women's Perspectives*. London: Earthscan.

Tan, M.L. (2001) 'Survival Through Pluralism: Emerging Gay Communities in the Philippines', *Journal of Homosexuality*, 40(3–4): 117–42.

Tickner, J.A. (2001) *Gendering World Politics: Issues and Approaches in the Post-Cold War Era*. New York: Columbia University Press.

Tickner, J.A. (2014) *A Feminist Voyage through International Relations*. Oxford: Oxford University Press.

United Nations (UN) (2011) *The Millennium Development Goals Report*. New York: United Nations. Available at: www.unmillenniumproject.org/goals/ (accessed 7 September 2015).

UN Women (2014) *The Global Economic Crisis and Gender Equality*. New York: UN Women, September. Available at: www.unwomen.org/en/digital-library/publications/2014/9/crisis-paper (accessed 8 April 2015).

Visvanathan, N., Duggan, L., Wiegersma, N. and Nisonoff, L. (2011) *The Women, Gender and Development Reader*. London: Zed Books.

Winter, S., Rogando-Sasot, S. and King, M. (2007) 'Transgendered Women of the Philippines', *International Journal of Transgenderism*, 10(2): 79–90.

World Health Organization (WHO) (2006) 'Gender and Human Rights'. Available at: www.who.int/reproductivehealth/topics/gender_rights/sexual_health/en/ (accessed 1 September 2015).

WHO (2015) 'What Do We Mean by "Sex" and "Gender"?' Available at: http://apps.who.int/gender/whatisgender/en/index.html (accessed 7 September 2015).

6

RETHINKING PRACTICES OF SECURITY IN AN AGE OF GLOBALIZATION

DAMIAN GRENFELL

INTRODUCTION

Human security has remained an important framework for security more than twenty years after the United Nations Development Programme (UNDP) made it the focus of its 1994 *Human Development Report*. While the meaning and relevance of a people-centred security has remained analytically contested, as an approach it has become embedded in a range of activities, programmes and policy frameworks in post-conflict and development contexts. That human security has remained popular can be understood for a range of reasons, not least because it appears to provide an integrated approach across different spheres of life. In stressing the need to build security in multidimensional ways, human security appears more comprehensive and progressive than state security, ostensibly moving beyond the conventional realm of nation-state politics and giving priority to people and a sense of utility in addressing people's day-to-day needs.

In shifting the security domain from between to within nation-states, the objectives associated with providing human security coalesce with those of international development, often to the extent that the two appear as virtually one and the same. While the discursive parameters at times remain differentiated, the securitization of poverty has been very powerful, to the extent that the principles of equality and human rights have been increasingly usurped by arguments that security can be achieved as poverty is reduced (see, for example, Brainard and Chollet, 2007, *Too Poor for Peace? Global Poverty, Conflict, and Security in the 21st Century*). In other words, while justifications for programmes may be different – one based in security, while the other in economic development – both require an intervention into the everyday fabric of societies. Framing the approach in this chapter is the concept of mental models (Denzau and North, 1994) that has been used through this collection, arguing that human security is one manifestation of a cognitive framework that dominates the world of security and development practitioners coming out of the global North. The 'modern' – treated in this chapter as one form of epistemology – is understood here as a kind of mental model that assists in understanding why human security has taken the form it has and in turn is bound up with expressions of power.

Contrary to common rhetoric, the key contention for this chapter calls into question the emancipatory potential of human security and how it intersects with development by arguing that to an important extent it has reflected the ideological and instrumental interests of the global North. In a seemingly contradictory way, as social relations become increasingly abstracted across the globe, human security provides a way to justify interventions into 'the body' of local populations. As a kind of 'beneficence as control', human security gives reason for the attempted recalibration of social relations in communities in two ways. First, human security programmes draw communities towards a particular form of community – the national – and within that, towards forms of market capitalism and ostensibly democratic political systems. In a second, and more clearly ontological way, the same process rests on assumptions that instilling a form of modernity is essential for peace. As such, human security has essentially remained an elite-level mechanism for change rather than driven and shaped by far more local-level efforts.

This chapter begins with a short orientating discussion of how security can be defined and the dominance of state security across the twentieth century. In the second section, key aspects of human security are discussed in the context of the ideological dominance of liberalism since the end of the Cold War. Where the global political context shaped the formation of human security, the traction it attained is examined in the third section in light of the argument that some kind of doctrinal response was required in order to respond to the kinds of violence and conflict that were emerging at that time. In the fourth section, the intersection between conflict and development is explored with reference to how economics have come to dominate understandings of how and why violence occurs, and the significance of this in terms of the role of modernization of societies treated at the edges of the global periphery. Lastly, and building on the claim that human security remains largely elite focused, this chapter will argue for the requirement of human security to be defined and shaped by the communities of people facing risks in order to achieve the emancipatory objectives at more than a rhetorical level.

SECURITY AND INTERNATIONAL RELATIONS

For all its importance in determining the quality of life, and to what end social resources are deployed, definitions of security often remain highly contested. 'Security' is often used interchangeably with terms such as peace or safety, or in the negative as insecurity, and conflated with terms such as risk, conflict, violence and threat. Scholars such as Anthony Burke have claimed that we no longer know what security is, suggesting that the confusion and questioning over its discursive structure and political implications is a reflection that the term 'no longer possesses credible wholeness' (2007: 27). Richard Falk defines security as 'the negation of insecurity' (Hough, 2008: 9), although such an approach can lead to limited understandings in that noting the absence of something tells us little about its actual presence.

Acknowledging its contestability, security is taken here to be the condition where the existences of threats are negated via some *agent* imbued with the value of providing protection. Where peace is taken to be the absence of threat, security is a response to some form of recognizable threat that serves to undermine the sense of safety of a particular *referent subject*; a community, state, individual, organization, a practice and so on. In its simplest terms, an agent is able to prevent the actuation of some form of identified threat upon a referent subject, such as a police force acting to protect a community. The agent may take many different forms, from private security guards through to family members, or surveillance technologies through to amulets imbued with spiritual value or power (see Wlodarczyk, 2009: 90). Of course, these are just analytical distinctions and, in practice, the production of security is far more complex once one enters into the detail of any given situation.

The break-up of empires, large-scale conflict, colonialism and anti-colonial movements across the nineteenth and twentieth centuries saw the concept of security develop in the context of the consolidation of the nation-state system. Given significant momentum in the United Kingdom and North America, the discipline of international relations developed as a way to understand interstate relations (Lawson, 2015: 20), with a concern for security a key element. While various associated theories developed across the twentieth century – Idealism, the English School, Liberalism, Marxist and Feminist approaches – the dominant theory was Realism in its various iterations in both scholarship and foreign policy (see Acharya and Buzan, 2007). Taking the state as the primary source of both risk to and protection of security, realism established a very clear distinction between the international and domestic spheres of politics. Violence and conflict emerged in the competition between states, driven by national interest and the defence of national sovereignty. Hans Morgenthau and his book *Politics amongst Nations*, first published in 1948, advanced the realist position that all politics was a struggle for power (2005). Other political interests and actions – including that of domestic politics, or trade between nations – was seen as 'low politics' and peripheral to the primary objectives of international relations. Realism gave a trans-historical (and retrospective) account for warfare from the writings of Thucydides forward (431 BC), significantly dominating foreign policy during the Cold War as security was seen to be achieved via 'balance of power' politics and the threat of 'mutually assured destruction' (Trachtenberg, 2012: 25).

There were attempts to widen and deepen the discourse of security by authors such as Buzan and Hansen (2009: 188), who argued for the inclusion of agents beyond the state and of threats beyond those military, although such analysis remained limited (Hough, 2008: 3) and still anchored in a world of state politics (for instance, Buzan, 1983, *People, States and Fear*). It was not, however, until the end of the Cold War that there was a possible space for alternative conceptions of security to gain traction. The break-up of the Union of Soviet Socialist Republics (USSR) in 1991 marked the ideological demise of soviet communism and the steep reduction in super-power rivalry between the USA and the Soviets, with a significant reduction in the risk of nuclear annihilation.

As examined over the following two sections, this created new political contingencies, as well as new needs and challenges, from which human security emerged.

HUMAN SECURITY AND THE LIBERAL DREAM

> Human security does not entail the threat or use of force or coercive measures. Human security does not replace State security.
>
>   (UN, General Assembly Resolution, 66/290, 2012)

The origins of 'human security' are typically attributed to the UNDP's 1994 *Human Development Report*. The UNDP, tasked with the objective of the material advancement of societies facing extreme poverty and working in a range of conflict sites and 'fragile states', used the report to argue for the need to address core deficiencies in the way security had typically been previously conceptualized.

Human security called for a de-centring of the state, limiting the extent to which it is perceived as an agent of security *as well* as the referent subject. While the shift to being 'people-focused' is frequently identified, the state is actually being de-centred in two ways. Firstly, human security is provided via both governments and civil society actors. Organizations outside of the state, such as the plethora of non-government organizations (NGOs) that operate from the local to the global, become increasingly important as human security calls for a shift to the individual so as to prioritize 'safety from such chronic threats as hunger, disease and repression', as well as 'protection from sudden and hurtful disruptions in the patterns of daily life – whether in homes, in jobs or in communities' (UNDP, 1994: 23). Such a broadening of conceptions of threat requires a far larger ensemble of actors with different capacities, skills sets and modus operandi than states, including those that juxtapose with war-fighting and peace-keeping typified by the military and police. By shifting the focus to people and securitizing everyday needs for their social life – economic, health, food, environmental, political, community and personal (ibid: 24–5) – the focus on the security of the state and the provision of security by the state, are both reduced as other actors, including multi-lateral agencies, civil society organizations and corporations, are seen as better positioned to work within these domains.

Human security has been given institutional legitimacy through its adoption by organizations such as the UNDP, as well as its uptake as a guiding principle in the foreign policies of a series of 'middle powers', including Norway, Japan and Canada (Behringer, 2005: 307, 309). Additionally, there was the creation of the United Nations Human Security Unit in 2004, a follow-up to the Commission of Human Security that produced the 2003 *Human Security Now* report, as well as other research efforts such as the Human Security Report Project (formerly the Human Security Centre) in Canada, the Human Security Initiative, the Human Security Network, and the Civil Society Network for Human Security. The concept has also been adopted by a wide range of NGOs, as well as aid agencies working in sites of conflict, and these have become important in moving the doctrine from idea to practice (see Murdie, 2014).

With the collapse of the Soviet Union in 1991 and the apparent triumph of liberal-capitalism, there was a much greater space for liberalism to gain traction, particularly in multilateral agencies and within the burgeoning domain of NGOs (Edwards and Hulme, 1995: 849). Rather than the conservatism of Cold War 'realpolitik', this was a period of 'liberal triumphalism'. Fukuyama for one took the demise of the Soviet Union as a 'liberal revolution' that constituted the culmination of a 'universal history of mankind in the direction of liberal democracy' (1992: 48). While this was one of the more hubristic moments, liberalism did come to permeate significant dimensions of and key actors within the security landscape.

Human security varies in regards to its interpretative framing, from the emancipatory through to more conservative iterations (Richmond, 2007). Nevertheless, even across these differences, it is difficult to avoid the underpinning liberalism that imbues key elements of the doctrine. The first – and perhaps most obvious articulation of this – is the ways in which human security gives priority to the 'person'. The individualism at the core of liberalism is echoed through human security as the key purpose for security is the 'good life' of the person and the role of the state should always be contained and limited. The role for civil society, and the market through economic development, also echoes to the long-term conceptions of freedom within liberalism. James (2014: 74) is right to point out that the focus on individuals is uneven across the various key reports produced to support human security, and by the 2012 UN Resolution it has moved to 'people and communities'. Although in the context of locating security within, rather than between, states – and treating people in terms of their communities, rather than the state – the individual person is still being given a priority that had previously been the case in approaches to security.

The influence of liberalism is evident in other elements of human security, such as the way it is seen to be universal in its application, and the faith that is placed in international and multi-lateral institutions to mediate its implementation. Moreover, in terms of what might be described as the expansion in the 'lateral normative range' by including freedom from 'fear' and 'want' (United Nations Trust Fund for Human Security, UNTFH, 2013), human security mimics liberal conceptions of negative and positive liberty. Even the 1994 UNDP report speaks in terms of a social contract (1994: 5–6) and, at a deeper level, Stern and Öjendal point to an underpinning teleological framing where the 'past' is presented as insecurity, 'now' as the promise of security, and the 'future' the achievement of security (2010: 14). Such teleology is hardly distinct to liberalism of course, but when coupled with meliorism that frames human security, the pathway to a peaceful world appears to be grounded in a liberal cosmopolitanism where the 'world community' can determine the 'future of humanity'.

An 'integrated approach' speaks to the need for multiple actors to achieve human security and that there is a complementarity between state and human security, as outlined clearly in the 2012 United Nations General Assembly Resolution:

> (g) Governments retain the primary role and responsibility for ensuring the survival, livelihood and dignity of their citizens. The role of the international community is to complement and provide the necessary support to Governments, upon their request, so as to strengthen their capacity to respond to current and emerging threats. Human security requires greater collaboration and partnership among Governments, international and regional organizations and civil society.
>
> (UN, General Assembly Resolution, 66/290, 2012)

Not only is state security still seen as a necessary part of the inter-relationship between nations, but states still provide security through military and policing efforts, resources through aid agencies and development programmes, giving sanction through international legal mechanisms (from the UN Resolutions to International Tribunals), offering diplomatic support, intelligence, and so forth. Put this way, it is difficult to imagine human security without the state. The state may be de-centred, but perhaps in the ultimate echo of liberalism, human security treats the state as both simultaneously necessary and regarded with suspicion. It is required but must always be contained and held in check. This point will be returned to later in the chapter, though to understand both the emergence of human security and its relationship to the state, it is important to briefly turn to the changing patterns of warfare and violence that was seen to come to the fore in post-Cold War global politics.

A NEW SECURITY FOR UNENDING VIOLENCE

The title on the front cover of a 2016 issue of *Time* magazine reads 'Iraq's Forever War' (4 July 2016).[1] An overview of the efforts by different combat forces unified only by their opposition to ISIS, the article uses the devastation in the Northern Iraqi town of Sinjar to argue the inevitability of future conflict even after their common enemy is defeated:

> Many of the houses have been tagged according to ethnicity and religion – Yezidi, Kurd, Sunni, Shi'ite – a haunting reminder of the sectarian program ISIS has carried out everywhere it can. But it's a warning as well, of the next war this multiethnic, multi-sect country may face, the morning after it finally defeats ISIS. (Malsin, 2016: 23)

The 'forever' in the title reflects the discourse of unending war (see Duffield, 2007: 126–31), not just a 'war on terror' without expiration, but also its well-spring in the inevitability of ethnic violence within nations. There is a kind of essentialism in play, not only representing the Middle East as inherently chaotic and driven by deep societal schisms, but of the idea that ethnicity and violence in the world are deeply and necessarily interwoven.

While the risk of global nuclear annihilation ebbed, the end of the Cold War meant that regimes that had drawn support from the USA or the Soviets could no longer continue the repression and centralized control that they had previously. Indonesia, for instance – a nation-state that emerged via anti-colonial warfare in the years following the Second World War and took on a repressive anti-communism from the mid-1960s – had long drawn on Western support to counter various secessionist threats. By the late 1990s, however, the dictatorship of Suharto collapsed as different territories pushed for independence, with Timor-Leste emerging as a new nation across 1999–2002 (Aspinall

---

[1]With increased acknowledgement that a 'good life' should be part of security discussions, this reframing of security made an equivalent move to that of Johan Galtung more than two decades earlier in his call for a 'positive peace' (1969: 183), an attempt which forced a consideration of the structural elements that are required for a good life, rather than the narrower focus on the prevention of identifiable threat.

and Berger, 2001: 1012). Rather than ushering in an 'end of history', the end of the Cold War was like a release valve on violent contestation for the control over existing states or the formation of new ones from Southern Europe to South East Asia and, as Kabia writes, through to different regions of Africa (Kabia, 2009: 41–2).

The wars that occurred over the 1990s appeared to be frequently marked by rigid demarcations based on identity and claims to territory at a sub-national level. Some of these conflicts – such as Timor-Leste – had been long-running secessionist move-ments that pressed the claim for national independence in the post-Cold War era, while others – the Balkans for instance – erupted as a consequence of the collapse of the Soviet Union. Other violence, for example in Rwanda, did not call for secession or devolution but political control via the homogenization of the ethnic composition of society (Brounéus, 2008; Hintjens, 2001).

Despite these different dynamics, a discourse of 'new wars' emerged as a way to rec-ognize distinctive changes to how warfare was evolving. Various characteristics appeared common including the collapse of a clear distinction between combatants and civilians, the multiplication of different parties to conflicts, the specific targeting of civilian group-ings via expulsion or massacre, the emphasis on ethnic and religious identity in claims for sovereign control of territory, and the ways in which demands for secession or devolution marked political conflicts. Authors such as Mary Kaldor (2001: 8–9) argued that what differentiated 'new wars' from 'old wars' was decentralized organization and integration into a 'global' war economy rather than being ordered via 'vertically organized hierarchical units'. All of these aspects were not necessarily novel in and of themselves. In terms of trends in warfare however, the de-centred nature of violence and the impact of technology was shifting the patterns of warfare to such an extent that it appeared very different to warfare waged between uniformed armies along 'fronts'.

The emergence of human security makes sense in the context of 'new wars' in the way it bypasses states that were often bound up with creating insecurity and penetrates local populations at points of tension. While discursively human security is concerned for the emancipation of people in a way that resembles a liberal faith, human security can be understood as a way of domesticating the will of the global North within states that are no longer able to repress populations and contain risk (Duffield, 2007).

Compounding the apparent need for doctrines such as human security were the longer-term prejudices of former colonial powers in the way violence is understood outside of the West, from the Congo to the Solomon Islands, Iraq and Syria. Violence emanating from intra-state wars has often been treated as a kind of 'new barbarism' (Beswick and Jackson, 2011: 46–7), depicted as a violent world of resurgent tribalisms, clans, blood-ties, revenge, ritual and savagery (Kaplan, 1993). The 'tribes' of Afghanistan, and Libya, and like those shaped by and that afforded protection to Saddam Hussein, act as signifiers of threat located outside of modernity and beyond the European Enlightenment (see, for instance, Harpviken, 1997; Ucko, 2008).

Such portrayals of re-tribalization miss how such forms of violence are bound to and are shaped by modernity itself (Appadurai, 1996: 15, 139–57; Straus, 2007: 610). While others, such as *Time* magazine's 'Forever War' in Iraq, represent a kind of essentialism common in the mass media repudiated, in the case of Africa at least, by authors such as Mkandawire, as 'often poorly veiled racist accounts' (2002: 183–4).

In a similar vein, Mark Duffield suggests that the 1994 violence in Rwanda was not represented as 'organized and systematic' but as 'anarchic and spontaneous blood frenzy born out of old ethnic hatreds' (2001: 111). Even as violence encroaches on Europe, explanations can hedge towards one of irrationalism. Michael Ignatieff, writing on the effects of destruction of a museum during the war between Croatia and Serbia, reflected that 'some dark spirit, stronger than truth, was at work here' (1993: 35). This 'dark spirit' emerges across the globe in the work of different writers such as Robert Harvey (2003), Richard Kaplan (1994), Samuel Huntington (1996) and Benjamin Barber (1995), among innumerable *Time* magazine-style descriptions that anchor war in essentialised representations of populations.

While, on the one hand, human security can be seen as part of the triumph of liberalism across the 1990s, it can also be understood as a response to these changing patterns of violence. Just as violence was seen to be extending out from inside societies there was a need to reach in and ensure change not only at the institutional level, such as the state, but also within the normative and discursive fabric of local society. In this regard, this can be seen as the attempt to shift the social and epistemological foundations – the mental models of peoples from a wide variety of localized epistemologies – to a cognitive framework shaped in terms of a liberal-style modernity. People became the subject in that global security and a universalization of the objectives of human security – is inversely dependent on recalibrating social relations to contain recalcitrant 'spoilers' and to weaken points of possible resistance at sites of risk and contagion.

SECURITY, DEVELOPMENT AND THE ECONOMY OF CONFLICT

In reflecting on the intersection of security and development, it is important to recognize that what may appear as recent trends or challenges nevertheless are shaped by long-forged contours in the socio-cultural exchange between warring parties. While human security remains a recent innovation, in key respects it is no more apart from Euro-centric world-views than state security is. Siracusa, reflecting on the assessment of Joseph Fairbanks and the US failure in the Vietnam War, speaks to the consequences of being unable to understand security as it is reproduced across very different social domains.

In Fairbank's words:

Ignorant of Buddhism, rice culture, peasant life, and Vietnamese history and values generally, we sent our men and machines to Saigon. Now we are out, and still ignorant, even of the depth of our ignorance. In contradistinction to successful American intervention in Europe in World Wars I and II, an area that admittedly shared a common Atlantic culture,

he continued, the United States disregarded 'the interests of the local people as they see them in their cultural terms' and, instead, and with disastrous consequences, imposed 'upon their situation our view of the world as seen in our cultural terms'. It could hardly have had a different outcome (Siracusa, 1976: 234, citing John K. Fairbank, *New York Review of Books*, 12 June 1975: 30–1).

This quote is from nearly two decades before the emergence of human security as a codified concept, and as an explanation for a conflict that was shaped by the Cold War rather than one that occurred in its aftermath. In this assessment, for all the military might that the US armed forces could muster, the disaster was in the inability to recognize the importance of different views of the world. There are important points that *prima facie* distinguish state security and human security, although this chapter will conclude with an argument that despite the focus on 'people and communities', in key respects human security carries the same risk as conventional state security as portrayed here. Namely that it is unable to accommodate different views of the world and is delivered in a way where both the cause and the resolution to violence are largely predetermined.

In many respects, human security can be treated as the securitization of development practice integrated with a recognition that a military presence is necessary. This is particularly the case in the 'new wars' discussed above, where the de-centred nature of warfare and the fusion between civilian and combatant necessitate that humanitarian and development work is undertaken alongside military actions. This dynamic has resulted in efforts towards civil–military cooperation and radically expanded the extent to which militaries undertake development work in addition to war fighting and peacekeeping.

In the reverse, the economic and social development dimensions of human security are understood as critical in that economic factors are central to the cause of conflicts and thus development is a critical way out of it. Often referred to as a 'security–development nexus' (Duffield, 2010; Stern and Öjendal, 2010), each are frequently treated as essential elements to one another and increasingly integrated.

That the economic dimensions to life are both seen as a cause of conflict and a route to peace have become almost the norm. In the years following significant internal conflict within Timor-Leste during 2006 to 2008, the state-adopted slogan '*Adeus Konfliktu, Benvindu Desenvolvimentu*' (Goodbye conflict, Welcome development) adorned banners, formal documents, and other state-produced paraphernalia. In other circumstances the slogan may have welcomed 'peace', and yet here development has been taken as the panacea for violence. Over recent decades, accounts for the cause of conflict have increasingly focused on economic drivers, typified by the uptake of analysis by Collier and Hoeffler (1998) that argues that economic factors are the primary cause of civil war.

Following Sen (2008: 8), poverty alone is not the cause for conflict, and approaching it this way takes a reductive pathway that ignores the fact that poverty and peace often co-exist. Nevertheless, human security is a doctrinal manifestation of the centrality given to economics, a policy instantiation of the belief that development will draw populations away from endemic violence. This can be seen as the guiding logic of various multi-lateral agencies as well as in human security programmes as they are implemented in communities (World Bank, 2011; UN, 2013). For instance, while more than eighty countries have different programmes funded by UNTFH, in sites where there has been extensive violence, efforts focus heavily on conflict mitigation initiatives, poverty alleviation, or both. By way of example, in Timor-Leste, the focus is on food security, education and water management; in Bosnia Herzegovina, it is 'community reconciliation through poverty reduction'; in Kosovo, human security initiatives include 'weapons in exchange for development', 'multi-ethnic partnerships for improved education, health and sustainable livelihoods'; and in the Solomon Islands, there are programmes for 'tensions reduction, reconciliation and rehabilitation' (UNTFHS, 2013).

While each of these programmes is applied in different contexts, they are drawn into a framework that is already largely predetermined with regards to what is needed. The more broadly human security is applied, as in 'freedom from fear' as well as 'freedom from want', the wider the legitimation is to intervene into societies in ways that work towards the adjustment of political structures (towards democratic representation), economies (market capitalism) and the health and education of at-risk populations, playing into the more general process of forming a liberal peace (Richmond, 2007: 472–4). Tool kits are developed and experts move from site to site as needs are seen as being the same. Adaption is understood to be required, but only to the extent that security is not grounded culturally, but becomes a technical exercise delivered increasingly by systems based on highly abstracted authority; the logic and rationality of all kinds of ratings, indices, rank-ings and measurements that indicate whether societies 'achieve' a quantifiable level of security within designated fields and sub-fields. The threats are delineated, interpreted, applied and evaluated by a global conglomerate of organizations tasked with re-ordering societies in a way that tilt them towards a modern-liberal subjectivity of progress and secular agency (Stern and Öjendal, 2010: 17). There is no need to know cultures at a localized level, as beyond minor adaptations or differences over when political liberaliza-tion should occur, multi-lateral agencies, civil society actors and states can impose 'upon their situation our view of the world as seen in our cultural terms' (Siracusa, 1976: 234).

By making the economy the central focus of understanding conflict, and also shifting debates within security so that they extend into the sphere of development practice, the terrain is laid to legitimate not only the extension of global capital to the global South, but also the latter's transformation (see Chandler, 2011). Security is achieved through intervening in societies and changing material and social conditions at the level of 'day-to-day life'; a remaking of security from within, albeit delivered by exogenous organiza-tions. This might only be focused at points of concentrated risk within communities, but then it is threaded alongside a whole series of other programmatic interventions, such as peace-building, state-building, other development programmes, and transitional justice. In a more ontological sense, this speaks to the deeper effect of modernization of societies, or at least the drawing of certain aspects of social life towards a liberal modernity. While the attempts to theorize the change from 'agrarian' and 'traditional' societies via processes of modernization are not overtly articulated in the way that they were during the 1960s and 1970s, the emphasis on 'good governance', economic development, human security and so forth are a continuum of the same mental model that means the 'good life' equates with that of Western societies.

The lack of space for local articulation of threats, in tandem with the inverse penetra-tion into communities without linking threats to broader social and political processes and their adjustment, means that much of human security can be seen as inextricably tied to the interests of the global North. Human security becomes part of an architecture of power that suggests a far closer relationship with state security than the complementarity argued earlier in this chapter. As Duffield suggests, 'the idea of human security embodies a mobilizing relation of governance able to bridge the worlds of sustainable development and inter-national security' (2007: 111). In practice, then, human security is directed at securing local populations in a way that ensures that risks are mitigated by making them self-reliant, at the same time as structuring them into a global order of capital and liberal governance (Goodman, 2008: 45–50; Kienscherf, 2011: 522). While, in response to the post-11 September attacks in the United States, there was a reversion to a more conventional state-centric security position (Battersby and Siracusa, 2009: 23), human security has continued to be part of the mainstream, to the extent that its central logics of integration of actors, penetration into communities, and securitization of poverty has become standard even when the concept of human security is not overtly alluded to. In this regard, then, human and state security appear to be on a continuum rather than being thoroughly different, especially when the latter is seen to be employed to recalibrate societies in order to mitigate risk to northern orders and interests.

ALTERNATIVES AND RETHINKING PRACTICE: CONCLUDING COMMENTS

In summary, this chapter has argued that human security gained traction in the post-Cold War years in part given the ascendancy of a form of liberalism, especially embedded in multilateral agencies as well as NGOs, and a need to contain shifting patterns of violence and conflict. In turn, human security has resulted in the securitization of development in a way that creates space for market capitalism as an agent in the building of security, while also remaking sites designated as conflict-prone into pliable domains for a shift towards a liberal modernity.

In concluding this chapter, it is acknowledged that the discursive shifts made from focusing on states to peoples was not insignificant, though the real change needs to come with how security is practised. In effect, the reproduction of security needs to be inverted so that it is determined by communities that are experiencing risk. By allowing for an end-user account for security, the aim is to provide a greater space for the subjectivities as well as historical and cultural contexts as responses to security are driven upwards from communities, rather than downwards by agencies. This approach is distinguished from thinkers such as Buzan and Waever (2009), who, while in recognition of non-military threats, still perceive state and institutions as the securitizing actors capable of endorsing and enacting measures and responses to threats and objects faced by 'referent objects'. The constitution of security is far more than an apparatus or service deliverable, and should be deepened to see it as an 'interlocking system of knowledges, representations, practices and institutional forms that imagine, direct and act upon bodies, spaces and flows in certain ways' (Burke, 2007: 28). McDonald argues that any definition of security 'suggests different articulations of political community and that community's core values' (2008: 64). Just as 'participation' has become a mantra in development practice that obfuscates the exercise of power rather than shifting the nature of the relationship between practitioner and recipient, great care would be required to ensure equivalent calls for human security do not replicate this. In contrast, achieving a form of security driven and defined locally, and with a much greater sense of mutuality and exchange, would amplify the priority given to culture, alternative centres of power and pathways to resolution. In the reverse, a move away from the genericism and largely unreflexive articulation of predetermined pathways would bring the focus onto what it means to be 'human' so as to ensure a richly defined security.

Questions for Discussion

1   What is new about human security? How does the concept differ from previous mental models of security?

2   Do you agree with the contention that states can no longer play the role of security guarantor to their populations?

3   In what ways might reflexivity, deliberation and mutuality offer a more secure future for people, communities and the global system as a whole?

FURTHER READING

Buzan, B. and Hansen, L. (2009) *The Evolution of International Security Studies*. Cambridge: Cambridge University Press.

James, P. (2014) 'Human Security as a Military Security Leftover, or as Part of the Human Condition', in P. Bacon and C. Hobson (eds), *Human Security and Japan's Triple Disaster*. London: Routledge. pp. 72–88.

Kaldor, M. (2013) *Human Security: Reflections on Globalization and Intervention* (online edn). Hoboken: Wiley Press.

Morgenthau, H. (2005) *Politics among Nations: The Struggle for Power and Peace* (7th edn). New York: McGraw-Hill Higher Education (1st edn, 1948).

Münkler, H. (2005) *The New Wars*. Oxford: Polity Press.

REFERENCES

Acharya, A. and Buzan, B. (2007) 'Why is There no Non-Western International Relations Theory? An Introduction', *International Relations of the Asia-Pacific*, 7(3): 287–312.

Appadurai, A. (1996) *Modernity at Large: Cultural Dimensions of Globalization*. Minneapolis, MN, and London: University of Minnesota Press.

Aspinall, E. and Berger, M.T. (2001) 'The Break-Up of Indonesia? Nationalisms after Decolonisation and the Limits of the Nation-State in Post-Cold War Southeast Asia', *Third World Quarterly*, 22(6): 1003–24.

Barber, B.R. (1995) *Jihad vs. McWorld: Terrorism's Challenge to Democracy*. New York: Times Books.

Battersby, P. and J. Siracusa (2009) *Globalization and Human Security*. Lanham, MD: Rowman & Littlefield Publishers.

Behringer, R.M. (2005) 'Middle Power Leadership on the Human Security Agenda', *Cooperation and Conflict: Journal of the Nordic International Studies Association*, 40(3): 305–42.

Beswick, D. and Jackson, P. (2011) *Conflict, Security and Development*. New York: Routledge.

Booth, K. (1991) 'Security and Emancipation', *Review of International Studies*, 17(4): 313–26.

Brainard, L. and Chollet, D. (eds) (2007) *Too Poor for Peace? Global Poverty, Conflict, and Security in the 21st Century*. Washington, DC: Brookings Institution Press.

Brounéus, K. (2008) 'Truth-Telling as Talking Cure? Insecurity and Retraumatization in the Rwandan Gacaca Courts', *Security Dialogue*, 39(1): 55–76.

Burke, A. (2007) *Beyond Security, Ethics and Violence: War Against the Other*. London and New York: Routledge.

Buzan, B. (1983) *People, States and Fear: The National Security Problem in International Relations*. Brighton: Wheatsheaf Books Ltd.

Buzan, B. and Hansen, L. (2009) *The Evolution of International Security Studies*. Cambridge: Cambridge University Press.

Buzan, B. and Waever, O. (2009) 'Macrosecuritisation and Security Constellations: Reconsidering Scale in Securitisation Theory', *Review of International Studies*, 35(2): 253–76.

Chandler, D. (2011) 'The Liberal Peace: Statebuilding, Democracy and Local Ownership', in S. Tadjbakhsh (ed.), *Rethinking the Liberal Peace: External Models and Local Alternatives*. Hoboken, NJ: Taylor & Francis, pp. 77–88.

Collier, P. and Hoeffler, A. (1998) 'On the Economic Causes of Civil War', *Oxford Economic Papers*, 50: 563–73.

Commission on Human Security (2003) *Human Security Now*. New York: Commission on Human Security.

Democratic Republic of Timor-Leste (RDTL) (2012) *'Goodbye Conflict, Welcome Development': AMP Government Snapshot 2007–2012*. Dili: Alliance of the Parliamentary Majority (AMP).

Denzau, A.T. and North, D.C. (1994) 'Shared Mental Models: Ideologies and Institutions', *Kyklos*, 47: 3–31.

Duffield, M. (2001) *Global Governance and the New Wars: The Merging of Development and Security*. London: Zed Books.

Duffield, M. (2007) *Development, Security and Unending War: Governing the World of Peoples*. Cambridge: Polity Press.

Duffield, M. (2010) 'The Liberal Way of Development and the Development–Security Impasse: Exploring the Global Life-Chance Divide', *Security Dialogue*, 41(1): 53–76.

Edwards, M. and Hulme, D. (1995) 'Policy Arena: NGO Performance and Accountability in the Post-Cold War World', *Journal of International Development*, 7(6): 849–56.

Fukuyama, F. (1992) *The End of History and the Last Man*. London: Penguin.

Galtung, J. (1969) 'Violence, Peace, and Peace Research', *Journal of Peace Research*, 6(3): 167–91.

Goodman, J. (2008) 'Global Capitalism and the Production of Insecurity', in D. Grenfell and P. James (eds), *Rethinking Insecurity, War and Violence: Beyond Savage Globalization?* Abingdon: Routledge, pp. 44–56.

Harpviken, K.B. (1997) 'Transcending Transnationalism: The Emergence of Non-State Military Formations in Afghanistan', *Journal of Peace Research*, 34(3): 271–87.

Harvey, R. (2003) *Global Disorder.* London: Constable and Robinson.

Hintjens, H.M. (2001) 'When Identity becomes a Knife: Reflecting on the Genocide in Rwanda', *Ethnicities,* 1(1): 25–55.

Hönke, J. and Müller, M. (2012) 'Governing (In)Security in a Postcolonial World: Transnational Entanglements and the Worldliness of "Local" Practice', *Security Dialogue,* 43(5): 383–401.

Hough, P. (2008) *Understanding Global Security* (2nd edn). Abingdon: Routledge. (1st edn, 2004).

Huntington, S.P. (1996) *The Clash of Civilizations and the Remaking of World Order.* New York: Simon & Schuster.

Ignatieff, M. (1993) *Blood and Belonging: Journeys into the New Nationalism.* New York: Farrar, Straus and Giroux.

James, P. (2014) 'Human Security as a Military Security Leftover, or as Part of the Human Condition', in P. Bacon and C. Hobson (eds), *Human Security and Japan's Triple Disaster.* London: Routledge. pp. 72–88.

Kabia, J.B. (2009) *Humanitarian Intervention and Conflict Resolution in West Africa: From ECOMOG to ECOMIL.* Aldershot: Ashgate Publishing Limited.

Kaldor, M. (2001) *New and Old Wars: Organised Violence in a Global Era.* Stanford, CA: Stanford University Press.

Kaplan, R. (1993) *Balkan Ghosts: A Journey through History.* New York: St. Martin's Press.

Kaplan, R. (1994) 'The Coming Anarchy: How Scarcity, Crime, Overpopulation, Tribalism, and Disease are Rapidly Destroying the Social Fabric of our Planet', *The Atlantic,* 273(2): 1–16.

Kienscherf, M. (2011) 'A Programme of Global Pacification: US Counterinsurgency Doctrine and the Biopolitics of Human (In)security', *Security Dialogue,* 42(6): 517–35.

Lawson, S. (2015) *Theories of International Relations: Contending Approaches to World Politics.* Cambridge: Polity Press.

Malsin, J. (2016) 'Iraq's Fight for Survival', *Time,* 4 July: 16–23.

McDonald, M. (2008) 'Constructivism', in P.D. William (ed.) *Security Studies: An Introduction.* Hoboken, NJ: Taylor & Francis, pp. 59–72.

Mkandawire, T. (2002) 'The Terrible Toll of Post-Colonial "Rebel Movements" in Africa: Towards and Explanation of the Violence against the Peasantry', *Journal of Modern African Studies,* 40(2): 181–215.

Morgenthau, H. (2005) *Politics among Nations: The Struggle for Power and Peace* (7th edn). New York: McGraw-Hill Higher Education (1st edn, 1948).

Murdie, A. (2014) *Help or Harm: The Human Security Effects of International NGOs.* Stanford, CA: Stanford University Press.

Richmond, O.P. (2007) 'Emancipatory Forms of Human Security and Liberal Peacebuilding', *International Journal,* Summer Issue: 459–77.

Sen, A. (2008) 'Violence: Identity and Poverty', *Journal of Peace Research,* 45(1): 5–15.

Siracusa, J. (1976) 'Lessons of Vietnam and the Future of American Foreign Policy', *Australian Outlook,* 30(2): 227–37.

Stern, M. and Öjendal, J. (2010) 'Mapping the Security–Development Nexus: Conflict, Complexity, Cacophony, Convergence?', *Security Dialogue,* 41(1): 5–30.

Straus, S. (2007) 'What is the Relationship between Hate Radio and Violence? Rethinking Rwanda's "Radio Machete"', *Politics and Society*, 35(4): 609–37.

Thucydides (431 BC) *The History of the Peloponnesian War.*

Trachtenberg, N. (2012) *The Cold War and After: History, Theory and the Logic of International Politics.* Princeton, NJ: Princeton University Press.

Ucko, D. (2008) 'Militias, Tribes and Insurgents: The Challenge of Political Reintegration of Iraq', *Conflict, Security & Development*, 8(3): 341–73.

United Nations (UN) (2012) General Assembly Resolution on Human Security (A/RES/66/290). Available at: www.un.org/humansecurity/sites/www.un.org.humansecurity/files/hsu%20documents/GA%20Resolutions.pdf (accessed 27 February 2017).

UN (2013) 'A New Global Partnership: Eradicate Poverty and Transform Economies through Sustainable Development: The Report of the High-Level Panel of Eminent Persons on the Post-2015 Development Agenda'. Available at: www.post2015hlp.org/wp-content/uploads/2013/05/UN-Report.pdf (accessed 27 February 2017).

United Nations Development Programme (UNDP) (1994) *Human Development Report 1994.* New York and Oxford: Oxford University Press.

United Nations Trust Fund for Human Security (UNTFHS) (2013) 'Human Security for All'. Available at: www.un.org/humansecurity/about-human-security/human-security-all (accessed 27 February 2017).

Wlodarczyk, N. (2009) *Magic and Warfare: Appearance and Reality in Contemporary African Conflict and Beyond.* New York: Palgrave Macmillan.

World Bank (2011) *World Bank Development Report 2011: Conflict, Security, and Development.* Washington, DC: World Bank.

PART II
MODELS OF JUSTICE

7

GLOBAL JUSTICE, INTERNATIONAL LAW AND DEVELOPMENT

PAUL BATTERSBY AND REBEKAH FARRELL

INTRODUCTION

Questions of justice and international law intersect with development practices at many levels and in many different issue domains across the global system. In previous chapters, we have examined policy interventions intended to equalize economic opportunities, increase political participation and provide a measure of security for people rather than for states. In this chapter, we turn our attention to the vast and expanding body of international law, understood conventionally as codified agreements between nation states in the form of conventions, treaties, agreements, resolutions and declarations.[1] The United Nations System is built upon a liberal idea of law and justice, where people are, in the ideal, entitled to enjoy rights to life, freedom, and equality, irrespective of their social status and irrespective of whether or not they constitute the majority (Rawls, 1971). International development, as conceived by states and those global institutions that administer assistance programmes, is primarily a matter of allocating resources to promote social and economic progress in areas of identified need in order that these rights be realized. Central to this official discourse is the assumption of a shared understanding as to the mutuality of economic justice, the rule of law and global security. Yet, there are

---

[1]An expanded definition would include agreements and arrangements made between and within international non-state organizations (see Noortmann, 2015). As will be touched upon, institutions, especially national judiciaries, play a significant role in 'making' international law through interpretation and application.

many models of global justice; from the liberalism of those advocating for the consolidation and extension of international human rights norms through law, to the globalism of those who assert that justice is unrealizable within the prevailing system of global governance (Wilson et al., 2013; Hardt and Negri, 2000; Steger, 2009). There are divergences between secular humanist universalism on the one hand, and the belief systems of people from diverse religious faiths on the other (see Chapter 9). There is also disagreement between absolutists and pragmatists on the flexible accommodation of law to practical imperative (discussed in Chapter 4).

All international laws are subject to interpretation and dispute, and compliance is rarely uniform, especially where legality conflicts with state security interests or constrains commercial opportunity. Often, decisions must be made about whose and which rights to prioritize, and to defend, and at what cost. This uncomfortable reality applies to humanitarian aid workers and organizations as it does to states and transnational corporations. Development practitioners must navigate a way across these unstable frontiers in a global system where enforcement remains contingent on the exercise of state power.

GLOBAL JUSTICE AND INTERNATIONAL ORDER

How much legal knowledge is necessary for those who do not practise law as a profession? Military personnel are expected to be aware of their obligations under the laws of war that govern the use of force. In the commercial world, compliance officers monitor company obligations under different national-level corporations, financial, contract laws, industrial relations and environmental laws, and public international laws, where these relate to crimes of corruption for example. The United Nations Human Rights Based Approach (HRBA) explicitly connects knowledge of international human rights law (IHRL) to action across the entire spectrum of development interventions (UNDG, 2003). All organizations, and not just those within the UN System, are enjoined to incorporate human rights norms into the fabric of their corporate governance (for a summary of development-related international laws, see Table 7.1 on p. 111).

In liberal institutionalist models of global justice, the principles that underpin a just international order are written in key public international law instruments. Foundational to this international rule of law is the *United Nations Charter* (1948), binding on all United Nations member states, which declares a decisive link between respect for law and 'international peace and security', where security is achieved through the promotion of human wellbeing and not merely the use of force. But how much human welfare can the existing international system provide and to what extent can international law provide any guarantee that rights and obligations will be respected? Even though the exponential growth of international law since the end of the Second World War lends a sense of solidity and solidarity to many fundamental development aims, both the laws and the institutions tasked with upholding them have fallen short of achieving universal compliance. This is because the interstate system is founded upon the principle of state sovereignty, which is enshrined in the UN Charter and to which there are only very limited and controversial exceptions.

There is no universal sovereign power that can enforce law in the international system, and there is the barefaced reality of consistent and extensive transgressions by states behaving contrary to their international legal obligations (Kratochwil, 2014; Blakeley and Raphael, 2013; Krasner, 1999). The International Criminal Court (ICC) is empowered to impose criminal penalties for war crimes, genocide and crimes against humanity, but only where the persons charged are either nationals of a state that is party to the *Rome Statute*[2] or have committed a crime within the territorial jurisdiction of the Court. While international humanitarian norms have legal force at the international level, international human rights norms stand on much shakier ground. The International Court of Justice (ICJ) has authority to determine if and where states have violated their obligations across the broad spectrum of international treaty law, but has no power to impose penalties for non-compliance (Cassese, 2008; Robertson, 2002). With the exception of international criminal law, therefore, in order for international norms to be given effect, they must be adopted into national legal codes and enforced through national-level criminal and civil processes, except where regional courts have jurisdiction, such as the European Court of Human Rights. Observance is consequently uneven, with China for example ratifying the *International Covenant on Economic, Social and Cultural Rights* (ICESCR, 1966) but not the coterminous *International Covenant on Civil and Political Rights* (ICCPR, 1966). And, while once it was commonplace for the USA and other Western powers to be outspoken about China's human rights record, criticism has become muted as China's global economic weight has increased. In an increasingly divergent global world, 'international human rights law', writes Stephen Hopgood, 'is no longer "fit for purpose"' (2013: 2).

One could be forgiven for succumbing to the notion that the idea of international law as the embodiment of universally agreed principles of justice and right is simply too fantastical. Critics of a conservative and nationalist persuasion argue that humanist legal transnationalism shackles sovereign states and prevents democratically elected governments from implementing their mandate to protect their country from attack (Kyl et al., 2013: 125). Liberal transnationalists decry the fact that, for reasons of diplomatic process, representatives from states with poor human rights records can nonetheless serve on international human rights bodies like the UN Human Rights Council (Neuer, 2016).[3] In the post-development quarter, the so-called international human rights 'empire' is denounced as an elite enterprise involving highly paid humanitarian lawyers and celebrity advocates for whom cases of human rights abuse are a *cause célèbre* (Hopgood, 2013: 2, 119; Kapoor, 2013). Worse still, arguably, that the institutions of humanitarian and human rights merely uphold the *status quo* in a global system of extreme inequality represents an unconscionable denial of economic justice to the billions of people living in the global South (Escobar, 1995; Sklair, 2002; Rajagopal, 2004; Hardt and Negri, 2000). International humanitarian and human rights regimes are criticized for undermining security and inhibiting justice, where the protection of fundamental rights becomes the pretext for military intervention (Duffield, 2007, 2010).

---

[2]Which therefore excludes nationals of the USA, which signed but withdrew its intention to ratify in 2002 (https://2001-2009.state.gov/r/pa/prs/ps/2002/9968.htm accessed 3 April 2017).

[3]The UN Human Rights Council comprises 47 national representatives, elected for three-year terms by the UN General Assembly, which, so the Council claims, weighs 'candidate States' contribution to the promotion and protection of human rights', available at: www.ohchr.org/EN/HRBodies/HRC/Pages/Membership.aspx (accessed 2 June 2016).

While we can identify, and magnify, frequent technical inadequacies and ethical shortcomings, the fact remains that many bodies of international law are routinely effective, where they serve systemically significant ends, to keep money, goods and people circulating around the world. The task, from a constructivist standpoint, is to realize the possibilities for 'resistance' to the moral hegemony of global elites and for 'recoding' laws to recognize the broad scope of human need and aspiration, especially, but not solely, in the global South (Rajagopal, 2004). International laws are made by global elites but it is possible to harness the discourses of liberal norms to empower people to challenge all forms of injustice and advocate for a more cosmopolitan world order (Held, 2010; Wheeler, 2010; Falk, 1999). To do this, of course, some knowledge is needed of what these norms are and how they are constituted, respected and transgressed (Noortmann, 2015).

INTERNATIONAL HUMAN RIGHTS LAW

The *Universal Declaration on Human Rights* (UDHR, 1948) is the fundamental legal document underpinning the post-1945 human rights regime. Unlike the UN Charter, which binds member states to act in accordance with its principles, the Declaration is non-binding in that it does not incur any formal legal obligations, even though all UN members are automatically party to it. However, it sets out minimum expectations for the recognition of fundamental rights defined positively as freedom of speech, association, religion and movement; and negatively as the freedom from political oppression, from exploitation and from discrimination. The document establishes equality of rights as a benchmark, from the equal right to a fair trial, to the right to a reasonable standard of living, to education and health care irrespective of social class, ethnicity, language or religion and to engage in representative politics. Two covenants spell out what are categorized as first- and second-generation rights: the ICCPR, stating the rights of individuals to freedom of speech and of trial by jury; and freedom from torture – termed first-generation rights because their recognition is seen as essential for the enjoyment of all other rights, and the ICESCR, setting forth second-generation rights, including the right to fair wages, the right to work and the right to food and shelter, enjoyed free of any discrimination based on gender, ethnicity or religion. Indeed, there has been a significant enumeration of human rights since the Declaration came into force, addressing the rights of refugees, the rights of the child, labour rights, women's rights and the rights of peoples with disabilities (Cassese, 2008; Clapham, 2007).

What are called third-generation rights, the rights of peoples, emerged in recognition of the special collective rights of minorities and indigenous populations. The principal instruments asserting this category of rights are the *African Charter on Human and Peoples' Rights* (1981), the *International Labour Organization Indigenous and Tribal Peoples Convention* (1989) and the *Declaration on the Rights of Indigenous Peoples* (UNDRIP) (2007). Indigenous rights also come within the purview of conventions addressing biological diversity and intellectual property. While genetic research delivers indisputable human health gains, biotechnologies have given food and drug companies the means to distil and manipulate the genetic structure of plants known to people in traditional communities for their medicinal qualities. This 'traditional knowledge', incorporating 'cultural expressions and genetic resources', is an integral part of an emerging indigenous rights regime but, while the principle appears uncontroversial, its codification requires that distinctions be made between what is traditional and natural and what is adapted or created through the application of scientific and technical knowledge.[4]

As stated, there is an evolutionary aspect to international law driven by the ongoing realization of omissions or gaps within legal instruments as well as tensions between law and social practice. The elevation of women's rights is a case in point. In the UDHR, the right to the presumption of innocence and a fair trial accords those charged the right to all legal means 'necessary for *his* [emphasis added] defence' (Article 11.1). Both the ICCPR and the ICESCR use gendered language to confer rights specifically upon men. For example, Part 3, Article 6.1 of the ICCPR expressly states that: 'no one shall be arbitrarily deprived of *his* life' (1976, emphasis added). The ICESCR, while striving to be balanced, nonetheless also privileges the rights of men with regard to trades union membership (Part 3, Article 8.1a) and living standards (Part 3, Article 11.1), echoing a time when men predominated in industrial workforces and were the principal bread-winners in the family home (1976). Feminist writers charge that human rights laws, while claiming to accord equal rights to all irrespective of gender, religion, ethnicity or social class, fail to accommodate the reality that each influences how rights are enjoyed in practice. Foundational international human rights laws are silent on the informal and deliberate exclusion and victimization of women, for which reason the *Convention for the Elimination of all Forms of Discrimination Against Women* (CEDAW) was brought into being (Brems, 2003: 103). But, even then, rights accorded to women in this document are not universally embraced.

The *Cairo Declaration on Human Rights and Islam* (1990) of the Organisation of Islamic Cooperation (OIC) asserts a position on human rights that is at odds with Western notions of gender equity and conflicts with CEDAW. In many societies in the Muslim world, women are subject to religiously sanctioned gender-based discrimination – from repressive dress codes to restrictions on freedom of movement and the denial of the right to tertiary education, or even the right to sign a bank cheque. Such discrimination constitutes a form of oppression that is not sanctioned by the Qur'an but is, nonetheless, widely tolerated, in Saudi Arabia for example, controversially elected to the UN Human Rights Council in 2013, along with China. However, secular human rights agendas, and secular regula-tion of religious practice, can lead to violations of cultural rights. It is 'hubris' (to borrow from Hopgood) to presume that national laws forbidding the wearing of traditional face

---

[4]The World Intellectual Property Organization (WIPO) has prioritized the development of spe-cific protections for traditional knowledge in intellectual property rights law. See: www.wipo.int/tk/en/igc/ (accessed 9 June 2016). For draft principles on intellectual property and genetic resources, see, Intergovernmental Committee on Intellectual Property and Genetic Resources, Traditional Knowledge and Folklore (2016) 'Consolidated Document Relating to Intellectual Property and Genetic Resources', 30th Session, Geneva, 30 May–3 June, WIPO/GRTKF/IC/30/4, available at: www.wipo.int/edocs/mdocs/tk/en/wipo_grtkf_ic_30/wipo_grtkf_ic_30_4.pdf (accessed 9 June 2016).

coverings, as introduced by France in 2010, for example, where the wearing of the *niqab* and *burkah* in public was rendered unlawful, are welcomed by Muslim women as steps towards their emancipation. In enacting the ban, which, despite extending prohibitions on the wearing of all head coverings, clearly targeted women of the Muslim faith, the French National Assembly acted contrary to the intent of international anti-discrimination norms. Perplexingly, however, the legislation was subsequently endorsed by the European Court of Human Rights (ECHR, 2014).

Currents of national politics inevitably affect the extent to which rights are enjoyed, and by whom. The 1951 Refugee Convention permits the seeking of asylum through irregular means outside the ambit of United Nations High Commissioner for Refugees (UNHCR). The Convention is a binding international treaty that confers the right to seek asylum and obliges states to afford assistance. Yet governments in the main recipient countries of Western Europe, North America, Australia and New Zealand, have turned to severe measures to arrest the flow of irregular refugee arrivals, including indefinite detention and *refoulement* (where a person seeking asylum is repatriated despite an ongoing risk of persecution in their country of origin), stretching the meaning of 'protection' to its epistemological limits ostensibly for reasons of border security (Flynn, 2014). Relations between governments and those providing humanitarian assistance to asylum seekers in detention have, consequently, become fraught. Although constrained by laws limiting their right to speak openly about their experiences, many NGO staff and health workers nonetheless have felt compelled to publicly criticize conditions within Australian administered centres and raise concerns about the physical and mental health of inmates.[5] In one much publicized case, workers for the INGO, Save the Children, were accused of colluding with detainees to subvert Australian immigration law and were expelled from an Australian-run offshore detention centre on the Pacific Island of Nauru (GDP, *c.* 2016; Greene, 2016).

The *United Nations Declaration on the Right to Development* (1986) reaffirms principles set down in ICCPR and ICESCR but offers no provisions for enforcement. Such sweeping declarations do little to resolve questions as to which and whose rights should take precedence where there is overlap or conflict, as with international intellectual property rights norms governing private pharmaceutical patents rights, which are either subordinate or prior to a person's right to health (Sonderholm, 2014).[6] The tide of global policy has veered towards the view that development is something to be earned through compliance with neoliberal development prescriptions (Cheru, 2016). 'New governance,' or neoliberal governance, supplants 'black letter law' with prescriptive principle, exemplified in the adoption by the UN and specialized agencies like the ILO of a programmatic approach, in which rights are 'mainstreamed' in organizational codes and practices and global goals, such as the SDGs, the ILO's Decent Work Campaign and the UN HRBA (Baccaro and Mele, 2012; ILO, 2007).

---

[5] See: https://www.savethechildren.org.au/about-us/media-and-publications/media-releases/media-release-archive/years/2015/in-its-last-act-on-nauru,-save-the-children-calls-for-independent-oversight-across-all-australian-run-processing-centres (accessed 27 February 2017).

[6] Except in circumstances of acceptable limitation, where one right is limited to ensure the enjoyment of another (goes to the discussion of absolute rights) ICCPR 18(3) as an example.

INTERNATIONAL HUMANITARIAN LAW

How much harder is it to guarantee rights observances in armed conflict? Bodies of law have emerged that seek to control the excesses of war, while falling short of outlawing war altogether. International humanitarian law (IHL), or the laws of war, is primarily concerned with conduct during and immediately after armed conflict (*in bello* and *post bellum*). The Geneva Conventions emerged out of a sense of common humanity and moral revulsion at the increasingly visible inhumanity of war. The first Convention (1864) established that the International Committee of the Red Cross (ICRC) should be granted access to war zones, where ICRC staff could provide medical aid to wounded soldiers on all sides – in effect, codifying the principle of neutrality to the benefit of future generations of humanitarian workers – provided, of course, that neutrality can be established and recognized in practice (Hilhorst and Pereboom, 2016). Three more followed: the second codified protections (in effect rights) for shipwrecked and wounded sailors; a third established the rights of prisoners of war and the fourth, in 1949, conferred specific protections on civilians in or near to combat zones. Central to the Geneva Conventions is the concept of protected persons being civilians or those with non-combatant status, who present no immediate military threat and are, therefore, not to be subjected to violence or inhumane treatment, and are entitled to safe passage or medical assistance or both within and beyond the field of battle. This requirement forms the substance of Common Article Three (so named because it is common to all four treaties). Two further protocols were attached to the Conventions in 1977 to strengthen civilian and non-combatant rights, with the Second Additional Protocol refining and extending the scope of protection in non-international armed conflicts (Cullen, 2010).

The Geneva Conventions are binding but enforcement depends on the willingness of states parties to recognize their obligations in practice and through their national justice systems. That said, Article Three is regarded as a peremptory norm which applies, in theory, to all states irrespective of whether they are signatories or not (Kolb, 2015).[7] The Conventions also apply to non-state armed actors which, where meeting the criteria for a combat force, are recognized as legitimate and whose armed combatants are entitled to the same observances offered to state armed forces personnel. This norm incurs obligations on all conflict parties not to act contrary to IHL. While intergovernmental organizations hesitate to negotiate with rebel forces, non-government organizations such as Geneva Call are able to initiate and sustain dialogues with such groups in an attempt to encourage them to respect, at the very least, the rights of civilians and captured soldiers (Geneva Call, 2014). Without the Conventions, humanitarian NGOs, for example, Médecins Sans Frontières (Doctors Without Borders), would find it harder to operate in conflict zones. IHL, also, arguably encompasses the activities of private companies and individuals. At the very least, there are recognized responsibilities not to act in ways that contravene international treaties, and which are increasingly evident in internal codes of conduct. Where businesses trade in the means of war however, or, more

---

[7]The Vienna Convention on the Law of Treaties (1969) defines peremptory norm as 'a norm accepted and recognized by the international community of States as a whole as a norm from which no legal derogation is permitted' (Article 53, UNTS, 1980: 344).

controversially, cooperate directly with incumbent regimes known to be responsible for gross inhumanity in conflict, the 'hypocrisies' of global politics insulate protagonists against criminal conviction (Krasner, 1999).

The scope of IHL has expanded to limit or prohibit the use of particular types of armaments, phosphorous shells and landmines for example, because of their indiscriminate impacts on civilians.[8] Outside, but related to IHL, the principle of civilian protection underpins the doctrine of the Responsibility to Protect (R2P), adopted at the 2005 World Summit to clarify grounds upon which state sovereignty could be overridden. The R2P norm grants the international community, in effect the UN Security Council, *ad bellum* authority to intervene militarily in the internal affairs of states where there is an immediate danger of massive loss of civilian life. However, military interventions in the first decades of the twenty-first century, in which humanitarian considerations were salient,[9] have had mixed results. The NATO-led Libyan intervention of 2011 ensured the defeat of the Muammar Gaddafi regime by a fractious rebel coalition but left a country in chaos. The Syrian civil war, which ignited in 2011, has proven beyond the capacity of the Security Council to resolve, because the conflict affects the interests of key antagonists, the USA and Russia and also the Gulf States, Saudi Arabia in particular, and Iran. Both cases exemplify the perplexities inherent in armed conflict and the practical limits of laws designed to define and limit unconscionable conduct (Kennedy, 2006).

INTERNATIONAL CRIMINAL LAW

Specific injunctions against 'cruel' and 'inhumane treatment', including torture and hostage-taking have become codified into international criminal law in the *Rome Statute of the International Criminal Court* (2002). In contrast to violations of non-binding international laws, international crimes incur criminal penalties, meaning that persons found guilty of war crimes, crimes against humanity and genocide,[10] as set down in the Rome Statute, face a custodial sentence commensurate with the harm or harms inflicted. These are crimes that, as the Preamble to the Statute claims, 'threaten the peace, security and well-being of the world' (ibid.: 7). Derogations on grounds of national interest are, according to the ICRC, increasingly unjustifiable in the face of what are, allegedly, accepted by states parties as universal customary norms (Meron, 2009: 624). And, yet, the Statute upholds the caveat of military necessity, thereby acknowledging the permissibility of attacks that harm civilians and civilian settlements where there is a justifiable military purpose and where the scale of harm is commensurate to the objective (Article 8.2a).

---

[8]The International Committee of the Red Cross explains the key areas of application and evolution at https://www.icrc.org/en/document/ihl-and-other-legal-regimes and https://www.icrc.org/en/war-and-law/weapons (accessed 2 June 2016).

[9]Therefore, excluding recurring armed interventions in Afghanistan and Iraq post-9/11.

[10]The definitions of these crimes are lengthy but, essentially, in the Rome Statute, the crime of genocide is the deliberate destruction 'in whole or in part, a national, ethnical, racial or religious group' (Article 6); crimes against humanity include 'murder', 'extermination', 'enslavement', 'torture' and 'rape' (Article 7); and war crimes are 'grave breaches of the Geneva Conventions' (Article 8.2a).

Convictions for international criminal acts are rare but attention-grabbing *cause célèbre*, like the trial of former Bosnian President Radovan Karadzic, sentenced to 40 years in prison for complicity in the 1995 Srebrenica genocide (Borger and Bowcott, 2016). The bar for proof of criminal complicity is set very high, rightly so given the serious implications for those convicted.[11] International criminal law also contains sufficient ambiguities as to sustain widely divergent judicial interpretations (Webb, 2013). Prosecution also requires conclusive evidence of direct involvement in criminal acts, beyond all reasonable doubt, and yet hard evidence of complicity in much of what transpires in the secretive world of national security, including the authorization of unlawful force, is unavailable to a court of law,[12] unless it is the leaders of a defeated state that are on trial, as happened at Nuremberg and Tokyo at the end of the Second World War.

It is impossible to bring to justice every person involved, directly or indirectly, in international crimes, which raises questions about the efficacy of trials and convictions in deterring future violations. Enforcement, while offering the promise of a future where respect for humanitarian principles and human rights is the norm, does little to guarantee their formal extension because so much depends upon extra-judicial factors (Hopgood, 2013). Political realities ensure that some protagonists will be allowed to escape responsibility, as was the case with Japanese doctors whose scientific experiments on Allied prisoners of war gave them skills and knowledge deemed useful to medicine and to the USA. While human rights advocates balk at the practice of granting amnesties to former dictators and their military supporters from Argentina to Afghanistan, such amnesties can serve a pragmatic purpose – to end a civil war by giving all parties to the conflict a reason not to defect, or to reassure demobilized militias and prevent their remobilization (Naqvi, 2003). Reconciliation through restorative justice, not retribution, is arguably a necessary part of any durable cessation to armed hostilities.

TRANSNATIONAL CRIMINAL LAW

Transnational criminal law is growing in international significance, supported by the entry into force of key crime conventions, the *UN Convention Against Corruption* (UNCAC) (2005) and the *UN Convention Against Transnational Organized Crime* (UNCTOC) (2003). The first strengthens the liberal norms governing international trade and investment relations by seeking to curb the influence of bribery and patronage in global business dealings. The second is recognition by states that they have a common security interest in cooperating to address the growth of transnational organized crime, inter alia, all forms of trafficking and smuggling, money laundering, embezzlement, fraud, and official corruption, which have a corrosive effect on governance and law enforcement. The CTOC's significance is amplified by international concern for the causes and the effects of globalized terrorism, which has led to the curtailment of fundamental civil and political rights (Rice, 2012). But, while the CTOC furthers the hegemonic discourse

---

[11]Two such tribunals were established in the 1990s to try persons for genocide in the Balkans wars of 1992–95, and the 'Rwandan Massacre' of 1994.

[12]Because details are kept secret by governments and their intelligence agencies.

of transnational organized crime as a convergent global security threat, it establishes international norms that can also potentially, and perversely, complement development and justice aims.

Official corruption undermines development programmes, skews wealth distribution and weakens governance institutions (see Chapters 4 and 10). Victims of crime are entitled to protection and rehabilitation. The duty to protect civilian populations extends to the reduction of gun violence and other firearms offences in peacetime, which can be achieved by restricting the global trade in weapons through more effective policing. Annexed to the CTOC are protocols, which encourage states parties to act in ways consistent with these priorities. For example, the Trafficking in Persons Protocol advises states to '*consider* the physical, psychological and social recovery of victims', which, though falling short of requiring fair and just treatment imply an entitlement or right to specific protections (UNODC, 2004: 43, emphasis added). The Trafficking in Firearms Protocol complements the Arms Trade Treaty (2014) in, among other things, calling for legislative and law enforcement steps to reduce the illicit manufacture and sale of 'any portable barreled weapon' (UNODC, 2004: 72). Admittedly, these norms are not couched in categorical language, leaving much latitude for states to determine how far they will comply, but they at the very least provide a basis for advancing broader humanitarian and development objectives.

INTERNATIONAL TRADE AND INVESTMENT LAW

International trade and investment treaties complement the pursuit of humanitarian and other normative ends, which we might for convenience refer to as a sustainable development. The 162 states party to the Marrakesh Agreement (1994), the founding document for the World Trade Organization (WTO), agree, in principle, to make: 'optimal use of the world's resources in accordance with the objective of sustainable development, seeking both to protect and preserve the environment and to enhance the means for doing so in a manner consistent with their respective needs and concerns at different levels of economic development' (WTO, 1994). While the language used does not impose binding obligations on WTO members, the Agreement implies an obligation to work in good faith towards the accommodation of sustainable development principles in the practices of international trade and investment. International treaties like the Convention on the Illegal Trade in Endangered Species (CITES), for example, and national custom and environmental laws prohibiting importation of illegally sourced forest and marine resources demonstrate states' interest in both preventing environmental destruction and further constraining the scope for transnational organized crime.

Although we might expect all humanitarian, human rights, and sustainability norms to run second to state and private commercial priorities, these are not incompatible ends (Desierto, 2015; Vadi, 2010). It is not uncommon for regional and bilateral treaties to incorporate stronger provisions to protect human rights. Assertion of ILO norms is likely to be robust where weak labour standards are interpreted by larger trading countries, the USA in particular, as a form of economic protectionism (Prislan and

Table 7.1   Development Priorities and International Law

Issue Area	Minimum Standards	Relevant Bodies of International Law*
Armed Conflict	Protection of civilians and non-combatants, medical assistance, safe passage for wounded and sick, neutrality (with the exception of conflict parties, of course)	Geneva Conventions, Rome Statute, UN Charter, UNDHR, ICCPR, Torture Convention, Genocide Convention, Refugee Convention OECD and IFC Guidelines
Human Health	Access to basic medical services, medicines, clean water, adequate nutrition, shelter, primary education, freedom from political and criminal violence, protection against exploitation	UDHR, ICCPR, ICESCR ICEAFRD[a], CEDAW UNCAC, CTOC Marrakesh Agreement FCPA
Gender Equity	Equal access to education, equality before the law, equal employment opportunity, access to finance	UDHR, ICCPR; ICESCR ICEAFRD[a] CEDAW, UN-DRIP, ILO Conventions (pertaining to hours of work, pay, and conditions of work including workplace safety)
Bio-diversity	Protection of terrestrial and marine habitats and ecosystems, limitations to human resource exploitation, codification of environmental crimes	Convention on Biological Diversity (CBD), UN-DRIP, ICESCR, UNCLOS, CTOC, CITES Marrakesh Agreement WIPO[b]

* These listings do not exhaust the field of relevance

a. International Convention for the Elimination of All Forms of Racial Discrimination, at: www.ohchr.org/EN/ProfessionalInterest/Pages/CERD.aspx (accessed 3 June 2016)
b. World Intellectual Property Organization, at: www.wipo.int/portal/en/index.html (accessed 3 June 2016)

Zandvliet, 2015: 398–99; Bürgi Bonanomi, 2015). It is not beyond the bounds of logic to imagine a scenario where a state's failure to achieve internationally agreed but economically costly sustainable development targets might be interpreted as yet another non-tariff protectionist measure.

TRANSNATIONAL LEGAL FUTURES

The development of transnational laws presents opportunities to those who suffer human rights abuses at the hands of multi-national corporations (MNCs). One of the more significant aspects to this evolution is the development of transnational tort law made possible through the extended extraterritorial reach of domestic civil laws. This development is evidenced through the rise of transnational tort litigation, with advocacy organizations and tort lawyers experimenting with the jurisdictional boundaries of common tort law in an effort to attribute accountability to MNCs operating in developing countries. Under the US *Alien Torts Statue* (ATS), foreign litigants have pursued claims for human rights abuses through the district court system against US-registered corporate entities and, despite efforts by the US Supreme Court to constrain legal interpretation of the ATS, new cases are still being brought in an attempt to reverse this trend and broaden the scope of ATS jurisdiction. Progressive movements also appear in transnational tort law in European jurisdictions. The recent Dutch case of *Friday Alfred Akpan v. Royal Dutch Shell* C/09/337050 / HA ZA 09-1580 (2013) in holding Dutch Royal Petroleum accountable for human rights violations offshore, may set a precedent for transnational tort litigation. In the UK context, plaintiffs seeking compensation for injuries sustained in South Africa and inflicted by the Anglo-American mining company have brought class actions against these companies in the South African High Court and through the use of transnational tort litigation in the UK High Court (*Vava & Ors v. Anglo American South Africa Ltd*, Claim No HQ11X03245).

A second relevant development in the transnational legal space is the increase of bilateral and multilateral agreements. A pertinent example of bilateral agreements includes the *1993 Agreement between the Government of Australia and the Government of Hong Kong for the Promotion and Protection of Investments (Hong Kong Agreement)*. This agreement has currently come into the public eye with the tobacco company, Phillip Morris' claim that the Australian Government's enactment of the *Tobacco Plain Packaging Act 2011* (Cth) breached its obligations under the agreement. Investor-state arbitration is on the rise by means of bilateral treaties and there are concerns that disputes could increase further with the advent of new multilateral trade and investment agreements. The most recent of these is the controversial Trans-Pacific Partnership Agreement (TPP). While these examples of bilateral and multilateral agreements may not, at this point, bode well for the protection of human rights, they demonstrate how the transnational space of law is constantly changing (Choudhury, 2005). Paradoxically, perhaps, they betray a willingness of both states and non-state actors to be held to account by, of all things, private international courts of arbitration that enjoy de facto universal jurisdiction.

CONCLUSION

The argument presented in this chapter is that, despite the many – valid – criticisms of the international legal establishment, the scope to pursue global justice through law is not exhausted or futile. Knowledge of international law can be a means to raise public awareness of rights and of injustices, and enable lay persons to conceive different legal pathways towards the realization of development and humanitarian ends. Thinking of international law as a creative space where there is scope for imagination and legal or regulatory innovation can generate incentives for development practitioners to engage with legal issues and work in closer cooperation with legal experts. The relationship of international law to development stretches far beyond war crimes trials in The Hague, or the human rights agendas of Amnesty International or Human Rights Watch, or, indeed, the UN's Human Rights Based Approach. This relationship encompasses routine legal investigation, monitoring and advocacy; the discovery of new regulatory possibilities in existing international treaties governing trade and investment. While this approach might be rejected as merely toying with a system that is fundamentally flawed because it is loaded in favour of states and transnational commercial interests, at the very least it opens fresh avenues to expose, challenge and restrain the exercise of arbitrary power.

Questions for Discussion

1   What purpose, if any, does international law serve?
2   Under what circumstances might 'necessity' be used to justify derogations from international humanitarian or human rights law?
3   How is compliance with international law policed?

📖 FURTHER READING

Choudhury, B. (2005), 'Beyond the Alien Tort Claims Act: Alternative Approaches to Attributing Liability to Corporations for Extraterritorial Abuses', *Northwestern Journal of International Law and Business*, 26(1): 43–75.

Clapham, A. (2007) *Human Rights: A Very Short Introduction*. Oxford: Oxford University Press, 2007, pp. 42–51.

Hopgood, S. (2013) *The Endtimes of Human Rights*. Ithaca, NY: Cornell University Press.

Kratochwil, F. (2014) *The Status of Law in World Society: Meditations on the Role and Rule of Law*. Cambridge: Cambridge University Press.

REFERENCES

African Charter on Human and Peoples' Rights ('Banjul Charter'), opened for signature 27 June 1981, CAB/LEG/67/3 rev. 5, 21 I.L.M. 58 (entered into force 21 October 1986).

Agreement between the Government of Australia and the Government of Hong Kong for the Promotion and Protection of Investments 1993 (Cth).

Al Jazeera America (2015) 'Johns Hopkins Sued over STD Study'. 1 April. Available at: http://america.aljazeera.com/articles/2015/4/1/johns-hopkins-sued-over-std-study-in-guatemala.html (accessed 23 July 2016).

Arms Trade Treaty (2014) Available at: https://unoda-web.s3-accelerate.amazonaws.com/wp-content/uploads/2013/06/English7.pdf (accessed 4 June 2016).

Baccaro, L. and Mele, V. (2012) 'Pathology or Path Dependence? The ILO and the Challenge of New Governance', *International Labor Relations Review*, 65(2): 195–224.

Blakeley, R. and Raphael, S. (2013) 'Governing Human Rights: Rendition, Secret Detention, and Torturn in the "War on Terror"', in S. Harman and D. Williams (eds), *Governing the World: Cases in Global Governance*. London: Routledge, pp. 160–79.

Borger, J. and Bowcott, O. (2016) 'Radovan Karadzic Criminally Responsible for Genocide at Srebrenica'. *Guardian*, 25 March. Available at: www.theguardian.com/world/2016/mar/24/radovan-karadzic-criminally-responsible-for-genocide-at-srebenica (accessed 28 May 2016).

Brems, E. (2003) 'Protecting the Human Rights of Women', in G.M. Lyons and J. Mayall (eds), *International Human Rights in the 21st Century: Protecting the Rights of Groups*. Lanham, MD: Rowman & Littlefield, pp. 100–37.

Bürgi Bonanomi, E. (2015) *Sustainable Development and International Law: International Food Governance and Trade in Agriculture*. Cheltenham: Edward Elgar.

Cassese, A. (2008) *International Criminal Law*, 2nd edn. Oxford: Oxford University Press.

Cheru, F. (2016) 'Developing Countries and the Right to Development: A Retrospective African View', *Third World Quarterly*, 37(7): 1268–83.

Choudhury, B. (2005), 'Beyond the Alien Tort Claims Act: Alternative Approaches to Attributing Liability to Corporations for Extraterritorial Abuses', *Northwestern Journal of International Law and Business*, 26(1): 43–75.

Clapham, A. (2007) *Human Rights: A Very Short Introduction*. Oxford: Oxford University Press, pp. 42–51.

Convention (I) for the Amelioration of the Condition of the Wounded and Sick in Armed Forces in the Field. Geneva, 12 August 1949. Available at: https://www.icrc.org/ihl.nsf/INTRO/365?OpenDocument (accessed 15 May 2016).

Convention (II) for the Amelioration of the Condition of Wounded, Sick and Shipwrecked Members of Armed Forces at Sea. Geneva, 12 August 1949. Available at: https://www.icrc.org/ihl.nsf/INTRO/370?OpenDocument (accessed 15 May 2016).

Convention (III) Relative to the Treatment of Prisoners of War. Geneva, 12 August 1949. Available at: https://www.icrc.org/ihl.nsf/INTRO/375?OpenDocument (accessed 15 May 2016).

Convention (IV) Relative to the Protection of Civilian Persons in Time of War. Geneva, 12 August 1949. Available at: https://www.icrc.org/ihl.nsf/INTRO/380 (accessed 15 May 2016).

Convention for the Protection of Human Rights and Fundamental Freedoms, opened for signature 4 November 1950, 213 UNTS 222 (entered into force 3 September 1953), as amended by *Protocol No 11 to the Convention for the Protection of Human Rights and Fundamental Freedoms*, opened for signature 11 May 1994, ETS No 155 (entered into force 1 November 1998) (*ECHR*).

Convention on the Elimination of All Forms of Discrimination Against Women (CEDAW) (1979) Available at: www.un.org/womenwatch/daw/cedaw/cedaw.htm (accessed February 2007).

Convention on the Rights of the Child, opened for signature 20 November 1989, 1577 UNTS 3 (entered into force 12 July 2002).

Cullen, A. (2010) *The Concept of Non-International Armed Conflict in International Humanitarian Law*. Cambridge: Cambridge University Press.

Desierto, D.A. (2015) 'The International Mandate for Development: Building Compliant Investment within the State's Development Decision Making Processes'. In S.W. Schill, C.J. Tams and R. Hofmann (eds), *International Investment Law and Development: Bridging the Gap*. Cheltenham: Edward Elgar, pp. 333–68.

Duffield, M. (2007) *Development, Security and Unending War: Governing the World of Peoples*. Cambridge: Polity.

Duffield, M. (2010) 'The Liberal Way of Development and the Development–Security Impasse: Exploring the Global Life-Chance Divide', *Security Dialogue*, 41(1): 53–76.

Escobar, A. (1995) *Encountering Development: The Making and Unmaking of the Third World*. Princeton, NJ: Princeton University Press.

European Court of Human Rights (ECHR) (2014) *S.A.S. v. France* [GC], No. 43835/11, Judgment of 1 July. Available at: www.law.umich.edu/facultyhome/drwcasebook/ Documents/Documents/7.1_CASE%20OF%20S.A.S.%20v.%20FRANCE.pdf (accessed 28 December 2016)

Falk, R. (1999) *Predatory Globalization: A Critique*. Cambridge: Polity.

Flynn, M. (2014) *How and Why Immigration Detention Crossed the Globe*. Global Detention Project Working Paper No. 8. Available at: www.globaldetentionproject.org/sites/ default/files/fileadmin/publications/Flynn_diffusion_WorkingPaper_v2.pdf (accessed 4 June 2016).

Friday Alfred Akpan v. Royal Dutch Shell C/09/337050 / HA ZA 09-1580 (2013).

Geneva Call (2014) *Annual Report 2014: Protecting Civilians in Armed Conflict*. Available at: www.genevacall.org/wp-content/uploads/dlm_uploads/2015/05/2014-Geneva-Call-Annual-Report-Short-version.pdf (accessed 21 May 2016).

Global Detention Project (GDP) (*c.* 2016) 'Global Detention Reports'. Available at: www. globaldetentionproject.org/publications/country-detention-reports (accessed 3 June 2016).

Greene, A. (2016) 'Save the Children Staff Forcibly Removed from Nauru Should be Paid Compensation, Departmental Review Says'. Available at: www.abc.net.au/news/2016-01-15/report-removal-charity-workers-nauru-recommends-compensation/7092338 (accessed 26 May 2016).

Hardt, M. and Negri, A. (2000) *Empire*. Cambridge, MA: Harvard University Press.

Held, D. (2010) *Cosmopolitanism: Ideals and Realities*. Cambridge: Polity.

Hilhorst, D. and Pereboom, E. (2016) 'Multi-Mandate Organisations in Development Aid', in Z. Sezgin and D. Dijkzeul (eds), *The New Humanitarians in International Practice: Emerging Actors and Contested Principles*. Abingdon: Routledge, pp. 85–102.

Hopgood, S. (2013) *The Endtimes of Human Rights*. Ithaca, NY: Cornell University Press.

International Covenant on Civil and Political Rights (ICCPR), Office of the High Commissioner for Human Rights. Open for ratification and signature, 16 December 1966 (entered into force, 23 March 1976). Available at: www.unhchr.ch/html/menu3/ b/a_ccpr.htm (accessed 24 January 2008).

International Covenant on Economic, Social and Cultural Rights (ICESCR), Office of the High Commissioner for Human Rights. Open for ratification and signature, 16 December 1966 (entered into force, 3 January 1976). Available at: www.ohchr.org/ EN/ProfessionalInterest/Pages/CESCR.aspx (accessed 4 July 2016)

International Labour Organization (ILO) (2007) *Toolkit for Mainstreaming Employment and Decent Work*. Geneva: ILO. Available at: www.ilo.org/wcmsp5/groups/public/— dgreports/—exrel/documents/publication/wcms_172609.pdf (accessed 29 January 29).

Kapoor, I. (2013) *Celebrity Humanitarianism: The Ideology of Global Charity*. London: Routledge.

Kennedy, D. (2006) *On War and Law*. Princeton, NJ: Princeton University Press.

Kolb, R. (2015) *Peremptory International Law – Jus Cogens: A General Inventory*. London: Bloomsbury.

Kranser, S. (1999) *Sovereignty: Organized Hypocrisy*. Princeton, NJ: Princeton University Press.

Kratochwil, F. (2014) *The Status of Law in World Society: Meditations on the Role and Rule of Law*. Cambridge: Cambridge University Press.

Kyl, J., Feith, D.J. and Fonte, J. (2013) 'The War of Law: How New International Law Undermines Democratic Sovereignty', *Foreign Affairs*, 92(4): 115–25.

Meron, T. (2009) 'The Geneva Conventions and Public International Law', *International Review of the Red Cross*, 91 (875), September. Available at: www.icrc.org/eng/resources/documents/article/review/review-875-p619.htm (accessed 10 November 2012).

Naqvi, Y. (2003) 'Amnesty for War Crimes: Defining the Limits of International Recognition', *International Review of the Red Cross*, 851: 583–624. Available at: www.icrc.org/Web/eng/siteeng0.nsf/htmlall/5SSDUX/$File/irrc_851_Naqvi.pdf (accessed 27 June 2008).

Neuer, H.C. (2016) 'Reform or Regression: Ten Years of the UN Human Rights Council', United Nations Watch, 17 May. Available at: www.unwatch.org/10837-2/ (accessed 1 June 2016).

Noortmann, M. (2015) 'Non-Governmental Organizations: Recognitio, Roles, Rights and Responsibilitties'. In M. Noortmann, A. Reinisch and C. Rynagaert (eds), *Non-State Actors and International Law*. Oxford: Hart Publishing, pp. 205–224.

Prislan, V. and Zandvliet, R. (2015) 'Mainstreaming Sustainable Development into International Investment Agreements: What Role for Labor Provisions', in S.W. Schill, C.J. Tams and R. Hofmann (eds), *International Investment Law and Development: Bridging the Gap*. Cheltenham: Edward Elgar, pp. 390–452.

(Protocol I) Protocol Additional to the Geneva Conventions of 12 August 1949, and Relating to the Protection of Victims of International Armed Conflicts (Protocol I), 8 June 1977, International Committee of the Red Cross. Geneva, 1977, pp. 3–87. Available at: www.icrc.org/ihl.nsf/INTRO/470 (accessed 5 December 2013).

(Protocol II) Protocol Additional to the Geneva Conventions of 12 August 1949, and Relating to the Protection of Victims of Non-International Armed Conflicts (Protocol II), 8 June 1977, International Committee of the Red Cross. Geneva, 1977, pp. 89–101. Available at: www.icrc.org/ihl.nsf/INTRO/475 (accessed 5 December 2013).

Protocol to Prevent, Suppress and Punish Trafficking in Persons, Especially Women and Children, Supplementing the United Nations Convention against Transnational Organized Crime (2000), United Nations Treaty Series A-39574. Opened for signature, 15 November 2000 (Entered into force 25 December 2003). Available at: https://treaties.un.org/Pages/ViewDetails.aspx?src=IND&mtdsg_no=XVIII-12-a&chapter=18&lang=en (accessed 1 June 2016).

Protocol against the Illicit Manufacturing and Trafficking in Firearms, Their Parts and Components and Ammunition, Supplementing the United Nations Convention against Transnational Organized Crime (2001). Opened for signature, 31 May 2001 (entered into force, 3 July 2005). Available at: www.unodc.org/unodc/en/treaties/CTOC/countrylist-firearmsprotocol.html (accessed 1 June 2016).

Rajagopal, B. (2004) *International Law from Below: Development, Social Movements and Third World Resistance*. Cambridge, MA: MIT Press.

Rawls, J. (1971) *A Theory of Justice*. Cambridge, MA: Harvard University Press.

Rice, S. (2012) 'Statement by the President of the Security Council'. United Nations Security Council, S/PRST/2012/16, 25 April. Available at: www.securitycouncil report.org/atf/cf/%7B65BFCF9B-6D27-4E9C-8CD3-CF6E4FF96FF9%7D/ IPS%20S%202012%2016.pdf (accessed 16 May 16).

Robertson, G. (2002) *Crimes against Humanity: The Struggle for Global Justice*, 2nd ed. London: Penguin.

Rome Statute of the International Court (2002) The Hague: ICC Public Information and Documentation Service.

Sklair, L. (2002) *Globalization, Capitalism and its Alternatives*. Oxford: Oxford University Press.

Steger, M. (2009) *The Rise of the Global Imaginary: Political Ideologies from the French Revolution to the Global War on Terror*. Oxford: Oxford University Press.

Sonderholm, J. (2014) 'A Critique of an Argument against Patent Rights for Essential Medicines', *Ethics and Global Politics*, 7(3): 119–36.

Tobacco Plain Packaging Act 2011. Commonwealth of Australia, No. 148, 2011. Available at: https://www.legislation.gov.au/Details/C2011A00148 (accessed 12 May 2016).

Trials of War Criminals before the Nuremberg Military Tribunals under Control Council Law No. 10, Vol. 2, Nuremberg (Washington, DC: US Government Printing Office, October 1946–April 1949).

United Nations Convention Against Corruption (UNCAC) (2005). Opened for signature, October 2003 (entered into force, 14 December 2005). Available at: https://www. unodc.org/unodc/en/treaties/CAC/index.html (accessed 4 November 2012).

United Nations Convention on the Law of the Sea (UNCLOS) (1982) United Nations Treaty Series I-31363 (entered into force 16 November 1994). Available at:www.un.org/depts/ los/convention_agreements/texts/unclos/UNCLOS-TOC.htm (accessed 5 June 2006).

UN Convention against Transnational Organized Crime (UNCTOC) (2003) Opened for signature, 12–15 December 2000 (entered into force, 29 September 2003). Available at: https://www.unodc.org/unodc/en/treaties/CAC/ (accessed 30 January 2012)

United Nations Declaration on the Right to Development (1986) Available at: www.un.org/ en/events/righttodevelopment/ (accessed 2 May 2014).

United Nations Development Group (UNDG) (2003) *The Human Rights Based Approach to Development Cooperation: Towards a Common Understanding among UN Agencies*. UN Practitioners' Portal on Human Rights Based Approaches to Programming. Available at: http://hrbaportal.org/the-human-rights-based-approach-to-development-cooperation-towards-a-common-understanding-among-un-agencies (accessed 12 September 2014).

United Nations Declaration on the Rights of Indigenous Peoples (UNDRIP) (2007) United National General Assembly A/Res/61/295. Available at: www.un.org/esa/socdev/ unpfii/documents/DRIPS_en.pdf (accessed 9 July 2009).

United Nations Office on Drugs and Crime (UNODC) (2004) *United Nations Convention against Transnational Organized Crime and the Protocols Thereto*. New York: UNODC. Available at: www.unodc.org/unodc/en/treaties/CTOC/ (accessed 4 July 2009).

Universal Declaration on Human Rights (UDHR) (1948). Available at: www.un.org/en/ universal-declaration-human-rights/ (accessed 24 March 2012).

Vadi, V.S. (2010) 'Access to Medicines Versus Protection of "Investments" in Intellectual Property: Reconciliation through Interpretation?', in A. Perry-Kessaris (ed.), *Law in the Pursuit of Development: Principles into Practice*. New York: Routledge, pp. 52–67.

Vava & Ors v. Anglo American South Africa Ltd, Claim No HQ11X03245.

Vienna Convention on the Law of Treaties, 1969. United Nations Treaty Series, 1980. Available at: https://treaties.un.org/doc/Publication/UNTS/Volume%201155/volume-1155-I-18232-English.pdf (accessed 2 June 2016).

Webb, P. (2013) *International Judicial Integration and Fragmentation*. Oxford: Oxford University Press.

Wheeler, S. (2010) 'Political Consumption: Possibilities and Challenges', in A. Perry-Kessaris (ed.), *Law in the Pursuit of Development: Principles into Practice*. New York: Routledge, pp. 10–25.

Wilson, E., Goodman, J. and Steger, M. (2013) *Justice Globalism: Ideology, Crises, Policy*. London: Sage.

World Trade Organization (1994) *Marrakesh Agreement* (also *Agreement Establishing the World Trade Organization*) (1994) Available at: www.wto.org/english/docs_e/legal_e/04-wto.pdf (accessed 3 May 2016).

8

MORAL DILEMMAS: ETHICS AND DEVELOPMENT PRACTICE

VANDRA HARRIS

INTRODUCTION

In a world in which news of crises and disasters spreads rapidly, more people are aware of their dire impact just as increasing numbers of people are affected by them. The desire to respond is rooted in many ethical frameworks, driving individuals, communities and governments to 'humanitarian' response. Such responses are as complex as the situations that inspire them, and this chapter aims to address some of the layers of complexity in humanitarian response. It first looks at the diverse ways of understanding and performing humanitarianism, it then explains the core values in the profession of humanitarianism and how these relate to ethics. Subsequently, it examines the dilemmas faced by humanitarian practitioners through a case study in the devastating Pakistan floods of 2010 to demonstrate the utility of the processes of ethical decision-making in the complex, political and often traumatic environments of conflict and disaster.

The term 'humanitarian' is widely understood as responding to need, and is generally associated with a sense of altruism, though this assumption may mask other motives. Within this very broad context sits the profession of humanitarian practice, which aims to 'save lives, alleviate suffering and maintain and protect human dignity' in crisis and disaster (GHA, 2016a), accepting a set of core values and minimum practice standards that will be expanded below. It is distinct from development practice, in that the focus is on immediate life-saving response, rather than durable improvements in quality of life. Based on the clearly expressed premise that 'all human beings are born free and equal in dignity and rights', the *humanitarian imperative* demands that 'action should be taken to prevent or alleviate human suffering arising out of disaster or conflict' (Sphere, 2011: 20).[1] This is the guiding concern for humanitarian practitioners, whose focus is 'first response' to acute human suffering as the result of natural or human catastrophe.

DEFINING THE HUMANITARIAN

Professional 'first responders' are not the only actors claiming the label of humanitarian practitioner. With such a ubiquitous term, it is inevitable that there will be broad mainstream uptake of the idea of humanitarianism. Indeed, the drive to respond to the needs of others can be called a basic human impulse (see Slim, 1997) so people giving coins to a homeless person can call themselves humanitarians, just as doctors and nurses providing medical aid in a war zone call themselves humanitarians.

At a finer level, professional humanitarians seek to maintain a clear distinction between development and humanitarian action that is not always embraced by development professionals, and is not extensively discussed in either literature. The distinction is most evident in funding streams (with increasing resources flowing to humanitarian emergencies), but is also evident in focus and practice. In practice, development organizations generally work to differing degrees with local authorities and government while humanitarians work to maintain a distance from any group, organization or mechanism that might be seen as partisan or party to the conflict, in order to protect staff and maintain access to vulnerable communities in the most volatile contexts (De Vos, 2015). A convenient distinction can be made in which development practice focuses on long-term improvements in quality of life, health and wealth (UNDP, 2015) while humanitarianism 'seeks to save lives and alleviate suffering of a crisis- affected population' (ReliefWeb, 2008). In the messy reality of humanitarian and development interventions, the differences in context are rarely so clear (OCHA, 2016), but there are important characteristics of a humanitarian approach that will be expanded below.

Another distinction between development and humanitarian assistance can be seen in the extensive work by the humanitarian sector to standardize and coordinate. Humanitarian agencies have agreed-upon principles, rights and duties that guide practice and distinguish them from other actors giving assistance. These humanitarian principles provide a foundational framework and guide for humanitarian actors in much the same way as applied ethics in other professions – and, for this reason, I term these actors 'principled humanitarians', as a means of distinguishing them from the vast wealth of actors responding to human need. This chapter examines how these humanitarian principles relate to other ethical frameworks and shape the responses of humanitarian actors facing complex choices. The framework does not reduce the complexity of these decisions,

---

[1]The Humanitarian Charter and Minimum Standards in Humanitarian Response (*The Sphere Handbook*) constitutes a 'voluntary code and a self-regulatory tool for quality and accountability' (Sphere, 2011: 8), setting out the core values of professional humanitarian response and strategies for putting those values into practice.

but, rather, gives practitioners a guide for navigating the ethical dilemma[2] of situations in which not everyone's needs can be met, and where these choices can genuinely mean the difference between life and death for individuals and for populations.

While the total number of humanitarian emergencies has decreased in the three years 2011–13 (the most recent period of data), the crises in this period have been 'mostly "complex" (conflict-related) in nature, and with larger human caseloads' (ALNAP, 2015). Thus, the demand on the humanitarian system continues to grow in spite of advances in resilience and preparedness of people, systems and the physical environment (McConnell, 2014; HLPHF, 2016). As well as being more complex and affecting more people, these crises are protracted, as revealed by the statistic that 84 per cent of countries receiving humanitarian assistance in 2014 had received it for five consecutive years, and 69 per cent for ten consecutive years (ALNAP, 2015). Thus, while Syria, South Sudan, Iraq, Palestine and Jordan were the top five recipients of international humanitarian assistance (IHA) in 2014, over the decade 2004–14 Sudan received 11 per cent of IHA, totalling $US11.3bn, while the occupied Palestinian territory, Pakistan, Ethiopia and Afghanistan each received 5–7 per cent of assistance in that period (totalling $US5.5bn–7.4bn per country) (GHA, 2016b).

DOMINANT ETHICAL MODELS

In its wide-ranging triennial report on *The State of the Humanitarian System*, ALNAP (2015) estimates that there are now 4,480 humanitarian organizations, of which 80 per cent are 'local NGOs working in-country' – which is to say that they are indigenous to the developing nation in which they operate, some partnered with larger international NGOs. This international group, which includes large organizations such as the Red Cross, World Vision and Save the Children, but also small, little-known, single-issue NGOs, is influential despite its relatively small size, due not least to the donor funding they bring with them (see Stoddard, 2003).

The power and dominance of these international organizations, especially in the humanitarian sector (Barnett, 2011), means that it is critically important to understand (and perhaps influence) their shared ethical framework as expressed through the Humanitarian Principles. This requires an understanding of the dominant ethical models that retain power and thus influence thought and action. The two key models of the twentieth-century West are the consequentialist model and the Kantian model of duty. Both are based on reason and find their provenance in the Age of Reason.

Consequentialism and its close cousin utilitarianism are based on a philosophy and decision rule that states that the ethically most desirable outcome is determined by the consequences of the action (Driver, 2014; Sinnott-Armstrong, 2015). Thus, for a consequentialist the best outcome will be that which produces 'the greatest good for the greatest

---

[2]Dilemma, in this context, has a specific meaning extending beyond a difficult decision, to a choice in which it is not clear which outcome is the best, or in which no outcome meets everybody's interests. The dilemma, therefore, is how one chooses between outcomes that are less than perfect – or, indeed, deeply damaging for some parties. See McConnell (2014).

number' or some similar formula (Pettit, 1993). For utilitarians, the decision is based on the notion of utility (the ability to bring pleasure or advantage, or prevent the opposite) (Gooden, 1993). Both consequentialism and utilitarianism are results-based approaches to ethical decision-making, which is to say that outcomes are the key element by which to judge the value of an action.

The Kantian model, named after the German philosopher Immanuel Kant (1724–1804), is concerned with 'doing the right thing' and gives a lesser priority to outcomes. Kant argued that humans, by application of their capacity to reason, could determine a rule for right action and that the rule could be expressed in the terms of a duty to act only according to principles which could be universally applied (Kant, 2005). Sometimes, more colloquially, it is expressed as 'doing to others as you would have them do to you'. This approach also gives rise to the establishment of rules or lists of behaviour that are seen to be in accord with one's duty (Johnson and Cureton, 2016). For Kant and his Enlightenment followers, these rules arise from reason and human intellect, but for others rules might arise from a god or other external agent. These ethical models are referred to as deontological in that they have a defined goal.

For decision-making in humanitarian situations, difficulties can arise when applying utilitarian and deontological systems, for there is no guidance for taking account of different views of utility (see Hall, 1997). This can be equally the case in determining Kantian universal principles of what one would do to others (or self). Even where there is a single tragically disadvantaged group with shared views of the utility of all possible actions and a single group of humanitarian agents with common views about the utility of the actions which might be undertaken, there is a high likelihood that these utility sets will not align and that calculations of the greatest good will be disputed, and may indeed change. The utilitarian emphasis on results can seem to accept results where the end justifies the means, which puts it in clear dispute with those who insist that no action contrary to the rules or beliefs be undertaken, regardless of any potential (utilitarian) benefit. This can be further complicated when there is dispute among the client and provider groups as to what is right. This is particularly so when there are strict prohibitions, taboos or legal constraints on action.

BROADENING THESE HORIZONS

There are alternatives to the utilitarian and Kantian approaches with their Western, 'Age of Reason' roots. Some have come to the fore relatively recently, driven in part by the needs set out above and by the growth of feminisms, post-colonial studies and the greater contact between belief systems brought about by globalization. Others have long been dominant in the majority world but largely ignored in Western philosophy despite being shared by such a large number of people. At a very general level, it is possible to highlight broad consistencies in some key non-Western ethical systems, notably a focus on communities rather than individuals, whereby good outcomes are achieved through actions that support or promote a harmonious society. These priorities can be found in Islamic, Confucian and 'Afro-communitarian' ethical frameworks (see, for example, Nanji, 1993; Lepard, 2002; Metz, 2013).

This orientation towards community and care is also evident in development ethics, a relatively recent field focused on development work to improve lives in the poorest countries. It is a field of applied, or practical ethics, a term that describes the consideration of ethics in relation to specific fields, notably business ethics, animal ethics and so on. It is quite simply 'the application of ethics ... to practical issues' (Singer, 1993: 1). Practical ethics is no less grounded in the great philosophical traditions, but it is concerned with the challenges faced in day-to-day life by people striving to live and work ethically. Most professions involve difficult choices, and practical ethics seeks to provide frameworks for approaching those decisions and weighing up the alternatives from a strong ethical foundation.

The field of development ethics is well established, and grounded in particular in the works of Denis Goulet (1931–2006) and Des Gasper (1953–). Its proponents contend that the objective of development practice must be to create an enabling environment in which people are able to live long, healthy and fruitful lives – in short, human flourishing. Addressing the human practice of ethics in the personal and professional spaces of development, development ethics is therefore focused on the impact of development on its recipients. Development work concerns people who are absolutely or relatively disadvantaged, often the poorest communities in the poorest countries, people whose capabilities are limited by factors including poverty, social exclusion, disability, displacement and marginalization, and whose own governments are unable or unwilling to meet their needs without external assistance. Development is therefore fundamentally concerned with power, and a key focus of development ethics is the question of how 'moral guidelines influence decisions of those who hold power' (Goulet, 2006: 19). Thus, development ethics insists that development cannot simply be palliative, but must also address structures of dominance.

As a result, development ethics is concerned with expanding capabilities, which has direct connections with the humanitarian commitment to humanity and dignity, which I will expand below. Developed and expanded by Amartya Sen (1993) and Martha Nussbaum (2000), the capabilities approach focuses on the way people's abilities interact with their environment to determine what choices and outcomes are realistically available to them. Within this understanding, importance is placed on those ends and outcomes that people have reason to value; in other words, not all possible outcomes are considered valuable, and priorities differ within and between communities, a point that speaks to the (assumed) universalism of the dominant Western ethical models addressed above. Development ethics thus asserts that development work is valuable when it expands people's opportunities to achieve their valued ends or functionings, and local priorities must therefore be central to any intervention.

HUMANITARIAN ETHICS

Humanitarian practice is not a sub-set of development work but it is intrinsically connected by the nature and location of the work, the primacy of those in greatest need, and the commonality of some organizations, including some intergovernmental organizations (UN, FAO) and NGOs that have mandates and funding for both. It is also true that there is rarely a clear distinction between a period of crisis requiring humanitarian intervention and times of severe disadvantage requiring development assistance. Ethical dilemmas arise when there is no obvious 'right' answer that meets everyone's needs, and this is characteristic of the humanitarian environment, in which practitioners are faced with a range of persistent, wicked challenges, not limited to the pressing issues of inadequate resources,[3] inability to determine or access those in greatest need, corruption and the danger of their work contributing to conflict (Anderson, 1999; Transparency International, 2010; GHA, 2016b).

Humanitarian practice is defined by four key principles: humanity, neutrality, impartiality and independence (see OCHA, 2012). They have their roots in the core principles of the International Red Cross and Red Crescent society, are enshrined in UN General Assembly Resolutions 46/182 (1991) and 58/114 (2004), and underpin the Humanitarian Charter, which together with the Minimum Standards in Humanitarian Response comprise the *Sphere Handbook*, a core guide to humanitarian practice (Sphere Project, 2011).

According to the Humanitarian Charter, the central humanitarian claim is the principle of *humanity*, the conviction that 'all human beings are born free and equal in dignity and rights' (Sphere Project, 2011). Flowing from this is the *humanitarian imperative*, that these rights (specifically the core rights to life with dignity, to humanitarian assistance, and to protection and security) correlate with a responsibility to respond to people affected by conflict and disaster, addressing any deficit in these rights.

Neutrality is the direction that humanitarian providers shall not take sides in any conflict or 'engage in controversies of a political, racial, religious or ideological nature' (OCHA, 2012). *Impartiality* requires that assistance be given according to need only, with priority determined by severity of distress rather than distinctions such as ethnicity, religion or gender. Finally, the principle of *independence* recognizes that it is critical that humanitarian actions be free from 'the political, economic, military or other objectives' held by any actor (UN, 2004). These principles set humanitarian actors apart and fundamentally shape their work.

Hugo Slim (2012) contends that the Humanitarian Principles constitute a framework that humanitarian actors use to make moral claims on others, particularly claims about assistance needs and priorities. I take it one step further and call the Humanitarian Principles the foundation of humanitarian ethics, in that they are normative claims about how the world, and the humanitarian profession, should be; they speak clearly to the value of both means and ends; they claim universal applicability; and they provide a clear framework for making judgements and decisions.

Humanitarian ethics must go further than the Humanitarian Principles, however, because the field cannot remain apolitical – if, indeed, it ever was. Barnett and Weiss point to the tendency to romanticize and depoliticize humanitarianism, negating the reality that 'the meaning and practices of humanitarianism have been as historically fluid as the world in which it operates' (2008: 10). To respond to people in crisis is a political act, an active statement that all people deserve support and succour in crisis and disaster. Human suffering is a tool of war, and to medicate it is to take a side; not with one of the warring

---

[3]UN-coordinated appeals for humanitarian assistance drew only 55 per cent of required funding in 2015, the lowest proportion recorded (Global Humanitarian Assistance (GHA), 2016b: 37).

parties, but with people in need of assistance, whether or not they have participated in the conflict in any way. In disaster, the political act may be to respond according to need rather than wealth, status or ethnic group. The radical call of humanity that all people are free in dignity and rights is heavily political in many parts of the world today.

At first sight, the notion of political humanitarianism may seem incompatible with neutrality and independence, but in reality they are very different demands. Neutrality and independence are concerned with taking a position or a side in a conflict that is causing the distress of the people being harmed, or being driven by concerns external to the human suffering at hand. They are intimately connected with the path-breaking work of Mary B. Anderson (1999), that identifies the ways in which development (and subsequently humanitarianism) becomes part of a conflict, and therefore demands that practitioners 'do no harm'. In disasters that are not affected by conflict, these principles take account of underlying tensions, disparities and political divisions that may otherwise impact on the impartial identification of need and delivery of assistance, or which may impose unacceptable costs on recipients, in forms including religious or political conversion, sexual services, debt or conscription.

A political version of humanitarianism is consistent with one of the two main schools of thought in humanitarianism. The first of these is focused exclusively on humanitarian response and committed to neutrality in its most literal form, while the second has an intent to address root causes and thus have political impact. Barnett (2011) describes these as emergency and alchemical humanitarianism respectively (ibid.: 10). I contend here that since the fundamental principle of humanity – given primacy in the Humanitarian Charter – places dignity and rights as the forefront of humanitarianism, to respond to matters of human dignity, to provide assistance according to need only, and to protect people from further harm all require, at times, a response that is political in the sense of responding to structural disadvantage and marginalization, advocating for change, or including people in decisions and actions who would normally be excluded. These kinds of actions are, in fact, central to the accepted goals and methods of humanitarian response, and reflect the reality that 'humanitarian good practice can change the balance of power' in communities affected by crisis (Slim, 2012).

ETHICAL CHOICES AND DECISION-MAKING

Humanitarian work by its nature involves serious and often life-changing decisions, as practitioners must determine who is (most) in need of what help, and how to balance that with limits on resources, and the accessibility of people and affected areas. This is hard enough outside of crisis situations, but disaster and conflict mean that humanitarian decisions are normally made under duress despite their importance, since they may well determine who lives through a crisis and how many are protected from further harm. In ethics terminology, they constitute a dilemma: a decision in which there is no clear 'right' choice or best outcome.

This kind of decision or challenge is absolutely characteristic of the humanitarian sector, where even the smallest choice can have major implications. For example, the days after a disaster are critical for rescue and survival, demanding immediate response; however, an appropriate and effective response requires a thorough assessment of needs, preferably with significant local input. Organizations must, therefore, make choices about how they structure their engagement: do they commence immediately and save lives but potentially miss opportunities and overlook marginalized or physically isolated groups? Do they conduct a thorough participatory assessment, knowing that people will die in the time this takes? Or, do they do a 'quick and dirty' assessment trying to compromise between these demands? Whichever choice is made, it is likely that not all lives will be saved, and this responsibility can weigh heavily on the conscience of humanitarian professionals.

According to Rest (1986), there are four steps in the ethical decision-making process: recognizing the moral issue (identifying the specific problem); making a moral judgement (choosing which values or rules to apply); establishing moral intent (deciding on action); and engaging in moral behaviour (following through with that action). While each of these steps brings challenges, a dilemma is most concerned with the second step, or the question of moral judgement or ethical identification. This may be identifying the issue, or more commonly, identifying an appropriate ethical response when none provides a completely satisfactory outcome. The interactionist model posits that it is not only the individual's ethical standpoint that influences the choices made, but also a range of contextual and individual factors (Aroskar, 1980). Thus, even those most committed to the Humanitarian Principles may come to different decisions about the same or similar dilemmas, and indeed it may be those contextual variables – including the immediate context of the crisis as well as the broader context of the humanitarian sector – that contribute to the difficulty of the dilemma.

In defining the Humanitarian Principles, the sector has given practitioners a set of guidelines for addressing these dilemmas. This in no way makes the decision-making process easy, but it provides a framework for both making and evaluating those choices, particularly in the high-pressure environment of crisis. This chapter draws on examples given in one interview conducted for a research project on NGO–military interaction in humanitarian environments.[4] While not held up as a representative humanitarian, focusing on one practitioner's story in this way helps us consider an event and related dilemmas in depth rather than skimming superficially over a collection of stories.

Text Box 8.1   Case Study: The Civil–Military Interface in Pakistan

With over fifteen years' experience with humanitarian NGOs, N17 worked in Pakistan following the 2010 floods which seriously affected over 20 million people, left over 4 million without shelter a month after their onset, and caused widespread destruction of infrastructure. In 2010, the United Nations Development Programme ranked

---

[4]Entitled 'The NGO–Military Interface in Post-Conflict and Post-Disaster Contexts', this research received funding from the Australian Civil Military Centre (Smith/2011/032986), the ethics approval from RMIT University (2000583-10/11) and the Australian Defence Human Research Ethics Committee (652-12). For anonymity, the interviewee is referred to as N17 only, and pronouns used do not necessarily reflect the participant's sex.

Pakistan 125th of 169 nations for human development,[5] with high rates of infant mortality (72 per 1,000 live births), 54 per cent adult literacy, 23 per cent of the population undernourished (UNDP, 2010) and 4 million refugees and internally displaced people as a result of both the 2005 earthquake and on-going conflict along the border with Afghanistan. Those most affected by the 2010 flooding 'comprise the lowest socioeconomic quintiles that were already facing neglect' (Warraich et al., 2011: 236). The extreme and disproportionate impact of the flooding on the poorest people exacerbated existing hardship and increased vulnerability.

The government of Pakistan had significant experience dealing with major disasters previously, particularly the 2005 earthquake, which led to the creation of the National Disaster Management Authority (NDMA). Writing in 2000, Rizvi reflected that:

> Pakistani society is now so fractured, inundated with sophisticated weapons, brutalized by civic violence and overwhelmed by the spread of narcotics that it is no longer possible for any civilian government to operate effectively without the Army's support. (2000: 53)

These challenges, significant inequality and government reliance on military action for a range of function, including responses to internal conflicts contributed to mistrust of the military within the population, which, in turn, led to increased caution amongst NGOs regarding collaborating with the Pakistani military, despite the logistical and 'boots on the ground' advantages they could bring.

With advance warning, N17's organization was able to deploy her before the flooding hit in a particular region, giving her the opportunity to assess existing local capacity and needs. This warning also meant that few people died in the floods themselves, after which:

> all the [affected] people went to camps – most of the camps were in schools. The living conditions were horrible. There was open defecation everywhere, and children were dying in camps, which really broke our hearts. There weren't a lot of people who had died from the floods, because there was a lot of early warning, and people knew that the water was coming. But there were so many [already] displaced and the living conditions of the displaced were so terrible, that it resulted in quite a lot of hardship. But also the pre-existing poverty just meant that people had very little resilience as well.

Humanity

The initial choice for humanitarians involved in the flood response was very much one of whether to respond immediately on the basis of superficial information and limited resources, or to respond in a more measured manner that might be more sustainable and perhaps more equitable but certainly slower. With such high numbers of people affected, spread over one-fifth of the country – 'an area larger than England', as widely reported (Gall, 2010) – the form of response was a critical question for humanitarian agencies. This will not always constitute a dilemma, since each agency is well aware of its strengths and resources, and those of others in the region, and will act within those bounds. Thus, an organization may identify WASH (water, sanitation and hygiene) as critical in the environment described above, but be aware of other agencies working effectively in this area, so stick with its own expertise, for example in providing temporary shelters.

(Continued)

---

[5]169 countries were ranked in 2010. Countries ranked 1–42 were considered to have very high human development, while those ranked 128–169 were considered to have low human development.

(Continued)

N17's part of her organization focused on food and nutrition in the first phase of their response, but the form of the relief posed a dilemma. The flood spread through irrigation channels, leading to the rapid destruction of crops and farm animals, limiting both the resources available in the local community, and the access to communities, particularly access for heavy vehicles carrying food aid. Just from a logistical perspective, the decision therefore involved whether to opt for significant expense to import food and time to establish distribution points or centres, with the risk of disrupting local economies with imported provisions; or to seek local food where supplies are extremely diminished and shops or other potential distribution points have been destroyed.

Financial constraints are among the real-world pressures that must influence organizational choices and, unfortunately, recognition of the entitlement to a humanitarian response is not sufficient to guarantee that response.

There is no 'best' answer when any equation includes lives that cannot be saved because choices must be made about how money will be expended. As with other ethical frameworks, political humanitarian ethics based on the Humanitarian Principles gives guidance or a framework for making such a decision, rather than a clear directive. It does not advise practitioners whether they must alleviate immediate suffering at the expense of sustainability, or whether to prioritize a strategic response that may be more equitable and save more lives in the medium term over an immediate response that saves those most imperilled in the first days. It simply tells practitioners that all affected people are entitled to an effective response and that responses must be impartial, neutral and independent.

Describing the way that international organizations partnered with local organizations to maximize impact, N17 noted that: 'each of the international NGOs worked slightly differently. I think the spread of the type of responses that they had were also good.' N17's organization chose to distribute a $US50 cheque to each of 20,000 households in the region, which it achieved in ten weeks before moving onto cash-for-work programmes that employed men to clear rubble and women to make traditional quilts (which the organization purchased and distributed to keep people warm through winter). She praised both the scale and the execution of the first two phases of the response, highlighting its success by critiquing another organization's choice to go down a more traditional food aid path, which meant that 'their response was only starting four months after, whereas we completed our response two months after the floods began'. These reflections illustrate that for N17, dignity (through control over the use of the money) and a quick response are central priorities. Other practitioners may well have praised the second organization's response for effecting a more equitable response that incorporated effective early assessments. Both are broadly consistent with the Humanitarian Principles.

Neutrality

The principle of neutrality demands that humanitarian workers do not take sides in a conflict. One of the four humanitarian principles, neutrality, is seen as conveying protection on practitioners by holding them to the side of hostilities, helping all people according to need, even those participating in the conflict. Ironically, onlookers may misinterpret this impartiality as demonstrating a lack of neutrality (they are helping the enemy, therefore they are on the enemy's side). In terms of protection of aid workers, *demonstration* of neutrality is as important as neutrality itself, and this is one reason that many organizations make an active choice not to work directly with militaries, particularly where the military is party to a conflict, although NGOs can be very nuanced in how they interact.

Given the Pakistani military's political influence and its strong relationship with the NDMA, it is to be expected that they would have a strong presence in the initial response. This was described by N17 as follows:

> The Pakistani military were there and they had their own camps that they set up.

> At first they had makeshift camps. I remember a camp by a petrol station which was just quite hideous. My recollection of the initial camp was that they were doing things like throwing food from trucks and stuff, and there were mad scrambles. There wasn't much dignity in the type of response they were doing. I was quite horrified by it all, so we kind of steered clear. We kind of went, 'well we're not going to get involved in this big shit fight'.

> Then, later on, they had these beautiful camps that looked like those picture perfect, with the tents and all that.

N17's organization made a deliberate decision not to work in these camps run by the Pakistani military for a range of reasons that did not, in this case, include neutrality:

> first of all, there was an assumption that if they're going to set up camps, they can do the WASH for those camps. They also can have the resources to actually figure out what kind of food security response there should be.

This is a logical decision about distribution of scarce resources. Beyond this, however, other factors were important in determining which camps they worked with and which groups they targeted:

> It was rumoured that [the Pakistani military] were quite selective about who actually went into the camps. We just didn't feel that it was reaching the most vulnerable, so we just decided to work more in informal camps, like the people who were on the side of the road or in the schools.

Thus, the decision not to work with the military was determined less by a concern for neutrality, and more a commitment to impartiality and providing assistance based on: 'need alone, giving priority to the most urgent cases of distress and making no distinctions on the basis of nationality, race, gender, religious belief, class or political opinions' (OCHA, 2012). Especially in light of the improvement of conditions in military camps described by N17, these camps were well resourced and managed by an entity with significant resources, thus able to meet the right to assistance of those within the camps. Given the concern that access to those camps was not impartial, the best response was identifying excluded groups and tending to them.

It was not only military-run camps that were cause for concern, however, as 'there were political parties who were setting up camps. Imran Khan[6] had tents with his face

(Continued)

---

[6]Imran Khan is a Member of the Pakistani National Assembly, who achieved international fame playing in (and at times captaining) Pakistan's national cricket team in 1971–92. He founded a political party in 1996, and is also known for his philanthropy.

(Continued)

printed on it. There were lots of political parties who just had their political party slogan on [the tents].' To work in these camps thus also carried the risk of perceptions of political affiliation, but they were equally easy to avoid due to the highly visible images and slogans branding the tents.

Impartiality and independence

Impartiality constituted a larger problem than neutrality and came from an unexpected source: local NGOs and community organizations. It is common practice for international NGOs (INGOs) to partner with local NGOs (LNGOs) – indeed, it is considered a strength of NGO practice, enhancing delivery capability, local engagement and understanding of community goals and values. N17 described the extensive uptake of this model in Pakistan:

> In the Pakistan context, I think the international NGOs were great because they had resources. Most of them partnered with local NGOs. So, for example, we partnered with many, many local NGOs and, to be frank, it was more like doing a hostile takeover of them. Because they just didn't have the capacity to do a response like that. So, we effectively said, we're coming in, we're taking over, we're effectively going to manage your staff and you. The local NGOs were good, because they had local knowledge, but they also didn't have the technical capacity. Also, a lot of them were corrupt. So, I think the partnership was really good and the reach was amazing.

A large-scale response to crises such as this benefits from experienced staff, strong systems and good resources, and adequate measures to address risks of organizational corruption.

It is very important to ensure that NGO–INGO cooperation takes the form of partnership rather than takeover, however, or concerns of independence and dignity may arise. The principle of independence (being free from non-humanitarian objectives) is an important concern for INGOs, but it should not be forgotten that it matters equally to LNGOs, who may feel compromised by the sheer power of their international counterparts in the relationship. There may also be a sense of loss of dignity, through being made to appear incapable and in need of foreign takeover, whether or not this is the INGO's intention. These partnerships must, therefore, be handled incredibly sensitively.

For the INGOs in N17's case, an unexpected area of concern with these partnerships arose from the affiliations of local NGOs and religious groups that they were partnering with. Several organizations were taken by surprise to discover that their local partners were not acting impartially, demonstrating that the INGOs had been 'a bit gung-ho', failing to take stock of local politics, religious arrangements and group relationships:

> Pakistan is so heavily political and tribal. To some extent, we were quite naïve in going there, not really understanding the political and tribal implications ... There were political parties that were aligned with tribes and we didn't know ... We had accusations that we were targeting certain tribes more than others ... Also, a lot of the local NGOs are affiliated with different tribes as well, which we hadn't realised.

Another challenge that we had was that there were Islamist groups as well, and some of the informal camps that we went to ... were in mosques. We went to give assistance at one of the mosques, thinking that, 'it's a mosque it's like a church, no big deal'. But, it turned out to be a mosque that was [associated with] an Islamist group, I can't remember which one, and [they had been presenting our work] as effectively their assistance.

These situations present new dilemmas for humanitarian organizations, long after they have determined the forms their assistance will take and how they will target it. Pragmatically, N17's organization prioritised humanity – the right to assistance – and chose to complete these programmes but to cease the relationships immediately upon conclusion of the programmes. Humanitarian Principles may at times constitute competing demands, posing a complex challenge to practitioners, for, although humanity is clearly the foundational principle, there is no guidance on how to prioritize or balance the remaining three.

CONCLUSION

Humanitarian response is more than just meeting humanitarian needs, and this is evident in the commitment to dignity expressed throughout the *Sphere Handbook* and in the reflection that: 'we are dealing with human beings. Just being safe is not enough' (Leahy, 2011). Many humanitarian agencies have transformative goals, in the sense that even seeking to treat female-headed households with the same value as male-headed ones during a crisis response is a decision that seeks to change a society to respond better to people who are arbitrarily marginalized. A key driving motivation for this is to increase resilience among the most vulnerable people in order that they may withstand future crises better. Slim (2012) calls this the irresistible moral logic of addressing the root causes of distress, grounded in the 'fundamental values of autonomy and dignity'. This is rarely seen as a dilemma by humanitarians since it makes sense that they should work to minimize threats to lives and livelihoods in future crises, as this would enable them to focus on ever-smaller groups of affected people and ensure greater survival and flourishing.

Concerned with people's desire to live peaceful, rich lives, and the need for special assistance for some whose capabilities are constricted, humanitarian assistance is firmly founded on a political humanitarian ethic. For many humanitarians – and certainly those interviewed for this research project – the goal is not just to ensure bare survival. Rather, they, like the communities they work with and for, believe in the right not only to dignity but also to human flourishing – what Freire (1970) called the vocation to become more fully human.

The political humanitarian ethic is firmly committed to humanity, impartiality, neutrality and independence, as well as the futility of a response that ignores root causes, marginalization and arbitrarily limitations on capabilities of certain individuals and groups. Although it is widely accepted across the humanitarian sector, individuals and organizations will still come to different conclusions as they respond to humanitarian challenges. This ethical framework, internalized by many humanitarian practitioners – provides guidance for decision-making that assists in identifying ethical issues, making judgements, determining a path of action and implementing it. It removes neither the ethical challenges of humanitarian response, nor the angst in responding to dilemmas. Rather, it helps practitioners work through ethical quandaries when they arise by reminding them of their core values as fundamental priorities in their decision-making.

> ## Questions for Discussion
>
> 1   Are there points of agreement between different mental models of ethical practice?
> 2   Is neutrality an impossible dream for humanitarian workers?
> 3   By what criteria should humanitarian workers judge the appropriateness of their ethical choices?

FURTHER READING

Anderson, M.B. (1999) *Do No Harm: How Aid Can Support Peace – or War*. Boulder, CO, and London: Lynne Rienner.

Barnett, M. (2011) *Empire of Humanity: A History of Humanitarianism*. Ithaca, NY, and London: Cornell University Press.

Metz, T. (2013) 'The Western Ethic of Care or an Afro-Communitarian Ethic? Specifying the Right Relational Morality', *Journal of Global Ethics*, 9(1): 77–92.

REFERENCES

Active Learning Network For Accountability and Performance (ALNAP) (2015) The State of the Humanitarian System, *ALNAP Study*. London: ALNAP/Overseas Development Institute (ODI).

Anderson, M.B. (1999) *Do No Harm: How Aid Can Support Peace – or War*. Boulder, CO, and London: Lynne Rienner.

Aroskar, M.A. (1980) 'Anatomy of an Ethical Dilemma: The Theory', *American Journal of Nursing*, 80(4): 658–60.

Barnett, M. (2011) *Empire of Humanity: A History of Humanitarianism*. Ithaca, NY, and London: Cornell University Press.

Barnett, M. and Weiss. T.G. (2008) 'Humanitarianism: A Brief History of the Present', in M. Barnett and T.G. Weiss (eds), *Humanitarianism in Question: Politics, Power, Ethics*. Ithaca, NY: Cornell University Press, pp. 1–48.

De Vos, M. (2015) '3 Positive Trends that are Bridging the Humanitarian–Development Divide', *Inside Development*. Available at: https://www.devex.com/news/3-positive-trends-that-are-bridging-the-humanitarian-development-divide-86598 (accessed 1 September 2016).

Driver, J. (2014) 'The History of Utilitarianism', in E.N. Zalta (ed.), *The Stanford Encyclopedia of Philosophy*. Available at: https://plato.stanford.edu/archives/win2014/entries/utilitarianism-history (accessed 6 June 2016).

Freire, P. (1970) *Pedagogy of the Oppressed*. New York: Continuum.

Gall, C. (2010) 'Pakistan Flood Sets Back Infrastructure by Years', *New York Times* (online). Available at: nytimes.com/2010/08/27/world/asia/27flood.html (accessed 27 February 2017).

Global Humanitarian Assistance (GHA) (2016a) 'Defining Humanitarian Assistance'. Available at: www.globalhumanitarianassistance.org/data-guides/defining-humanitarian-aid/ (accessed 17 January 2016).

GHA (2016b) *Global Humanitarian Assistance Report 2016*. Available at: www.global humanitarianassistance.org/report/gha2016 (accessed 27 February 2017).

Gooden, R.E. (1993) 'Utility and the Good', in P. Singer (ed.), *A Companion to Ethics*. Malden, MA, Oxford and Carlton: Blackwell, pp. 241–80.

Goulet, D. (2006) *Development Ethics at Work: Explorations 1960–2002*. London and New York: Routledge.

Hall, B.J. (1997) 'Culture, Ethics and Communication', in F.L. Casmir (ed.), *Ethics in Intercultural and International Communication*. New York and London: Routledge, pp. 11–42.

High Level Panel on Humanitarian Financing (HLPHF) (2016) 'Too Important to Fail: Addressing the Humanitarian Financing Gap'. *High Level Panel on Humanitarian Financing – Report to the Secretary-General*. United Nations.

Johnson, R. and Cureton, A. (2016) 'Kant's Moral Philosophy', in E.N. Zalta (ed.), *The Stanford Encyclopedia of Philosophy*. Available at: https://plato.stanford.edu/archives/win2016/entries/kant-moral (accessed 6 June 2016).

Kant, I. (2005) *Fundamental Principles of the Methaphysics of Morals*. Mineola, NY: Dover.

Leahy, P. (2011) Address at the Launch of the 2011 Sphere Manual, MCG Melbourne, by Peter Leahy, Principal Executive International Programs, CARE Australia. 14 April 2011.

Lepard, B. (2002) *Rethinking Humanitarian Intervention: A Fresh Legal Approach Based on Fundamental Ethical Principles in International Law and World Religions*. University Park, PA: Pennsylvania State.

McConnell, T. (2014) 'Moral Dilemmas', in E.N. Zalta (ed.), *The Stanford Encyclopedia of Philosophy*. Available at: https://plato.stanford.edu/archives/fall2014/entries/moral-dilemmas/ (accessed 6 June 2016).

Metz, T. (2013) 'The Western Ethic of Care or an Afro-Communitarian Ethic? Specifying the Right Relational Morality', *Journal of Global Ethics*, 9(1): 77–92.

Nanji, A. (1993) 'Islamic Ethics', in P. Singer (ed.), *A Companion to Ethics*. Malden, MA, Oxford and Carlton: Blackwell, pp. 106–19.

National Disaster Management Authority (NDMA) (2010) *Flood 2010*. National Disaster Management Authority. Online, Government of Pakistan.

Nussbaum, M. (2000) *Women and Human Development: The Capabilities Approach*. Cambridge: Cambridge University Press.

Office for the Coordination of Humanitarian Affairs (OCHA) (2012) 'OCHA on Message: Civil–Military Coordination'. Available at: www.unocha.org/what-we-do/coordination-tools/UN-CMCoord/overview (accessed 23 October 2012).

OCHA (2016) 'From a Shock-Driven to a More Predictable Response System', *Thematic Areas: Humanitarian Development Nexus*. Available at: www.unocha.org/what-we-do/policy/thematic-areas/humanitarian-development-nexus (accessed 4 August 2016).

Pettit, P. (1993) 'Consequentialism', in P. Singer (ed.), *A Companion to Ethics*. Malden, MA, Oxford and Carlton: Blackwell, pp. 230–40.

ReliefWeb (2008) 'Glossary of Humanitarian Terms'. Available at: http://reliefweb.int/report/world/reliefweb-glossary-humanitarian-terms (accessed 24 July 2016).

Rest, J. (1986) *Moral Development: Advances in Research and Theory*. Westport, CT: Praeger.

Rizvi, H.-A. (2000) *Military, State and Society in Pakistan*. Houndsmills and London: Macmillan.

Sen, A. (1993) 'Capability and Well-Being', in M. Nussbaum and A. Sen (eds), *The Quality of Life*. Oxford: Oxford University Press, pp. 30–53.

Singer, P. (1993) *Practical Ethics*. Cambridge: Cambridge University Press.

Sinnott-Armstrong, W. (2015) 'Consequentialism', in E.N. Zalta (ed.), *The Stanford Encyclopedia of Philosophy*. Available at https://plato.stanford.edu/archives/win2015/entries/consequentialism/ (accessed 6 June 2016).

Slim, H. (1997) 'Relief Agencies and Moral Standing in War: Principles of Humanity, Neutrality, Impartiality, and Solidarity', *Development in Practice*, 7: 342–52.

Slim, H. (2012) *Essays in Humanitarian Action*. eBook. London: Oxford Institute of Ethics, Law and Armed Conflict. Available through ELAC/Kindle.

Sphere Project (2011) *The Sphere Handbook: Humanitarian Charter and Minimum Standards in Humanitarian Response*. Rugby: Practical Action Publishing.

Stoddard, A. (2003) 'Humanitarian NGOs: Challenges and Trends', in J. Macrae and A. Harmer (eds), *Humanitarian Action and the 'Global War on Terror': A Review of Trends and Issues*. London: Overseas Development Institute, pp. 25–35.

Transparency International (2010) *Preventing Corruption in Humanitarian Operations*. Available at: www.transparency.org, Transparency International (accessed 1 July 2016).

United Nations (UN) (2004) UN General Assembly Resolution 58/114: Strengthening of the Coordination of Emergency Humanitarian Assistance of the United Nations United Nations General Assembly. New York: United Nations.

United Nations Development Programme (UNDP) (2010) *The Real Wealth of Nations: Pathways to Human Development - Human Development Report 2010*. Available at: hdr.undp.org, UNDP (accessed 1 July 2016).

UNDP (2015) 'About Human Development,' *Human Development Report* (accessed 1 July 2016).

Warraich, H., Zaidi, A.K. and Patel, K. (2011) 'Floods in Pakistan: A Public Health Crisis', *Bulletin of the World Health Organization*, 89: 236–7.

9

RELIGION AND INTERNATIONAL DEVELOPMENT

DESMOND CAHILL

INTRODUCTION

According to the psychologists, religion is about believing, bonding, behaving and belonging (Saroglou, 2011). The overwhelming majority of peoples across the world consider that religion is important or very important in their daily lives (Pew Research Center, 2015). Contrary to the expectations of such luminaries as Friedrich Nietzsche (1844–1900), Bertrand Russell (1872–1970) and the death-of-God theologians of the 1960s who argued for a transformed post-Christian vision, one of the great surprises of the twentieth century was that religion not only survived but even prospered, except in most parts of the developed world with the continuous growth of secular humanism, neo-atheism and nihilistic agnosticism.

The last four decades have seen a religious resurgence with the emergence of Islam as a political force, beginning with the Iranian Revolution in 1979 under Ayatollah Khomeini (Jones and Petersen, 2011). This was followed by the fall of the Soviet Union and the resurgence of Russian Orthodoxy after its long Soviet dormancy with Patriarch Kiril as the current leader strongly supported by Vladimir Putin. China has seen the revival of neo-Confucianism and the spread of Protestant Christianity and, to a lesser extent, of patriotic Catholicism alongside the persecuted Vatican loyalists. Lastly, we have seen the growth of Evangelical Pentecostalism with its prosperity gospel across many parts of the globe, not least in Latin America, and the growth of Buddhism and Hinduism in the developed world with some militant movements in their heartland countries (Carbonnier, 2013). Tomalin (2012) notes that both US President George W. Bush and UK Prime

Minister Tony Blair pushed a global faith agenda, spurred on by the religious right, with Blair subsequently quite active in the interfaith movement. During the Bush era, US government funding for faith-based organizations doubled from 10.5 to 19.9 per cent in 2005 (Jones and Petersen, 2011).

According to the latest in a series of population projections of the Pew Research Center (2015), the religious profile of the world is rapidly changing. If current trends continue, it is projected that by 2050:

- Muslim numbers will nearly equal the number of Christians across the world and Muslims will make up about 10 per cent of the European population.
- Atheists, agnostics and those unaffiliated with any religion, although increasing in many developed countries, will represent a declining share of the world's population.
- The total Buddhist population will remain at about the same size, while the Hindu and Jewish populations will be larger than they now are.
- India will remain as a Hindu majority nation, but it will have the largest Muslim population of any country, surpassing Indonesia.
- Four out of ten Christians will live in sub-Saharan Africa.

This chapter recognizes that development is not exclusively a secular humanitarian space, but one that includes many 'faith-based organizations' (FBOs), to some of which, secular liberal development presents a significant normative challenge. Religious orders were once the main source of humanitarian assistance and religious concerns were central to the formation of many international non-governmental organizations active in development today. Indeed, religious missions still underpin the operations of globally significant NGOs. The development literature is replete with examples of Northern NGO practice, but the intersections of religion and development in the Islamic world especially are of potentially greater global significance, not least because of the association of 'Islamic' NGOs and political extremism in the Middle East. If development cooperation is to be just that, then there has to be more wide-ranging correspondence between religious and secular models of development.

RELIGION AND INTERNATIONAL DEVELOPMENT: THE SURPRISING LACK OF SCHOLARLY DIALOGUE

Notwithstanding the personal importance of individual faith and the changing religious profile, the academic and professional dialogue between religious studies and international development experts has, until quite recently, been almost non-existent, although religious organizations and their religious scholars, especially the Christian missionologists, were themselves not inactive. From one perspective, this lack of dialogue was not surprising, given that most social scientists and economists either ignored religion or thought it would soon become defunct in the face of the modernist and post-modernist movements (Jones and Petersen, 2011). The religious illiteracy of development researchers, policy-makers and practitioners still remains an issue (Rakodi, 2012a). Rakodi (2012b) suggests that the situation has arisen as a result of the secularization of state and of society, particularly in Europe, as well as the process of modernization in which religion was identified with past and dying traditions.

All this has been reinforced by the dominance of neoliberal economic frameworks since the 1980s (ibid.). Most eminent economists who have been influential in formulating development theories ignore religion as they do entrepreneurship (Heslam, 2014). This lack of dialogue is surprising. In 1905, Max Weber had published his *Protestant Ethic and the Spirit of Capitalism,* in which he argued that economic development which had been fostered in the European countries such as Germany and Great Britain, had been underpinned by their various Protestant world views, relationships and institutions and by the core values of hard work, diligence, frugality, a sense of vocational calling and the rational and productive stewardship of resources (Carbonnier, 2013; Heslam, 2014). On the other hand, the Catholic and Christian Orthodox countries of Southern and Eastern Europe such as Italy, Spain and Russia had been essentially imitative of the development success of the Protestant countries from the industrial revolution onwards.

Peter Berger (2003) argues that contemporary Evangelical Pentecostalism is a reincarnation of Weber's thesis and Yining (2012) applies this to the spreading influence of Protestantism in China. Its global growth is attributable to its prosperity gospel, which teaches that God's redemption extends to the realm of personal finances where it replaces poverty with riches for those with faith (Heslam, 2014). Heslam (ibid.) argues that in contrast to the Marxist notion of religion as the opium of the people, Christianity generally offers the attributes of a deep sense of calling, an optimistic sense of the future, a deferral of gratification, a spirit of stimulative entrepreneurship, a rationalist approach freed from witchcraft and superstition and the creation of voluntary associations. However, he also notes that many Pentecostal organizations can be over-dependent on founder leaders. Rew and Bhatewara (2012) have noted the same thing in their Maharashtra study of Hindu, Muslim and Sikh organizations, where the influence of charismatic founders can lead to unquestioned implementation of one person's ideas about development and educational programmes.

Even though they share much common ground, the lack of dialogue between the disciplines of religious studies and development studies is surprising (Marshall, 2014). Many of the world's humanitarian and international development agencies have been inspired by religiously motivated people, beginning with the Red Cross. Local and international faith-based organizations sponsor schools, universities, health services, HIV and AIDS agencies, water investments and microfinance organizations in the developing world (ibid.). The beginning of a dialogue was probably triggered by the collaboration in 1998 between George Carey, Archbishop of Canterbury, who made a well-publicized visit to the southern part of the Sudan, and James Wolfensohn, head of the World Bank (Jones and Petersen, 2011), which sponsored the three-volume *Voices of the Poor* study (Narayan et al., 2000). While the study contained some negative references to religion, it was widely quoted as suggesting that religion should be brought into the development equation (White et al., 2012). It was also driven by the impact of post-9/11 politics (Green et al., 2012; Jones and Petersen, 2011). However, the World Bank engagement became derailed due to diverging perceptions of poverty and development between government and religious bodies and suspicion and distrust in collaborative efforts (Haynes, 2013). Dialogue has been much furthered by a 2012 double issue of the journal *Development in Practice*, edited by Carole Rakodi (2012a).

In this chapter, after examining the lessons to be learned from the origins of the principal agencies, we will look at three vexed issues in scoping this difficult terrain: the difficulty of delineating the separation line between faith-based organizations and secular humanitarian and development agencies; the alleged comparative advantage of faith-based organizations and, lastly, religion and proselytization in development countries.

THE EMERGENCE OF FAITH-INSPIRED HUMANITARIAN AND INTERNATIONAL DEVELOPMENT AGENCIES

The Pre-First World War Era

While there is a longer history of welfare and humanitarian agencies, especially in regard to orphanages and hospitals, at the international level the birth of the Red Cross, seemingly of Christian origins with its name and emblem, was of Calvinist inspiration when founded by the Swiss businessman Jean-Henri Dunant and the jurist Gustave Moynier in Geneva in 1863. The Red Cross has always proclaimed itself an impartial, areligious, neutral and independent organization. It grew out of Dunant's witnessing of the appalling suffering in the Battle of Solferino in June 1859, during the Austro-Sardinian War. However, his Christian faith seems not to have been his main motivating factor as he became non-religious in his later years, even attacking Calvinism and all organized religion (Boissier, 1985).

After its enormous work during the First World War, in 1919, after some political bickering, the International Federation of the Red Cross and Red Crescent was formed as a way to legitimize its neutrality and to incorporate the global Islamic brotherhood within the broad umbrella. The Red Crescent emblem had been worn in the armed conflict between Russia and the Ottoman Empire in 1877–78. To counter the Turkish argument that the Red Cross emblem had its origins in Christianity, there was promoted the questionable idea that the Red Cross flag was nothing but a reversing of the colours of the Swiss flag (Boissier, 1985). In 2005, the Red Crystal emblem, officially known as the Third Protocol Emblem, was approved to accommodate Israel's presence after a failed five-decade-long lobbying campaign to have the Red Star of David (Magen David Adom) as the Jewish emblem.

The second significant organization to emerge prior to the Second World War was Caritas, founded in 1897 by a German Catholic priest and social worker, Lorenz Werthmann. However, given Germany's vicissitudes in the first half of the twentieth century, it was not until the 1920s that it became an international organization and not until 1947 that it was approved by the Vatican's Secretariat of State. It sees itself as a Catholic relief, development and social service organization with the aim to build a better world and has 170 member nations now headed by the Filipino *papabile* Luis Cardinal Tagle.

The birth of another significant pre-Second World War organization was in the UK in 1919 with Save the Children, today known as the Save the Children Fund. It was founded by two sisters, Eglantyne Jebb, an Anglican primary school teacher, and

Dorothy Buxton, who later became a Quaker. A few months later, surprisingly, the fledgling organization received the support of Pope Benedict XV in pre-ecumenical days. Its work began with the alleviation of the starvation of children, both in Germany and in the remains of the Austro-Hungarian Empire, as a result of the Allied blockade which extended beyond the 1918 Armistice. This initial effort was soon followed by the Russian famine in 1921 (Mulley, 2009). Another pre-War organization to emerge was the International Rescue Committee, begun in 1933 at the suggestion of Albert Einstein to rescue Jews in Nazi Germany and which has continued its humanitarian work ever since. Its response to the worst humanitarian crises is to restore health, safety, education, economic wellbeing and power to people devastated by conflict and disaster. Its origins were very secular, for it grew out of the International Relief Association founded in Germany in 1931 by the Communist Party and the Socialist Workers' Party to aid victims of Nazi oppression and persecution.

The Post-Second World War Era

With the 1940s and the Second World War, other humanitarian and development organizations emerged. Oxfam, originally known as the Oxford Committee for Famine Relief, was formed during the Second World War by a number of Quakers, an Anglican canon, social activists and Oxford academics to help relieve famine in Greece. While not directly religiously inspired, it had strong connections with people of faith. The first meeting was in the Old Library of the Anglican University Church of St Mary the Virgin in Oxford. It has now evolved into an international humanist confederation of seventeen organizations working in about 100 countries. Operating within a rights framework, it has four target areas: economic justice, essential services, rights in crises and gender justice. Part of its work is the resettlement of refugees.

In 1945, CARE – which originally stood for Co-operation for American Remittances to Europe – emerged in the USA soon after the end of the war to send food parcels to Europe. It was a consortium of 22 civil, religious, cooperative, farm and labour organizations, now with its headquarters in Atlanta. In 1950, in California, a Baptist minister, Robert Pierce (1914–78) formed World Vision within an evangelical Christian vision and initially framed within an anti-Communist framework – it now has the largest budget (US$2.72 billion in 2011) of all human and developmental non-government agencies (Jones and Petersen, 2011).

Another separate but interlinked Catholic organization is CIDSE, the French acronym for International Cooperation for Development and Solidarity, with eighteen member organizations from Europe and North America and its headquarters in Brussels, probably to be near the EU headquarters and away from Rome. Within its umbrella are the huge German development organization Misereor that works closely with the German government and was formed by German bishops in 1962; the UK CAFOD (Catholic Agency for Overseas Development), created in 1960 from the National Board of Catholic Women; the USA's Center of Concern, formed in 1971 by the nation's bishops; and Ireland's Trocaire, established in 1973. Post-Second World War Two, Catholic developments have been influenced by the 1967 encyclical of Pope Paul VI, *Populorum Progressio*, which applied Catholic social teaching (which had begun to be enunciated in the 1890s) to the emerging Third World, where, since the sixteenth century, the Church has been heavily involved in tandem with European colonization enterprises. The encyclical also partly led to the emergence of liberation theology in Latin America.

Text Box 9.1   Faith-Inspired Organizations: Islam

Other major faith traditions have been slower to form organizations. Petersen (2012) has scoped the under-researched area of more than 400 transnational Muslim NGOs, many funded by Saudi Arabia. The emergence began in the 1970s because the perception of many Muslim NGOs was that Western NGOs were proselytisers of atheism in contrast to the strong Islamic monotheism, which cannot imagine a world without God. Petersen describes four types: da'watist, jihadist, solidarity-based and secularised organizations.

Prince Aga Khan Development Network, including the Aga Khan Foundation, is the largest with, in 2012, a budget of US$320 million but, like the Red Cross, it does not consider itself a Muslim NGO. It was founded in 1967 by Prince Shah Karim Al Hussain, Aga Khan IV, born in 1936, the head imam of Nizari Ismailism within Shia Islam. Besides the Foundation, there are the Aga Khan Health Services and the Aga Khan Educational Services among others, all working in developing countries, usually but not always where there is a Muslim community. The International Islamic Charitable Agency was founded by some Kuwaitis as a direct reaction to an initiative in 1978 in Colorado that some Christian missionaries intended to invest one billion dollars to proselytise African Muslims (Benthall and Bellion-Jourdan, 2003). In 1979, the International Islamic Relief Organization (2012 turnover of $47 million) was founded in Saudi Arabia. In the United Kingdom, Islamic Relief ($96 million) was founded by two Egyptian doctors in 1984, and in the following year members of the UK Bangladeshi and Pakistani communities formed Muslim Aid ($73 million). As one example, Islamic Relief works with imams in Bangladesh to disseminate information on children's rights. The main Turkish NGO is Deniz Feneri Association ($46 million), and there is also the Saudi Committee for the Relief of the Palestinian People ($40 million), and the Qatar Charitable Society ($31 million) (Petersen, 2012).

Text Box 9.2   Faith-Inspired Organizations: Hindu, Sikh and Buddhist

Hindu-inspired international development organizations have been slow in their emergence: 'Compared to Islam and Christianity, we do not find as many development organizations linked to the Hindu tradition that are international in reach, possibly because most Hindus live in India' (Tomalin, 2013: 210). However, the Hindu diaspora has begun spawning several, including Hindu Aid founded in the UK to act as a coordinating body for the many Hindu charitable organizations. The diaspora has also established a Disaster Task Force in response to catastrophes (ibid.). In the USA, there is the Hindu American Seva Charities that links into Seva (Sanskrit for 'service') International. Like Hindu Aid, the UK Sikh community has established Khalsa Aid to act in a coordinating role and in the Punjab in India there is the Global Sikh Educational Society. The efforts of these Hindu and Sikh organizations are directed at India and Nepal, but their activities are also focused on responding to disasters in other parts of the world.

The Buddhist situation is even more complex, with many Buddhist-majority coun-tries and with many different traditions in Asia and across the Buddhist diaspora. Watts (2004) has documented how Buddhist NGOs in Japan – as a rich country with Buddhist traditions – emerged in the early 1980s as a result of the Vietnamese refugee crisis and, later on, the Hanshin earthquake in 1995. Often their Buddhist identity is thin. However, there had been earlier initiatives that had begun with their focus on Japan, which, in some cases, evolved internationally. The Buddhist NGO Network of Japan had spawned the Light Up Your Corner Movement founded in 1969 by the founder of the Tendai sect, Dengyo Daishi. The Buddhist Aid Centre was founded in 1982 by priests from the Nichiren sect in response to press criticism that Buddhism had reached its use-by-date and that Buddhist monks had no concern for the general wellbeing of Japanese or world society (Watts, 2004). The Rissho Koseikai movement, founded in 1938, launched the Donate a Meal Campaign in 1974, which encouraged the skipping of a meal twice a month and donating the savings. It initially focused on Japan but then expanded internationally. It also launched the Niwano Peace Foundation in 1978 for research into world peace, based on generating peace dividends from the Hiroshima bombing (Anderson, 1994) and fulfilling the notion of 'Engaged Buddhism' with the International Network of Engaged Buddhists.

WHAT IS A FAITH-BASED ORGANIZATION?

This brief overview highlights how the development, aid and charitable activities of most of these organizations are intertwined with religious traditions to a greater or lesser or negligible extent though many who head secular humanist agencies have strong religious affiliations. These various birth accounts of well-known international non-government organizations across the various world faith traditions highlight their differences and the difficulty in scoping the intellectual and research terrain of religion and development as researchers began to do in the 1990s. It was helped along by the focus that the World Bank gave to religion through the leadership of Katherine Marshall, which has led to the emergence of the World Faith Development Dialogue (Jones and Petersen, 2011). But, in her view, bridging the gap has been 'torturous' with mutual suspicions running high (Marshall, 2014). Notwithstanding the tensions, religion and development 'share much common ground in a concern for human dignity and welfare and for translating these ideals into reality' (ibid.: 384).

Scoping the terrain has been further hindered by an essentializing of the concept of religion itself and nor is there scholarly consensus on the notion of development except that it is linked to wellbeing and welfare and certainly not on how it is achieved. Rakodi (2012a) suggests that the links are immensely complex and so no theory has been devel-oped though she herself has outlined a complex model. Academic work in the area of their proliferation has also brought into relief the difficulty in developing a typology of faith-inspired organizations delivering programmes in developing countries.

The term 'faith-based organizations' (FBOs) has emerged, although Smith and Sosin (2001) prefer 'faith-related' since the faith basis of many organizations such as World Vision and even the Red Cross is implicit. Their proliferation has resulted from many factors, including: (i) the emergence of a transnational civil society where FBOs are prominent players; (ii) the support for charitable enterprises from transnational diasporic communities; (iii) the decline of communism and the rise of organizational identity politics; (iv) the rise of NGOs pursuant to the economic structural adjustments of the 1970s and 1980s with the decline of the welfare state; (v) the growth of the Christian Right; and (vi) the growth of Islam, including Muslim organizations (Clarke, 2008).

Various typologies have as a consequence emerged that have taken a worldview approach, rather than a faith approach, because of the difficulties of defining religion, describing a faith-based organization and, lastly, the fact that the religious/secular dichotomy reflects a Western Christian philosophical and theological approach. Clarke (ibid.) outlined five types: (i) representative religious organizations or apex bodies; (ii) religious charitable or development organizations; (iii) religiously inspired sociopolitical organizations; (iv) religious missionary organizations; and (v) radical, illegal or terrorist organizations. Heffernan et al. nominate six organizational types on a sliding scale: (i) faith-permeated; (ii) faith-centred; (iii) faith-affiliated; (iv) faith-background; (v) faith-secular partnership, and (vi) secular (2009); although, given the problems associated with the word 'secular' it would be preferable to label it as 'humanist' or 'secular humanist' (Bouma et al., 2011).

In an international survey of religious and secular humanist informants, Noy (2009) identified six ideal type models of development, only one being purely secular. It was concluded, however, that specific religious adherence is not the only or even the most important criterion for classifying the various visions of international development. It has been asked whether it is even worthwhile to attempt to develop a typology (ibid.; Rakodi, 2012b). Sider and Unruh (2004) take a different approach, suggesting the preferable bases for categorization are: (i) mission statement; (ii) founding circumstances; (iii) affiliation networks; (iv) controlling authorities; (v) senior management profile; (vi) other support staff profile; and (vii) sources of support.

Accordingly, while in most situations it is clear whether an organization is or is not faith-inspired, there is a large grey area, complicated by the fact that some large organizations while seemingly of some religious inspiration stridently claim that they are non-sectarian and humanitarian.

THE COMPARATIVE ADVANTAGES OF FAITH-BASED ORGANIZATIONS

Behind the definitional and typological discussions has been the question of whether faith-inspired organizations have a comparative advantage in achieving developmental objectives. It is argued that as local grassroots communities they are better equipped to deliver or help to deliver development initiatives. Rakodi (2012b) suggests that it is not possible to provide a simple answer. Perhaps it is not possible to provide even a complex answer or perhaps it is not even worthwhile asking the question, given the huge differences in religious, cultural, economic and political contexts that characterize each developmental initiative. This is being confirmed by the particular case studies that have begun to emerge.

Two Indian studies highlight how positive stereotypes of religion, development and welfare are not necessarily true. They question the claims that religions are close to the poor and they have been and can be more effective deliverers of welfare programmes. White et al. (2012) studied two urban and two rural sites in Orissa (relatively poor, Hindu dominant) and the Punjab (relatively wealthy, Sikh dominant), each with smaller Muslim presences. In Orissa, they found considerable fluidity in religious identification and influences, most especially among the low caste Dalits, who, ambivalent about their Hinduism, often visited other places of worship to avoid discrimination. In the Punjab, Sikh communities had a strong commitment to hospitality with the provision of guest rooms and free food (the *langar*), which was given out at the local gurdwara. Except for this widespread Sikh tradition, Hindus, Muslims and Sikhs provided very little in the way of social welfare (ibid.). In fact, they noted that the flow was otherwise – many adherents gave of their own free time and money to help the local place of worship and there was some questioning of the character and commitment of the imams and priests.

More positive scenarios, although not unproblematic, have come from other contexts. In their study of the Sarvodaya movement in Sri Lanka, Daskon and Binns (2012) claim that the strong role of Buddhism in social and economic development has gone largely unnoticed in the West. They are critical of the capitalist development process because it creates unavoidable economic competition. However, it must also be noted the Sri Lankan Buddhist leaders did not play an especially positive role in helping to unite Sri Lanka and prevent or mitigate its civil war. Sarvodaya – which is the Sanskrit word used by Gandhi to describe his own political philosophy – was founded in 1958 by Dr Ahangamage Ariyaratne as a grassroots development movement, seeing development as a process of awakening and empowering people in making their own decisions and determining their own values, priorities and capacities, incorporating multiple paradigms such as sustainability in development, environmentally friendly practices, the participation of local people and the importance of networking (Daskon and Binns, 2012):

> Sarvodaya implements its development strategies in accordance with *sathara viharas* (four sublime abodes), the four principles of personality development as described in Buddhism. These include *metta* (loving-kindness and caring), *mudita* (joy of the accomplishment of a person), *karuna* (wishes for all sentient beings to be free from suffering) and *upekkhja* (equanimity). (Ibid.: 869)

Now working in 15,000 Sri Lankan villages, it emphasizes social equality in its rejection of Hindu casteism. The study found much change in attitudes and practices such as cleaner villages, the philosophy of shared labour and the establishment of small-scale enterprises. Much insistence is placed on 'the righteous way of living' with the Noble Eightfold Path of Buddhism (ibid.).

Leurs (2012) compared evangelical Christian, Muslim and secular organizations in two states in Nigeria in the HIV/AIDS area, finding that the faith-based organizations demonstrate some distinctive features and comparative advantages but cautions against any simplistic division between religious and secular organizations. But he could not determine if either had some comparative advantages as the issue is largely determined by context. Donors preferred to fund the faith-based agencies as the people trusted religious leaders, while government agencies were seen as incompetent and corrupt. Olivier and Wodon (2012) cautioned against questionable claims. Using the image of the broken telephone, they analyzed the various claims that 30–70 per cent of health care is provided by faith-based organizations, suggesting the data base is 'fragmented'. Certainly, mission-based hospitals have been important but careful research has been lacking. The claims are driven by vested interests (ibid.).

However, several studies have highlighted that religious attitudes towards women can be a development hindrance, given that the education of women is considered central to well-founded development progress. Jones and Petersen (2011) note that the emphasis on religion's positive values has led to the neglect of the negativities of gender inequality and social hierarchies. In a study in Pakistan of religious leaders, teachers and *madrassa* schools, Bradley and Saigol (2012) found that religious men were more closely aligned to patriarchalism and the gendered division of labour than religious Pakistani women. The more religious the respondents were, the more likely they were to be opposed to co-education. Prior to the study, girls' schools in Pakistan had been torched and bombed – the religious respondents explained it in terms of conspiracy and blaming foreigners while secular humanist respondents blamed the Taliban and religious militants (Bradley and Saigol, 2012).

Adams (2015) has studied the situation in Bangladesh, where, since independence in 1971, the empowerment of women has been a central focus following the brutal violence against women in the liberation war of separation from West Pakistan. In Bangladesh, historically, the Sufi influence has been a mitigating factor in gender inequality though the nineteenth-century Islamic reform movements emphasized orthodoxy restorationism, which stressed religious devotionalism and moral purity. The targeting of women in Bangladeshi development programmes has led to much lower maternal mortality rates, increased educational level of girls and greater political participation of women. Notwithstanding this, these Islamic reform movements, in stressing women's education, have targeted the religious education aspect in promoting piety and religious practice (ibid.).

Another finding to emerge from the various studies is that there are limitations to what even large faith-based organizations can achieve. In a study of the Anglican Church in South Sudan and the role of its international linkages, Kinney (2012) found that the Church, in calling on the resources of these linkages, was able to support and improve the wellbeing of local communities through development activities and service provision. But the faith-based organizations did not have the resources to develop large-scale projects in education, agriculture, health, sanitation and transportation.

Another related focus has been the performance of Pentecostal Christian initiatives. Early on, Meyer (1998) had studied Pentecostalism in southeastern Ghana from a commodities and globalization perspective. The aim of the fast-growing faith is to purify and de-demonize through prayer goods and commodities gained by these born-again Christians:

> It takes as a point of departure both the desire to have access to the world and existing fears about the nature of the world market and one's connection to it. Affirming that the market is an abode of invisible satanic forces, adherents can claim that a Pentecostal religion is needed in order to profit from, rather than fall victim to globalisation. (Ibid.: 774)

Profit is God! In Malawi, in a programme delivered by the Living Waters Church to 110 local congregations, James (2012) found that they had been empowered in their visions and attitudes to start local social development programmes. Zalanga (2010), in an Africa-wide review, found that the Pentecostal faith-based gospel laced with the hate of Islam has not fundamentally addressed Africa's realities, even though it does contain a useful theology of entrepreneurship.

RELIGION AND PROSELYTIZATION IN DEVELOPMENT CONTEXTS

An issue that has tended to poison the dialogue about religion and development is proselytization, which is a loaded and unhelpful word. Missionization and evangelization are too over-loaded with Christian connotations and so conversion and exposure are being used in some studies. Proselytism is extremely widespread in most societies in convincing people to change the way they think or act, as happens in universities, schools and in community campaigns through advertisements or making students read an article. Religious proselytism is little different. Hence, the issue is not whether it happens but how it happens. Mussolini legislated against proselytizing by 'sects' such as Seventh-Day Adventists and Jehovah's Witnesses (Homer, 2004), while the US Supreme Court has allowed Jehovah's Witnesses to enter private property and knock on doors to spread their message (Bouma et al., 2011).

Religious freedom is not merely the right to worship and build places of worship but also the right to participate and engage with civil society (ibid.). And it also implies the freedom to change one's religion or to become areligious. But does this imply the right to proselytize or try to convince people to change their religious affiliation, particularly in Third World contexts where the religious group is delivering welfare or development services? Is it compassion with strings? Does the opportunity to make conversions lead to instability and violence as political and religious elites claim? It is a debate that reaches back, especially to nineteenth-century India. Almost all major world religions to a greater or lesser extent are committed to converting others to their tradition. Freedom to change one's religion is protected under Article 18(b) in the 1967 International Covenant of Civil and Political Rights. Proselytism has become more contestable with increasing secularisation together with attempts to domesticate religion and with the growth of civil society and the secular state (Barnett, 2015).

Within a colonial history perspective, Woodberry (2012) suggests that the free competition between the conversionary Protestant missionaries working usually in tandem with the colonial authorities led directly in the colonized countries to an increased level of education, the greater use of print technology, an expansion in voluntary organizations, an increase in economic development, a lengthening of life expectancy, a reduction in infant mortality and perhaps to political democracy. Eschewing the word 'proselytism', Woodbury usefully distinguishes between four levels: (i) incentivized exposure like advertisements on television or on the Internet; (ii) forced exposure such as being required to go to school which exposes students to something religious beyond the academic subjects. More problematic are: (iii) incentivized conversion; and (iv) forced conversion, with the last certainly unacceptable.

Incentivized conversion where there is a quid pro quo is more problematic though it has been quite common. India has been its epicentre, where the colonial heritage overhangs the controversy and where converts fear nationalist Hindutvas who argue that Christian missionaries are preying on the vulnerability of the poor. In India, conversions have typically occurred amongst the poor such as low-caste Hindus, tribal people and outcasts (Shah and Shah, 2013). They have shown that by converting to Pentecostal Christianity Dalit women have been assisted to overcome poverty. The entry of missionaries has generated a veritable religious market place and, as one example, spurred the growth of Hindu hospitals.

Woodberry suggests that:

> In the long run, religious competition undermines abuses. For example, the people who convert to Islam, Buddhism and Hinduism in the United States are dispro- portionately groups that Christians have discriminated against. Blacks are more likely to convert to Islam because white Christians enslaved and discriminated against them. Gays and lesbians are more likely to convert to Hinduism, Buddhism et cetera. People who have been exploited are more likely to convert. That happens all over the world and if the dominant religious group wants to stop it, the best thing to do is to stop discriminating or exploiting the group that is converting. (2015: 16–17)

Additionally, NGOs, whether religious or secular, have been acting on an implied agree- ment that all humanitarian and development aid should be impartial, independent and neutral. But, in the view of Barnett (2015), this commitment has been diminishing.

CONCLUSION

In summary, this overview has brought to the fore that generalizations are dangerous in the interface between religion and development, both heavily contested notions, and that there is the need to heavily contest any simplistic division of the religious from the secular. It might be preferable to examine the issue through the lens of civil society-based organizations, both humanist and religious, which have differentiating worldviews, value systems and organizational practices. Indeed, this book is organized around the notion of mental models and this study of religion in development further expands the range of beliefs and ideologies that frame development practice and to which development practitioners must be sensitive, be they secular or committed to a particular faith.

The religion–development dialectic provides one often-crucial perspective in the design, delivery and evaluation of development aid programmes and in the selection of appropriate local and international partners. For faith-based organizations themselves, reflection on the dialectic provides the necessary planning, implementation and ethical parameters and limitations in addressing poverty, social participation and wellbeing in collaborating successfully with other government and non-government agencies. Until now, in the limited number of formal academic studies, much light has been shone. But more studies are needed. They are needed in non-Christian contexts and taking into account the multifaith and interfaith perspectives. The global insight that to be reli- gious is to be interreligious has almost become a slogan. But it is an important slogan. Researchers bridging the two areas need to have a quite deep appreciation not only of religion and spirituality, but of the particular religions themselves, their historical and theological traditions and their values and practices, both positive and negative, and their interfaith perspectives. As is often said, religion is part of the problem, but it is also part of the solution.

Questions for Discussion

1 Should development or humanitarian assistance be used as an opportunity to proselytize?
2 In what ways do faith-based and secular organizations work cooperatively together? How significant are distinctions between these broad categories of development actor?
3 Why do religious studies scholars and development studies scholars struggle to comprehend each other?

 FURTHER READING

Adams, N. (2015) *Religion and Women's Empowerment in Bangladesh*. Occasional Paper, Berkley Center for Religion and World Affairs, Georgetown University, in association with World Faiths Development Dialogue, Washington, DC.

Daskon, C. and Binns, T. (2012) 'Practising Buddhism in a Development Context: Sri Lanka's Sarvodaya Movement', *Development in Practice*, 22(5–6): 867–74.

Leurs, R. (2012) 'Are Faith-Based Organisations Distinctive? Comparing Religious and Secular NGOs in Nigeria', *Development in Practice*, 22(5–6): 704–19.

Tomalin, E. (2013) *Religions and Development*. New York: Routledge.

REFERENCES

Adams, N. (2015) *Religion and Women's Empowerment in Bangladesh*. Occasional Paper, Berkley Center for Religion and World Affairs, Georgetown University, in association with World Faiths Development Dialogue, Washington, DC.

Anderson, R. (1994) 'Eissho Koseikai and the Bodhisattva Way: Religious Ideals, Conflict, Gender and Status', *Japanese Journal of Religion and Culture*, 21(2–3): 312–37.

Barnett, M. (2015) 'Historical Perspectives in Proselytism, Humanitarianism and Development'. Roundtable Discussion, Berkley Center for Religion, Peace and World Affairs, Georgetown University, 15 March. Available at: http://berkleycenter.georgetown.edu/events/sharing-the-message-proselytism-and-development-in-pluralistic-societies-a-public-dialogue (accessed 27 February 2017).

Benthall, J. and Bellion-Jourdan, J. (2003) *The Charitable Crescent: The Politics of Aid in the Muslim World*. London: I.B. Tauris.

Berger, P. (2003) *Questions of Faith: A Skeptical Affirmation*. New York: Blackwell.

Boissier, P. (1985) *History of the International Committee of the Red Cross and the Protection of War Victims*. Geneva: ICRC & Mamillan.

Bouma, G., Cahill, D., Dellal, H. and Zwartz, B. (2011) *Freedom of Religion and Belief in Twentieth-Century Australia*. Sydney: Australian Human Rights Commission.

Bradley, T. and Saigol, R. (2012) 'Religious Values and Beliefs and Education for Women in Pakistan', *Development in Practice*, 22(5–6): 675–88.

Carbonnier, G. (2013) 'Religion and Development: Reconsidering Secularism as the Norm', in Geneva Graduate Institute International Development Policy, International Development Policy: Religion and Development. Basingstoke: Palgrave Macmillan.

Clarke, G. (2008) 'Faith-Based Organizations and International Development: An Overview', in G. Clarke and M. Jennings (eds), *Development, Civil Society and Faith-Based Organizations: Bridging the Sacred and the Secular*. Basingstoke: Palgrave Macmillan pp. 17–45.

Daskon, C. and Binns, T. (2012) 'Practising Buddhism in a Development Context: Sri Lanka's Sarvodaya Movement', *Development in Practice*, 22(5–6): 867–74.

Green, M., Mercer, C. and Mesaki, S. (2012) 'Faith Informs: Civil Society, Evangelism and Development in Tanzania', *Development in Practice*, 22(5–6): 721–34.

Haynes, J. (2013) 'Faith-Based Organisations, Development and the World Bank', *International Development Policy*, 4(1): 49–64.

Heffernan, T., Adkins, J. and Occhipinti, L. (2009) 'Faith-Based Organizations, Neo-Liberalism and Development: An Introduction', in T. Heffernan, J. Adkins and L. Occhipinti (eds), *Bridging the Gaps: Faith-Based Organizations, Neoliberalism and Development in Latin America and the Caribbean*. Lanham, MD: Lexington Books pp. 1–34.

Heslam, P. (2014) 'Christianity and the Prospects for Development in the Global South', in P. Oslington (ed.), *The Oxford Handbook of Christianity and Economics*. Oxford: Oxford University Press, pp. 359–83.

Homer, M. (2004) 'New Religions in the Republic of Italy', in J. Richardson (ed.), *Regulating Religion: Case Studies from Around the Globe*. New York: Kluwer Academic/Plenum, pp. 203–12.

James, R. (2012) 'Addressing Dependency with Faith and Hope: the Eagles Relief and Development Programme of the Living Waters Church in Malawi', *Development in Practice*, 22(5–6): 883–92.

Jones, B. and Petersen, M. (2011) 'Instrumental, Narrow, Normative? Reviewing Recent Work on Religion and Development', *Third World Quarterly*, 32(7): 1291–306.

Kinney, N. (2012) 'The Role of a Transnational Religious Network in Development in a Weak State: The International Links of the Episcopal Church of Sudan', *Development in Practice*, 22(5–6): 749–62.

Leurs, R. (2012) 'Are Faith-Based Organisations Distinctive? Comparing Religious and Secular NGOs in Nigeria', *Development in Practice*, 22(5–6): 704–19.

Marshall, K. (2014) 'Faith, Religion and International Development', in P. Oslington (ed.), *The Oxford Handbook of Christianity and Economics*. Oxford: Oxford University Press, pp. 384–400.

Meyer, B. (1998) 'Commodities and the Power of Prayer: Pentecostalist Attitudes towards Consumption in Contemporary Ghana', *Development and Change*, 29: 751–76.

Mulley, C. (2009) *The Woman Who Saved the Children: A Biography of Eglantyne Jebb*. London: Oneworld Publications.

Narayan, D., Chambers, M., Shah, K. and Petesch, P. (2000) *Voices of the Poor: Crying out for Change*. New York: World Bank and Oxford University Press.

Noy, D. (2009) 'Material and Spiritual Conceptions of Development: A Framework of Ideal Types', *Journal of Developing Societies*, 25: 275–307.

Olivier, J. and Wodon, Q. (2012) 'Playing Broken Telephone: Assessing Faith-Inspired Health Care Provision in Africa', *Development in Practice*, 22(5–6): 819–34.

Petersen, M. (2012) 'Trajectories of Transnational Muslim NGOs', *Development in Practice*, 22(5–6): 763–78.

Pew Research Center (2015) The Future of World Religions: Population Growth Projections, 2010–2050. Available at: www.pewforum.org/2015/04/02/religious-projections-2010-2050/ (accessed 27 February 2017).

Rakodi, C. (2012a) 'Religion and Development: Subjecting Religious Perceptions and Organizations to Scrutiny', *Development in Practice*, 22(5–6): 621–33.

Rakodi, C. (2012b) 'A Framework for Analysing the Links between Religion and Development', *Development in Practice*, 22(5–6): 634–50.

Rew, M. and Bhatewara, Z. (2012) 'Pro-Poor? Class, Gender, Power and Authority in Faith-Based Education in Maharashtra, India', *Development in Practice*, 22(5–6): 851–66.

Saroglou, V. (2011) 'Believing, Bonding, Behaving and Belonging: The Four Big Religious Dimensions and Cultural Variation', *Journal of Cross-Cultural Psychology*, 42(8): 1320–40.

Shah, R. and Shah, T. (2013) 'Pentecost Amid Puja: Charismatic Christianity in the Lives of Dalit Women in 21st-Century Bangalore', in R. Hefner (ed.), *Global Pentecostalism in the 21st Century*. Bloomington, IN: Indiana University Press, pp. 194–222.

Sider, R. and Unruh, H. (2004) 'Typology of Religious Characteristics of Social Service and Educational Organizations and Programs', *Nonprofit and Voluntary Sector Quarterly*, 33(1): 109–34.

Smith, S. and Sosin, M. (2001) 'The Varieties of Faith-Related Agencies', *Public Administration Review*, 61(6): 651–70.

Tomalin, E. (2012) 'Thinking about Faith-Based Organizations in Development: Where Have we Got to and What Next?', *Development in Practice*, 22(5–6): 689–703.

Tomalin, E. (2013) *Religions and Development*. New York: Routledge.

Watts, J. (2004) 'A Brief Overview of Buddhist NGOs in Japan', *Japanese Journal of Religion and Culture*, 31(2): 417–28.

White, S., Devine, J. and Jha, S. (2012) 'The Life a Person Lives: Well-Being and Development in India', *Development in Practice*, 22(5–6): 651–62.

Woodberry, R. (2012) 'The Missionary Roots of Liberal Democracy', *American Political Science Review*, 106(2): 244–74.

Woodberry, R. (2015) 'Historical Perspectives in Proselytism, Humanitarianism and Development'. Roundtable Discussion, Berkley Center for Religion, Peace and World Affairs, Georgetown University, 15 March. Available at: http://berkleycenter.georgetown.edu/events/sharing-the-message-proselytism-and-development-in-pluralistic-societies-a-public-dialogue (accessed 27 February 2017).

Yining, L. (2012) *Economic Reform and Development in China*. Cambridge: Cambridge University Press.

Zalanga, S. (2010) 'Religion, Economic Development and Cultural Change: The Contradictory Role of Pentecostal Christianity in Sub-Saharan Africa', *Journal of Third World Studies*, 27(1): 43–62.

10

CORRUPTION AND DEVELOPMENT

ROBERT KLITGAARD

INTRODUCTION

Corruption is frequently cited as a key obstacle to economic development and the fair and efficient distribution of aid and development finance. Sustained campaigns by international agencies focus public attention on corruption's consequences and, yet, corrupt practices remain the norm in many developing societies (see, for example, Chapter 4). Around the world, corruption is a remarkably salient political issue. In 2013, for example, WIN/Gallup International surveyed almost 70,000 people in 69 countries, and corruption was deemed the world's number one problem (Holmes, 2015: xii). In autumn 2014, the World Economic Forum and several collaborating institutions surveyed 1,089 people aged 18 to 34 in 102 countries. Of the respondents, 72 per cent agreed that 'corruption is holding my country back' and that 'corruption is causing lost opportunities for my generation'. Only 10 per cent agreed with the statement: 'Corruption is a necessary part of functioning in society.'[1] In the *American Economic Review*, David Benjamin and his colleagues (2014a–b) assembled 136 different attributes of wellbeing. They then asked individuals for their *tradeoffs* among pairs of these. Among all the public goods (or policies) rated by respondents, the most important contributor to people's wellbeing was 'freedom from corruption, injustice, and abuse of power in your country'.

Many elections feature corruption as a key issue, and protests against corruption are widespread. In early 2014, I asked Kasit Piromya, the former foreign minister of Thailand, how his Democrat Party could be opposed to democratic elections. 'What has been happening in Thailand during the past ten years,' he answered via email, 'is similar

---

[1]'The Impact of Corruption: Perspectives from Millennial Voices', available at: http://widgets. weforum.org/partnering-against-corruption-initiative/ (accessed 27 February 2017).

to Turkey, Tunisia, Egypt, Russia, Ukraine, Venezuela, etc., namely elected governments have become illiberal, abusive; using the argument of the majority voice to overcome and ignore the concept of check and balance, rule of law, independent media and judiciary.' Soon after, Thailand experienced a military coup, which the generals excused in part by the need to counter corruption.

Political leaders are also speaking loudly about the fight against corruption. In 2014, Chinese President Xi Jinping told a closed-door meeting of the Politburo that he is disregarding 'life, death and reputation' to combat corruption (Zhai, 2014). Bhutan is one of the least corrupt of the developing countries, yet its government perceives corruption as a threat. On 17 December 2014, King Jigme Khesar Namgyel Wangchuck focused his National Day Speech on the topic:

> The main aspiration of the people is that the 11th plan will succeed, and prosperity will grow all around the country. The realization of this goal depends more than ever on the government's commitment to good governance, which should include check and balance, openness and transparency … The highest probable risk to development that I foresee is corruption. Our national development efforts will be hindered by unchecked corruption … Corruption is unambiguous – there is no great or small corruption. And no one can be above the law:

Note one of the key costs of corruption that the King identified:

> But there is an even greater threat – ignoring corruption. When the corrupt are not held to account, those who observe due diligence, work hard and professionally are most likely to be discouraged. We mustn't allow the latter to lose morale by rewarding everyone indiscriminately, irrespective of his or her performance. That is why, corruption must be curtailed and, more than ever before, extraordinary service must be recognized and rewarded.

But what is it, exactly, that the King, President Xi and people around the world are talking about?

1. What is 'corruption'? Isn't the concept hopelessly diffuse? And isn't it culturally specific? In particular, isn't corruption a Western concept that ill fits the global South and East?
2. Second, how could we ever measure corruption? Since bribery is illegal and secretive, hard evidence about its extent and effects is episodic at best. And, again, doesn't Western bias enter? Many prevailing measures concern 'perceptions' of corruption. Whose perceptions? Westerners'?
3. Third, how harmful are various forms of corruption?
4. Finally, what can a president, a king or anyone else do about corruption?

WHAT IS CORRUPTION?

Almost all concepts that matter in the social and behavioural sciences, and in public policy, are latent and contestable. By 'latent', I mean something that we cannot directly measure. 'Contestable' means that people do not agree on definitions and, perhaps, never can. Almost all important concepts? Yes: just consider these. Mental health. Democracy. Economic development. Sustainability. Intelligence. Happiness. Even seemingly technical terms like 'unemployment', 'literacy' and 'poverty' are latent and contestable. Just after winning the 2015 Nobel Prize for Economics, Angus Deaton, an expert on poverty lines, said, 'Focusing on the number of people who are below the line is like chasing an [*sic*] unicorn through the woods' (Giuliagno, 2015).

So, with regard to corruption, let's not begin with an abstract definition. Let's start instead with real examples:

- A president wins an election thanks to fraud. His campaign and the fraud were importantly financed by organized crime.
- Procurement for road building is ostensibly competitive, but actually there is a parallel system where some unqualified firms can pay to be qualified, where losers in the competition can pay to be winners, and where after contracts are awarded, there are renegotiations that raise the price, dividing the increase between contractors and public officials. The cost of roads can rise by a third, and quality declines.
- Health systems for the rural poor involve practices such as having to pay for an eligibility card. Warehouses for duty-free pharmaceutical imports also contain massive amounts of television sets and cases of alcohol.
- When Congress builds an addition and does a renovation of another part, a Congress member's sibling gets the contract without competitive bidding, and each member gets a $5,000 gift.
- In another country, many Congress members are financed by organized crime – not only their campaigns, but also their votes on particular bills.
- The kinds and levels of public services are not decided by a professional civil service or by local votes but by local elites who have captured local governments. Contracts favour the elites, not the poor. In one country, health ID cards bear the picture of the local Congress-person.
- The police practise no-fault corruption. You were speeding; please pay the fine to me.
- The tax system features bribery (a lower tax in exchange for a bribe), extortion (pay me or I'll assess you more), theft, counterfeiting (phony certificates for cigarettes and alcohol), and nepotism (positions are bought).
- Hospital employees routinely practise extortion for things such as pain medication.
- School officials accept bribes, or demand them, for students to pass examinations.
- Customs bureaux let trucks pass uninspected, in exchange for an envelope full of cash.

Would each of us call each of these acts 'corruption'? Perhaps not. But in fact, most of these acts are illegal in most countries of the world, whatever their religion, culture or historical background.

These phenomena share common features. The authority of office is abused for illicit ends. Corruption classically referred to such things as 'the turning of the head' of a judge: instead of being blindfolded with a fair scale, the judge shifts her gaze and tips the scale toward the one who pays her a bribe. 'The core of the concept of a bribe,' writes Noonan (1984: xi), 'is an inducement improperly influencing the performance of a public function meant to be gratuitously exercised.'

Corruption can occur in government, business, civil society organizations and international agencies. Corruption goes beyond bribery to include nepotism, neglect of duty and favouritism. Corrupt acts can be internal to an organization (theft, embezzlement, some kinds of fraud) or involve parties outside the organization (in transactions with clients and citizens, such as extortion and bribery). Each of these varieties has the dimension of scale, from episodic to systemic.

Many typologies of corruption have been advanced. For example, Michael Johnston (2005) distinguishes four regimes of corruption: Influence Markets (including countries such as Germany, Japan and the USA); Elite Cartels (Botswana, Italy and Korea); Oligarchs and Clans (Mexico, the Philippines and Russia); and Official Moguls (China, Indonesia and Kenya).

At the broadest level, then, corruption is the misuse of office for unofficial ends. Office is a position of duty, or should be; the office-holder is supposed to put the interests of the institution first. A society deems that certain goods and services are not for sale but should be apportioned by need, merit, seniority, election or random allotment. Systemic corruption undermines duty, office, merit and democracy. It creates shells of institutions, full of official ranks and rules but hollow, cynical and ineffective.

What about those cultural differences? The propensities do vary over time and place; culture, class, education, even genes may play an explanatory role in these variations. But, this is not to say that corruption is differently defined or valued. As we shall see, structures of power, information and incentives lead to different equilibria, in which people pay bribes even when their personal values decry doing so. In fact, every religion condemns bribery. In fact, every country has laws against it. In fact, in most countries, large numbers of citizens and businesses are angry about corruption and the abuse of power.

MEASURING CORRUPTION

The sociologist Troy Duster once described social movements this way: 'No movement is as coherent and integrated as it seems from afar, and no movement is as incoherent and fractured as it seems from up close' (Duster, 1973: 7). His remark also applies to measures of 'corruption', 'rule of law' and 'governance'. Up close, the measures seem incoherent and fractured. Stepping back, though, they may appear coherent and integrated.

Incoherent and Fractured Up Close

Up close, the concepts and measures of corruption look complex, if not chaotic.

Conceptually, Rothstein and Teorell (2012) say that it has proven impossible to reach agreement on definitions of corruption, rule of law, government efficiency, normative and procedural fairness, etc. In his criticism of 'governance', Fukuyama (2013) notes that existing definitions confuse process, capacity, outcomes and autonomy.

Empirically, up close there are signs of chaos. During the past decade, Ciudadanos al Día, a Peruvian non-profit organization, has sponsored large-scale surveys of citizens to rate the quality of service and the corruption across Peruvian agencies, cities and hospitals. In 2013, it was found that 79 per cent of Peruvians believed that 'corruption has gained ground in the country'. Across agencies, an average of 70 per cent of respondents believed that the staff is not honest. And yet, only 4 per cent of respondents said they were asked to pay bribes. If 'corruption' does not refer to bribery, to what does it refer?[2]

Analyzing questions about governance-related issues (such as how long it takes to start a business or get a licence) in relevant surveys,[3] answers given by firms do not coincide. Firms' responses in Enterprise Surveys reveal 'massive variance across firms', which may reflect corruption and 'favoured firms'. This variation is said to undercut the meaningfulness of the Doing Business country averages and rankings (Hallward-Driemeier and Pritchett, 2011).

Consider the example of Norway. Its national measures of governance are superb, including world-class political rights and civil liberties, strong rule of law, effective bureaucracy and low corruption. Yet, the five-year Norwegian Study of Power and Democracy revealed how Norwegians disparage the quality of their government institutions (Haugsvær and Eckmann, 2003; Ringen, 2004). How can macro-measures and micro-perceptions differ so radically?

The challenges of concept and measurement are exacerbated when cultural differences are considered. For example, does the word 'corruption' mean the same thing in Mauritania as in Mexico or Myanmar? Do 'impartiality' and 'fairness' mean the same thing in cultures characterized by differences in Geert Hofstede's cultural measures such as individualistic-collectivistic or power distance?[4] These rhetorical questions seem to lead to only one answer: 'No.'

Coherent and Integrated from Afar

Stepping back, much of the apparent chaos dissipates, but new puzzles arise. Condemning corruption is virtually universal. No culture or religion endorses corruption.[5] All governments have laws against bribery, extortion and related practices. Anthropological

---

[2]Boza (2013), a founder of Ciudadanos al Día, hypothesises that what Peruvians mean by corruption is not limited to bribery. When government employees use their monopoly power and discretion to avoid providing proper public services, she says, this is perceived as an 'abuse of power' and 'dishonesty', and then equated to corruption. 'When a public entity offers a service monopolistically and is the only entity that can make the changes to offer the service in better conditions, not to do so is to use inadequately the power that this institution has received to offer the service. And this improper use of power is perceived by citizens as evidence of dishonesty. It is dishonest for a public servant to have accepted a job that he does not know how to fulfill or does not want to fulfill. And this dishonesty on the part of the public servant, in the mind of the citizen who is not thinking of a legal or penal concept, is an act of corruption' (author's translation, p. 30).

[3]World Bank Enterprise Survey (www.enterprisesurveys.org) and World Bank Doing Business Survey (www.doingbusiness.org/rankings) (both accessed 27 February 2017)..

[4]Geert Hofstede. See: http://geert-hofstede.com (accessed 27 February 2017).

[5]For example, the Malaysian sociologist Syed Hussein Alatas (1968), argued strenuously against the Western idea that non-Westerners accept corruption for cultural reasons. His book provided copious evidence of concern about the abuse of public office in Muslim and Chinese cultural traditions.

studies in Bangladesh, Ghana and the Philippines show that peasants understand well the difference between a gift and a bribe – and they loathe the latter.

Across cultures and countries, different measures of concepts such as corruption, rule of law, impartiality and efficiency turn out to be well behaved in terms of statistical criteria such as coherence and stability. Importantly, most of the measures turn out to be highly correlated. For example, at the country level, the bivariate correlations among three widely used measures – Transparency International's Corruption Perceptions Index (CPI) and the World Bank's Rule of Law Index and Government Effectiveness Index – exceed 0.90, which is about as high as correlations between imperfect social science measures can be. The CPI is correlated 0.91 with a composite of three quality-of-government indicators of the PRS Group's *International Country Risk Guide* (ICRG) (PRS Group, 2012).

High correlations also exist among very different country-level measures. In 2013, the International Finance Corporation's Ease of Doing Business aggregate measure was correlated 0.83 with the World Economic Forum's Global Competitiveness Index (GCI). Although these two measures do not directly gauge governance or corruption, they correlate highly with the CPI, the World Bank's Worldwide Governance Indicators and the three ICRG indicators. For example, the GCI rating turns out to be correlated 0.84 with the CPI and 0.84 with the combination of three ICRG measures.

Text Box 10.1   Measures of Corruption

A number of researchers and groups have recently developed new measures of corruption and the quality of governance. Remarkably, they turn out to correlate highly with the existing measures, as discussed below.

Impartiality

Rothstein and Teorell (2012) have criticized existing measures of governance and corruption as theoretically ungrounded. In response, they and their colleagues developed a new measure of 'impartiality' in government. After a multi-year data collection effort, their measure turns out to correlate over 0.86 with existing measures of good governance such as the CPI and the various World Bank Worldwide Governance Indicators.

Rule of Law Index

The World Justice Project (WJP) decomposes the rule of law into eight concepts: absence of corruption; constraints on government powers; open government; fundamental rights; order and security; regulatory enforcement; civil justice; and criminal justice (World Justice Project, 2015). These eight are, in turn, disaggregated into 47 'sub-factors'. The WJP carried out two surveys in countries around the world, one of the public and another of local legal experts. The most recent iteration surveyed over 100,000 respondents and 2,400 respondents in 102 countries.

It turns out that the WJP's dimensions of the rule of law are highly intercorrelated, despite their conceptual differences and wide variety of measures. This was revealed

(Continued)

(Continued)

in an outside 'statistical audit' of an earlier year's results, which found that the WJP's dimensions:

> share a single latent factor that captures 81% of the total variance. This latter result could be used as a statistical justification for aggregating further the nine [the previous version included informal justice] dimensions into a single index by using a weighted arithmetic average. (Saisana and Saltelli, 2012: 2)

Two other new measures go beyond perceptions to more objective indicators.

Public Administration Corruption Index (PACI)

Escresa and Picci (2015) painstakingly created another new measure of corruption across countries. Their Public Administration Corruption Index (PACI) is based on the geographic distribution of public officials involved in cross-border corruption. The index examines 816 cross-border corruption cases pursued between 1998 and 2012 by courts in Germany and the USA with 122 foreign countries. Various ways to compute the PACI have rank correlations between 0.80 to 0.93. The log of the authors' preferred version of the PACI turns out to be correlated over 0.85 with both the Transparency International Corruption Perceptions Index and the World Bank's Control of Corruption Index.

'Letter grades'

Chong et al. (2014) mailed letters to non-existent business addresses in 159 countries (10 per country, 2 to each of the five largest cities). They measured whether the letters came back to the return address in the USA and, if so, how long it took. They argued that their results 'provide new objective indicators of government efficiency across countries, based on a simple and universal service' (ibid.: 277).

Their new indicators turn out to be significantly correlated with 25 existing measures of the quality of government: '[I]t is "better" governments – more democratic, more accountable, less corrupt – that perform better on returning letters, even if we hold per capita income constant' (ibid.: 385). The authors observe: 'Interestingly, when we conduct the principal components analysis that includes our postal variables and several other measures of quality,[6] only the first principal component is significant. It appears that the quality of government is driven by a one factor model' (ibid., 2012: 5–6).

Index of Public Integrity (IPI)

In 2016, this new index was released for 105 countries. It combines expert judgements and objective indicators across six categories: judicial independence; 'administrative burden'; trade openness; budget transparency; 'e-citizenship'; and freedom of the press. The resulting IPI turns out to be correlated 0.89 with the 2014 CPI (Mungiu-Pippidi and Dadašov, 2016: 17).

---

[6]Such as the Property Rights Index (Heritage Foundation), the Doing Business Rank, the government effectiveness score (Worldwide Governance Indicators, World Bank), the Infrastructure Quality Index (World Economic Forum), the ICRG Corruption Index and the Democracy Index (Polity IV).

Despite the chaos from up close, measures of corruption, good governance and competitiveness are highly correlated at the national level. These measures are capturing something at the national level that has important statistical associations: they also correlate strongly with development outcomes.

HOW HARMFUL IS CORRUPTION?

Some of the older scholarly literature, whose main points are sometimes heard today, noted that corruption might not be negatively related to development outcomes. 'What is the problem about corruption?' was the title of a 1965 article by Colin Leys (1965). With reasoning reminiscent of Robert Merton or Niccolò Machiavelli, Leys' answer was that corruption is not much of a problem for development. Leys noted that corruption has its functions, sometimes even its benefits. Under awful conditions, bribery may be socially, not just privately, beneficial. A few years later, Samuel Huntington noted: 'In terms of economic growth the only thing worse than a society with a rigid, over-centralized, dishonest bureaucracy is one with a rigid, over-centralized, honest bureaucracy' (1968: 386). For years, it was impermissible to mention corruption in dialogues between countries. Even researchers shied away, in what Gunnar Myrdal in the 1960s called 'diplomacy in research' (Myrdal, 1968).[7] Myrdal recounted the excuses used by South Asians and Westerners to avoid taking corruption seriously – excuses that are still occasionally heard today, around the world.[8]

However, by the late 1980s, informed by theory, case studies and quantitative research, corruption's many costs had become clear (Klitgaard, 1988: chapter 2). Later research has elaborated how systemic corruption distorts incentives, undermines institutions and redistributes wealth and power to the undeserving (see, for example, OECD, 2014; Runde et al., 2014). Corruption

---

[7]'The taboo on research on corruption is, indeed, one of the most flagrant examples of this general bias ... [which] is basically to be explained in terms of a certain condescension on the part of Westerners' (Myrdal, 1968: 938).

[8]Corruption:

> is rationalised, when challenged, by certain sweeping assertions: that there is corruption in all countries (this notion, eagerly advanced by students indigenous to the region, neglects the relative prevalence of corruption in South Asia and its specific effects in that social setting); that corruption is natural in South Asian countries because of deeply ingrained institutions and attitudes carried over from colonial and pre-colonial times (this primarily Western contention should, of course, provide an approach to research and a set of hypotheses, not an excuse for ignoring the problem); that corruption is needed to oil the intricate machinery of business and politics in South Asian countries and is, perhaps, not a liability given the conditions prevailing there (again, this mainly Western hypothesis about the functioning of the economic and social system should underline, rather than obviate, the need for research): that there is not as much corruption as implied by the public outcry in the South Asian countries (this claim needs to be substantiated, and if it is true, the causes and effects of the outcry should be investigated). These excuses, irrelevant and transparently thin as they are, are more often expressed in conversation than in print. (Myrdal, in Heidenheimer and Johnston, 2001: 266–7)

undercuts democracy and decentralization; it erodes public services and reinforces personalism (Holmberg et al., 2009; Wright, 2010). Not always, but usually, corruption erodes incentives to invest and slows economic progress.[9] Corruption undercuts trust: 'Since social trust is an important intrinsic value (personal happiness, optimism about the future) and also has a political value (support for fair institutions, minority rights, tolerance, etc.) and an economic value (its positive relation to individual earnings and aggregate economic growth), it may be that dysfunctional government institutions are the worst social ill of all' (Rothstein, 2011: 162).

New research links fighting corruption and improving government efficiency[10] to increases in citizens' expressed wellbeing.[11] Helliwell et al. (2014) carried out an econometric analysis of a panel of 157 countries, using a variety of estimation techniques:

> The new results are able to show not just that people are more satisfied with their lives in countries having better governance quality, but also that actual changes in governance quality since 2005 have led to large changes in the quality of life. This provides much stronger evidence that governance quality can be changed, and that these changes have much larger effects than those flowing simply through a more productive economy. For example, the ten most-improved countries, in terms of delivery quality changes between 2005 and 2012, when compared to the ten countries with most worsened [sic] delivery quality, are estimated to have thereby increased average life evaluations by as much as would be produced by a 40% increase in per capita incomes. When we explain changes in average life evaluations over the 2005 to 2012 period, just as much was explained by changes in governance quality as by changes in GDP, even though some of the well-being benefits of better governance are delivered through increases in economic efficiency and hence GDP per capita. Our new results thus confirm that quality of governance affects lives via many channels beyond those captured by GDP per capita, and also that important improvements can be achieved within policy-relevant time horizons. (Ibid.: 4)

So, aggregated national measures of corruption and governance have practical and theoretical importance. The high correlations among measures of such different provenance undercut the view that corruption cannot be measured, that perceptions of corruption are unreliable and biased, that aggregated data are meaningless.

---

[9]Wei (2000) calculated that reducing the level of perceived corruption in Mexico to that in Singapore would have the equivalent effect on investment as lowering the tax rate by over 20 percentage points. Lambsdorff (2003) estimated that improving Colombia's perceived 'level of integrity' to that of the United Kingdom would increase net yearly capital inflows by 3 per cent of GDP. In the Middle East and North Africa, 'improved governance institutions [including political rights, civil liberties, and corruption and bureaucratic quality] would greatly stimulate private investment'. An improvement of one standard deviation 'would ... boost private investment by 3.5% of GDP per year' (Aysan et al., 2007: 446).

[10]The measure used was the country's average on four measures from the World Bank's Worldwide Governance Indicators: government effectiveness, regulatory quality, rule of law, control of corruption.

[11]The data come from the annual Gallup World Polls and represent the country's mean response to this question: 'Please imagine a ladder, with steps numbered from 0 at the bottom to 10 at the top. The top of the ladder represents the best possible life for you and the bottom of the ladder represents the worst possible life for you. On which step of the ladder would you say you personally feel you stand at this time?'

What is true, however, is that national-level scores on governance indices, just like national-level data on income or employment or carbon emissions, are limited in meaning and usefulness. Many policies demand finer geographic discrimination, as well as the examination of relevant subgroups (age, industry, ethnicity and more). Using governance indices to monitor progress, just as with other outcome measures, should control for factors beyond a responsible entity's control that affect the outcome. A general theory of choosing and using performance measures enters here (Klitgaard et al., 2005).

WHAT CAN BE DONE?

Some people, tired of corruption and endless chatter about it, may rightly wonder if change is even possible. Why would politicians ever want to reform corrupt institutions or systems? Politicians are ready to move when several forces converge. Expanding opportunities for international trade, investment and financing mean that lagging countries will lose investment opportunities. International institutions pressure for change. Emerging industries that depend on fast-moving knowledge and innovative styles breed young entrepreneurs with little tolerance for corrupt practices. Finally, anti-corruption is a major force behind popular unrest in countries as diverse as Brazil, Greece, Guatemala, Honduras, India, Iraq, Kazakhstan, Kenya, Lebanon, Malaysia, Mexico, Moldova, Romania, South Africa, Sri Lanka, Thailand, Tunisia, Turkey, Ukraine and Venezuela.

In my experience, many new presidents, governors, ministers and mayors are eager to reduce corruption. They know that corruption is constraining development. What government leaders need is help that recognizes that corruption is a system that needs a hard-headed, politically tuned strategy. Politicians must see that fighting corruption can help them win elections as well as advance their economies. Here there is good news. Even in very corrupt settings, corruption can be reduced, leading to greater investment and public satisfaction. And the success stories exhibit some common principles, regardless of cultural setting.

'Success' means significant improvement in governance measures, followed by increases in investment and improvements in public services. Success is always incomplete, and the risk of corruption re-emerging is always a threat. The success stories range from classic cases such as Singapore and Hong Kong, China (Klitgaard, 1988) to more recent examples of progress such as Colombia, Georgia, the Philippines, Qatar and Rwanda (ibid., 2015). Some would include Indonesia, which moved in the first decade of the twenty-first century from about the 6th percentile to the 40th percentile on the Corruption Perceptions Index, and Malaysia, despite the personal travails of Prime Minister Najib Razak. A number of cities have also made impressive progress against corruption. Case studies exist for Bogotá and Medellín, Colombia; Campo Elias, Venezuela; Naga City, the Philippines; La Paz, Bolivia; and Mandaue, the Philippines (Devlin and Chaskel, 2010a–b; González de Asís, 2000; Puatu, 2012; Klitgaard et al., 2000; Mahoney and Klitgaard, 2016). Craiova, Romania, and Martin, Slovak Republic, won the United Nations Public Service Awards in 2011 for their reforms against corruption (Transparency International, 2011).[12] The remarkable collection of cases at Princeton's Innovations for Successful Societies contains many examples of fighting corruption. None of these successes is perfect; progress means improvement, not eradication. For example, Qatar and Rwanda have been praised for reducing corruption but criticized for favouritism and a lack of transparency (Mungiu-Pippidi et al., 2014). In some cases, subsequent administrations reversed many of the anti-corruption policies, which led to the re-emergence of corruption (Klitgaard et al., 2000; Klitgaard, 2013). Like inflation, success by one government or central bank in quelling corruption does not guarantee that another administration's policies will not rekindle it.

WHAT SUCCESSFUL STRATEGIES SHARE

Successful strategies are consistent with some economic principles (Klitgaard, 1988). Corruption is an economic crime, not a crime of passion. Givers and takers of bribes respond to economic incentives and punishments; corruption follows a formula: $C = M + D - A$. Corruption equals monopoly plus discretion minus accountability. To reduce corruption, limit monopoly and enhance competition. Circumscribe official discretion, and clarify the rules of the game. Enhance accountability about processes and results in many ways, including citizen- and business-driven scorecards for government agencies and programmes.

Lessons can also be discerned about the politics of anti-corruption. Undermine political equilibria dominated by powerful interests that benefit from systemic corruption. Fry big fish. Diagnose and subvert corrupt systems (Klitgaard, 2006). Do a few things that can show results in six months, to build momentum. Don't try to do everything at once.

Here are two more lessons for reformers. Don't think of corruption primarily as a legal or moral issue. In very corrupt countries, new laws, codes of conduct and better training for public officials will, alas, make little difference. Second, think of collaboration across the public–private–nonprofit divide. Business and civil society can play key roles. They are part of corrupt systems, stuck in a corrupt equilibrium. To get out, they have to be given ways to expose corruption without taking personal risks. Ipaidabribe.com in India is a promising example. Successful partnerships, such as Ciudadanos al Día in Peru and the Bangalore Agenda Task Force in India, exploit credible information supplied by NGOs and the pressure, resources and technical expertise of the business community.

CONCLUSION: AN OPTIMISTIC PREDICTION

The final word goes to John T. Noonan, author of *Bribes* (1984), the best book ever written on corruption. He concludes this magisterial tome with a prediction about corruption:

---

[12]See: 'How Martin Became Transparent and Won a UN Public Service Award', Space for Transparency blog, Transparency International, 18 May 2011. Available at: http://blog.trans parency.org/2011/05/18/how-martin-became-transparent-won-a-un-public-service-award/ (accessed 3 April 2017).

As slavery was once a way of life and now … has become obsolete and is incomprehensible, so the practice of bribery in the central form of the exchange of payment for official action will become obsolete. (Noonan, 1984: 706)

Slavery persists in many forms but it can no longer be considered morally acceptable. Noonan says that the moral condemnation of corruption will grow, for four reasons:

- Bribery is shameful. (In all cultures.)
- Bribery is a sell-out to the rich. (And no one wants plutocracy.)
- Bribery is a betrayal of trust, which is 'a precious necessity of every social enterprise' (ibid.: 704).
- Bribery violates a divine paradigm.

Noonan argues that our collective repulsion will eventually change practice and render corruption extinct. *How* that will happen, Noonan leaves to the machinery of history.

As we have seen, many people around the world join Noonan in condemning corruption. But Noonan's prediction will not be realized without determined effort. To eliminate corruption, we need practical, feasible strategies to do such things as weed out monopolies, increase accountability, align incentives, create coordinated government approaches, enlist the cooperation of businesses and civil society and empower the public to expose corrupt practices. And, perhaps to make progress on these practical, locally tailored steps, we need to bracket for a moment some of the debates over definitions, measures and estimates of harmfulness. The challenge for development practitioners is a complex one, that is to shape law and governance at the national/local level while recognizing the limits of formal legal means, and at the same time to encourage indigenous modes of knowing and challenging corruption.

Questions for Discussion

1 For development practice, how would you define 'corruption'?
2 Are development practitioners potentially as capable of behaving corruptly as politicians, government officials and corporate executives?
3 If you encountered corruption in a development NGO, how would you apply the principles in this chapter in the diagnosis and care?

📖 FURTHER READING

Holmes, L. (2015) *Corruption: A Very Short Introduction.* Oxford and New York: Oxford University Press.

Klitgaard, R. (2015) *Addressing Corruption Together.* Paris: OECD.

Wright, J. (2010) 'Aid Effectiveness and the Politics of Personalism', *Comparative Political Studies,* 43(6): 735–62.

REFERENCES

Alatas, S.H. (1968) *The Sociology of Corruption: The Nature, Function, Causes and Prevention of Corruption.* Singapore: D. Moore Press.

Aysan, A.F., Nabil, M.K. and Véganzonès-Varoudakis, M.-A. (2007) 'Governance, Institutions, and Private Investment: An Application to the Middle East and North Africa', in M. K. Nabli (ed.), *Breaking the Barriers to Higher Economic Growth: Better Governance and Deeper Reforms in the Middle East and North Africa.* Washington, DC: World Bank, pp. 423–464.

Benjamin, D.J., Heffetz, O., Kimball, M.S. and Rees-Jones, A. (2014a) 'Can Marginal Rates of Substitution be Inferred from Happiness Data? Evidence from Residency Choices', *American Economic Review*, 104(11): 498–528.

Benjamin, D.J., Heffetz, O., Kimball, M.S. and Szembrot, N. (2014b) 'Beyond Happiness and Satisfaction: Toward Well-Being Indices Based on Stated Preference', *American Economic Review*, 104(9): 698–735.

Boza, B. (2013) *Manual CAD de Anticorrupción.* Lima: Ciudadanos al Día.

Chong, A., La Porta, R., Lopez-de-Silanes, F. and Andrei, S. (2012) 'Letter Grading Government Efficiency', NBER Working Paper 18268 (August). Available at: http://cdi.mecon.gov.ar/doc/nber/w18268.pdf (accessed 1 July 2016).

Chong, A., La Porta, R., Lopez-de-Silanes, F. and Andrei, S. (2014) 'Letter Grading Government Efficiency', *Journal of the European Economic Association*, 1(2): 277–99.

Devlin, M. and Chaskel, S. (2010a) *Conjuring and Consolidating a Turnaround: Governance in Bogota, 1992–2003.* Princeton, NJ: Innovations for Successful Societies, Princeton University.

Devlin, M. and Chaskel, S. (2010b) 'From Fear to Hope in Colombia: Sergio Fajardo and Medellín, 2004–2007'. Princeton, NJ: Innovations for Successful Societies, Princeton University, December.

Duster, T. (1973) 'Introduction', in G. Napper, *Blacker than Thou: The Struggle for Campus Unity.* Grand Rapids, MI: Eerdmans, pp. 1–7.

Escresa, L. and Picci, L. (2015) 'A New Cross-National Measure of Corruption', *World Bank Economic Review*, 24 July. Available at: doi: http://dx.doi.org/10.1093/wber/lhv031.

Fukuyama, F. (2013) 'What is Governance?', *Governance*, 26(3): 347–68.

Giuliagno, F. (2015) 'Nobel Prize Winner Angus Deaton Shares 3 Big Ideas', *Financial Times*, 12 October. Available at: www.ft.com/intl/cms/s/0/b60c2e76-70f0-11e5-ad6d-f4ed76f0900a.html#axzz423eMMu8n (accessed 1 July 2016).

González de Asís, M. (2000) 'Reducing Corruption: Lessons from Venezuela', PREM Note, No. 39. Washington, DC: World Bank. Available at: http://siteresources.worldbank.org/INTWBIGOVANTCOR/Resources/premnote39.pdf (accessed 1 July 2016).

Hallward-Driemeier, M. and Pritchett, L. (2011) 'How Business is Done and the "Doing Business" Indicators: The Investment Climate when Firms Have Climate Control', *Policy Research Working Paper.* Washington, DC: World Bank.

Haugsvær, S. and Eckmann, C.B. (2003) 'Main Conclusions of the Norwegian Study on Power and Democracy', August. Paris: OECD. Available at: www.oecd.org/norway/33800474.pdf (accessed 1 July 2016).

Heidenheimer, A. and Johnston, M. (eds) (2001) *Political Corruption: Concepts and Contexts*. New Brunswick, NJ: Transaction Publishers.

Helliwell, J.F., Huang, H., Grover, S. and Wang, S. (2014) 'Good Governance and National Well-Being: What are the Linkages?', *OECD Working Papers on Public Governance*, No. 25. Paris: OECD Publishing. Available at: http://dx.doi.org/10.1787/5jxv9f651hvj-en. (accessed 1 July 2016).

Holmberg, S., Rothstein, B. and Nasiritousi, N. (2009) 'Quality of Government: What You Get', *Annual Review of Political Science*, 12: 135–61.

Holmes, L. (2015) *Corruption: A Very Short Introduction*. Oxford and New York: Oxford University Press.

Huntington, S.P. (1968) *Political Order in Changing Societies*. New Haven, CT: Yale University Press.

Johnston, M. (2005) *Syndromes of Corruption: Wealth, Power, and Democracy*. Cambridge and New York: Cambridge University Press.

Klitgaard, R. (1988) *Controlling Corruption*. Berkeley and Los Angeles, CA: University of California Press.

Klitgaard, R. (2006) 'Subverting Corruption', *Global Crime*, 7(3–4): 299–307. Also in *Finance & Development*, 37(2), June 2000.

Klitgaard, R. (2013) *Tropical Gangsters II: Adventures in Development in the World's Poorest Places*. KDP Select Books. Available at: www.amazon.com/Tropical-Gangsters-II-Adventures-Development-ebook/dp/B00C9GEQ58 (accessed 1 July 2016).

Klitgaard, R. (2015) *Addressing Corruption Together*. Paris: OECD.

Klitgaard, R., Fedderke, J.W. and Akramov, K.A. (2005) 'Choosing and Using Performance Criteria', in R. Klitgaard and P.C. Light (eds), *High-Performance Government: Structure, Leadership, Incentives*. Santa Monica, CA: Rand Corporation, pp. 407–46. Available at: www.cgu.edu/include/MG256-ch14.pdf (accessed 1 July 2016).

Klitgaard, R., MacLean-Abaroa, R. and Parris, H.L. (2000) *Corrupt Cities: A Practical Guide to Cure and Prevention*. ICS Press and World Bank Institute. Available at: http://wwwwds.worldbank.org/servlet/WDSContentServer/IW3P/IB/2000/10/07/000094 946_00092605362082/Rendered/PDF/multi_page.pdf (accessed 1 July 2016).

Lambsdorff, J.G. (2003) 'How Corruption Affects Persistent Capital Flows', *Economics of Governance*, 4: 229–43.

Leys, C. (1965) 'What is the Problem about Corruption?' *Journal of Modern African Studies*, 3(2): 215–30.

Mahoney, M. and Klitgaard, R. (2016) 'From Reform to Implementation: Mandaue, the Philippines', two-part case study, Claremont Graduate University, CA.

Mungiu-Pippidi, A. and Dadašov, R. (2016) 'Measuring Control of Corruption by a New Index of Public Integrity', *European Journal on Criminal Policy and Research*, 22(3): 1–24. First online: 27 July.

Mungiu-Pippidi, A. (ed.) (2014) *The Anticorruption Frontline*. The ANTICORRP Project, Vol. 2. Opladen, Berlin and Toronto: Barbara Budrich Publishers. Available at: www.budrichverlag.de/upload/files/artikel/00001003_010.pdf?SID=26b2da27bfe 338432130d2e09ea406c2 (accessed 1 July 2016).

Myrdal, G. (1968) *Asian Drama: An Enquiry into the Poverty of Nations, Vol. 2*. New York: Twentieth Century.

Noonan, J.T., Jr. (1984) *Bribes*. New York: Macmillan.

OECD (2014) 'The Rationale for Fighting Corruption', Brief, CleanGovBiz. Paris: OECD. Available at: www.oecd.org/cleangovbiz/49693613.pdf (accessed 1 July 2016).

PRS Group (2012) 'International Country Risk Guide Methodology'. East Syracuse, NY: PRS Group, Inc. Available at: www.prsgroup.com/wp content/uploads/2012/11/icrgmethodology.pdf (accessed 1 July 2016).

Puatu, A.K.S. (2012) 'Community Capacity Building and Local Government Leadership: Describing Transformational Leadership Practices, Naga City, the Philippines', in K. Miyoshi, Y. Okabe and C.L. Banyai (eds), *Community Capacity and Rural Development*. Kyushu International Center, Japan International Cooperation Agency and Ritsumeikan Asia Pacific University. Available at: www.apu.ac.jp/rcaps/uploads/fckeditor/publications/journal/RJAPS_V28_Ana.pdf (accessed 1 July 2016).

Ringen, S. (2004) 'Wealth and Decay: Norway Funds a Massive Political Self- Examination – and Finds Trouble for All', *Times Literary Supplement*, 13 February.

Rothstein, B. (2011) *The Quality of Government: Corruption, Social Trust, and Inequality in International Perspective*. Chicago, IL, and London: University of Chicago Press.

Rothstein, B., and Teorell, J. (2012) 'Defining and Measuring Quality of Government', in S. Holmberg and B. Rothstein (eds), *Good Government: The Relevance of Political Science*. Cheltenham: Edward Elgar, pp. 13–39.

Runde, D.F., Hameed, S. and Magpile, J. (2014) *The Costs of Corruption: Strategies for Ending a Tax on Private Sector-Led Growth*. Washington, DC: Center for Strategic and International Studies. Available at: http://csis.org/files/publication/140204_Hameed_CostsOfCorruption_Web.pdf (accessed 1 July 2016).

Saisana, M. and Saltelli, A. (2012) 'The World Justice Project: Rule of Law Index Statistical Audit', World Justice Project. Available at: http://worldjusticeproject.org/sites/default/files/statistical_audit.pdf (accessed 1July 2016).

Wei, S.-J. (2000) 'How Taxing is Corruption on International Investors?', *Review of Economics and Statistics*, 82(1): 1–11. Available at: http://users.nber.org/~wei/data/wei2000a/wei2000a.pdf (accessed 1 July 2016).

World Justice Project (2015) *WJP Rule of Law Index 2015*. Washington, DC: World Justice Project.

Wright, J. (2010) 'Aid Effectiveness and the Politics of Personalism', *Comparative Political Studies*, 43(6): 735–62.

Zhai, K. (2014) 'Xi's "Shockingly Harsh" Politburo Speech Signals Tensions over Anti-Graft Crackdown', *South China Morning Post*, 5 August. Available at: www.scmp.com/news/china/article/1567026/xis-shockingly-harsh-politburo-speech-signals-tensions-over-anti-graft?page=all (accessed 1 July 2016).

PART III
NEW MODELS OF PRACTICE

11

ENVIRONMENTALLY SUSTAINABLE DEVELOPMENT IN PRACTICE

ANIL HIRA

INTRODUCTION

Denzau and North (1994: 3) stress that 'uncertainty, not risk, characterizes choice making'. Under such conditions, mental models are constructed to create heuristics for decision-making to summarize learning for the next instance. The heuristics morph into ideas, ideologies and cultural perspectives, including 'myths, dogmas, and taboos' as they become shared. This ensures divergence in the inputs for rational decision-making.

Postmodernists such as Michel Foucault go much further, suggesting that a discourse or conversation occurs around major issues in society over time. The discourse has an essentially artificial nature, used by the powerful to construct social relations and ideologies that help to maintain their position. Reality for these authors, then, is essentially subjective. Foucault (1966) uses the examples of the varying definitions of insanity, criminality and sexuality to illustrate his points. They would certainly reject the Denzau and North approach that subjectivity only enters in to the point of helping one to learn from uncertain and dynamic situations.

In my own work (Hira, 2015), I point to examples of human decision-making that defy Denzau and North's approach, such as prolonged conflict or credit card debt. Even in the most charitable light, there is no uncertainty that humans are making irrational decisions. However, unlike the postmodernists, I posit that there are evolutionary roots that create patterns to explain such behaviour. The three key explanations lie in understanding hierarchy (power), emotions and group think.

In this chapter, we will explore sustainable development discourse and practice over time. The three approaches noted above will all shed light on the complexities involved in what would seem to be a straightforward concept, and thereby explain why policy action towards sustainability has been so challenging.

SUSTAINABLE DEVELOPMENT – BIRTH AND GROWTH OF A CONCEPT

Treasuring the environment is nothing new. Some religions, such as Japanese Shinto, and cultures, such as that of native Americans, worshipped nature for centuries before the term sustainable development was ever heard. Love for the environment is also part of modern Western culture. Isaac Walton wrote the book *The Compleat Angler* about fishing conservation in 1640. The settling of the USA is replete with a love of nature, from Thoreau's famous *Walden* to the development of modern conservation efforts by President Theodore Roosevelt in the early 1900s. In sum, arguably the ideas behind sustainable development have deep evolutionary roots, a recognition of both the beauty and the vitality of nature for our preservation, from weather affecting harvests to our own health. But vitality also entails the fact that for most of human history nature was not experienced as a natural preserve of beauty but as a threat to our livelihood, directly through danger during a hunt or indirectly through pestilence of crops. Thus, from an evolutionary perspective, we naturally have a contradictory approach to nature.

The 1987 UN Report *Our Common Future* by the Brundtland Commission (WCED, 1987), also known as the Brundtland Report, attempted to link environmental issues with economic costs. First, environmental stresses can be linked to direct economic costs. For instance, deforestation leads to soil erosion and negative effect on rivers and lakes. Second, economic policies can be linked to direct environmental costs. For example coal-based energy generation leads to greenhouse gas emissions and climate change. Third, environmental and economic problems are also interconnected with political and social issues, such as population growth and environment. Fourth, these linkages are not only local, but also global. In short, the Commission attempted to make the connections between environment, economy and society which in turn leads to the synergy between traditional economic 'development' and environmental 'sustainability' together creating a new model of development which is 'sustainable development' (Baker, 2006).

We also see the uncertainty and discourse aspects of sustainable development. The concept has morphed over time. Egelston (2013: 26) suggests that there are at least 57 different uses of the term sustainable development. She traces the first use of the term to the Stockholm environmental conference in 1972; however, it morphed to include both environmental preservation and basic human needs by the time of the Brundtland Report. That document set out the idea that there are natural limits to economic growth, echoing the Malthusian approaches to population growth that became re-popularized in the 1970s, such as *The Population Bomb* (Ehrlich, 1968). Yet, one of the most commonly used definitions of sustainable development, to ensure that needs of the present are met without compromising those of the future, as coined by the same Brundtland Commission, papers over its contradiction with natural limits. Such documents and the current discourse push the idea that environmental preservation and raising of standards of living of a world population that could reach 11 billion by 2050 are quite compatible, a convenient but questionable premise, revealing the somewhat artificial nature of sustainable development as might be posed by postmodernists.

Despite the pretence towards convergence after Brundtland, sustainable development remains an elusive concept. For example, sustainable development (SD) is sometimes used to include factors outside of environmental preservation and standards of living (generally posed as 'social wellbeing'). These variously include political and financial sustainability. Political sustainability is generally used to discuss the need for more participatory, i.e. grassroots, decision-making. This has been a largely unsuccessful attempt to move SD out of the technocratic realm in which it thrives and into discussions about global justice. The issue is a lot more tangled in practice than the tendency to accept the principles that the world should be just and the environment preserved (Lélé, 1991). What exactly entails participatory development and how it is to be promoted are largely unresolved questions, reflecting another central contradiction, namely that the international organizations who are the main promoters of SD are funded and made up by states as member organizations, and therefore constitutionally apolitical. Financial sustainability is a lot more easily put into practice by international organizations, such as the World Bank, where it is part of their mission statement (2013). It figures largely in terms of the post-Cold War period of shrinking aid budgets and results-based management, to show measureable results and cost recovery from aid projects to sceptical policymakers with competing domestic priorities.

Furthermore, the axis of growth vs. preservation itself creates a variety of potential equilibria as Denzau and North would put it, around possible solutions. Ulrich Beck's (1992) famous work on modernity suggests that uncertainty and risk go together. In regard to modern technology, whether nuclear energy (Chernobyl), genetically modified organisms, or, in this case, climate change, new technology outpaces our ability to calculate risks. Moreover, both environmentalists and those concerned with population growth suggest that there are limits to the 'carrying capacity' of the Earth (Arrow et al., 1995). Others are optimistic about the ability to find balanced growth. Authors who discuss the 'environmental Kuznets curve', suggest that as economic growth continues environmental preservation and sustainability become increasingly important as income increases; yet other authors challenge whether such a trajectory actually exists (Stern, 2004). Even aside from predicting outcomes or stable patterns of growth and preservation, mainstream economists are confident that a property rights and trading regime that allows for appropriate valuation and preservation of the environment while using modified market forces can be created (Conrad et al., 2005). On the other side are ecological economists such as the celebrated Herman Daly (1996), who call for a complete revision of economics to consider sustainable use of resources. Daly's principles include the ideas that waste products should be limited to the absorptive capacity of the environment; harvest rates for renewable resources should be limited to levels where they are not depleted; and for non-renewable resources, depletion should follow the rate at which substitutes can be developed. These are forward-looking principles but difficult to operationalize.

The COP21 Paris Agreement reached in 2016 perhaps marks a turning point from the benign interpretation of the growth-preservation axis. For the first time, countries voluntarily agreed to reduce emissions, requiring moving towards renewable resources as well as likely reductions in consumption, or at least, more costly consumption. Moreover, the agreement recognized the fundamentally distinct places that Northern and Southern countries occupy on the growth-preservation axis. However, enforcement, which must be completed by individual countries, in a time of political tumult related to economic unease, remains fraught as we discuss below.

SUSTAINABLE DEVELOPMENT IN PRACTICE

A new database of international environmental agreements (www.iea.uoregon.edu) demonstrates that, notwithstanding the conceptual confusion, activity at a bilateral level dates back at least to 1351 and at a multilateral level to 1857. Agreements in the pre-1970s period tend to centre around specific areas of concern, such as whaling rights and phytosanitary regulations. The number of agreements picks up after the 1950s, but they still are limited to multiple states, as opposed to representing global agreements.

The multilateral nature of agreements after 1973 represents a growing recognition of the global scope of environmental problems, amply illustrated by the destructive power of nuclear weapons. Such recognition was part of the growing environmental movement pushed forward by environmental disasters. Authors such as Rachel Carson, who wrote *Silent Spring* in 1962 to much acclaim, about the deleterious effects of pesticides on the environment, helped to raise awareness that led to activism. Greenpeace was founded in 1971, with an attempt to disrupt a US nuclear weapons test. Key events such as the Chernobyl nuclear meltdown in 1986 reinforced such efforts. Activism based on major newsworthy events speaks to the emotional and groupthink aspects that create new policy trajectories. The International Convention for the Prevention of Pollution from Ships (MARPOL) was signed in 1973 and amended in 1978 in response to oil tanker accidents. The Convention on International Trade in Endangered Species of Wild Fauna and Flora (CITES) was also signed in 1973 amidst reports of possible extinction of species, with the number of countries signing eventually reaching 170.

Climate change is relatively recent, with the 1992 UN Framework Convention on Climate Change declaring intentions to begin to address greenhouse gas emissions. The Kyoto Protocol from 1997 set up the principle of binding targets for emissions reductions, over two periods, from 2008–12 and 2012–20. However, the Protocol was never ratified by the USA, and it withdrew in 2001. Canada withdrew after not meeting its targets in 2012. Thus, most activity occurred in the European Union, leading to dissatisfaction and a push for a more comprehensive agreement culminating in Paris in 2016.

The fundamental incorporation of sustainability as an integral part of development is illustrated by the transformation of the UN Millennium Development Goals – set up in 2000 and to be reached by 2015, with mixed results – into the Sustainable Development Goals (SDGs), set up in 2015 and to be reached by 2030 (Table 11.1). The SDGs include many more objectives specifically around environmental preservation and sustainability. Every aid agency appears to have adopted sustainable development, often referring to the SDGs, as part of its agenda. What this means in practice, of course, differs widely from agency to agency and even bureau to bureau.

Not surprisingly, the outcomes have been generally limited given the challenges with monitoring (e.g., measuring ocean fish stocks) and enforcement endemic to all global regimes. In certain areas, such as the phasing out of CFCs as set out by the Montreal Protocol of 1987, and particularly in areas of limited scope and geographical coverage such the air pollution

Table 11.1   The United Nations Sustainable Development Goals

1. No poverty	11. Sustainable cities and communities
2. Zero hunger	12. Responsible consumption and
3. Good health and wellbeing	production
4. Quality education	13. Climate action
5. Gender equality	14. Life below water
6. Clean water and sanitation	15. Life on land
7. Affordable clean energy	16. Peace, justice and strong institutions
8. Decent work and economic growth	17. Partnership for the goals
9. Industry, innovation and	
infrastructure	
10. Reduced inequalities	

Source: https://sustainabledevelopment.un.org/sdgs (accessed 1 June 2016)

('acid rain') treaty between Canada and the USA signed in 1991, there certainly have been triumphs. However, on a broader scale, from endangered species to climate change, advances in addressing sustainable development have been alarmingly slow. In terms of climate change, a perusal of basic emissions and consumption statistics demonstrates that there are reasons to doubt the benign aspects of the environmental Kuznets curve, or the effectiveness of current policy efforts. As we see in Figure 11.1, as China's economic growth has picked up, so have its emissions. In some Western countries, emissions have plateaued and experienced slight declines, but this is counteracted by significant increases in China and India.

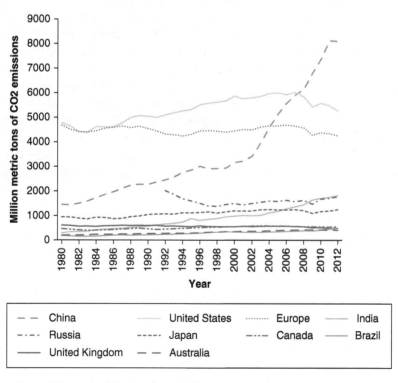

Figure 11.1   Largest Emitters of Carbon Dioxide Emissions, 1980-2012

Source: Author, Umair Suhail from US Energy Information Association

We see that emissions are concentrated in Western countries and a handful of rapidly growing Southern giants. This has brought out the question of justice, based not only on present levels, but also the history of global emissions, almost all of which have come from Western countries. This justice question generally figured as a background question to climate change agreements, until the growth of China from the 2000s made it impossible to sidestep.

Despite the halting progress of global agreements, efforts on the national and local level have been considerable in some pockets. For example, Denmark achieved approximately 41.7 per cent of electricity from renewable energy in 2012 according to the World Wildlife Fund, with 30 per cent coming from wind energy. The country has goals to reach 100 per cent renewable energy by 2050. At the municipal level, cities around the world are vying for the title of 'greenest city'. While a number of the leaders are not surprisingly in Western Europe, select cities such as Curitiba, Brazil, have also gained recognition. Initiatives at this level cover a wide range of activities, from planning for greater density to reduce commuting to developing environmentally pro-active building standards. San Francisco, for example, created a zero waste policy to be achieved by 2020 to enforce recycling and proper disposal of all rubbish. Because battery life has so far limited the range of electric vehicles, extending public transport remains one of the most active sectors for municipalities.

While laudable, such efforts can only have a limited impact, given the concentration of pollution in the West and a few rapidly growing developing countries, and the halting efforts at the national level to enact more pro-active measures. The International Energy Agency (IEA) estimated that fossil fuel energy subsidies totalled $493 billion in 2014. This refers to direct subsidies, primarily in developing countries where they are used to reduce energy costs. In Venezuela, for example, such subsidies reached $21.1 billion in 2014. The IEA does not have estimates about the types of tax breaks and other favouritism given to oil companies, in part because oil markets are marked by many state-owned enterprises where such information is not disclosed. In a series of reports, the International Institute for Sustainable Development (https://www.iisd.org/gsi/fossil-fuel-subsidies) estimates the global total to be something closer to $600 billion annually. The IEA puts renewable subsidies at one fourth as much. Considering the plunge in oil prices in 2008 from approximately $125/barrel to $28/barrel in 2015, the market incentives as well as inadequate national policies seem to ensure a continuation of fossil fuel dominance for energy supplies for the foreseeable future.

UNDERSTANDING CHALLENGES TO SUSTAINABLE DEVELOPMENT

The lack of what would be a rational response to impending doom in the form of loss of biodiversity, desertification, collapses of agriculture and fish stocks, flooding of cities and states, etc., defies a simple explanation. Mainstream economics points to the problem of 'externalities', whereby a polluter does not reap but a fraction of the costs of contamination that he creates, thus the true costs of production are not reflected in business decisions. Such problems have been overcome in some places through domestic regulation of an extremely varied nature; however, overcoming externalities remains elusive on the multilateral level. One of the best answers as to why is given by the theories of collective action (Olson, 1965) and the tragedy of the commons (Hardin, 1968). Olson points to the costs of organizing groups in terms of ensuring that everyone does their fair share to avoid 'free riders' (as in a bus metaphor). As a group gets larger, enforcement costs also increase. Thus, it is much more likely to have an effective group that has wealthy members with clearly defined common interests. Olson thereby explains some of the sources of power differences between lobby groups for economic growth vs. those for preservation. These differences, along with the fact of sunk costs, such as existing economic infrastructure built around fossil fuels, are often referred to as 'carbon lock in' (Unruh, 2000). We can combine this with the commons problem, whereby a common use area, such as international waters, is more likely to be degraded because no one is willing or able to take responsibility. Even though long-term degradation would hurt each member, in the short term, each is likely to overharvest as it benefits them individually. This explains the real challenges to protecting the environment on a global scale, where air and water are shared.

Mainstream economists commonly suggest the solution lies in market-based mechanisms. The foundation of many of these arguments is the Coase Theorem (1960), whereby the problem of the commons is solved by awarding property rights. In an area such as common grazing land, fencing off areas for private property incentivizes each owner to take responsibility for the long-term preservation of the land. Mainstream economists have extended the thought process towards a variety of policy instruments, such as auctioning off rights to pollute up to a certain limit ('cap and trade') that could be offset by purchasing assets such as forests that reduce carbon emissions. This has continued even further in the literature on ecosystems, whereby natural environmental systems such as water purification through the precipitation cycle are given economic value (Gómez-Baggethun et al., 2010).

However, in practice, such efforts have been haphazard. The Kyoto Protocol from 1997 set up the principle of offsets, whereby Northern countries could purchase or create projects that would reduce carbon (such as preserving a forest or adding scrubbers to a coal plant) in the developing world through what came to be known as the Clean Development Mechanism (CDM). According to the CDM website,[1] as of 30 April 2016, there have been a total of 7,923 projects leading to approximately 1.7 billion certified emissions reduction (CER) credits issued. There are no data on the total value of projects so far. The site reports that from 2004–15, 49 per cent of projects were in China, 21 per cent in India, 4 per cent in Brazil, 3 per cent in Vietnam and 2.5 per cent in Mexico; all other countries were less. The counterpart for trading emissions credits among Northern countries was called the Joint Implementation. This was accompanied by an Adaptation Fund, deriving revenues from the CDM. The Adaptation Fund spent $338.5 million across 61 countries from 2010–16 according to their website.[2] The offsets would allow countries to meet their emissions targets to supplement and ease the burden of reducing their own emissions. This was later expanded to the voluntary carbon offset markets allowing individuals or companies to purchase 'carbon credits' elsewhere, as advertised by airlines.

---

[1] See: https://cdm.unfccc.int/Statistics/Public/CDMinsights/index.html (accessed 20 May 2016).

[2] See: www.adaptation-fund.org/about/governance/ (accessed 20 May 2016).

In conjunction, a European trading system, the 'European Emissions Trading System', created in 2005, has had limited success. There are a number of reasons posited for its overall failure, beginning with the fact that it is limited to one part of the world. These reasons are typical of environmental policy failures. The CDM has been dogged by ambiguity in valuation and the natural suggestion that it amounts to evasion of reducing emissions (Bumpus and Liverman, 2008; Olsen, 2007). There are also concerns that CDM biases towards large infrastructure projects, with inadequate concern for local communities (Mathur et al., 2014). The price of CERs collapsed in 2012, revealing perhaps that both the recession and a natural reduction in emissions from increasing use of natural gas and renewables were occurring. There are other problems as well, from a lack of policy harmony between Europe and the other smaller carbon-trading markets, such as New Zealand and Québec, to the ceilings for carbon being placed so high that fossil fuels industries remain more competitive. In addition, there are concerns about the distributional effects of carbon pricing (Newell et al., 2013).

More fundamentally, measurements of pollution are exceedingly complex, beginning with which variables to measure. Kates et al. (2005: 15) point out that environmental sustainability indices abound in differing variables and methodologies; the ones they survey range from 6 key variables to 159! The issue, more generally, is how to set valuations for such things as pollution permits, and where to set limits and how fast they should creep downwards. The valuation issue is even problematic if we consider that the valuation of preserving resources to future generations is extremely ambiguous. Economists use the term discount rate to explain our preference for immediate as opposed to future use; however, how to calculate it for resources is unknown and likely to depend upon subjective inputs. For some, particularly activists, the very act of attaching economic prices to the environment confines its importance through 'commodification' (Norgaard, 2010), thus reducing its meaning and implications to purely economic concerns.

The general market-reliant approach of economists clashes with the basic human rights/needs for environmental preservation as reflected among some aid agencies and the SDGs. Yet, both ignore the possibility of overall limits to growth as embraced by more strident environmental preservation groups such as Greenpeace. The differences among the approaches are made more stark when comparing the methods and solutions sets of the different groups. Whereas economists and aid agencies largely ignore politics, or confine it to part of their technocratic approach under 'effective governance', environmental activists see politics at the heart of the problem. They use terms such as indigenous traditional knowledge to suggest that Western property rights ignore the appropriate and just returns to the use of resources, in this case for the discovery of new drugs. Some Southern states also decry the injustice of the distribution and history of Western use of resources as opposed to the developing world, yet their agenda is almost universally as growth centred as that of the technocrats. Thus, it is not surprising that a technocratically based approach clashes with an emotionally based one, creating a continual tension over the meaning of and path towards sustainable development.

One illustration of the elusiveness of policy consensus is the idea that there is an overall carrying capacity for the Earth. If this is the case, the priority should be the reduction of population. However, the role of women and their access to education and work, as well as reproductive rights, are tied up in differences in cultural values. Thus, conventional rationality falls apart. One could go even further, as I do (2015) in examining the role of consumption for social status, emotional comfort, and a strong linkage to a sense of identity. If consumption ultimately needs to be reduced, we are a long way from acknowledging it, let alone embracing a new definition of progress and quality of life more generally. This would require a great breakdown of the precept that growth and sustainability are compatible, or that a reasonable level of wealth then affords one the ability to turn to environmental values (Inglehart, 1971). The possibility that sustainable development is an oxymoron in a future 11 billion-person planet has not been seriously considered.

SUGGESTED SOLUTIONS

While the reductions in emissions set by the Paris Agreement are a promising step forward, they still lack the 'teeth' of careful monitoring and enforcement. Optimistically, as seen in Figure 11.1, the handful of states responsible for emissions will self-enforce as they also capture a larger share of the benefits. Focusing on the activities of a few states also reduces monitoring costs. As we have seen, however, North America lags behind Europe in policy measures, and China and India are even more likely to resist vigorous measures.

The natural tendency is to rest upon the hope that technological breakthroughs can solve the possible tradeoffs between standard of living and conservation. There are some reasons for optimism on this front. For example, solar panel costs dropped by > 50 per cent over the period from 2009–15 (Bolinger and Seel, 2015). New electric vehicle manufacturer Tesla created a Gigafactory in 2016 that they suggested would reduce battery costs by 30 per cent. However, the differences in the retail price and driving range between conventional gasoline and electric vehicle engines remain a substantial stumbling block, exacerbated by low oil prices. Such developments do not touch on the justice of resource distribution and use. Moreover, technology is a multi-faceted phenomenon. As in the case of natural gas fracking, market pressures often incentivize reduction of costs in fossil fuels more so than renewables, as fossil fuel infrastructure, market size, capitalization, and supply chains are already built. The potential phase-out of fossil fuels through market evolution will likely too slow to avoid a 'tipping point' of climate change, whereby earth systems from weather to currents undergo irreversible change (Lenton, 2011).

The issue of the usefulness of property rights for sustainable development remains unresolved. Mainstream institutions would suggest that adjustments to the trading model and the creation of a truly global trading system lie at the heart of failures thus far. Some environmental activists, by contrast, believe that property rights are part of an unjust system of resource exploitation led by multinational companies, as reflected in numerous global protests. Many would hope that global ties among likeminded people could be created to counteract this power imbalance. Celebrated economist Elinor Ostrom suggested (1990) that property rights were not necessary if a clear set of rules and monitoring system was put in place. However, most of her examples were on a small scale where monitoring could occur by peers. This brings up a point I raise in regard to rational choice-based institutional theory. If enforcement costs are high, then compliance largely rests upon shared values. Such is the case with compliance with tax rules in many Western states. A bigger question for Ostrom and others who are rule-oriented, is how to shift values so that selective enforcement becomes possible. Shifting values away from consumption and towards higher cost but sustainable production systems is not an object of focused discussion, but may be slowly happening by virtue of the discourse itself.

CONCLUSION

Our analysis leaves us with two issues that deserve more attention as foundational pieces for a long-term solution. The first is distributional and equity questions and the second is to shift values by engaging the public. Underlying these two issues is the fact that sustainable development discourse has largely ignored power differentials through different crucial relationships, among governments, companies, non-governmental organizations and communities.

In terms of distributional issues, according to the World Bank,[3] approximately 896 million people lived on less than $1.90/day in 2012, a dramatic reduction from previous years, but still 13 per cent of the world. Poverty is also concentrated, as East Asia saw the most dramatic reductions over the last two decades. Fully 78 per cent of the extremely poor live in South Asia (309 million) and sub-Saharan Africa (388.7 million). The price of energy figures large in household incomes in much of the developing world, and removing subsidies will have uneven effects. Similarly, poverty can be linked to environmental destruction. For example, slash and burn agriculture of rainforests, sometimes linked to global beef markets, is often spearheaded by marginal income groups who have no income alternatives. Although environmental destruction will hurt their livelihoods in the long run, in the short run desperation wins out. Equity also looms large in climate change. Discussions of North-South responsibility reflect not only historical colonialism and Western preponderance in the supply chains and consumption of global resources, but also the fact that climate change will likely have more concentrated effects in parts of the South. For example, Pacific island and coastal nations such as Bangladesh are already concerned about the possibilities for losing their land as sea levels rise. Desertification could affect large parts of the developing world as temperatures rise and precipitation patterns shift. Regardless of where climate change is felt most acutely, developing nations and the poor more generally will have a harder time adapting given their limited means.

In turn, the issues of equity reflect major issues with knowledge gaps, again reflecting the largely technocratic circles in which sustainable development policies have been developed and the lack of engagement with the public in formulating either analysis or solutions. The gap helps to explain why the push for climate change policies have been irrationally slow. Leiserowitz (2006), for example, points out that the

---

[3] See: www.worldbank.org/en/topic/poverty/overview (accessed 20 May 2016).

US public is knowledgeable about climate change but does not think that it will affect them personally. Other priorities, particularly economic conditions, take precedence. Recognizing that greater diffusion of knowledge and participation are needed is still a far cry from having ready tools for doing so, a subject still in its infancy (Cash et al., 2000; Reed, 2008).

The values shift can be seen on the academic side in terms of new analytical tools for understanding sustainability. For example, the number of publications around life cycle analysis has increased markedly since 2000. Life-cycle analysis seeks to measure the costs of the entire production process from raw material to finished product or service, including all environmental effects and externalities. It is still in its infancy and the methodology for using it is highly contentious. From the ecosystems perspective, resources should no longer be thought of in terms of their usefulness and costs in the production process, but also in terms of the costs of their depletion.

These new trends suggest that a more momentous shift in both rationality and values might be starting to take place, namely a shift from a linear production and consumption process to starting to think about production in a more circular fashion, so that every item that is produced considers the reuse of all materials. A starting point would be to consider environmental outcomes in product and process design (Zhang et al., 1997), as part of a broader movement of corporate social responsibility to embrace environmental conservation as in their own long-term interests, including avoiding public regulation (Shrivastava, 1995). This would likely require a wholesale shift in the way in which market pricing operates, where the costs of disposal and environmental effects are part of the costs of production. As I highlight in a forthcoming publication, several companies in the sharing economy are starting to show that consumption could take on a different direction whereby lightly used assets, such as autos, are now shared, reducing overall production requirements, as less people would have to own them, as well as providing more ready secondary markets of used items. Internet communication apps are enabling the coordination of the use of such assets.

Uncertainty around the costs, valuation and levels of destruction of the environment as highlighted by climate change, lend themselves readily to an interpretation of slowly evolving convergence around the definition of and need for action around sustainable development as a gradually developing shared mental model, shifting from a linear production model to one that is more circular in nature. At the same time, the remaining ambiguity and challenges in measurement underline the partly artificial nature of the construct, largely ignoring centuries of previous thought and action on the environment in creating a new term. A discourse approach also reveals the very real power differentials that create doubts around the efficacy and equity of what has so far been a largely technocratic process and one that assumes uncritically that growth and conservation are compatible. Last, but not least, sustainable development touches on group values and emotions, as highlighted by contentions around just behaviour, social movements that identify clear pollution enemies, the appropriate role of the market vs. regulation, and the failure to reach global consensus on much-needed collective action. Humans remain as contradictory as ever in regard to nature, at once seeing it as a tool as well as an asset marked by beauty of immeasurable value to be preserved.

Questions for Discussion

1   What is meant by the term 'sustainable development'?
2   How accurate are the predictions of impending environmental catastrophe made by scholars such as Rachel Carson and others in the 1960s and 1970s?
3   In what ways do dominant mental models of economic development need to change for the SDGs to be realized?

ACKNOWLEDGEMENTS

The author would like to thank Umair Suhail and Anna Kim for their research assistance, funded by Simon Fraser University's work-study programme.

 # FURTHER READING

Hira, A. (2015) *Three Perspectives on Human Irrationality: The Book of Rules*. Hove: The Book Guild.

Kates, R.W., Parris, T.M. and Leiserowitz, A.A. (2005) 'What is Sustainable Development? Goals, Indicators, Values, and Practice', *Environment: Science and Policy for Sustainable Development*, 47(3): 8–21.

Meadows, D.H., Meadows, D.L., Randers, J. and Behrens III, W.W. (1972) *The Limits to Growth: A Report for the Club of Rome's Project on the Predicament of Mankind*. Washington, DC: Universe Books.

Turner, G. and Alexander, C. (2014) 'Limits to Growth was Right: New Research Shows we are Nearing Collapse', *Guardian*, 2 September. Available at: https://www.theguardian.com/commentisfree/2014/sep/02/limits-to-growth-was-right-new-research-shows-were-nearing-collapse (accessed 1 July 2016).

REFERENCES

Arrow, K., Bolin, B., Costanza, R., Dasgupta, P., Folke, C., Holling, C.S., Jansson, B.-O., Levin, S., Mäler, K.-G., Perrings, C. and Pimentel, D. (1995) 'Economic-Growth, Carrying-Capacity, and the Environment', *Science*, 268 (5210): 520–1.

Baker, S. (2006) *Sustainable Development*. New York: Routledge.

Beck, U. (1992) *Risk Society: Towards a New Modernity*. London: Sage.

Bolinger, M. and Seel, J. (2015) 'Utility-Scale Solar 2014: An Empirical Analysis of Project Cost, Performance, and Pricing Trends in the United States'. Report LBNL-1000917. September. Berkeley, CA: Lawrence Berkeley National Laboratory.

Bumpus, A.G. and Liverman, D.M. (2008) 'Accumulation by Decarbonization and the Governance of Carbon Offsets', *Economic Geography*, 84(2): 127–55.

Cash, D.W., Clark, W.C., Alcock, F., Dickson, N.M., Eckley, N., Guston, D.H., Jäger, J. and Mitchell, R. (2000) 'Knowledge Systems for Sustainable Development', *PNAS*, 100(14): 8086–91.

Coase, R.H. (1960) 'The Problem of Social Cost', *Journal of Law and Economics*, 3(1): 1–44.

Conrad, R.F., Gillis, M. and Mercer, D.E. (2005) 'Tropical Forest Harvesting and Taxation: A Dynamic Model of Harvesting Behaviour under Selective Extraction Systems', *Environment and Development Economics*, 10(5): 689–709.

Daly, H.E. (1996) *Beyond Growth: The Economics of Sustainable Development*. Boston, MA: Beacon Press.

Denzau, A.T. and North, D.C. (1994) 'Shared Mental Models: Ideologies and Institutions', *Kyklos*, 47(1): 3–31.

Egelston, A.E. (2013) *Sustainable Development: A History*. New York: Springer.

Ehrlich, P.R. (1968) *The Population Bomb*. New York: Sierra Club/Ballantine Books.

Foucault, M. (1966) *The Order of Things: An Archaeology of the Human Sciences*. Paris: Gallimard.

Gómez-Baggethun, E., de Groot, R., Lomas, P.L. and Montes, C. (2010) 'The History of Ecosystem Services in Economic Theory and Practice: From Early Notions to Markets and Payment Schemes', *Ecological Economics*, 69: 1209–18. Available at: www.cepal.org/ilpes/noticias/paginas/7/40547/the_history_of_ecosystem.pdf (accessed 27 February 2017).

Hardin, G. (1968) 'The Tragedy of the Commons', *Science*, 162(3859): 1243–8.

Hira, A. (forthcoming) 'Prospects for the Sharing Economy and Development', working title, *Journal of Developing Societies*.

Hira, A. (2015) *Three Perspectives on Human Irrationality: The Book of Rules*. Sussex, UK: Book Guild.

Inglehart, R. (1971) 'The Silent Revolution in Post-Industrial Societies', *American Political Science Review*, 65: 991–1017.

Leiserowitz, A. (2006) 'Climate Change Risk Perception and Policy Preferences: The Role of Affect, Imagery, and Values', *Climatic Change*, 77: 45–72.

Lélé, S.M. (1991) 'Sustainable Development: A Critical Review', *World Development*, 19(6): 607–21.

Lenton, T.M. (2011) 'Early Warning of Climate Tipping Points', *Nature Climate Change*, 1(4): 201–9.

Mathur, V.N., Afionis, S., Paavola, J., Dougill, A.J. and Stringer, L.C. (2014) 'Experiences of Host Communities with Carbon Market Projects: Towards Multi-Level Climate Justice', *Climate Policy*, 14(1): 42–62.

Newell, R.G., Pizer, W.A. and Raimi, D. (2013) 'Carbon Markets 15 Years after Kyoto: Lessons Learned, New Challenges', *Journal of Economic Perspectives*, 27(1): 123–46.

Norgaard, R.B. (2010) 'Ecosystem Services: From Eye-opening Metaphor to Complexity Blinder', *Ecological Economics*, 69: 1219–27.

Olsen, K.H. (2007) 'The Clean Development Mechanism's Contribution to Sustainable Development: A Review of the Literature', *Climatic Change*, 84: 59–73.

Olson, M. (1965) *The Logic of Collective Action: Public Goods and the Theory of Groups*. Cambridge, MA: Harvard University Press.

Ostrom, E. (1990) *Governing the Commons: The Evolution of Institutions for Collective Action*. Cambridge: Cambridge University Press.

Reed, M.S. (2008) 'Stakeholder Participation for Environmental Management: A Literature Review', *Biological Conservation*, 141: 2417–31.

Shrivastava, P. (1995) 'The Role of Corporations in Achieving Ecological Sustainability', *Academy of Management Review*, 20(4): 936–60.

Stern, D.I. (2004) 'The Rise and Fall of the Environmental Kuznets Curve', *World Development*, 32(8): 1419–39.

Unruh, G.C. (2000) 'Understanding Carbon Lock-in', *Energy Policy*, 28: 817–30.

World Bank (2013) *The World Bank Group Goals: End Extreme Poverty and Promote Shared Prosperity*. Washington, DC: World Bank.

World Commission on Environment and Development (WCED) (1987) *Our Common Future*. New York: UN.

Zhang, H.C., Kuo, T.C., Lu, H. and Huang, S.H. (1997) 'Environmentally Conscious Design and Manufacturing: A State-of-the-Art Survey', *Journal of Manufacturing Systems*, 16(5): 352–71.

12

SITUATING THE PRACTITIONER AS CO-LEARNER AND CO-PARTICIPANT IN GLOBAL DEVELOPMENT

JOSE ROBERTO GUEVARA, KENT GOLDSWORTHY AND ALEXANDER SNOW

INTRODUCTION

Employing globalization as a framework for analyzing global development presents theoretical and practical challenges for development professionals. The reality of cross-border and cross-cultural projects has often been provided as the rationale for preparing development professionals to be culturally aware and sensitive. However, there is less emphasis placed on the need for a heightened level of self-awareness to navigate the wicked social problems, made more complex by a context of uncertainty, that exist at the nexus of local–global interactions. Heightened self-awareness fosters a deeper level of knowing, particularly in terms of our identities, our roles within institutions we work with, and consequently, our contribution. This proposition aligns with the argument of Denzau and North (1994), that individuals construct mental models to make sense of the world, which in turn inform their ideologies and the institutions that are established. We argue that this level of self-awareness of one's own 'mental models' facilitates empathy and provides impetus for effective social action. Rather than assert the need for mental models to change, this chapter examines the evolution of shared mental models in an education for development setting.

One core element of this level of self-awareness has been to develop the capacity for critical self-reflection, which, from our experience, does not come easily or indeed naturally for a lot of us who wish to contribute to development work. This observation is the result of a history of top-down and North–South development approaches that must fit within a logical framework approach to planning, delivering and evaluating (Dearden, 2005; Gasper, 2000; Hummelbrunner, 2010) and an equally long history of a 'banking' approach to education and learning (Freire, 2000) within our educational institutions that is equally mirrored in the types of training conducted within development work.

While there has been on-going recognition of the importance of participatory approaches to development (Chambers, 1983, 2004, 2013) to address the failure of top-down and Global North–South approaches, there is equally a strong critique that these participatory approaches continue to be framed around getting the 'beneficiaries' who need to be 'developed' to participate.

In this chapter, we propose to examine the value and the process for enhancing the capacity for critical self-awareness of development practitioners, as a significant element in contributing to effective global development. We argue that this level of self-awareness involves being alert to their identity, their role and their objectives as a co-learner and co-participant in global development. To illustrate this argument, we shall draw from our own experiences and learning, as development practitioners, primarily from our roles in a postgraduate subject within the Master in International Development at RMIT University, Melbourne, Australia entitled 'Learning and Participation in Development' (L&P) from 2009 to 2016, but also from our respective development experiences outside of the university.

Our examination of the argument draws from key educational frameworks that have influenced development work, such as adult education (Knowles et al., 2014), transformative learning (Mezirow, 1991; Mezirow and Taylor, 2011), popular education (Freire, 2000) and adult education for development (Rogers, 1992, 2005). We also draw from the theory and practice of participation in development based on the works of Robert Chambers (1983, 2004, 2013) and of Stan Burkey (1996). Two processes of engagement embedded within L&P are Most Significant Change (Davies and Dart, 2005) and Freirean Culture Circles, that have their roots in the Brazilian Union movement of the 1930s (Taylor, 1993: 22), and which we have called 'Learning Circles'. Finally, these theoretical frames and practices are drawn together by the work of Donald Schon (1983) on the self-reflective practitioner.

Methodologically speaking, writing this chapter has been a collaborative and participatory process informed by the principles of participatory research, an educational tool that provides a concomitant production, and subsequent ownership, of knowledge (Conrad, 2004). In the 1970s, Paulo Freire instigated the 'popular education movement' where he invited a critical consciousness from ordinary people in critiquing the world. Freire wanted people to be active in shaping the social contexts of their lives; in an educational sense this reflected a movement away from orthodox methods of 'banking' where the students were passive recipients of knowledge. This new process encouraged a critical thinking and mobilized the people toward collective social action (Conrad, 2004).

The evolution of participatory research provides a marked difference from conventional research methods as its focus is to research 'with' the people, rather than 'on' the people.

DEVELOPING CRITICAL SELF-AWARENESS OF DEVELOPMENT PRACTITIONERS

We identified five themes that illustrate our examination of both the value and the process for facilitating the development of critical self-awareness for development practitioners. These themes are: (i) the evolution of the L&P subject from 2009 to 2016; (ii) our own changing understanding and engagement with the role of the student as co-learner and co-participant; (iii) the value and process of collective learning; (iv) the evolution of the role of the academic staff as equally co-learner and co-participant; and (v) the clarification of the idea of the classroom as a *site of development*.

Subjects delivered within the formal education system have traditionally involved the delivery of ideas and theories from a teacher to a student. Paulo Freire (2000) refers to this normative approach to learning as 'banking': the teacher has knowledge that the student doesn't, but wants/needs, and through the transfer of this knowledge the student learns. However, from the beginning, the L&P subject had maintained a commitment to utilizing a participatory approach informed by adult learning theory (Knowles et al., 2014) that students had their own life experiences, had clear motivations to prepare them for learning, and therefore the challenge was to find a process of learning that values these experiences and motivations within the context of international development. Chambers argued for a 'pedagogy for the non-oppressed' (2004: 2) to countenance the lack of action in development, particularly from people with power. It was this notion of power and the understanding and practice of this within the structure of a university subject that facilitated the on-going adaptation or what we called progressive contextualization, defined as the on-going process of adapting the curriculum to the local context of the participants and their community (Guevara, 2002, 2012).

EVOLUTION OF LEARNING AND PARTICIPATION AS A DEVELOPMENT STUDIES SUBJECT

Learning and Participation evolved out of an elective subject entitled 'Participatory Approaches in Development'. This elective focused on developing the students' critical understanding and skills in the utilization of participatory approaches to development. As one might expect, the subject covered an introduction to the history and philosophy of participatory approaches, examined some of the main approaches in participatory development, such as Rapid Rural Appraisal (RRA), Participatory Rural Appraisal (PRA) and Participatory Action Research (PAR), and explored the limitations and potential of these. However, instead of the narrow focus on PRA, on assuming responsibility for the subject, Guevara introduced a greater emphasis on the ability to understand the application of the tools in different contexts. This involved inviting speakers to share their experiences of using PRA tools with women and with young people. Students worked in teams to develop a training design for a specific group of participants and then used role-play to work through the practicalities of implementation.

In 2011, Guevara engaged Goldsworthy to co-facilitate the expanded Participatory Approaches elective into a core course, which was then called 'Practising Development'. The learning objectives were expanded and fine-tuned to emphasize inclusion, learning and professional collaboration, and cultural diversity (of development and policy professionals and the intended beneficiaries of participatory development programmes). Alex Snow, who was then a student enrolled in the 2011 subject, recalls how the subject challenged normative learning and affirmed the Freirian principles of education: knowledge is not owned by anyone, learning takes place through critical self-reflection, and the goal is conscientization (self-actualization). Snow describes how the subject, despite the modified objectives, continued to focus on developing a training design that was sensitive to context.

Text Box 12.1   Critical Reflections from Student to Tutor

As a Masters of International Development student at RMIT, I enrolled in one of the core subjects, 'Practising Development', in 2011. The focus was on learning and participatory approaches to development, and, in particular, the role the practitioner played in the processes of participatory development: how did they design and implement participatory approaches to development? How did they conceptualize learning? To explore this, I was asked to decide on a development challenge that interested me and design a participatory project that addressed the challenge. My focus was the lack of theatre education institutions in Cambodia. The response was a peer-to-peer training programme for young artists. To this end, the subject felt like a participatory project planning experience (Aune, 2000; Cohen and Uphoff, 2011). Imperative to designing an appropriate participatory approach is being attuned to the various 'context(s)': individual, community, state, national, global. The subject utilized the principles of Robert Chambers' Participatory Rural Appraisal (PRA) to underpin this notion of contexts: equity and sustainability. In his seminal text, *Rural Development: Putting the Last First* (1983), Chambers argues that in this initial phase of decision-making local needs must be highlighted and local actors must participate in determining how to incorporate those needs into the project design.

As a student, I was told that design process fosters capacity building and lays an enabling precedent for all future forms of participatory action and decision-making (Cohen and Uphoff, 2011). It was this process of participatory planning, learning and capacity building that the subject embodied. Students were afforded the opportunity to experience participatory practices in order to learn *about* participation *through* participation.

Despite the focus of the learning task on participatory project planning, a change agent was still required to facilitate the learning process. In the university context, this is the teacher in the classroom; while in the project context, it is the development professional in the 'field'. This dual dynamic may cause some tension when taken in concert with Freire's critique of the 'banking' approach to education: Is the change agent as teacher merely banking information? Or is the change agent as development professional facilitating a process of change? Or can we play both roles together?

In 2013, I began teaching in the same core subject, now called Learning and Participation in Development, and the focus had shifted to the practitioner as a learner and participant.

The subject had always highlighted the need for a critical examination of the world (Freire, 2000). Now, though, it was explicit that both students and teachers were practitioners in a community where power is and should be shared. Central to this is that the students recognize that they have power, as individuals in a Western education system studying a programme that assumes they will be part of the 'solution'. Power resides in the powerful and educated and this must be acknowledged if participatory practices are to be taught, learned, and applied in order to contribute to social change and global development, i.e. the fair and contextually appropriate lifting of people out of poverty. As Arnstein argues, the danger in promoting participatory practices in social reform is that without the redistribution of power, participation 'is an empty and frustrating process for the powerless ... [as] it allows the power holders to claim that all sides were considered' (2011: 4) while actually only benefiting some.

This shift toward a truly (as true as possible) participatory subject resulted in the expected tension in terms of the role of the teacher as facilitator, plus most students had expectations from a masters subject: readings, essays, guidance and answers. When definitive answers weren't given but rather explored together through a process of critical self-reflection, the trained and institutionalized administrative learner resisted! Freire acknowledges that 'pushback' may occur when people believe they are powerless to change the way things are or are resistant to change, often due to fear of uncertainty. To counteract this 'pushback', in 2015 and 2016, Goldsworthy and I introduced a second subject theme of 'change', with a dual focus on the students in our community and the people in the broader development community. Utilizing the Most Significant Change (MSC) technique (Davies and Dart, 2005), we note that change is a process, not an event, and that it is often the unexpected change that fosters critical learning.

The subject today reflects two intellectual and practical activities. Firstly, the on-going proposition-making undertaken over time in regard to the role and the identity of the development practitioner specifically; and, secondly, question-making in regard to the function of a development studies postgraduate programme in relation to that role and identity. The experience of each preparation and delivery of the subject, with the proposition and question in mind, motivated each iteration of the subject to the point that acknowledgment of the evolution has itself become a feature in the delivery of the recent versions. Students are now told the story of the subject as a form of evidence, and example, of the reflexivity that the subject coordinators and tutors have experienced and applied. In this way, the narrative of the subject's evolution is told to the students as a story of community development. It reflects the original aim of the subject to demonstrate the valuable influence of context in the practice of learning and participation in development and equally demonstrate in practice the concept of progressive contextualization (Guevara, 2002, 2012).

THE ROLE OF THE STUDENT

Participatory approaches to development are often explored by teaching a technique or offering a tool kit for participation as illustrated by the design of the 2009 subject delivery. This approach presumes that participation is a linear process that can be measured or quantified. However, despite the observed growth of the practice of participation in development, one of the underlying reasons for participation has a tendency to be lost, namely the opportunity for learning for the organization and the practitioner. A conventional classroom setting often inhabits the same power asymmetries that play out between Northern development professionals and Southern community members, mediated through the teacher-student relationship.

Instead of trying to fill an empty glass, or 'bank' information into an empty student, we know that the glass is not empty, even more since the students are adults, with life experiences enrolled in a postgraduate degree. Therefore, the first role of the teacher is to facilitate the opportunity for the students to share the contents of their glass with each other, to share and create knowledge and the second role is to introduce new knowledge that can help to connect or deepen the shared knowledge. This very much aligned to Freire's (2000) challenging the banking system of learning and Malcolm Knowles' (Knowles et al., 2014) adult learning theory. Therefore, it requires that we have overtly expressed roles for the student in the delivery and on-going development of the subject.

Development Practitioner or Development Technician?

Teaching students the PRA tools alone, without the deeper understanding of the underlying philosophy of PRA, is similar to preparing students to become development 'technicians'. We draw this description of 'technicians' from the argument of Westoby and Dowling in their book entitled *Dialogical Community Development* (2009: 7), where they argue for the need to make 'a distinction between tradition and technique in community development'. They describe technique-based solutions as problematic because they can have a quick fix-it approach to social problems and therefore give the false impression that all we need to do is to master the technique, such as PRA, and the problems will be solved. From experience, we know this is not the case. The use of proper 'techniques are essential; but they must be put in their right context … informed by an understanding of the tradition of community development work' (ibid.: 8). Without this deeper understanding, teaching PRA methods alone diminishes the potential of students to become reflective practitioners. Inquiry-based processes are preferred to instruction, where identifying a question or a set of questions that interest the student, or even better that challenges them, is the starting point of the learning process. Initially, this involved hypothesizing about development that takes place 'over there', manifested in class through what we called 'The Development Challenge' assessment task.

Co-Learner and Co-Participant in Development

Upon reflection, we realized that the focus needed to be on the students themselves as learners and participants in their own development. Overtly, students are told via the content of their subject guide and in the early sessions of the semester, that the teaching staff are engaging with them as co-learners and practitioners, that we are a community, and that our classroom is a site of community development. In early versions of the subject, this message was more 'quietly' stated for various reasons, including our own confidence in how to actually do this.

The inquiry questions have shifted from 'The Development Challenge' of the 'other' towards more self-reflective questions:

- Who are you 'in Development', right now?
- Who do you want to be 'in Development' sometime in the future?
- What do you perceive is meant by thinking of the Development Practitioner as Learners and Participants?
- What kind of Learner are you?

These questions reorientate the focus of learning onto the student, i.e. how we participate and move toward self-actualization, and the role of the self-reflective practitioner (Schon, 1983). To reflect on their identity in relation to their role and position in our community the student must be critically self-aware, first identifying their inherent knowledge base, and then their learning needs. In the context of L&P, they then consciously explore their learning in seminars and workshops before using the MSC technique (Davies and Dart, 2005) to identify the change that has taken place in themselves. Using the MSC technique, students identify unexpected changes that took place during the semester and acknowledge the impact on their learning; and thus subsequent practice.

The Self and 'the Other' in Development

Despite the shift of the focus on the students themselves, for most, thinking about development is still synonymous with thinking about 'the other'. Usually an 'other' imagined as 'some person (possibly community)' in the grips of 'some version of political, cultural or economic injustice', 'somewhere' very far from the classroom in which they sit. This is unsurprising, considering the well-established nature of labelling in the development discourse: from Truman's 1949 inaugural address (Haslam et al., 2012: 5) describing 'underdeveloped areas', a term not far removed from the previously prevalent 'backward countries', to the politically charged Cold War language of 'The Third World', to the 'Developing World'. Even with the more 'enlightened' vocabulary of the World Bank and OECD, labels and classifications have their consequences. Each of these labels is 'othering'; a process of 'locating [sic] a person or group of persons outside the centre, on the margins'. Such a process, left unattended, serves to diminish critical attention to post-colonial critique of 'the self' – the self, in this instance, being the prospective development professional.

Students bring into the subject a particular identity, and very often, multiple identities. These identities then dictate the role the student presumes they will take in completing the subject. In addition to the 'student' identity, these multiple identities are usually one or a combination of, a good person wanting to do good, a customer, a career-changer, a career-developer, part of 'a solution' to a development or humanitarian 'problem', and change agent. In the alternative approaches utilized in the L&P subject, claiming any one or any combination of these identities does not necessitate that a student acknowledge them, yet each of these identities is clearly, maybe unconsciously, positioning itself in relation to 'the other'. The L&P subject argues that this positioning necessitates interrogation if the subject's central proposition is to be upheld. At the most basic level, the student's role is to be an active participant in this process of interrogation. Hopefully, the initial confrontation or discomfort morphs into motivation and confidence and ideally to the extent that their development practice benefits from the consciousness achieved as a co-learner and participant in development.

THE ROLE OF COLLECTIVE LEARNING

The myriad and complexity of socio-economic challenges facing the planet today requires a number of actors to engage in collaborative efforts of knowledge and resource sharing to address these challenges. This ideal of collaboration resource sharing opened up two areas of work, namely: (i) to establish the class as a community of development practitioners who all share a commitment to contributing to positive change; and (ii) to therefore work and learn together to achieve this commitment through learning circles. Each of these areas is elaborated in the following sub-sections.

Establishing a Sense of Community

Most students readily recognize themselves as enrolled in the Masters of International Development degree programme generally, and the L&P subject specifically. Except perhaps for a small number who enrol in the subject as an elective, the rest of the students take L&P as a required subject. However, early in the semester we attempt to establish a sense of community, beyond their enrolment. However, this recognition of being part of a community does not automatically translate into the recognition of the potential for collective learning (Steiner and Hanks, 2016). This potential needs to be stated and developed to a level of understanding if it is to be actualized. This challenge is often addressed by requiring students to engage in group work and develop teamwork skills. However, time and again students have responded negatively to group tasks given the difficulty of finding time, the tendency for tasks to be distributed unevenly, and the marks not being equitable to the amount of work each student has invested.

To address this, the L&P subject elaborates on Freire's Culture Circles (Souto-Manning, 2010) for reflexive practice through dialogic engagement with peers. Students identify from two to six other students to be part of their Learning Circles. The concept of circles has also been practised as with Action Learning Circles, whose formulation can be traced from the works of Burnard (1988) and Wade and Hammick (1999), both drawing on the work of Kolb (1984) for adult education. In the Practising Development subject in 2011, Learning Circles were created but it involved students working with other students on shared tasks. As expected, it was: (i) seen as group work and therefore mostly disliked; and, (ii) thought of as an opportunity for cheap marks. This predisposition to group work is based on assumptions of shared responsibility toward shared outcomes. In the process, some are left behind without contributing (often voluntarily) and others are left to do all the contributing (also often voluntarily, despite remarks to the contrary).

Learning Circles and 'Circle Work'

Participatory approaches to development recognize people are not homogenous. Groups of people are also not homogenous. And, therefore, the process of self-actualization (raising one's consciousness) will be very different for different people and is influenced by the people around you. Freire's Culture Circles have functioned to facilitate making evident these varied processes; learning potentially occurs through knowledge exchange with other individuals (circle members and teachers). But the end point is not marked nor is it necessarily shared. In recent years, we have been much more explicit in pointing out this difference between group work and circle work. Circles are formed early in the semester, which involves introducing the students to the theory and concept, some organizing principles to ensure that everyone will be in a Learning Circle, and finally time constraints to establish these Circles. After the briefing, the students then set about a supported exercise, which should see them finish the session in a Circle.

That done, each semester a variation on the 'Can I move from my Learning Circle if I don't like it?' will be asked at some point soon after. In response, a student will typically hear something like 'If you want to', to which they will then typically ask 'Which one should I join?' The student is then told that that is likely to depend on which Circle will be ready to accommodate them. At this point, we experience a few different types of reactions. Some students, thinking that organizing themselves (rather than the staff doing it) is going to be more effort than it is worth, will simply decide to stay with the Circle they're in. Others will initiate and ultimately achieve a move. In either case, our experience has been that students report feeling that the academic staff are not fulfilling their role using invested authority – students have reported thinking that staff should have been able to just answer, 'Yes, you can' or 'No, you can't,' or that the student should have been better supported with their dissatisfaction with the Circle in which they found themselves in.

A very common observation to the initial establishment of Circles is: 'I won't learn as much in a bad Circle.' Our response is always that, as stated above, a Circle's function is not to produce something between yourselves, but rather to share knowledge in order to raise your consciousness of how *you* learn, what methods and theories resonate for *you*, and how you might apply that in this community (and later others). Therefore, we argue that it is not possible to be in a 'bad' Circle. In following on from Arnstein's (2011: 13) critique on the redistribution of power vis-à-vis participation, she argues that it is at the fifth stage on her participation ladder, that of partnership and the third highest level of citizen participation, where 'power is in fact redistributed through negotiation between citizens [students] and power holders [teachers]'. The Circles thus become a living example of our attempt at this power shift toward shared learning, as well as in organizing and sustaining this process of shared learning.

There are multiple collectives existing in the makeup of the subject. There is the total cohort, inclusive of staff, and there are the Learning Circles. During the early weeks of semester, just after the Circles are formed, and often for quite some time into the semester, students don't see a distinction between what we called circle work, which they are all experiencing for the first time, and group work which they all have experienced, either in other subjects in the programme, or in previous study at undergraduate level. It is very common when in discussion that students will say 'my group', when referring to their Learning Circle. From the outset of the semester, we make a point of pulling-up students when they use 'group' to refer to their Learning Circle. This is another potential source for unsettled experiences. But, over the duration of the semester, it is revealing of a student's learning and understanding of the important distinction when students themselves start to correct each other, and the staff.

Challenges of Doing 'Circle Work'

Operating within an institutional environment presents a number of challenges for a subject that utilizes a Freirian framework that espouses collective learning. Padaki (2007) discusses the contradictory nature that exists between the ideals of empowerment and participation for a project's beneficiaries and the technocratic linear processes that form an organization's structure and dictate their actions. Time is one significant challenge. Time is a valuable commodity in a neoliberal, user-pay environment – time equals money. We only have 12 weeks to deliver sophisticated content and meet tightly held objectives, and each week we only have two hours. While professing to foster a participatory process of empowerment for the participants (students), for a while we were left feeling that the process was stuck, reflected by the students' inability to take control of their learning and development. Further evidence of this is that most students didn't recognize the value of the subject until much later down the track. For us, recognition must be given to the centrality of the student as primary stakeholders, not only as participatory planners, but also as co-learners and subsequently co-authors throughout the development intervention: the L&P subject!

Every week, we, the 'lecturers and tutors', would meet as our own Learning Circle after class to reflect on the students' feedback – both positive and negative – to ensure that we were engaging in a live dialogue underscored by Freire's (2000) principles of dialogic, activist and de-socialist education. This brings us smoothly into the role of the academic staff in this community.

THE ROLE OF THE ACADEMIC STAFF

International development has long been predicated on the need for external experts to facilitate the process of change. As Chambers (2013) and subsequent post-development authors (see Rahnema and Bawtree, 1997) challenged this top-down approach to development, the need to mirror this shift and embed critical reflection in the classroom is essential. If students of development are subservient to the outside expert, there is a danger that this learned behaviour is transferred into other fields/sites of development, and thus perpetuated. The role of the academic staff is to shift this dynamic. As Freire (2000) argues, education is not done to you by someone but is, rather, a process of negotiated activity that is inquiry based and motivated by desiring change:

> The teacher is of course an artist, but being an artist does not mean that he or she can make the profile, can shape the students. What the educator does in teaching is to make it possible for the students to become themselves. (Horton and Freire, 1990: 181)

During this process, the teacher must also be critically reflecting on their role, identity and the power they bring to the classroom so that they too are a party to the process of learning and change.

As with the role of the student in the subject, and the consequent influence of their adopted identity, the role of the academic staff similarly influences the students' participation and learning in the subject – with one significant and important distinction to be noted; that distinction being produced through the repeat experiences of attention to the design and delivery of the subject, as well as through a far more progressed understanding of the theoretical foundations and the practical implications of conscientization with learning and participation in development.

Staff as Subject Designer and Lecturer

In the role of educator and subject administrator, pre-semester, the academic staff prepares a comprehensive subject guide which sets-out subject materials including set readings, plans including sequence of topics, activities and the assessment pieces. Then, on commencement of the semester, in the very first seminar, time is devoted to a 'walk-through' of that subject guide and presentation of the subject theme and of the proposition that development practice benefits when the practitioner is self-aware: alert to their role, identity and their objectives as learner and participant in development.

An objective of that walk-through is to establish the set of 'non-negotiables' – the academic staff, after all, is making decisions to meet institutional compliance, trying to effectively manage subject administration, and overtly setting a very particular direction ideologically and pedagogically. But, those non-negotiables in the subject are finite.

Staff as Facilitator of Learning

The functioning role of the academic staff varies with identity: teacher, coach, facilitator, leader, practitioner, role model, disciplinarian, researcher and administrator. At one time or another, each of these identities is present. At times, the academic staff themselves 'take' an identity and work to that role. At others, students (the community) seem to project an identity onto the staff, and not always one that is consistent with that that the staff is taking or wants to take. A consistently present version of such a circumstance is with the 'Can I?' permission-type questions, such as the earlier example of asking, 'Can I move from my Learning Circle if I don't like it?' We have observed this attitude to extend to other areas such as assignments, readings, etc.

How do we respond? How do we negotiate these expectations on our roles as teachers? We need to weave more effectively the different roles and how we negotiate them – what is prescribed by the university, what is ascribed by the students, and what we ourselves adapt.

THE CLASSROOM AS SITE OF DEVELOPMENT

If orienting students towards seeing themselves as subjects of development is a challenge in pursuit of the educational perspective, it is at least in part because, as with preconceptions of 'the other', there are preconceptions about where development activity takes place. That place, if it has a name, is 'in the field'. The field, this pre-conception holds, is most certainly not a university classroom in a 'developed' country.

Yearly, we conduct a workshop activity that adapts a PRA mapping tool (Robinson-Pant, 1995), where the room is 'mapped' to represent different regions of the world. Students are then asked to imagine that they have a plane ticket that will allow them to travel anywhere in the world to do development work. Students are then asked to locate themselves on the map by moving to the part of the room where they'd like to work. Typically, international students will move themselves to the 'home' country or region, while local students will move themselves to locations conventionally associated as being sites of humanitarian assistance or development work in the 'developing' world. This typical response, while not exclusively the case, is certainly dominant enough to underline the relevance of the need to address the questions 'Who am I in development?' but also the 'Where am I in development?'

While we are able to bring interactive and participatory activities into the classroom, the notion of 'where' am I in development continues to be dominated by the assumption that one has to be out there, meaning outside the classroom or even better outside Australia, to be engaged in development. These observations were confirmed when we would encounter our students outside of the classroom, particularly those who are working in development, and be amazed by the confidence and skill they would demonstrate. However, this level of confidence seems to disappear when they enter the classroom. We therefore realized a need to facilitate a process whereby students recognize the experience, knowledge and skills they possess as adults and challenge the very notion of power within the classroom – thus problematizing the place of learning as a site of development practice.

As has been noted in previous parts of the chapter, we employ the same participatory methods that are employed in communities across the world. For example, we utilize Stan Burkey's (1993) proposition on Self-Reliant Participatory Development (SRPD) as a framework to conduct a needs analysis for the students. Burkey claims that SRPD has eight components: '(a) educational and (b) empowering, (c) process in which people in (d) partnership with each other and with those (e) able to assist them, identify problems and needs, (f) mobilize resources, and (g) assume responsibility themselves to plan, manage, control and assess the individual and (h) collective actions that they themselves decide upon' (Burkey, 1993: 205).

The extent of readiness of the students to accept themselves as learner and participant in development (simply by being enrolled in the subject and degree programme) runs in concert with their readiness to accept the classroom as a site of community development. If we are a community of learner participants in development, as previously defined in the section that explored Learning Circles, and we are here together in this classroom, then development is taking place here. The classroom involves multiple stakeholders who are operating from differently resourced contexts. In development, those contexts are typically categorized into North–South stereotypes that embody the dichotomous relationship between service providers, i.e. Northern NGOs (NNGOs) and donors, and service receivers, i.e. Southern NGOs (SNGOs) and beneficiaries (McFarlane, 2006). In our class community, we had people who identified as coming from the global North as well as from the global South. And we have the service provider, the University! As such, the same power dynamics play out in a classroom and the same principles of development can be applied at various stages.

CONCLUSION

Global development is a rapidly shifting and hotly contested field of work that requires the various actors at play to be, critically self-aware to their role, their identity and continuously reflecting in action. By utilizing the classroom as a site of development and seeing the students and staff as a community of practitioners, we have been able to critically reflect in action (Schon, 1983) while also acting as co-researchers investigating the value of experiential learning and participatory approaches to development. This experience and process that we have shared in this chapter recognizes that this self-awareness, of our own and our shared mental models (Denzau and North, 1994), has been primarily about the transformation of ourselves as learners, educators and development practitioners located in the Global north, who are seeking to effect change.

As Chambers (2013) recently highlighted, reflective practice should be embedded in all university subjects teaching development that includes both students and staff. By recognizing that the classroom is a site of development, we are learning with our students and preparing them for development practice by engaging with them as a community of practitioners: from varied geographical contexts, with diverse knowledge bases, and harbouring different levels of power.

Establishing Learning Circles and engaging in circle work, informed by Freire's own Culture Circles, allows that knowledge to be shared and discussed, which fosters a critical consciousness and alerts participants to the nuances of learning and participating in a community. As facilitators, we are part of this process. Collective learning involves both external and internal people (students and staff), and while a change agent is often required, they must be a party to the process of learning. Change manifests in us all, and within this context of a university subject, that has meant a constant evolution of content, the subject structure and how it is delivered. And after another year it looks like, thankfully so, this process is only going to continue!

Questions for Discussion

1   How relevant is Paulo Freire's critique of the 'banking' system of education to your own experiences of education? How might these experiences shape your development practice?
2   Is the ideal development practitioner a reflective learner? Why?
3   How applicable is the individual practice of learning through critical reflection to large international development institutions?

📖 FURTHER READING

Bolton, G. (2014) *Reflective Practice: Writing and Professional Development* (4th edn). London: Sage.

Chambers, R. (2012) *Provocations for Development* (1st edn) Rugby: Practical Action Publishing.

Freire, P. (2000) *Pedagogy of the Oppressed*, 30th Anniversary Edition. New York: Continuum.

REFERENCES

Arnstein, S.R. (2011) 'A Ladder of Citizen Participation', in A. Cornwall (ed.), *The Participation Reader.* London: Zed Books, pp. 3–18.

Aune, J.B. (2000) 'Logical Framework Approach and PRA – Mutually Exclusive or Complementary Tools for Project Planning?', *Development in Practice,* 10(5): 687–90. http://doi.org/10.1080/09614520020008850.

Burkey, S. (1993) *People First: A Guide to Self-Reliant Participatory Rural Development.* London: Zed Books.

Burnard, P. (1988) 'Experiential Learning: Some Theoretical Considerations', *International Journal of Lifelong Education,* 7(2): 127–33. http://doi.org/10.1080/0260137880070204.

Chambers, R. (1983) *Rural Development: Putting the Last First.* Harlow: Longman.

Chambers, R. (2004) *IDS Working Paper Ideas for Development: Reflecting Forwards* (No. 238). Brighton. Available at: www.ids.ac.uk/publication/ideas-for-development-reflecting-forwards (accessed 27 February 2017).

Chambers, R. (2010) *IDS Working Paper Paradigms, Poverty and Adaptive Pluralism* (No. 344). Brighton. Available at: www.ids.ac.uk/go/idspublication/paradigms-poverty-and-adaptive-pluralism-rs (accessed 27 February 2017).

Chambers, R. (2013) *Participation for Development: Why is this a Good Time to be Alive?* Available at: https://participationpower.wordpress.com/?s=why+it+is+a+good+time+to+be+alive (accessed 27 June 27 2016).

Cohen, J. and Uphoff, N. (2011) 'Participation's Place in Rural Development: Seeking Clarity through Specificity', in A. Cornwall (ed.), *The Participation Reader.* London: Zed Books, pp. 34–56.

Conrad, D. (2004) 'Exploring Risky Youth Experiences: Popular Theatre as a Participatory, Performative Research Method', *International Journal of Qualitative Methods,* 3(1): 12–25.

Davies, R. and Dart, J. (2005) 'A Dialogical, Story-Based Evaluation Tool: The Most Significant Change Technique', *American Journal of Evaluation,* 24(2): 137–55.

Dearden, P. (2005) 'A Positive Look at Monitoring, Review and Evaluation International Development Experiences Affecting Regeneration Work in the UK'. Available at: http://pdf2.hegoa.efaber.net/entry/content/881/A_positive_look_at_Monitoring__Review_and_Evaluation_.pdf (accessed 9 December 2016).

Denzau, A. and North, D.C. (1994) 'Shared Mental Models: Ideologies and Institutions', *Kyklos,* 47(1): 3–31.

Freire, P. (2000) *Pedagogy of the Oppressed,* 30th Anniversary Edition. New York: Continuum.

Gasper, D. (2000) 'Evaluating the "Logical Framework Approach" toward Learning-Orientated Development Evaluation', *Public Administration and Development,* 20: 17–28.

Guevara, J.R. (2002) 'Popular Environmental Education: Progressive Contextualisation of Local Practice in a Globalising World'. PhD Thesis. Victoria University of Technology.

Guevara, J.R. (2012) 'Progressive Contextualisation: Developing a Popular Environmental Education Curriculum in the Philippines', in P. Westoby and L. Shevellar (eds), *Learning and Mobilising for Community Development: A Radical Tradition of Community Based Education and Training.* Farnham: Ashgate, pp. 177–90.

Haslam, P. A., Schafer, J. and Beaudet, P. (2012) *Introduction to International Development: Approaches, Actors, and Issues* (2nd edn). Oxford: Oxford University Press.

Horton, M. and Freire, P. (1990) *We Make the Road by Walking: Conversations on Education and Social Change*. B. Bell, J. Gaventa and J.M. Peters (eds). Philadelphia, PA: Temple University Press.

Hummelbrunner, R. (2010) 'Beyond Logframe: Critique, Variations and Alternatives', in N. Fujita (ed.), *Beyond Logframe: Using Systems Concepts in Evaluation*. Tokyo: Foundation for Advanced Studies on International Development, pp. 1–35. Available at: www.fasid.or.jp/_files/publication/oda_21/h21-3.pdf (accessed 9 December 2016).

Knowles, M., Holton, E., III and Swanson, R. (2014) *The Adult Learner* (8th edn). Abingdon: Routledge.

Kolb, D.A. (1984) *Experiential Learning*. Upper Saddle River, NJ: Prentice Hall.

McFarlane, C. (2006) 'Crossing Borders: Development, Learning and the North: South Divide', *Third World Quarterly*, 27(8): 1413–37.

Mezirow, J. (1991) *Transformative Dimensions of Adult Learning*. San Francisco, CA: Jossey-Bass.

Mezirow, J. and Taylor, E.W. (2011) *Transformative Learning in Practice: Insights from Community, Workplace, and Higher Education*. San Francisco, CA: Jossey-Bass.

Padaki, V. (2007) 'The Human Organisation: Challenges in NGOs and Development Programmes', *Development in Practice*, 17(1): 65–77.

Rahnema, M. and Bawtree, V. (1997). *The Post-Development Reader*. London: Zed Books.

Robinson-Pant, A. (1995) 'PRA: A New Literacy?', *PLA Notes*, 24. London: IIED, pp. 78–82.

Rogers, A. (1992) *Adults Learning for Development*. London: Cassell Education Ltd.

Rogers, A. (2005) *Non-Formal Education: Flexible Schooling or Participatory Education?* Hong Kong: Comparative Education Research Centre, University of Hong Kong.

Schon, D. (1983) *The Reflective Practitioner – How Professionals Think in Action*. New York: Basic Books.

Souto-Manning, M. (2010) *Freire, Teaching, and Learning: Culture Circles Across Contexts*. New York: Peter Lang Publishing.

Steiner, R. and Hanks, D. (2016) 'The Development Conundrum', in R. Steiner and H. Duncan (eds), *Harnessing the Power of Collective Learning: Feedback, Accountability and Constituent Voice in Rural Development*. Abingdon: Routledge, pp. 1–15.

Taylor, P. (1993) *The Texts of Paulo Freire*. Buckingham and Philadelphia, PA: Open University Press.

Wade, S. and Hammick, M. (1999) 'Action Learning Circles: Action Learning in Theory and Practice', *Teaching in Higher Education*, 4(2): 163–78, doi: 10.1080/1356251990040202.

Westoby, P. and Dowling, G. (2009) *Dialogical Community Development*. Queensland: Tafina Press.

13

NAVIGATING DUALITIES: A CASE STUDY OF ORGANIZATIONAL GOVERNANCE IN CAMBODIAN CIVIL SOCIETY

LOUISE COVENTRY

INTRODUCTION

Models of governance used in large Western corporations and international non-government organizations (NGOs) are often assumed to be relevant to civil society organizations (CSOs) in developing contexts and with differing political regimes (Carver and Carver, 2001). Yet, this assumption is dubious on two counts. First, there is increasing evidence that Asians think differently and follow different social norms and mental models than do Westerners (Nisbett, 2003; World Bank, 2014). Second, the research community is still undecided about the extent to which insights from corporate governance can be applied to civil society organizations (Willems et al., 2016). This chapter focuses primarily on the first of these concerns. South East Asian polities, such as Cambodia, which generally attribute high value to the maintenance of social hierarchy, harmony and collectivist ideals and which are themselves governed in neo-patrimonial ways are unlikely to be well served by the wholesale application of Western and corporatist models; these models are not generally well-attuned to the challenges of governance in societies with a long history and culture of patronage. There is additional evidence that governance models need to be contextualized – culturally, politically, sectorally and otherwise – in order to ensure their relevance and applicability (Cornforth, 2014; Freiwirth, 2014; Ostrower and Stone, 2010). Demand for better governance, especially in fragile states and states emerging from conflict and in transition, typically comes from the broader international community more so than from citizens within these states, even though the intent is to build such demand among the local citizenry. Hughes (2013) goes so far as to argue that the international effort to instil 'good governance' in developing contexts is 'an imposition on local cultures that has a deadening impact on the possibility for a local emancipatory politics' (ibid.: 144).

This chapter opens with a review of (mostly Western) theories about how civil society organizations are – or should be – governed, juxtaposed with an outline of traditional and contemporary national governance practices in Cambodia. Current governance practices of civil society organizations in Cambodia are then described, elucidating the mismatch between international expectations and local/national practices. Civil society leaders have shown resilience by matching the new concepts to local requirements and generating advice for how others can do likewise. The process of adaptation outlined here yields important lessons for those wishing to contribute to governance theory and practice in non-Western contexts.

GOVERNANCE OF CIVIL SOCIETY ORGANIZATIONS

The governance of civil society organizations refers to the systems and processes by which organizational stakeholders ensure the overall direction, control and accountability of a NGO. Boards are sometimes equated with governance (Renz, 2013). However, changes in the complexity, pace, scale and nature of community concerns and demands means that the domain of governance has moved beyond the domain of the board (ibid.). Cornforth (2012) argues that governance extends well beyond boards and that the focus on boards at the expense of broader issues has not served institutions well.

Like the focus on governance-as-board, subsequent models used to establish boards for NGOs are similarly narrow. Commonly, a corporatist policy governance model is adopted. Corporate (or policy) governance rests on several assumptions, including that the civil society organization is performing actions required by stakeholders, that the stakeholders will judge the outcomes, that the board members are elected and that the board is independent of management (Hasan and Onyx, 2008).

A major proponent of the policy governance approach is John Carver (2006). Carver's work is perhaps foremost in a burgeoning popular literature recommending certain practices and processes to assist boards fulfil their responsibilities. 'How-to' guides informed by Carver's approach have proliferated. Most of this literature is generic and offers one-size-fits-all solutions to governance problems that vary across types of NGOs and between non-government and commercial organizations (Friedman and Phillips, 2004).

Research into organizational governance is generally informed by a small range of key theories, chief among them being principal–agent (agency) theory, stewardship theory, resource dependence theory and institutional theory (Cornforth, 2014; Renz and Andersson, 2014). Agency theory is the dominant mainstream theory informing governance research.

It underpins Carver's policy governance model (Jegers, 2009), and, significantly, informs the legal framework for NGOs in most jurisdictions (Renz and Andersson, 2014). Agency theory is deductive in its methodology and is focused on the relationship between principals (owners) and agents (executives) who manage on their behalf (Jegers, 2009; Stone and Ostrower, 2007). Agency theory is an awkward and ill-fitting match to NGO contexts because it is not immediately obvious who is the principal and the agent in the context of NGOs: NGOs have no clearly defined owner and answer to multiple stakeholders (Renz and Andersson, 2014). Nonetheless, as agency theory forms the basis for much legal guidance and donor advice to NGOs, it cannot be ignored.

Contrary to agency theory's pessimistic assumptions about the self-interested and self-serving motives of executives, stewardship theory suggests the potential for 'pro-organizational' motives of directors. It purports that problems of governance potentially lay not in the self-interest of managers but rather in the assumptions made by distant others as to the managers' self-interested motives (Van Puyvelde et al., 2012). Most NGOs appear to operate from a governance logic that is better described by stewardship theory than agency theory. Building on stewardship theory, stakeholder theory focuses on how organizational governance enables the management of relationships with stakeholders (Young, 2011).

Resource dependence theory, unlike agency theory, is inductively derived from empirical studies. It suggests that organizations are dependent on external actors for their resources, and that they therefore will act to reduce uncertainty and manage their dependence. Similar to resource dependence theory, institutional theory's central premise is that organizations are shaped by their institutional environment and seeking legitimacy from external stakeholders improves performance and the prospects of sustainability. NGOs could, for example, adopt the prevailing norms and values of the prevailing institutions within their environment, in order to secure legitimacy (Renz and Andersson, 2014). According to Renz (2007), institutional theory suggests a maintenance role for boards, whereby the board identifies with societal expectations, whereas resource dependency theory implies that board members should focus on their linking role (as a network of interlinking directorates).

The major theories described here are apt for explaining only some aspects of governance, sometimes at the expense of other theories. More recent studies have addressed some of the shortcomings of single theories by combining them for new insights (Harrison and Murray, 2012; Kreutzer and Jacobs, 2011; Renz 2007; Van Puyvelde et al., 2012). Given that it is unlikely that a grand theory of civil society governance can be found, a meta-theoretical approach that draws from various perspectives would appear more promising (Cornforth, 2014). In particular, new theories informed by an understanding of complexity, paradox and contingencies seem likely to be useful for a rapidly changing, global world.

Bradshaw (2009; Bradshaw et al., 1998) has been a leading proponent of the use of contingency theory in governance research. Contingencies to be considered include organizational size and complexity, mission, life stage and environmental conditions. Ostrower and Stone (2010) similarly argue that governance can be understood as a conditional phenomenon meaning that different governance features can be influenced by different contingencies but, moreover, the same contingency may affect the same board or governance feature differently. Summarizing the situation, Bradshaw and her colleagues explained: 'Having reviewed the normative and academic literatures on governance in not-for-profit organizations, we conclude that there is no consensus about an ideal way of governing non-profit organizations' (Bradshaw et al., 1998: 11).

Traditional and radical alternatives to the dominant corporate (or policy) governance model exist, some of which are informed by dialogic and relational approaches such as Theory U (Scharmer, 2007), complexity theory, democratic and critical perspectives (Guo et al., 2014), and storytelling (Bradshaw, 2002), and many of which are also informed by ideas of network or relational governance. Relational governance can be understood as a strategy for managing the imperative to join up service delivery in response to 'wicked problems' (Phillips and Smith, 2011). Wicked problems are ambiguous, complex issues, which involve numerous interdependent factors. Often, they are 'long-term social and organizational planning problems' which require coordination between many actors to tackle effectively.[1] Relational governance mirrors wicked problems by focusing on interdependence rather than power relationships, and negotiation and persuasion rather than control (ibid.).

In the face of new relational and networked systems of governance within civil society, fresh approaches for theorizing governance are needed (Cornforth, 2014). Inspiration for creative thinking can be drawn from self-organizing systems, models focused on emergent leadership drawn from complexity science (Hazy et al., 2007), generative relationships (Zimmerman and Hayday, 1999), Community-Engagement Governance™ (Freiwirth, 2014), storytelling organizations (Bradshaw, 2002), and dialogic, learning organizations (Isaacs, 1999; Jacobs and Wilford, 2010; Wheatley, 2009). Such fresh approaches can usefully be applied to explore network and collaborative governance, the governance of hybrid organizations and alternative governance designs, especially in the global South, and especially using action-based research (Bradshaw et al., 1998; Cornforth, 2012, 2014; Guo et al., 2014; Ostrower and Stone, 2010; Renz and Andersson, 2014; Stone and Ostrower, 2007).

GOVERNANCE IN CAMBODIA

As already noted, the governance of civil society organizations is a phenomenon distinct from public and corporate governance. Yet, civil society governance is embedded in and informed by national and other forms of public governance (Steen-Johnsen et al., 2011). Hence, it is important to understand the broader social and political context in which civil society governance is located.

Little information is available about traditional governance in Cambodia. Chandler (2008), a leading scholar of Cambodia, understands the Cambodian term *rajakar*,[2] literally 'royal work', to most closely approximate *governance*, as commonly understood. Traditionally, *rajakar* was the privilege enjoyed by people freed in some way from the

---

[1] T. Ritchey (2005, revised 2013) 'Wicked Problems – Structuring Social Messes with Morphological Analysis', available at: www.swemorph.com/wp.html (accessed 15 July 2015).

[2] Alternative spelling: *reichkar*.

obligation of growing their own food (ibid.: 3). The governed grew food for those above them in exchange for their protection. During the Angkorean period, families succeeded in securing these freedoms – and controlling land and labour – primarily through their connection with royally sponsored religious foundations. Kings were expected to grant land and slaves to these foundations (Mabbett and Chandler, 1995). When these foundations were replaced by Theravada Buddhist temples, the forms of social mobilization that characterized Angkor broke down, inspiring significant out-migration. The experiences of villagers at this time is impossible to fathom as no data is available (Chandler, 2008). However, the essence of *rajakar* held firm through the period of French colonial rule. Through French eyes, royal work enabled the extraction of revenue from peasants in exchange for 'guidance' (ibid.: 170).

After the republic of Cambodia was formed, and in particular during the period of Khmer Rouge rule, the word for governance changed. It became 'state work' (*rothkar*), not royal work. The word subsequently reverted back to 'royal work' in the 1980s during the period of the People's Republic of Kampuchea, possibly as a backlash against the Khmer Rouge regime, but this word is again unpopular.[3] The word *rajakar* has been unpopular, most notably since the coup d'état of 1997 (in which the Cambodian People's Party apparently orchestrated the deaths of leading FUNCINPEC party members, leading to several party luminaries fleeing the country, e.g. Sam Rainsy, Prince Norodom). *Rajakar* has recently further reduced its popularity, perhaps in response to the death of the King Father in 2012. Since the 1990s, *rajakar* has been progressively replaced by *ak phibalkech*, a new alternative and more technical word for governance associated with the process of decentralization and deconcentration (Affiliated Network for Social Accountability in East Asia and the Pacific, 2010). Poorly understood, especially outside the capital city, it generally refers to the functional, responsive and accountable administration of the state (ibid.). When paired with the word 'good' (*la'ar*), it refers to an ideal type of benevolent leadership characterized by transparency, accountability and the absence of corruption. This brief review of the etymology of 'governance' in Cambodia points to an alienation of Cambodian people from the responsibilities of governance; governance is seemingly either poorly understood or deemed more rightly the work of others.

Contemporary national governance in Cambodia is weak and poor (Ear, 2013; Jacobsen and Stuart-Fox, 2013; Malena and Chhim, 2009; Un, 2011). Cambodia is notionally a democracy, although it may also be described, following the liberal scholar of democracy, Larry Diamond, as a 'competitive authoritarianism' (Mantel, 2010). In practice, the dominant form of governance in Cambodia is patronage, or more precisely, neo-patrimonialism (Ear, 2013; Springer, 2009).

Neo-patrimonialism is the socio-political dominance of patron-client relations, which ensures that existing power relations are protected or at least not challenged (Springer, 2009). Pak and colleagues (2007: 43) explain neo-patrimonialism as a hybrid of two forms of governance and power, being patronage networks and legal-rational bureaucracy. Key characteristics of neo-patrimonialism, in Cambodia as elsewhere,

---

[3]Personal communication with Mr Chum Samnang, 18 May 2013.

include highly personalized power, co-option of formal and informal mechanisms of governance to gather personal wealth through rent-seeking, disruption of core services and functions, the creation of inequity and high resistance to reforms (Pak et al., 2007). Values in Cambodia that support neo-patrimonialism include the personalization of power (Jacobsen and Stuart-Fox, 2013) and the prevalence of interpersonal obligations and chains of unequal reciprocity and expectations around wealth formation (Horng et al., 2007; Pak et al., 2007). Governance in Cambodia is thus relational more than transactional (Hughes, 2013). Patrons in Cambodia are mostly politicians who have emerged in the post-Khmer Rouge era and who combine political, military, economic and administrative power to exploit resources and disrupt core administrative functions and service delivery (Pak et al., 2007). Patronage is supported and maintained by rural political support, especially through the giving of material gifts to villagers (Hughes, 2006; Pak et al., 2007; Un, 2005).

CIVIL SOCIETY GOVERNANCE IN CAMBODIA

Consistent with the 'post-Washington consensus', many look to civil society as the key to wider governance reform in Cambodia (Ear, 2013; Un, 2011), although the capacity of civil society to lead such reforms has been questioned (Ear, 2013; Merla, 2010; Springer, 2009). Most registered NGOs in Cambodia have a board and attempt to follow the corporate model of governance: nearly 80 per cent of respondents to the 2011 NGO Census report that they have a governing body such as a board of directors or trustees (Cooperation Committee for Cambodia, 2012). Similarly, almost all organizations surveyed by Suárez and Marshall (2014) have a board of directors (88 per cent of local NGOs and 93 per cent of international NGOs). Most boards are quite small, with an average of six members, and boards meet approximately three times a year. Suárez and Marshall (ibid.) found statistically significant differences between international and local NGOs, with boards of international NGOs involving more members and meeting more regularly.

The relative infrequency of local NGO board meetings suggests weak NGO-board ties. Alarmingly, Henke's recent study found one-quarter of sampled Cambodian NGOs to have serious financial system weaknesses and weak governance: one in five to seven Cambodian NGOs is affected by fraud (Henke, 2015). Suárez and Marshall's (2014) finding that 20 per cent of NGO leaders surveyed did not know how many members were on their board or how frequently the board met is similarly concerning. It appears that many NGOs under-use their board, regarding it as a peer support network for the director, a provider of general advice and inputs and, sometimes, a rubber stamp.[4] Underscoring the potentially tokenistic role of the board, the Royal Government of Cambodia, while requiring NGOs to have a board, in practice does not accord legal authority to the board. In instances where the board has attempted to remove an executive director, the Royal Government of Cambodia has taken the side of the director against the board. Indeed, there are some local examples of directors of NGOs sacking the entire board.

---

[4]Minutes of a meeting held on 18 March 2013 in Phnom Penh, attended by nine international donor organizations, to discuss how best to develop the capacity of board members of NGOs.

Many donors active in Cambodia require a commitment to corporate governance practices as a condition of receiving funds, consistent with practice in other Asian countries (Hasan and Onyx, 2008). Notably, however, foreign funding generally requires a board, but not a membership base nor an annual general meeting or any other indicators of stakeholder input into decision-making processes (ibid.).

Almost all respondents to the 2011 NGO Census (97 per cent) report that they have a written constitution or statutes and by-laws (which are also required by Cambodian law), and a little over two-thirds (68 per cent) that they produce a strategic plan. A substantial majority (88 per cent) say that they produce an annual financial report, with the same number producing an annual programme report. External auditing of accounting and financial situations is undertaken by 65 per cent of respondents, mostly annually (Cooperation Committee for Cambodia, 2012).

While NGOs themselves report relatively high capacity for governance (Yin and Sok, 2012), Suárez and Marshall (2014) identified governance as one of the more significant capacity challenges for NGOs. Key (self-identified) areas for improvement include long-term monitoring and evaluation planning, interpretation of vision and mission statements, functioning of boards, strategic planning and managing diversions from plans in response to donor agendas and objectives (Yin and Sok, 2012).

It is often the largest and most formal NGOs that participate in national census and other local research initiatives. Yet, civil society in Cambodia is diverse and alternative forms of civil society are numerous (Coventry, 2016). Among other less formal civil society organizations, it is often a respected elder who is the founder and who makes all key decisions associated with its management. Some organizations may be founded by well-meaning expatriates or local elites, including returnees. Visitors may return to their home country and raise funds to start an organization in Cambodia, or long-term residents may identify and then seek to fill a particular need within Cambodian society. Examples abound and include Sunrise Cambodia, Empowering Youth in Cambodia, VBNK, Social Services Cambodia, Kaleb and the Somaly Mam Foundation. Expatriate-founded organizations may quickly become formal and resemble NGOs described above, but in smaller and less formal organizations initiated by local elders, different characteristics may be observed (ibid.). For example, membership may be understood as a given and not subject to change. While elite-sponsorship, as an approach to governance, is open to abuse and corruption, it rests on time-honoured traditions of personal integrity, tradition and maintenance of social harmony. Governance frameworks are often adopted which allow the founder to continue to be influential, consistent with the role of a patron. The founder may collect a mix of expatriate and local individuals to assist in the governance, perhaps forming a board; however, organizational ownership is unlikely to rest with that group. Rather, the sense of ownership (the 'principal' of agency theory) stays with the founder or at least is perceived as being with the founder (Block and Rosenberg, 2002). While many founders seek to empower others and act with enormous integrity, the recent negative publicity of Somaly Mam[5] and her subsequent resignation from her eponymous

---

[5]See: www.newsweek.com/2014/05/30/somaly-mam-holy-saint-and-sinner-sex-trafficking-2516 42.html (accessed 21 July 2015).

foundation[6] illustrates some of the dangers of reliance on a single charismatic individual. O'Dwyer and Unerman (2010) confirm that international NGOs are aware that some local NGOs in developing contexts are increasingly managed by local elites, partly in response to the need to comply with increasingly stringent donor requirements for accountability. In their conclusion, they caution that without increased attempts at more direct oversight of local NGOs' relations with beneficiaries (by donors), then limited consultation and representativeness among local elites, where it exists, may go unchecked and possibly restrict beneficiaries from driving the focus of development efforts more directly.

An earlier review of the NGO sector in Cambodia (Bañez-Ockelford and Catalla, 2010) recommended that the sector critically analyze the governance concepts that have been introduced by international donors, and examine how these can be practised through maximizing some traditional practices and informal structures or relationships within society. For example, according to these authors, it may be useful to examine from within a patronage system, how 'affection-based connections between networks such as friendship, kinship and loyalty' (ibid.: 46) or how the Buddhist concept of karma can be used to enhance accountability. Similarly, it is useful to challenge donors/development partners to take greater account of the unique context of Cambodia in determining their expectations of governance practice and to reassess their approach and strategies of working with NGOs (ibid.).

A MISMATCH

Before taking up the recommendations of Bañez-Ockleford and Catalla (ibid.), it is important to reflect on the significant mismatch of ideas thrown into relief by the above canvassing of international (Western) literature and the description of historical and contemporary practices in Cambodia. This mismatch is apparent in the theoretical foundations of governance, in board practices and in the uneasy co-existence of patronage and corporatism. In terms of the theory underpinning Cambodian governance, unlike most jurisdictions across the developed world, the new law for NGOs in Cambodia is not premised on agency theory. Yet, this approach continues to inform donor interventions, as evidenced, for example, by donor requirements for a board and audit statement. Of mainstream governance theories, institutional theory is perhaps most relevant to Cambodia in that many NGOs seem to adopt the prevailing norms and values of the prevailing institutions within their environment, in order to secure legitimacy. As already explained, prevailing institutions are neo-patrimonial in character, and so too are boards. They often meet irregularly, and wield little power in practice although they serve important symbolic functions and, through their very existence, comply with donor requirements. Consistent with Renz's (2007) prediction, boards in Cambodia are often focused on maintenance functions. Specifically, for many boards, this means adopting a minimalist approach, although being attentive to donor requirements is itself demanding. A complex and multi-relational balance is struck – simultaneously attending and responding to international

---

[6]See: www.newsweek.com/somaly-mam-foundation-closes-278657 (accessed 21 July 2015).

donor standards and conforming to broader societal expectations of non-interference, respect for elites, and limited involvement in decision-making. Gaps in understanding remain especially in regard to how downward accountability works in the context of neo-patrimonialism, and what possibilities and opportunities may exist for Cambodian NGOs to transcend the limits of national governance. This tangled, patchy backdrop formed the context in which ethnographic, participatory action-research was undertaken in Cambodia.

Text Box 13.1   Case Study: A Cooperative Inquiry into Civil Society Governance in Cambodia

A cooperative inquiry into civil society governance, conducted in partnership with seven Cambodian co-researchers from NGOs, examined options for strengthening governance and demonstrating accountability to organizational stakeholders. Cooperative inquiry is a participative research methodology with roots in humanist psychology (Reason, 1999). During 2014, seven Cambodian NGO staff, advisors, executive directors and board members met together on 15 occasions to reflect critically on Cambodian NGO governance. These group meetings were mostly four hours, allowing each group member to complete at least six cycles of planning, action and reflection. A cumulative total of more than 50 specific actions were planned, undertaken and subjected to group reflection. An average of six group members attended each meeting. Additionally, and mostly to catch up on missed meetings, group members met individually with the author on more than 20 occasions. Field visits were undertaken to group members' organizations, and workshops took place with group members' boards. To analyze the data generated, a collective mind map was created by the group twice during the planning-action-reflection process. Each group member also created a personal learning trajectory. Initial findings were presented for validation by co-researchers to a community of peers in Phnom Penh (December 2014), and subsequent deeper analysis by the author yielded new and sharper insights.

The cooperative inquiry group sought to identify alternative, indigenous models of governance in Cambodia, but found only boards and patronage. Confirming earlier descriptions of Cambodian governance practices presented above, the cooperative inquiry group found that corporate models of governance are notionally the preferred model, but patronage co-opts and works around the corporate model of governance, co-existing awkwardly and creating a complex dual system of governance that does not ultimately serve organizational beneficiaries. Patronage influences NGOs in that NGOs are often treated as a business, sometimes as a family business. Executive directors were found to act as the absolute power and 'owner' of the NGOs. Directors sometimes appoint board members as an exchange of favours: 'I will sit on your board, if you sit on mine.' In this respect, NGO governance practices tend to mirror patterns of national governance in which a shadow state of myriad family and business connections and networks of patronage are ultimately more powerful and influential than the formal channels for decision-making and the exercise of authority. While this dual system of governance for NGOs is generally unacknowledged, it is sub-textual in current legislation: The *Civil Code of Cambodia 2007* treats executive directors as the ultimate authority of NGOs, instead of boards or other governance mechanisms.

Stories of three cooperative inquiry group members show how civil society leaders can – and do – respond and adapt constructively to this duality, finding creative ways to blend newly imported models of governance with local knowledge and requirements, and identifying options that (they believe will) better serve organizations and their constituents.

Phallika was employed by a large membership organization and served as secretariat to a broad coalition of civil society actors advocating for improved water governance. She was interested to learn how Buddhist precepts and frameworks could be used to support improved governance, and especially downwards accountability, among civil society organizations. She talked to monks and former monks working in leadership roles in civil society. Phallika became most excited when a monk explained to her how he uses the cycle of a monk's day to understand community development processes. A monk's day is characterized by mindfulness. In the early morning, monks walk local streets to collect alms. During their walk, they have an opportunity to be present with people, assess the mood in the community, and observe and identify emerging issues of concern. In returning to the pagoda, they pass on their observations to senior clerics and laypeople. This information is used to help determine where the monks should spend the remainder of their morning – visiting communities, offering a spiritual and stabilizing presence, sharing teachings and presiding over ceremonies of various types. After their extended community visits, monks can then reflect on what they have learned in communities, and bring their reports back to the pagoda. In the afternoon, monks spend time in prayer and devotion, often with the communities with which they have just worked in mind; this can be understood as interceding on behalf of the needy to a divine power, a form of advocacy. In the early hours of the morning, there is time again for deep reflection and meditation, which helps the monks to determine which communities are the priority to visit for the collection of alms. Phallika explained how the descriptions of a monk's daily tasks are well understood in Cambodia, even if they are not closely followed. She immediately recognized the parallels between these five activities and community development and engagement processes: rapid initial assessment (1), review and planning (2), deeper engagement and interventions (3), advocacy (4) and reflection/evaluation/learning (5). Phallika has commenced using the cycle of a monk's day to inform and teach others about how to engage communities in a reflective manner and demonstrate downwards accountability.

Consistent with the dual model of governance, board reliance on executive directors is a significant problem in Cambodia. Many executive directors 'govern' as well as 'manage' their NGOs. Board members are also often directors of other NGOs and, overall, the composition of boards is relatively homogenous and insular. More positively, the cooperative inquiry group learnt about the possibilities for change when one group member managed to awaken his 'sleeping' board through careful and systematic work towards this end. Teng was on a mission. As executive director of a small, provincial NGO, he had identified even before the research had begun, the urgency of reforming his board such that they could enact their roles and responsibilities. He talked of this as 'awakening the sleeping board'. He came to the first meeting with his precious 'Book of the Board' (by David Fishel) cradled in his arm and he had clear ideas that the policy approach to governance would serve him and his organization best. Using the research process as his support, Teng worked methodically towards his vision. Interestingly, he began by using a relational and personal approach, typical of patronage models of governance: He picked off board members one by one, asking them what they thought about the quality of the board's function and sharing his concerns. To a person, they agreed and supported him. Only then, the issue was discussed more formally in a board meeting, and board members could 'save face' by raising the issues themselves. The board asked for assistance in learning more about their roles and responsibilities and how to fulfil them and

(Continued)

(Continued)

so Teng arranged a capacity development workshop for them. The board also then recruited additional members similarly sympathetic to following corporate governance principles and they appointed a new chair. Fortunately, the newly recruited board members were able to participate in the planned workshop. The workshop helped the board members to understand their roles and responsibilities, using patron-client relationships as the foundation and starting point for learning new models of governance. Teng advises that his board meetings are now much better attended, more frequent, he no longer leads the meetings by default, and he is getting the support that he needs and wants from the board.

Importantly, the cooperative inquiry found that the quality of a board's function was determined by how well members understand their roles. This contrasts to assumptions held by many Cambodians (which would appear to have roots in a deep understanding of patronage systems) that celebrities and high-profile board members will bring 'quality' to the board. Predictably, the roles and responsibilities of board members, from a corporatist perspective, were found to be poorly understood. More positively, board members were often found to be committed and willing to learn, challenging locally received wisdom that board members are time-poor and unwilling to commit the time required for effective governance. Indeed, board members often have more resources than they realize, such as networks, commitment and passion. Cooperative inquiry group members found that board members are inspired when they understand their roles and responsibilities clearly and feel valued and acknowledged. Sopeat's story shows this clearly.

Sopeat was newly appointed as the inaugural chair of a fledgling organisation. Her first experience of involvement in a board, Sopeat was anxious to do a good job. Sadly, the board had a rocky start when a decision made by the board was overturned by staff who claimed that, because the organisation was still in the process of registering, the board was not legally constituted and could make only non-binding decisions. Sopeat decided to ask her fellow board members directly what they needed and wanted. She was struck by the profound nature of the responses especially given the simplicity of the question. She learned that board members wanted:

- Support to develop their capacity – access to knowledge, opportunities to develop their skills, and mentoring especially by board members of other organizations.
- Acknowledgement and respect and a sense of being valued by the organization and publicly.
- Recognition from donors and other agencies and appropriate introductions to others, as required.
- Enough power to make decisions (sometimes, power is not real or genuine, especially relative to senior staff).
- Accessible, convenient, well-resourced and well-planned meetings.

As the issue was not raised by Sopeat's informants, the cooperative inquiry challenges the locally prevailing assumption – as expressed at multiple public meetings about governance – that board members want compensation for their efforts. To help strengthen the board's capacity, Sopeat contributed to planning and facilitating a workshop for her board. A highlight of this workshop, a powerful and emotionally charged moment, was when each board member stood, in turn, to articulate the strengths that he or she was bringing to the board, and received an ovation from their peers.

THE EMERGENCE OF HYBRID MODELS OF GOVERNANCE – IDEAS FOR ACTION

New challenges are emerging which add weight to the urgency of untangling the governance challenges facing civil society organizations in Cambodia. These new challenges are an increasing imperative to work in partnership across diverse organizations and the emergence of hybrid organizations that traverse the space of business, government and civil society, each of which further complicate issues of governance (Billis, 2010).

The cooperative inquiry group identified a range of ideas, based on their own experiences of attempting to reform and improve governance in their own organizations, for improving civil society governance in Cambodia. These ideas centre on deepening community understandings of governance, using patron–client relationships as the foundation and starting point for learning new models of governance and articulating functional options for hybridity (of patronage and corporate governance models).

Taking account of the history and culture of patronage in Cambodia, boards could consider appointing a meeting facilitator rather than a chairperson, thereby disrupting the hierarchical power relations typical of patronage. Boards may also choose to rewrite by-laws to confirm that the chairperson (or equivalent) cannot make decisions on the board's behalf. Alternatively, boards may draw relationships between organizational stakeholders and examine how these connect to the board members and, potentially, also connect individual board members to a personal constituency or client base, thereby creating a functional form of patronage for organizational stakeholders who may otherwise be overlooked.

Boards in Cambodia require greater diversity, at least to the extent that boards and NGOs, or their donors, continue to choose to follow a corporate or policy model of governance. It could be wise for NGOs to consider including representatives of government, business and beneficiaries on the board, such as school principals, subnational councillors, and to recruit for gender balance. Former auditors can be good board members as they have skills in financial oversight, which may otherwise be difficult to secure. Boards can usefully consider creating a policy nominating a waiting period before former staff can be recruited, e.g. one year. Setting, and then following, mandates for the term of board members could assist in ensuring that the board is fresh or regularly reinvigorated.

According to the corporate/policy model of governance followed – and preferred – by most NGOs in Cambodia, the board leads recruitment of new board members, unless there is an election of board members by ordinary members (as is common among membership organizations). A good process for recruitment – learnt from the current practice of Banteay Srei, a Cambodian NGO focused on women's civil and political participation – could involve two formal interviews, the first as a background check and to ensure that there are no obvious conflicts of interest, the second for a discussion of roles and responsibilities. Clear, written instructions about expectations, roles and responsibilities could sensibly be provided to each potential new board member, as well as detailed information about the NGO. Board members can be asked to visit projects within the first year of their membership on the board, and be asked to sign a contract or similar document to this effect.

Board members will likely need a capacity development plan, separate from staff. Remembering that capacity for governance is values-based, it is useful to meet with individual board members, one by one, find a change agent on the inside, if possible, and identify a trigger to start the conversation about improving governance. Then, board members can be invited to a planning event at which a strengths-based, empowering approach can be used to facilitate discussions. In Cambodia, it seems that board members are willing to learn more. In planning for developing their capacity, the cooperative inquiry group can advise that boards will likely need extra support to find ways to hear and engage voices of beneficiaries in decision-making.

CONCLUSION

Civil society organizations in Cambodia have, by and large, embraced donor interpretations of what constitutes good governance. However, implementation of these ideas is patchy at best and deeply dysfunctional at worst. Western models of 'good governance' sit uneasily and awkwardly with local models of patronage creating a complex dual system of governance that does not ultimately serve organizational beneficiaries. Here, the creative efforts of civil society leaders to navigate this duality in ways that do serve organizational beneficiaries have been showcased. Civil society leaders have matched new governance concepts to local requirements and generated advice for how others can do likewise. The process of navigation and adaptation is complex and non-linear. Sometimes, leaders feel the need to resist one model and embrace a second; on other occasions, this is reversed. Mindful reflection on governance, peer-supported learning and a sustained commitment to improving outcomes for a range of organizational stakeholders, especially beneficiaries, have enabled careful decisions to be made and new practices adopted. Overall, the co-researchers' reflections on their experiences and ideas for action make a significant contribution to understanding and enhancing the quality of civil society governance in developing South East Asian contexts.

Questions for Discussion

1   In what ways do approaches to organizational governance in Cambodia differ from Western models and ideals?
2   What is meant by the term 'relational governance' and where might this fit within the taxonomy of governance forms proposed in Chapter 4?
3   How might participatory and/or action research approaches, such as cooperative inquiry, be useful tools with which to build governance capacity within small development organizations?

📖 FURTHER READING

Ear, S. (2013) *Aid Dependence in Cambodia: How Foreign Assistance Undermines Democracy*. New York: Columbia University Press.

Hasan, S. and Onyx, J. (eds) (2008) *Comparative Third Sector Governance in Asia: Structure, Process and Political Economy*. New York: Springer.

Jacobs, A. and Wilford, R. (2010) 'Listen First: A Pilot System for Managing Downward Accountability in NGOs', *Development in Practice*, 20(7): 797–811.

REFERENCES

Affiliated Network for Social Accountability in East Asia and the Pacific (2010) *The Evolving Meaning of Social Accountability in Cambodia*. Manila: ANSA-EAP.

Bañez-Ockelford, J. and Catalla, A.P. (2010) *Reflections, Challenges and Choices: 2010 Review of NGO Sector in Cambodia*. Phnom Penh: Cooperation Committee for Cambodia.

Billis, D. (2010) 'Towards a Theory of Hybrid Organisations', in D. Billis (ed.), *Hybrid Organizations and the Third Sector: Challenges for Practice, Theory and Policy*. Basingstoke and New York: Palgrave Macmillan, pp. 46–69.

Block, S.R. and Rosenberg, S. (2002) 'Toward an Understanding of Founder's Syndrome: An Assessment of Power and Privilege among Founders of Nonprofit Organizations', *Nonprofit Management and Leadership*, 12(4): 353–68.

Bradshaw, P. (2002) 'Reframing Board-Staff Relations: Exploring the Governance Function Using a Storytelling Metaphor', *Nonprofit Management and Leadership*, 12(4): 471–84.

Bradshaw, P. (2009) 'A Contingency Approach to Nonprofit Governance', *Nonprofit Management and Leadership*, 20(1): 61–81.

Bradshaw, P., Hayday, B., Armstrong, R., Levesque, J. and Rykert, L. (1998) 'Nonprofit Governance Models: Problems and Prospects', Paper Presented to ARNOVA Conference, Seattle, WA.

Carver, J. (2006) *Boards that Make a Difference: A New Design for Leadership in Nonprofit and Public Organizations* (3rd edn). San Francisco, CA: Jossey-Bass.

Carver, J. and Carver, M. (2001) 'Carver's Policy Governance Model in Nonprofit Organizations'. Available at: www.carvergovernance.com/pg-np.htm (accessed 7 July 2016).

Chandler, D.P. (2008) *A History of Cambodia* (4th edn). Boulder, CO: Westview Press.

Cooperation Committee for Cambodia (2012) *CSO Contributions to the Development of Cambodia, 2011*. Phnom Penh: Cooperation Committee for Cambodia.

Cornforth, C. (2012) 'Nonprofit Governance Research: Limitations of the Focus on Boards and Suggestions for New Directions', *Nonprofit and Voluntary Sector Quarterly*, 41(6): 1116–35.

Cornforth, C. (2014) 'Nonprofit Governance Research: The Need for Innovative Perspectives and Approaches', in C. Cornforth and W.A. Brown (eds), *Nonprofit Governance: Innovative Perspectives and Approaches*. Abingdon and New York: Routledge, pp. 1–14.

Coventry, L. (2016) 'Civil Society in Cambodia: Challenges and Contestations', in S. Springer and K. Brickell (eds), *Handbook of Contemporary Cambodia*. Abingdon: Routledge, pp. 53–63.

Ear, S. (2013) *Aid Dependence in Cambodia: How Foreign Assistance Undermines Democracy*. New York: Columbia University Press.

Freiwirth, J. (2014) 'Community-Engagement Governance: Engaging Stakeholders for Community Impact', in C. Cornforth and W.A. Brown (eds), *Nonprofit Governance: Innovative Perspectives and Approaches*. Abingdon and New York: Routledge, pp. 183–209.

Friedman, A. and Phillips, M. (2004) 'Balancing Strategy and Accountability: A Model for the Governance of Professional Associations', *Nonprofit Management and Leadership*, 15(2): 187–204.

Guo, C., Metelsky, B.A. and Bradshaw, P. (2014) 'Out of the Shadows: Nonprofit Governance Research from Democratic and Critical Perspectives', in C. Cornforth and W.A. Brown (eds), *Nonprofit Governance: Innovative Perspectives and Approaches*. Abingdon and New York: Routledge, pp. 47–68.

Harrison, Y.D. and Murray, V. (2012) 'Perspectives on the Leadership of Chairs of Nonprofit Organization Boards of Directors: A Grounded Theory Mixed-Method Study', *Nonprofit Management and Leadership*, 22(4): 411–37.

Hasan, S. and Onyx, J. (eds) (2008) *Comparative Third Sector Governance in Asia: Structure, Process and Political Economy*. New York: Springer.

Hazy, J., Goldstein, J. and Lichtenstein, B. (eds) (2007) *Complex Systems Leadership Theory: New Perspectives from Complexity Science on Social and Organisational Effectiveness*. Mansfield, MA: ISCE.

Henke, R. (2015) *NGO Governance in Cambodia: Service and Support Options for Improving Financial Management*. Phnom Penh: Southeast Asia Development Program.

Horng, V., Pak, K., Eng, N., Ann, S., Kim, S., Knowles, J. and Craig, D. (2007) *Annual Development Review 2006–07*. Phnom Penh: CDRI, Chapter 8: 'Conceptualising Accountability: The Cambodian case'.

Hughes, C. (2006) 'The Politics of Gifts: Tradition and Regimentation in Contemporary Cambodia', *Journal of Southeast Asian Studies*, 37(3): 469–89.

Hughes, C. (2013) 'Friction, Good Governance and the Poor: Cases from Cambodia', *International Peacekeeping*, 20(2): 144–58.

Isaacs, W. (1999) *Dialogue and the Art of Thinking Together*. New York: Doubleday.

Jacobs, A. and Wilford, R. (2010) 'Listen First: A Pilot System for Managing Downward Accountability in NGOs', *Development in Practice*, 20(7): 797–811.

Jacobsen, T. and Stuart-Fox, M. (2013) *Power and Political Culture in Cambodia*. Singapore: National University of Singapore, Asia Research Institute.

Jegers, M. (2009) '"Corporate" Governance in Nonprofit Organizations', *Nonprofit Management and Leadership*, 20(2): 143–64.

Kreutzer, K. and Jacobs, C. (2011) 'Balancing Control and Coaching in CSO Governance: A Paradox Perspective on Board Behavior', *Voluntas*, 22: 613–38.

Mabbett, I. and Chandler, D. (1995) *The Khmers*. Oxford: Blackwell.

Malena, C. and Chhim, K. (2009) *Linking Citizens and the State: An Assessment of Civil Society Contributions to Good Governance in Cambodia*. Phnom Penh: World Bank.

Mantel, B. (2010) 'Democracy in Southeast Asia', *CQ Global Researcher*, 4(6): 131–56.

Merla, C. (2010) *Strengthening Democracy and Electoral Processes in Cambodia: Civil Society Empowerment and Democratic Governance in Cambodia.* Phnom Penh: UNDP.

Nisbett, R. (2003) *The Geography of Thought: How Asians and Westerners Think Differently ... and Why.* New York: Free Press.

O'Dwyer, B. and Unerman, J. (2010) 'Enhancing the Role of Accountability in Promoting the Rights of Beneficiaries of Development NGOs', *Accounting and Business Research,* 40(5): 451–71.

Ostrower, F. and Stone, M.M. (2010) 'Moving Governance Research Forward: A Contingency-Based Framework and Data Application', *Nonprofit and Voluntary Sector Quarterly,* 39(5): 901–24.

Pak, K., Horng, V., Eng, N., Ann, S., Kim, S., Knowles, J. and Craig, D. (2007) *Accountability and Neo-Patrimonialism in Cambodia: A Critical Literature Review.* Phnom Penh: Cambodia Development Resource Institute.

Phillips, S. and Smith, S.R. (2011) 'Between Governance and Regulation: Evolving Government – Third Sector Relationships', in S. Phillips and S.R. Smith (eds), *Governance and Regulation in the Third Sector.* London: Routledge, pp. 1–37.

Reason, P. (1999) 'Three Approaches to Participative Inquiry', in N. Denzin and Y. Lincoln (eds), *Strategies of Qualitative Inquiry.* London: Sage, pp. 261–90.

Renz, D.O. (2013) 'Reframing Governance II', *Nonprofit Quarterly.* Available at: https://nonprofitquarterly.org/2013/01/01/reframing-governance-2/ (accessed 19 May 2014).

Renz, D.O. and Andersson, F.O. (2014) 'Nonprofit Governance: A Review of the field', in C. Cornforth and W.A. Brown (eds), *Nonprofit Governance: Innovative Perspectives and Approaches.* Abingdon and New York: Routledge.

Renz, P. (2007) *Project Governance: Implementing Corporate Governance and Business Ethics in Nonprofit Organisations.* Heidelberg: Physica-Verlag.

Scharmer, C.O. (2007) *Theory U: Leading from the Future as it Emerges.* Cambridge, MA: Society for Organisational Learning.

Springer, S. (2009) 'Neoliberalizing Violence: (Post)Marxian Political Economy, Poststructuralism and the Production of Space in "Post-Conflict" Cambodia', Vancouver: University of British Columbia.

Steen-Johnsen, K., Eynaud, P. and Wijkström, F. (2011) 'On Civil Society Governance: An Emergent Research Field', *Voluntas,* 22: 555–65.

Stone, M.M. and Ostrower, F. (2007) 'Acting in the Public Interest? Another Look at Research on Nonprofit Governance', *Nonprofit and Voluntary Sector Quarterly,* 36(3): 416–38.

Suárez, D. and Marshall, J.H. (2014) 'Capacity in the NGO Sector: Results from a National Survey in Cambodia', *Voluntas,* 25(1): 176–200.

Un, K. (2005) 'Patronage Politics and Hybrid Democracy: Political Change in Cambodia, 1993–2003', *Asian Perspective,* (29)2: 203–30.

Un, K. (2011) 'Cambodia: Moving Away from Democracy?', *International Political Science Review,* 32(5): 546–62.

Van Puyvelde, S., Caers, R., Du Bois, C. and Jegers, M. (2012) 'The Governance of Nonprofit Organizations: Integrating Agency Theory with Stakeholder and Stewardship Theories', *Nonprofit and Voluntary Sector Quarterly,* 41(3): 431–51.

Wheatley, M. (2009) *Leadership and the New Science: Discovering Order in a Chaotic World* (3rd edn). San Francisco, CA: Berrett-Koehler Publishers Inc.

Willems, J., Andersson, F.O., Jegers, M. and Renz, D.O. (2016) 'A Coalition Perspective on Nonprofit Governance Quality: Analyzing Dimensions of Influence in an Exploratory Comparative Case Analysis', *Voluntas*: 1–26, doi:10.1007/s11266-016-9683-6.

World Bank (2014) *World Bank Development Report 2015: Mind, Society and Behavior*. Available at: www.worldbank.org/en/publication/wdr2015 (accessed 27 February 2017).

Yin, S. and Sok, S. (2012) *Needs Assessment on Capacity Development and Learning of Civil Society Organizations (CSOs) in Cambodia*. Phnom Penh: Cooperation Committee for Cambodia.

Young, D.R. (2011) 'The Prospective Role of Economic Stakeholders in the Governance of Nonprofit Organizations', *Voluntas*, 22: 566–86.

Zimmerman, B. and Hayday, B. (1999) 'A Board's Journey into Complexity Science: Lessons from (and for) Staff and Board Members', *Group Decision and Negotiation*, 8(4): 281–303.

14

COMMUNICATING DEVELOPMENT: TOWARDS STRATEGIC, INCLUSIVE AND CREATIVE APPROACHES

MARIANNE D. SISON

INTRODUCTION

This chapter examines the interplay between media and communication and development within a complex and global context. The blurring of geographical boundaries, the emergence of new media and communication technologies and an increasingly fragile economic and political environment demand sophisticated and, yet, culture-sensitive approaches to communication. Social issues, previously the domain of governments, are now being integrated into business practices by the private sector as part of their commitments to sustainability and social responsibility. As many scholars (Berry and Kamau, 2013; Couldry et al., 2010; Jamieson and Campbell, 2000) contend, media and communication as processes, structures and technologies shape and influence political and societal discourses. And, as such, the role of communication is critical to engendering development and social change.

There is a prevailing view that new technologies make a difference to the lives of poor and marginalized people because these allow them to join the global knowledge economy (Unwin, 2009). This area of practice, dubbed ICT4D (information and communication technology for development), aims to improve the digital readiness of developing countries to get people connected by making telecommunications links, Internet service providers and public access points available where these facilities are thinly spread or absent. It also includes advocacy campaigns to reform ICT policy environments, as well as community development projects that use ICT to provide content and services to the poor. While access to previously inaccessible 'communication tools' may help reduce inequities in society, understanding 'communication processes' that enable effective communication is equally valuable. In this context, it is important to understand some of the traditional and contemporary communication theories and models that have been applied in the development field. Then, I discuss two sub-disciplines of communication that inform the practice of communication in the international development. The third section argues for critical and creative engagement, before I conclude with a case study of SCG's participatory community engagement.

Communication, and specifically public relations, practitioners used to be employed primarily by the private sector and all levels of governments. However, there is a growing interest in strategic communication, incorporating public relations, from NGOs including development agencies. While communication practitioners were once predominantly employed in the private sector, this is no longer the case.

THEORETICAL CONTEXTS: TOWARDS A MULTIPLE PERSPECTIVE APPROACH

Although communication existed as a field of practice in ancient times, the study of communication only began in the twentieth century. The communication discipline emerged from scholarly inquiries in psychology, sociology, literature and linguistics. While communication research has progressed because of its inter- and cross-disciplinarity, Craig (1999: 122) argued that this 'productive fragmentation' constrained the growth of communication theory.

To understand the origins and synergies of communication within the development field, it is useful to briefly describe the seven communication traditions summarized by Craig (1999). The rhetorical tradition examines the art of discourse, the communicator, audience, strategy, and the interplay of ethos, pathos and logos as part of persuasive communication. Semiotics focuses on the subjective understanding of signs, symbols, language and texts. Phenomenological approaches interrogate communication from the experience of otherness, and the value of dialogue, genuineness and respecting differences. The cybernetic tradition explores communication as information processing as a mechanistic function. The sociopsychological focuses on how expression, interaction and influence impact on behaviours. The sociocultural approach problematizes conflict, alienation and identity construction because of societal structures and cultural rituals. And critical traditions theorize communication as discursive reflection through problems of hegemony, ideology, oppression and emancipation.

Changing the discourse is critical to shifting the paradigms towards inclusion and social justice. This is why some writers prefer to reframe some of the terms such as 'developing countries' to 'emerging economies', 'beneficiaries' to 'constituents', and for references to the 'developed/developing' or Western/non-Western countries to 'global North' and the 'global South'. Similarly, C.K. Prahalad, in discussing his concept of Fortune at the Bottom of the Pyramid (2005), argues that companies should view the poorest of the poor not as 'victims' but as partners in the economy. Framing the discourse from 'victim' to 'entrepreneur' already provides a sense of empowerment and recasts notions of dependency to one of financial independence.

While each of these theoretical approaches privilege a particular paradigm or ideology, a singular approach is not sufficient for the current global environment. A multiple perspective approach to communication, which incorporates systems/functionalist, interpretive/rhetorical and critical/dialectical perspectives, provides a richer and more realistic understanding of the context in which practitioners work. In development practice, a multiple perspective approach to communication involves a consideration and sensitivity to the local context and existing worldviews. While intervention may often veer towards more participatory and critical approaches, understanding the roles of the various stakeholders and the structures in which they operate, and how they interpret and negotiate the discourses, enables more meaningful engagement.

DEVELOPMENT COMMUNICATION TO C4D: TRANSMISSION TO PARTICIPATION

Jo Ellen Fair (1989, cited in Servaes, 2008: 16) analyzed development communication studies between 1958 and 1986 and found they were predominantly influenced by Lerner's modernization study that media had 'powerful effects on Third World audiences' and magnified 'the benefits of development'. A later study by Fair and Shah (1997), however, revealed that between 1987 and 1996, the field had embraced participatory development and a postmodern orientation (cited in Servaes, 2008).

One of the early transmission models, reflective of the cybernetic tradition, used in the development field was rural sociologist Everett Rogers' Diffusion of Innovations theory (1995). Rogers (ibid.: 5) defined diffusion as 'the process by which an innovation is communicated through certain channels over time among the members of a social system'. This theory suggests that any new idea, product or service can be disseminated through communication channels that will effect a behaviour change or adoption. Drawn from work by American scholars Paul Lazarsfeld, Harold Lasswell, Carl Hovland, Wilbur Schramm, Shannon and Weaver, who invented 'hypodermic needle' or 'magic bullet' theories popular during the 1950s, diffusion theories reflected linear, cause-and-effect relationships between the sender, message, channel and the receiver (SMCR). While the classic diffusion model was a popular framework used by developing countries to evaluate the impact of development programmes in agriculture, family planning, public health and nutrition, it had its limitations. Because external 'experts' are expected to provide interventions, the model is criticized as modernist, elitist and essentially 'top-down' in orientation, thus simplistically treating communication as one way and assuming that audiences are passive (Servaes, 2008). Moreover, the diffusion model tends to disregard other contextual factors such as environmental 'noise', feedback, context and the predispositions of both sender and receiver. These models also reflect largely Western schools of thought.

Scholars (Dutta, 2011; Manyozo, 2012) from the global South, however, argue for the integration of post-colonial responses to development communication. Manyozo (2012) argues that different schools of thought, not just Western development theory, shaped the emergence and growth of the field. He argues that communicating development from various geographical locations required a post-colonial response that included 'another' kind of communication that met 'the challenges of rural poverty, underdevelopment, inequality and global imperialism' (ibid.: 2). Philippine scholar Nora C. Quebral introduced the term 'development communication' as part of a research programme on how communication can address the issues of rural development. First articulated at the University of the Philippines College of Agriculture in Los Baños in 1971, Quebral defined 'development communication' as:

> the art and science of human communication applied to the speedy transformation of a country and the mass of its people from poverty to a dynamic state of economic growth that makes possible greater social equality and the larger fulfillment of the human potential. (2011: 4)

Quebral and her colleagues clearly distinguished 'development communication' from advertising and propaganda in that it 'educates for purposes of greater social equality and larger fulfillment of the human potential' (Manyozo, 2012: 199). However, Quebral (2011) emphasized that development communication is evolving and needs to be examined from the local context. As such, she recently redefined 'development communication Los Baños version' as: 'the art and science of human communication linked to a society's planned transformation from a state of poverty to one of dynamic socio-economic growth that makes for greater equity and the larger unfolding of individual potential' (ibid.: 6). She highlights three aspects critical to communication for development: that it 'focuses on human beings and media technologies are just instruments' for this agenda; as participation which allows for the 'articulation and incorporation of multiple voices and interests in the design, implementation and evaluation of development policy'; and that strategies are driven by 'coherent theory and clear methods in order to strengthen external validity' (cited in Manyozo, 2012: 9).

From its origins as 'agricultural extension work', development communication has transitioned to a more participatory approach that incorporates two-way dialogic communication. Adopted by various international agencies such as the World Bank and explicated by scholars in Latin America, Africa, Asia and Europe, the model has now evolved to what is more commonly known in development circles as ICT4D and C4D. More recently, development communication scholars have framed their scholarship as Communication for Social Change (CSC) or Communication for Development and Social Change (CDSC). Underpinning this evolution is a focus on communities developing their own media systems, content and communication processes. Scholars rejecting the top-down approaches from governments and international agencies have since highlighted the value of participatory, bottom-up, communication (see Dutta, 2011; Servaes, 2008). However, Manyozo (2012: 9–10) argues the importance of focusing on changing the political economy: 'No matter how participatory or bottom-up development communication approaches can be, as long as the dominant political economy framework of development (that promotes inequality and underdevelopment) is in place, there will be no sustainable positive change in society.'

Drawing from the work of Paulo Freire (see Chapter 12), participatory communication 'stresses the importance of cultural identity of local communities and of democratization and participation at all levels – international, national, local and individual' (Servaes, 2008: 21), and focuses on dialogue (Huesca, 2008). Servaes posits that the participatory communication model has the following characteristics: (1) it sees people as controlling actors or participants for development, local culture is respected; (2) it sees people as nucleus of development, educating and stimulating people to be active; and (3) it emphasizes the local community rather than nation-state; and involves the redistribution of power (2008: 202). Resonating with community development principles that value local knowledge, culture, resources, skills and processes (Ife, 2013), Servaes proposes a continuum where conventional mechanistic (and behaviourist) communication models are on one end, and organic, participatory and spiritually oriented models are on the other end (see Servaes, 2008: 216–17).

Tufte and Mefalopulos (2009) suggest that participatory communication is guided by the following principles: (1) dialogue; (2) voice; (3) liberating pedagogy; and (4) action-reflection-action. Moreover, they propose that participatory communication strategies may include the traditional media as well as folk, community media and events such as theatres and concerts. For instance, community groups in rural Pakistan and India have used street theatre as a means of increasing awareness on social issues such as women's health and gender issues. Part of the performances included workshops as well as being accompanied by a medical team while focusing on socio-political concerns and human rights issues (Rashid, 2015).

Questions have emerged on whether participation is conceived as a means or an end (Jacobson, 2003). When used as a *means*, participatory communication focuses on teaching skills, meeting objectives and producing media products (Huesca, 2008). Moreover, when participation is used as a means to achieve 'buy-in' to a project, it can be manipulative and therefore not considered authentic participation (Jacobson, 2003). For activities that view participation as an *end*, the role of communication is 'aimed at organizing movements, transforming social relations and empowering individuals' (Huesca, 2008: 188). Other issues in participatory communication relate to the stage where participation starts, its applicability to large-scale programmes, the role of culture in social change, and determining authentic participation (Jacobson, 2003). However, it is possible to see the 'means' and 'end' as a continuum rather than binary opposites. For example, the International Association for Public Participation (IAP2) developed a Public Participation Spectrum with five goals: inform, consult, involve, collaborate and empower. They define public participation as a process that involves those who may not be stakeholders in solving problems and making decisions (www.iap2.org.au/Resources/IAP2-Published-Resources).

Communication for development acknowledges how communication processes are integral to human development. While focusing on empowerment, the term, 'communication for development' (C4D) has evolved over the years. In 1997, the United Nations adopted this definition: 'Communication for development stresses the need to support two-way communication systems that enable dialogue and that allow communities to speak out, express their aspirations and concerns and participate in the decisions that relate to their development.'

Then, in 2006, the Rome Consensus from the World Congress on Communication for Development (World Bank, 2006) defined communication for development as:

> a social process based on dialogue using a broad range of tools and methods. It is also about seeking change at different levels, including listening, building trust, sharing knowledge and skills, building policies, debating and learning for sustained and meaningful change. *It is not public relations or corporate communications.* (emphasis added, p. xxiii)

The explicit distancing and distinction from public relations or corporate communication positions C4D as an externally oriented activity based on dialogue. Moreover, it assumes that public relations and corporate communication reflect organization-centric approaches whose purpose is to merely promote organizational interests. While this may be true, the United Nations and its international agencies are organizations that employ corporate communication and public relations strategies.

Servaes and Malikhao (2015: 22) believe that 'major aspects of many projects and programs currently being promoted are nothing but "public relations and corporate communication"'. They also suggest that many development practitioners are not overly concerned with what the approach is called or how it is communicated, but, rather, the tools they have to achieve the objectives of sustainable development.

The effectiveness of these tools, processes and interventions, however, will need to be evaluated. For instance, analyzing the impact of individual media technologies on a community will require assessing all modes of communication – mediated, interpersonal, formal, informal – as well as the infrastructure that enables the communication – roads, trains, buses, private and public spheres (Lennie and Tacchi, 2013).

STRATEGIC COMMUNICATION FOR DEVELOPMENT: FINDING COMMON GROUND

While Servaes (2008: 16) argues that participatory communication is often confused by laypersons with 'public relations, public information, corporate communications and other media-related activities', he admits that skill sets from these fields are used in participatory communication activities. Despite the criticisms against public relations, international development agencies have adopted strategic communication for development (see Cabañero-Verzosa, 2003; UNICEF, 2005).

Strategic communication, although generally associated with management, marketing, public relations, advertising and organizational communication, is defined as an organization 'communicating purposefully to advance its mission' (Hallahan et al., 2007: 4). Here, the authors specify that 'organization' can refer to governments, profit and not-for-profit organizations, activist groups, nongovernment organizations, political parties or movements or those promoting social change. Thus, they posited that strategic communication is a deliberative communication practice 'on behalf of organizations, causes and social movements' (ibid.: 4).

Strategic communication, however, has not been fully explored among communication for development and social change scholars. Part of the reason is because the term 'strategic' is often associated with modernist, rationalist management approaches, which 'privileges a management discourse and emphasizes upper management's goals for the organization as given and legitimate' (ibid.: 11). This top-down approach is hardly consistent with the bottom-up and grassroots-based approaches by development communication scholars and practitioners. While the ideologies of organizations and groups may differ, they share a common ground in the deliberative use of communication, through various strategies and tactics, to achieve their respective organizational goals.

Alternative notions of strategy have its challenged top-down, asymmetric interpretations. Citing Quinn's (1978) notion of emergent strategy that argues that strategy comes from prior experience and action, thus legitimizing the values and actions of employees at all levels in the organization, Hallahan et al. (2007: 10) suggest that strategic communication 'recognizes that purposeful influence is the fundamental goal of communications by organizations'. Although strategic communication tends to focus on how the organization engages with its stakeholders for the organizational benefit, it is also concerned with the organization's role in society 'as a social actor in the creation of public culture and in the discussion of public issues' (Hallahan et al., 2007: 27). Applied to development practice, emergent strategy implies that developing a strategy from the experience, values and actions of all stakeholders at all levels – governments, NGOs, local community residents and corporations – is valid. As such, it allows for participatory communication practices to be integrated in stakeholder engagement and change management.

Critical to the notion of strategic communication for development is the locus of power. In 'traditional' strategic communication, the communication expert is expected to drive and lead the change. However, there are three other roles that the practitioner can play aside from being the expert: the communication technician; the communication facilitator; and the problem-solving process facilitator role (Broom, 1982). Although the communication process is often driven and controlled by 'organizational experts', these facilitator roles provide rich opportunities to integrate participatory approaches especially in stakeholder engagement activities. Similarly, participatory communication specialists can learn from strategic communication practitioners.

Strategic communication practitioners can provide a streamlined purposeful and systematic approach to advocacy, with a view to influencing critical actors in business and government. Advocacy has been defined to be the 'attempt to influence public policy, either directly or indirectly' (Pekkanen and Smith, 2014: 3). Advocacy, which is different to influence, is a 'question of articulating a position and mobilizing support for it' (Jenkins, 2006: 309). Advocacy can take the form of a range of activities such as letters to the editor, coalition building, undertaking research and using various channels including social media networks. Pekkanen and Smith (2014: 6–7) distinguish lobbying as a sub-set of policy advocacy, which involves 'communicating the organization's positions to policymakers (direct lobbying) or by mobilizing the general public (grassroots lobbying)'. Framing messages is a critical element of advocacy as is joining together with other like-minded organizations to build a coalition. Given the diminishing resources governments are allocating to development projects, and the need for a broader whole-of-society approach to many social issues such as climate change, poverty alleviation and food security, creative and more strategic advocacy and lobbying efforts are needed. The plethora of global issues that compete to be prioritized and funded, coupled with the openness of social media networks, require development communication practitioners to be innovative and imaginative to be heard and rise above the 'noise'. While activism, social movements and protests have their own strategic value, advocacy and lobbying with or through partners one would otherwise not have considered in the past may be as effective.

For instance, public health advocates would not previously have thought that Microsoft Corporation founder Bill Gates would be interested in joining their advocacy. Although the Bill and Melinda Gates Foundation's advocacy is backed by their generous philanthropy, they have worked with governments, NGOs, civil society and other private sector organizations and philanthropists such as Warren Buffett to reduce inequity through Global Health, global development and education programmes. While the Foundation primarily provides grants to groups that align with their strategic priorities, they also work with local organizations in over a hundred countries. However, what is not clear is the extent to which the grantees and community 'beneficiaries' are involved in the communicative processes of the Foundation.

C4D highlights the need for authentic community participation where messages and processes are co-created with grassroots communities. Waisbord (2014: 149) argues that strategic communication needs to be integrated in participatory perspectives that 'links communication, collective action and politics'. He posits that strategic communication in the development communication field be foregrounded with collective action. He suggests that participatory principles be integrated in problem definition, where multiple actors define and negotiate the social problem, goals selection, strategy and tactic development and in assessing motivations for change. Instead of information dissemination and top-down persuasion, Waisbord (ibid.: 164) redefines communication as 'strategic political action that needs to be mindful of stakeholders, interests, opportunities and other issues' and acknowledges this approach might not align with organizational cultures in public agencies and private organizations.

In addressing inequities of power, particularly of the poor and marginalized, development, C4D and critical communication scholars promote the notions of multiplicity and pluralism. Authentic dialogue is critical to these processes. Authentic communication, or dialogue, is defined as being 'founded on the experience of direct, unmediated contact with others' (Craig, 1999: 138), or from the phenomenological perspective, as one that 'requires congruency between the experience and the expression' (ibid.: 141). Authenticity has also been explicated in terms of relationships between organizations and publics and ethical communication. Public relations scholars have defined authenticity as 'conforming to fact' (Page, 2007: 15), consistency (Molleda, 2010), good character, sincerity and moral autonomy (Stoker and Rawlins, 2010), and ethical leadership, genuineness, transparency and truthfulness (Bowen, 2010). They argue that authenticity and ethical practice is key to developing trust.

Trust is a critical factor in the establishment, cultivation and maintenance of relationships, whether these relationships are between individuals, communities or organizations. Developing and nurturing these intra- and inter-organizational relationships (Ferguson, 1984) are critical responsibilities for communication practitioners in their roles as either 'boundary-spanner' or 'cultural mediator' between organizations and their publics. Establishing mechanisms for dialogue to occur in a safe and protected environment for all participants is a necessary condition to build trust.

Trust between corporations and NGOs as well as NGOs and governments is an essential prerequisite before any meaningful conversation can begin. The 2016 Edelman Trust Barometer revealed that NGOs were trusted more than business, media and government and that search engines were more trusted than traditional media (www.edelman.com/insights/intellectual-property/2016-edelman-trust-barometer/). The global study indicated also inequities in trust and an increased influence of peers and employees instead of institutional leaders. While these findings are based on perceptions of trust, how an organization communicates shapes these perceptions.

For example, in the mining sector, governments and corporations are often perceived to be in collusion and local community residents are perceived as activists or victims. While each sector will have its own interest, these 'mental models' of each other will define the types of engagement. But, how do we validate if these perceptions are accurate? And how do we shape the discourse and engender change, if we do not engage with the 'enemy'? Engaging with the 'other' is a necessary first step in reducing distrust. Communication is key to establishing trust and developing partnerships.

CRITICAL AND CREATIVE ENGAGEMENT IN DEVELOPMENT PRACTICE

The United Nations, through its Global Compact, has acknowledged the importance of involving the private sector in its goals towards sustainable development. The UN Global Compact was developed to provide a framework 'designed to help advance sustainable business models and markets' (www.unglobalcompact.org/AboutTheGC/index.html). The voluntary initiative is meant to encourage business to commit to the ten principles, which cover human rights, labour, environment and anti-corruption. Similarly, the World Bank highlights corporate responsibility on its website and mentions its partnership with other international institutions, donors and civil society to achieve its twin goals of ending extreme poverty and boosting shared prosperity (www.worldbank.org/en/about).

Scholars and practitioners agree that collaboration is the key to addressing sustainable development and other social issues such as poverty, public health and education (Austin, 2000; Armitage et al., 2007; Vazquez-Brust et al., 2014). Multi-sectoral and multi-stakeholder collaboration underpinned by values of co-creation and inclusion is necessary to achieve the sustainable development goals. Social issues and their solutions are not, and should not be, exclusive to particular ideologies. The idea behind collaboration, dissensus, pluralism, requisite variety and dialectics is an openness to listen and learn from different perspectives. Dialogic communication facilitates this process and we must aim to engender a safe and nurturing environment for this dialogue to occur for all participants, regardless of their background.

Partnerships between business and civil society organizations are not new. However, the nature of the relationships has often taken the form of philanthropy through charity and event sponsorship. Austin (2000) posits that partnerships between the private sector and non-profit organizations go through a 'collaboration continuum' with three stages: philanthropic, transactional and integrative. In the philanthropic stage, the relationship tends to be one-way where the business takes the role of 'benefactor' and the recipient group the 'beneficiary'. This type of collaboration is characterized by limited engagement and fit. The next stage is transactional and reflects a mutually beneficial relationship between the business and the NPO. At this stage, the two parties identify a similarity in their values, increase their interactions and leverage this exchange for their respectivebenefits. Austin (ibid.) describes the third stage of integration as the point when the organization's boundaries disappear and notions of 'them' and 'us' shift to 'we' when they do things together. At this stage, the relationship goes beyond the leaders and advocates and involves most organizational members. A later conceptualization added a fourth stage – transformational – to the collaboration continuum (Austin and Seitanidi, 2012). They suggest that transformational collaborations involve partners learning about their social needs and roles in meeting those needs and could take the form of collaborative social entrepreneurship, where a large segment of the society is benefited (ibid.). Moreover, because this type of collaboration promotes interdependence and collective action, they contend that the transformative effects of collaboration go beyond social, economic and political systems but also within organizations and their individual employees.

Scholars in development communication (Manyozo, 2012), organizational communication (Putnam and Mumby, 2014; Mumby and May, 2005) and public relations (Bardhan and Weaver, 2011; Sison, 2010) agree that globalization and the rapid advancement of communication and media technologies require broader and more inclusive worldviews to deal with an increasingly borderless world. At the same time, the persistence of 'wicked' problems such as climate change, poverty and inequality require more creative and collaborative approaches. Acknowledging that each sector has a particular worldview and language is an important starting point.

Co-orientation theory suggests that individuals must recognize and be aware of how the other people in the relationship might think about or perceive an issue. While co-orientation theory aims for consensus, dissensus (Holtzhausen and Voto, 2002) or 'agonistic pluralism' (Burchell and Cook, 2013) could also be a preferred outcome. In examining NGO-business relationships within a corporate social responsibility (CSR) context, appropriation and co-optation of the sustainable development language into neo-liberal and managerial contexts is a real threat. Burchell and Cook (ibid.) propose adopting Mouffe's (1999) framework of 'agonistic pluralism'. 'Agonism', according to Mouffe (1999, cited in Burchell and Cook, 2013: 749), is a position wherein 'conflicts exists between "adversaries" who oppose one another but who regard each other as holding "legitimate" views'. As with Lyotard's notion of dissensus, agonistic pluralism acknowledges difference and conflict that will lead groups to interact and make decisions. While these interactions do not necessarily have to result in consensual decisions (Burchell and Cook, 2013), engaging in a continuing dialogue that aims to present conflict, rather than contain the issue, enables NGOs and activists to continue the pressure and influence responsible business practices.

Drawing from Edward Hall's oft-quoted notion that 'culture is communication, and communication is culture', critical public relations scholars (Bardhan and Weaver, 2011; Curtin and Gaither, 2012) highlight the value of communication as a process of meaning making. They posit that communication practitioners 'serve as cultural intermediaries to create shared meanings, or discourses surrounding globalization issues, thus legitimizing certain norms and values' (Curtin and Gaither, 2012: 11).

Curtin and Gaither (ibid.) admit that while public relations has generally been associated with transnational companies and their hegemonic practices, they posit a reframing of public relations toward social justice. Echoing Sachs' (2008) view that multilateralism may solve the excesses of globalization, the authors suggest that when 'corporations, governments, NGOs and activists work together, diplomacy becomes an attainable standard that trumps the unilateral interests of one organization' (Curtin and Gaither, 2012: 310). Moreover, they argue that social issues such as human trafficking, for example, require systemic changes that governments, NGOs, activists or corporations cannot handle on their own. As such, communication practitioners play an integral role in refocusing organizational and public discourse towards social justice issues as well as in building relationships between these global actors to drive social change.

Critical communication scholars argue for a shift from an organization-centric approach to a community-centric approach in both research and practice. While this may be a given for development practitioners, it is not necessarily the case for most corporate communication practitioners who also have to focus on other stakeholders such as government, employees and shareholders. It could be argued that this renewed focus on the 'local' has emerged from criticisms of globalization. Questions about universal 'one size fits all' global standards have generated protests from scholars and practitioners from the 'global South' who find Western models of practice inappropriate at best, useless at worst. At the same time, there are calls from development communication scholars (Waisbord, 2014; Wilkins, 2014) to reconfigure practitioner roles as 'experts' to that of 'facilitators'. By playing a facilitative role, practitioners enable communities to discuss and define the problems, identify the approaches and solutions from a context that is appropriate to their local environment. External 'experts' are often criticized for trying to impose their 'best practice' knowledge and processes, which may not necessarily be appropriate for the local culture and context.

While the private sector has been criticized for its focus on profits above all else, a shift occurred around the 1990s with the introduction of Triple Bottom Line (TBL) reporting. Coined by activist John Elkington of SustainAbility in his book *Cannibals with Forks* (1997), the triple bottom line framework urged companies to evaluate their business models and performance against social (people), environmental (planet) and financial (profits) considerations. Inspired by the Brundtland Commission's *Our Common Future* (WCED, 1987), Elkington's work also aligned with the re-emerging interest in corporate social responsibility (CSR). Business and social responsibility is not new, with Carroll (1999) tracing its beginnings to the 1950s. In 1970, the Philippine Business for Social Progress (PBSP), comprising 50 businessmen, committed to set aside 1 per cent of their companies' net income toward social development programmes (Tan and Bolante, 1997).

After the 1992 Rio Summit, a group of business leaders committed to sustainable development established the World Business Council on Sustainable Development (WBCSD). They have hosted a roundtable (1997) and debates (2006) between CEOs, leading civil society representatives and government representatives to discuss how the private sector can play a role in advocating for sustainable business practices. In 2000, the UN launched the Global Compact to urge the private sector 'to align strategies and operations with universal principles on human rights, labour, environment, anti-corruption, and take action that advance societal goals' (https://www.unglobalcompact.org/what-is-gc).

Anita Roddick's Body Shop claims to be one of the pioneers in naturally inspired products; however, more and more companies are espousing their sustainability credentials. For instance, Unilever, the company behind brands such as Lifebuoy, Omo, Magnum and Lipton, has integrated 'sustainable living' in its business plan. Under this plan, they aim to improve the health and wellbeing of more than a billion people, halve the environmental footprint of their products, and source 100 per cent of their agricultural raw materials sustainably while enhancing the livelihoods of people across their value chain (https://www.unilever.com/about/who-we-are/about-Unilever/). Unilever's commitment to collective action enabled them to work with NGOs such as Direct Relief, businesses such as Lafarge Holcim's Geocycle and philanthrophic organizations such as Ford Foundation, to address issues of skin care in areas of conflict, waste management and empowering women farmers. Their website reveals the scale and scope of their interventions but also the stories from their work in Asia, Africa and Latin America. This corporate discourse around sustainability is not unique. Although small- and medium-sized enterprises still face challenges with integrating sustainability in their business models, social enterprises such as KOTO (Know One, Teach One) in Vietnam have been established to provide training and livelihood programmes for young people (www.koto.com.au/about-koto/what-is-koto).

Critics might argue that the private sector has 'commodified' development initiatives and that communicating about one's 'good deeds' raises more scepticism about what companies 'say' and what they 'do'. The reality is that private, public and civil society organizations all need to establish their trust and reputation in order to effectively engage with their stakeholders. As we found in our studies in Vietnam, corporates are not the only ones who select their partners or 'beneficiaries' for strategic alignment. Well-established charity organizations also undertake a rigorous screening process when choosing their corporate partners (Sison and Hue, 2015). Thus, strategic communication helps organizations position themselves in the increasingly competitive funding environment. As we have seen from the examples mentioned, social justice and human empowerment are ideologies that are not exclusive to NGOs or activist groups. Partnerships with the private sector, which has extensive resources and global infrastructure, are necessary to scale up local community projects that could effect systemic change.

Nevertheless, we need to be vigilant and continue to keep all organizations accountable and transparent. Meanwhile, governments, civil society and the private sector need to continue communicating and working with each other. And communication practitioners must be involved at the start, during the planning stage, of any project, and not just called on to implement a programme or to manage a crisis. Because, through nuanced and culturally sensitive research, listening, negotiating and interpreting, we can develop strategic, inclusive and creative communication that will empower us to address the global issues that we all face.

Text Box 14.1   Case Study: Integrating Participatory and Creative Strategic Communication[1]

Thailand conglomerate SCG (Siam Cement Group) was established in 1913 under the decree of King Rama VI to support the country's modernization and infrastructure projects. Its philosophy of doing business with righteousness has continued with its more recent commitment to be a leader of sustainable development in the ASEAN

---

[1] I would like to acknowledge SCG for coordinating the interviews, and my research assistant, Ms Chayanit Vivatthanavanich, PhD student at Chulalongkorn University, who helped collect interview data on which this discussion is based.

region. To achieve this, the company adopted three stages of 'green implementation': green manufacturing; sustainability supply chain; and eco-value labels and products (Leelakulthanit, 2014). One of its key projects, SCG Conserving Water for Tomorrow, was conceived in 2003 after the King remarked that 'water is life'. The project is underpinned by a belief that water conservation is critical to a better environment and quality of life. They adopted the business concept of 'where our factories are, there's lush green forest'. The project started in Lampang, in Northern Thailand, where they helped restore the degraded forests surrounding the plant. They planted trees in the nearby forests but the drought reduced the foliage and caused forest fires. Aside from the farmers in nearby ricefields, many of the plant employees also lived in the surrounding communities affected by the fires. The company decided to learn about watershed management in one of the King's study centres in 2003. Company representatives learned to construct small 'check dams' made of locally available materials such as rocks, logs, branches and soil. Since this 'technology' can impact the surrounding communities, and is relatively easy to teach, SCG saw an opportunity to engage the community and approached them to join the project.

Initially, the community resisted and was distrustful of SCG's intent. The village leader was concerned about the company's pollution, and 40 per cent of the community refused to participate in the 'dam building activity'. The NGO leader echoed his distrust: 'My NGO skeptical thought is that industry is an evil to the environment.' However, the community relations manager who grew up in the area and spoke the language persisted and developed a relationship with the NGO leader. To establish trust, the community relations manager patiently explained their green concept, and organized a community trip to their plant in the central region. They showed how their plant was designed with a semi-open-cut system with environmentally friendly technology imported from Germany. The system has won best practice awards and the company organized open houses so the community can visit when they want.

Once the NGO leader was on side, the community relations manager brought a few of the village leaders to the King's study centre to show how check dams are built and what the result can be. To empower them in water conservation, SCG acted as mentors while the community was made to run and manage the project, exploring and testing their ideas. The project implementation was neither designed nor implemented, nor dictated by SCG. While the company suggested the idea to the community, the community developed the project and now hosts an annual community event with farming and non-farming families, SCG employees including executives and the media. Since 2003, there are now more than 70,000 checked dams in the area, of which 55,000 were built with SCG involvement. The company's community relations manager admitted that they changed their paradigm from 'giving' to 'participation' in 2008.

The community project not only increased the knowledge of the village members but also restored the forest's biodiversity. SCG commissioned Chiang Mai University to survey the flora and fauna and found that the number of bird species increased, and that local residents were also able to collect mushrooms and other plants for their consumption. One female leader we interviewed also revealed how the return of the water to the forest brought water to her house through pipes, ending her days of walking for many kilometres, hiking up and down the mountain, to collect water for her family's use.

As the community relations manager said, 'They have the knowledge from learning process and can survive without our guidance. It was difficult to change the locals' attitude when SCG changed its paradigm. It took three years for (the) community to understand but seven years for full participation. Now the locals can do the research.'

(Continued)

(Continued)

The community's success has also enabled them to share their knowledge with other nearby villages.

The success of the highly participative project was attributed to an integrated communication process, which targeted the needs of each stakeholder group. Moreover, involving media practitioners, spiritual leaders and NGOs to join employees, residents and other volunteers in building the dams enabled them to experience the process 'hands-on'. At the same time, they launched a public awareness campaign on water conservation, using TV, radio commercials, print ads, articles and an illustrated guidebook. In addition, SCG collaborated with a production company to develop a four-episode music documentary featuring well-known Thai musicians.

CONCLUSION

Globalization has enabled more interconnections between peoples of the world, through trade, migration, travel and media and communication technologies. Given the complexity and speed with which technologies and environments are changing, we need to understand how strategic communication is integral in international development. Further, in this new information-rich global universe, it is possible, indeed, necessary, to rethink development strategies to engage proactively with private companies, with the expertise and financial resources to support development projects in the communications field. That said, there is no urgency to adopt new technologies and, indeed, doing so, risks adoption for adoption's sake without any appreciation of context or need. The case study demonstrates how integrating participatory and creative strategic communication with traditional media techniques helped community members empower themselves and redevelop their previously drought-stricken village to a lush, productive and sustainable environment.

Questions for Discussion

1 What is 'social entrepreneurship'?
2 How can trust between communities and corporations be built in ways that encourage sustainable practice?
3 Are development outcomes likely to be 'better' when local communities are involved in project planning and implementation?

FURTHER READING

Burchell, J. and Cook, J. (2013) 'Sleeping with the Enemy? Strategic Transformations in Business–NGO Relationships through Stakeholder Dialogue', *Journal of Business Ethics*, 113(3): 505–18.

Elkington, J. and Hartigan, P. (2008) *The Power of Unreasonable People: How Social Entrepreneurs Create Markets that Change the World*. Boston, MA: Harvard Business Review Press.

Luke, B. and Chu, V. (2013) 'Social Enterprise Versus Social Entrepreneurship: An Examination of the "Why" and "How" in Pursuing Social Change', *International Small Business Journal*, 31(7): 764–84, doi: 10.1177/0266242612462598.

REFERENCES

Armitage, D., Berkes, F. and Doubleday, N. (eds) (2007) *Adaptive Co-Management: Collaboration, Learning and Multi-Level Governance*. Vancouver: UBC Press.

Austin, J.E. (2000) 'Strategic Collaboration Between Nonprofits and Businesses', *Nonprofit and Voluntary Sector Quarterly*, 29(1): 69–97.

Austin, J.E. and Seitanidi, M.M. (2012) 'Collaborative Value Creation: A Review of Partnering Between Nonprofits and Businesses: Part 1. Value Creation Spectrum and Collaboration Stages', *Nonprofit and Voluntary Sector Quarterly*, 41(5): 726–58.

Bardhan, N. and Weaver, C.K. (2011) *Public Relations in Global Cultural Contexts: Multi-Paradigmatic Perspectives*. London: Routledge.

Berry, D. and Kamau, C. (2013) *Public Policy and Media Organizations*. Aldershot: Ashgate Publishing.

Bowen, S.A. (2010) 'The Nature of Good in Public Relations: What Should be its Normative Ethic?', in R.L. Heath (ed.), *The SAGE Handbook of Public Relations*. Thousand Oaks, CA: Sage, pp. 569–83.

Broom, G. (1982) 'A Comparison of Sex Roles in Public Relations', *Public Relations Review*, 8(3): 17–22.

Burchell, J. and Cook, J. (2013) 'Sleeping with the Enemy? Strategic Transformations in Business–NGO Relationships through Stakeholder Dialogue', *Journal of Business Ethics*, 113(3): 505–18.

Cabañero-Verzosa, C. (2003) *Strategic Communication for Development Projects: A Toolkit for Task Team Leaders*. Washington, DC: World Bank.

Carroll, A. (1999) 'Corporate Social Responsibility: Evolution of a Definitional Construct', *Business & Society*, 38(3): 268–95.

Couldry, N., Hepp, A. and Krotz, F. (eds) (2010) *Media Events in a Global Age*. Abingdon: Routledge.

Craig, R.T. (1999) 'Communication Theory as a Field', *Communication Theory*, 9(2): 119–61.

Curtin, P.A. and Gaither, T.K. (2012) *Globalization and Public Relations in Postcolonial Nations: Challenges and Opportunities*. Amherst, NY: Cambria Press.

Dutta, M.J. (2011) *Communicating Social Change: Structure, Culture, and Agency*. New York: Routledge.

Elkington, J. (1997) *Cannibals with Forks: The Triple Bottom Line of Twenty-First Century Business*. Oxford: Capstone.

Ferguson, M.A. (1984) 'Building Theory in Public Relations: Inter-Organizational Relationships', Paper Presented to the Public Relations Division, Association for Education in Journalism and Mass Communication, Gainesville, FL, August.

Hallahan, K., Holtzhausen, D., van Ruler, B., Vercic, D. and Sriramesh, K. (2007) 'Defining Strategic Communication', *International Journal of Strategic Communication*, 1(1): 3–35.

Holtzhausen, D. and Voto, R. (2002) 'Resistance from the Margins: The Postmodern Public Relations Practitioner as Organizational Activist', *Journal of Public Relations Research*, 14(1): 57–84.

Huesca, R. (2008) 'Tracing the History of Participatory Communication Approaches to Development: A Critical Appraisal', in J. Servaes (ed.), *Communication for Development and Social Change*. New Delhi: Sage, pp. 180–98.

Ife, J. (2013) *Community Development in an Uncertain World: Vision, Analysis and Practice*. Melbourne: Cambridge University Press.

Jacobson, T.L. (2003) 'Participatory Communication for Social Change', *Communication Yearbook*, 27: 87–123.

Jamieson, K. and Campbell, K.K. (2000) *The Interplay of Influence: News, Advertising, Politics, and the Mass Media*. Belmont, CA: Thomson Wadsworth.

Jenkins, J.C. (2006) 'Nonprofit Organizations and Political Advocacy,' in W.W. Powell and R. Steinberg (eds), *The Nonprofit Sector: A Research Handbook*, 2nd edn. New Haven, CT: Yale University Press, pp. 307–32.

Leelakulthanit, O. (2014) 'Sustainability: The Case of Siam Cement Group (SCG)', *Journal of Business Case Studies*, 10(4): 441–5.

Lennie, J. and Tacchi, J. (2013) *Evaluating Communication for Development: A Framework for Social Change*. Abingdon: Routledge.

Manyozo, L. (2012) *Media, Communication and Development: Three Approaches*. New Delhi: Sage.

Molleda, J.C. (2010) 'Authenticity and the Construct's Dimensions in Public Relations and Communication Research', *Journal of Communication Management*, 13: 223–36.

Mumby, D.K. and May, S. (2005) 'Introduction: Thinking about Engagement', in D.K. Mumby and S. May (eds), *Engaging Organizational Communication Theory & Research*. Thousand Oaks, CA: Sage, pp. 1–14.

Page Society, A.W. (ed.) (2007) *The Authentic Enterprise*. New York: Arthur W. Page Society.

Pekkanen, R. and Smith, S.R. (2014) 'Nonprofit Advocacy: Definitions and Concepts', in Y. Tsujinaka, S.R. Smith and R. Pekkanen (eds), *Nonprofits and Advocacy: Engagement Community and Government in an Era of Retrenchment*. Baltimore, MD: Johns Hopkins University Press, pp. 1–20.

Prahalad, C.K. (2005) *The Fortune at the Bottom of the Pyramid*. Upper Saddle River, NJ: Pearson Education, Inc.

Putnam, L.L. and Mumby, D.K. (2014) 'Introduction: Advancing Theory and Research in Organizational Communication', in L.L Putnam and D.K. Mumby (eds), *The SAGE Handbook of Organizational Communication*. Thousand Oaks, CA: Sage, pp. 1–18.

Quebral, N.C. (2011) 'Devcom Los Baños Style', Paper Presented at Honorary Doctorate Celebration Seminar, University of London, December 2011.

Rashid, T. (2015) 'Theatre for Community Development: Street Theatre as an Agent of Change in Punjab (Pakistan)', *India Quarterly*, 7(4): 335–47.

Rogers, E. (1995) *Diffusion of Innovations* (4th edn). New York: Free Press.

Servaes, J. (ed.) (2008) *Communication for Development and Social Change*. Thousand Oaks, CA: Sage.

Servaes, J. and Malikhao, P. (2015) 'Communication for Development: Three Development Paradigms, Two Communication Models, Many Applications and Approaches', in J. Hong (ed.), *Introduction to Communication Studies*. Beijing: Tsinghua University Press, pp. 20–44.

Sison, M.D. (2010) 'Recasting Public Relations Roles: Agents of Compliance, Control or Conscience', *Journal of Communication Management*, 14(4): 319–36.

Sison, M. and Hue, D.T. (2015) 'CSR Communication and NGOs: Perspectives from Vietnam', Paper Presented at the the 3rd International CSR Communication Conference, Ljubljana, Slovenia.

Stoker, K. and Rawlins, B. (2010) 'Taking the B.S. out of PR: Creating Genuine Messages by Emphasizing Character and Authenticity', *Ethical Space: The International Journal of Communication Ethics*, 7: 61–9.

Tan, V.E. and Bolante, M.P. (1997) *Philippine Business for Social Progress*. Synergos Institute Voluntary Sector Financing Program.

Tufte, T. and Mefalopulos, P. (2009) *Participatory Communication: A Practical Guide*. Washington, DC: World Bank.

UNICEF (2005) *Strategic Communication - For Behaviour and Social Change in South Asia*. Retrieved from Kathmandu: www.unicef.org/cbsc/files/Strategic_Communication_for_Behaviour_and_Social_Change.pdf (accessed 27 February 2017).

Unwin, T. (2009) 'Introduction', in T. Unwin (ed.), *ICT4D: Information and Communication Technology for Development*. Cambridge: Cambridge University Press, pp. 1–6.

Vazquez-Brust, D.A., Sarkis, J. and Cordeiro, J.J. (eds) (2014) *Collaboration for Sustainability and Innovation: A Role for Sustainability Driven by the Global South?* Greening of Industry Networks Series. Dordrecht: Springer.

Waisbord, S. (2014) 'The Strategic Politics of Participatory Communication', in K. Wilkins, R. Obregon and T. Tufte (eds), *The Handbook of Development Communication and Social Change*. Hoboken, NJ, London: Wiley-Blackwell, pp. 147–67.

Wilkins, K.G. (2014) 'Advocacy Communication', in K. Wilkins, R. Obregon and T. Tufte (eds), *The Handbook of Development Communication and Social Change*. Hoboken, NJ: Wiley-Blackwell, pp. 57–71.

World Commission on Environment and Development (WCED) (1987) *Our Common Future*, Brundtland Commission. New York: UN.

15

FINANCIAL INCLUSION AS PRACTICE: MICROFINANCE AND MOBILE MONEY

SUPRIYA SINGH

INTRODUCTION

Financial innovation in development practice was once viewed predominantly through a microfinance lens, with microenterprises supported by credit facilities offered through NGOs, such as Grameen Bank. Mobile technologies are, however, opening up new worlds for the 'unbanked', empowering financial inclusion as women, especially, become better skilled and more adept at managing money, from work, family remittances, business income and investment. In this dynamic economic sphere, we find telecommunications companies, financiers and financial institutions offering new tools for development which leapfrog established banking systems to render money a more mobile resource.

This chapter addresses the challenges faced by global development practitioners as they work in partnership with governments, international, non-government and philanthropic organizations, and the private sector, to imagine and refine mental models of financial innovation. These challenges relate to working within a changing regulatory structure, adopting a customer-centric approach to see how the financial strategy works in the context of social relationships and cultural values. In other words, established models in which finance is conceived as an impersonal 'thing' need to be replaced by contextualized models of the understanding and use of money by people. Practitioners must now also ensure that impact can be measured and understood, instead of assuming that financial inclusion will automatically lead to development.

In order to understand financial inclusion as practice, we need to embed its study in the social and cultural meanings of money. This is particularly important when forging pathways for accessing formal credit as with microfinance and making payments and transferring via the mobile phone. Implementing financial innovations in the global South requires an understanding of the distinctiveness of money, family and gender in a cultural context. Money is a social phenomenon. It belongs to personal life as well as the market. Money shapes and is shaped by social relationships and cultural values. This is particularly important when dealing with gender issues around money (Hart, 2007; Zelizer, 1994, 2005, 2011). These are tied up with the position of the woman in the family and kinship context, the woman's place in the labour market and the economy and the management and control of money in the home. Women's economic empowerment goes together with gender equity in society (Woetzel et al., 2015).

UNDERSTANDING THE SOCIAL AND CULTURAL CHARACTERISTICS OF MONEY

Countries of the global South have roughly similar understandings about money and family in some respects. In the global South, money is shared across generations in the family, whether it is nuclear or extended. Parents and grandparents give to their children, and children and grandchildren also see it as their duty to give money to the parents, grandparents and extended kin (Singh, 2013a). Money is the preferred gift at births, marriage and death. The gifting of money converts money to a currency of care (ibid., 1996). The morality of money in the family underlies the importance of remittances, domestic and international in developing countries (ibid., 2013a, forthcoming). This is why sending money home, domestically, remains the core function of mobile money (Omwansa and Sullivan, 2012).

This intergenerational morality and reciprocity of money is different from that in the global North. This is because care in the family is displayed through action, visits, communication rather than money. A son would take the mother shopping, banking, to the doctor. A daughter most likely will phone the mother every day. This also rests on the fact that, most often, there is a welfare buffer for the older generation (Singh, 1997).

Money in the global South is male in a more pronounced way than in the global North. Globally, women – if they earn a wage – earn 24 per cent less than men (UN Women, 2015). Women own less wealth than men. In the USA, single women own 36 cents for every dollar of wealth owned by single men. This wealth gap persists even for women in their twenties and thirties (Chang, 2010). In the global South, women's position with wages and wealth is more precarious. Women are at the bottom of global supply chains and are more often in the informal economy. There has been uneven legislative change relating to equal property rights in marriage and inheritance (UN Women, 2015). However, legislative change does not always lead to women equally inheriting property (Singh, 2013a). The one universal about women and money is that women use more of their money, compared with men, on their children and the household (Zelizer, 2011).

FINANCIAL INCLUSION IS A MAJOR POLICY FOCUS FOR
THE GLOBAL SOUTH

Irene, Rina and Khadijah's stories below illustrate the everyday realities of women's financial exclusion. Irene, in Papua New Guinea, has no bank account for there is no bank
branch in her remote village, and she as yet does not have her own mobile phone. Rina, in
an urban village in India, is excluded because money is seen as male in her patrilineal joint
family. For Khadijah, in Bangladesh, microfinance is one of the ways she and her husband
cope with poverty, while sending money to her husband's family. These sketches illustrate
the social and cultural contexts of financial exclusion – lack of access to a financial institution, the exclusion of women in patriarchal societies, money as a currency of care in the
sending of remittances and some of the innovative financial strategies that have evolved
in the global South. This is the situation the development practitioner has to address in
combating financial exclusion.

The basic indicator of financial exclusion is not having an account with a formal financial institution. A financial account is a necessary, though not always a sufficient condition
for access to deposits, formal credit, payments and transfers and insurance. The passion
behind achieving financial inclusion goes further than economic growth. Giving women
the ability to save and the possibility of formal credit and insurance gives them greater
agency in shaping their own lives. Financial inclusion increases a person's freedom and
capability to choose the kind of life she or he wants individually and for the family. This,
in turn, is central to the concept of human development (Nussbaum, 2011; Sen, 1999).

Globally, financial inclusion is included in the targets for achieving six of the 17
sustainable development goals (SDGs) for attaining economic, social and environmental development by 2030. Financial inclusion is important as a necessary condition
for achieving the goals of no poverty, zero hunger, gender equality, decent work and
economic growth, industry, innovation and entrepreneurship, and reduced inequalities
(United Nations Department of Economic and Social Affairs, 2015a–b).

Having access to a financial institution is not in itself an elixir. Making credit
available to persons without the ability to repay can lead to disastrous outcomes. The
sub-prime crisis in the USA, the microfinance debacle in Andhra Pradesh in India and
the credit card crisis in Chile are important warnings (Han, 2012; *Indian Express*, 2015;
Rajan, 2010).

MEASURING FINANCIAL INCLUSION

Measuring financial inclusion makes possible a road map for addressing financial exclusion.
It establishes a base line against which financial innovation can be evaluated in terms of
impact. Governments in the global South place financial inclusion as a central part of economic and social policies because of its demonstrable potential for improving the welfare
of the household and increased economic growth (Cull et al., 2014). Achieving women's
financial inclusion is part of achieving gender equality, which could add 26 per cent to
annual global GDP in 2025 (Woetzel et al., 2015).

Financial inclusion is important for the poor. One of the myths is that the poor have no money to save or manage. But, as recent research has shown, the poor need effective and reliable financial services in order to save, borrow, insure, pay and have resilience to face emergencies. They have little or no buffer to withstand emergencies. Their cash flows are irregular and unstable. So, they need financial services that will help them manage money on a daily basis. They need to be able to build savings for the long term a step at a time. They also need to be able to borrow for all purposes at affordable rates with ease and speed (Collins et al., 2009).

In 2014, 2 billion persons over 15 years of age, that is 38 per cent of the global adult population, remained financially excluded. They did not have an account with a financial institution or a mobile money account. Women were the majority of the excluded, numbering 1.1 billion. It was found that 58 per cent of the women were banked compared with the men, at 65 per cent (Demirguc-Kunt et al., 2015).

There has been progress since 2011, when nearly half the world (49 per cent) was unbanked. Much of this progress has been in sub-Saharan Africa and due to mobile money – payments that go from one mobile phone to another with or without a bank account. Disparities relating to financial inclusion persist in the developing world. In the Middle East, only 14 per cent are banked, while in East Asia and the Pacific, 69 per cent are banked (ibid.).

The persistent issues with financial inclusion remain the greater exclusion of women and the poor. There also remains persistent regional diversity in financial inclusion. The Middle East and South Asian regions have the largest gender gaps. More than half the adults (54 per cent) in the poorest 40 per cent of the households are unbanked, that is 1 billion persons (Demirguc-Kunt and Klapper, 2012; Demirguc-Kunt et al., 2015).

ENABLING REGULATION

Financial inclusion is a necessary condition for development and the expansion and deepening of the financial sector. Hence developing countries see it as a priority. When Central Bank governors of the global South meet – that is, Asia, Africa, Latin America, the Middle East and the Pacific – they share their experiences around financial exclusion. Of the regulators in 143 jurisdictions, 67 per cent have a mandate to promote financial inclusion (Demirguc-Kunt et al., 2015). It is the countries of the global South that have the greatest problems and have also been the most innovative in addressing financial exclusion (Singh, 2013a).

Regulators chart the policy levers relating to financial inclusion and the pathways that are permitted. They discuss the challenges of increasing financial inclusion, enabling innovation, together with consumer protection. So, in India, there has been a gradual reshaping of the banking industry to include different kinds of banks so that mobile money and microfinance come under the financial regulator (*Mint Asia*, 2015). In Kenya, there has been an increased enablement so that formal mobile international remittances are possible in specified countries in Africa. At the same time, regulations are being considered to encourage greater competition in mobile money (Scharwatt and Williamson, 2015).

In Brazil, banking correspondents have been the means for increasing access to branchless banking. The number of banking correspondents slowly increased since they were introduced in the 1970s. Their ability to enable deposits, withdrawals, credit, payments and foreign exchange transactions slowly increased. They have become the most used channel for paying utility bills and credit transfers (Singh, 2013a). Brazil also used Bolsa Familia, its conditional cash transfer programme to help the very poor achieve better health and education outcomes for the children. It also meant that 99 per cent of its recipients have an account with a financial institution (Winn, 2016).

MICROFINANCE: SUCCESS, STUMBLES AND REGULATION

The challenges for development practitioners lie in examining how microfinance and mobile money succeeded, stumbled and grew in different countries. This section examines how microfinance and mobile money have increased the financial reach of the previously unbanked. The strategies themselves have had to be adapted to different regulatory environments, cultural contexts and financial needs. Most often, they began with one aim, which then changed as they saw that customers were using it for a different need. They then modified their approach, building on patterns of customers' use. It has become central in today's partnership model to evaluate the impact of these financial strategies on the alleviation of poverty and gender empowerment, in order to ensure funding and measure whether the SDGs are being reached.

It is inspirational to hear Muhammad Yunus talk of the beginnings of the Grameen Bank in 1976. He overturned the long-held belief that it is risky lending to the poor and especially to women. He was able to build a sustainable enterprise by lending small amounts of money, mainly to women, to set up microenterprises. This lending was based on peer-group relationships, supplemented by mentoring and training.

Microcredit spread across much of the global South and to parts of the global North. In 2015, Women's World Banking, the world's largest network of microfinance institutions and banks, worked with 38 microfinance institutions (MFIs), operating in 27 countries (Women's World Banking, 2015). Figures for 2012 show that there were 91.4 million borrowers with $81.5 billion in loans. The majority of the borrowers remain in South Asia, followed by East Asia and the Pacific (*Microfinance Barometer*, 2014). Microcredit took different organizational forms and worked in different regulatory environments. Even in Australia, the philosophy of microcredit is behind the no-interest and low-interest loans (Cabraal, 2011). Yunus and the Grameen Bank were awarded the Nobel Peace Prize in 2006.

MICROCREDIT STUMBLES

The inspirational script about microcredit has been challenged on a number of fronts. Anthropological studies showed the majority of women gave the loans to their husbands to control. These loans also led to increased domestic violence against the women (Johnson, 2004). This was only one side of the story. When the women themselves evaluated microcredit, they said that the loans had given them greater management and control over some parts of household money. Microcredit had increased their sense of agency and given them greater capabilities (Sanyal, 2009). As discussed later in this section, formal evaluation later substantiated that microfinance did empower, though it did not necessarily reduce poverty.

The rapid and competitive growth of microcredit in India nearly strangled it in 2010, as it moved from a social enterprise to a for-profit organization. It was alleged that farmers in Andhra Pradesh committed suicide because of multiple microfinance loans at high interest rates. The state government retroactively waived loans sparking massive defaults. Gradually, microfinance recovered as the Central Bank set up a national licensing system. Interest rates were capped at 10–12 per cent points above their borrowing costs. Investment slowly returned to the sector in 2012–13 (*The Economist*, 2013).

The impact of microfinance is being questioned. There has been a call for evidence to question the impact of microcredit on the alleviation of poverty, the empowerment of women and its transformational effects. A World Bank study based on panel household survey data over 20 years in 87 villages in rural Bangladesh found that lending to women, particularly, has reduced poverty (Khandker and Samad, 2014). It says:

> group-based credit programs have significant positive effects in raising household welfare including per capita consumption, household non-land assets and net worth. Microfinance increases income and expenditure, the labor supply of males and females, non-land asset and net worth as well as boys' and girls' schooling. Microfinance, especially female credit, also reduces poverty. (Ibid.: 28)

Randomized controlled trials (RCTs), however, found that microcredit was 'modestly positive' but not transformative. There was no clear evidence that microcredit reduced poverty or improved living standards. It, however, did increase freedom of choice relating to occupations, business scale, consumption, female decision power and improved risk management. This evidence confirmed that microcredit has not been harmful, even when it has a high real interest rate (Banerjee et al., 2015). The reaction to the Andhra Pradesh debacle was intense for the demise of microfinance would leave the rural poor with no alternative to moneylenders, who charged 60 to 120 per cent a year. They also often enforced repayment by illegal and exploitative means (Banerjee et al., 2010).

MICROFINANCE IN A CHANGED REGULATORY CONTEXT

The 40-year history of microcredit shows how it has gradually transformed to microfinance offering savings, pensions and insurance. Attention is focused on how microfinance providers address user demands in the giving of information and designing their products. Part of this change has been due to user demand. Over the years, Grameen Bank itself moved to a broader set of services including savings and pensions. Credit became more flexible for poor households and was not tied to microenterprises. Savings were included. Customers had shown their key need was to be able to borrow for all needs when income was uncertain and insufficient for immediate needs (Collins et al., 2009). This wider offering has been more favourably judged (Ehrbeck, 2014; Singh, 2013a).

In India, regulatory change has meant that some of the large microfinance institutions are becoming part of the banking regulatory system. The Reserve Bank of India introduced a range of banking licences in 2015. The largest microfinance financial institution, Bandhan, was given a commercial bank licence and began operating as Bandhan Bank in August 2015. Another large MFI, Ujjivan, and seven other MFIs were given an in-principle small finance bank licence in September 2015. This licence will allow these MFIs to take in deposits, and lend mainly to small borrowers and enterprises in rural and semi-urban areas. Samit Ghosh, Founder and Managing Director of Ujjivan Financial Services, says that the ability to take in deposits will allow the MFIs to lower their deposit costs and thus decrease their lending interest rates. It will also allow them to offer working capital loans to micro-entrepreneurs. The hope is that the MFIs will build on their present reach to the unbanked to mobilize savings. They will also be able to expand to lending to small business (*Mint Asia*, 2015).

MOBILE FINANCIAL SERVICES ENABLE FINANCIAL INCLUSION

Mobile money, that is money transmitted via the mobile phone to another mobile phone without necessarily having a bank in the middle, has resulted in a large increase in financial inclusion between 2011 and 2014. Mobile money in itself is a payment or a transfer of value, but it often facilitates a savings and credit account with a financial institution.

Mobile money was first introduced in the Philippines in 2001, but it was M-PESA, which started in Kenya in 2007, that has become the global success story followed by other developing countries. Later, Bangladesh with B-Kash became the country with the fastest growth in mobile money. Hence, mobile money has become a global South phenomenon.

The importance of mobile money changed the way financial inclusion was measured by 2014, in that it included adults with accounts in financial institutions as well as those with mobile money accounts. Between 2011 and 2014, mobile money was mainly responsible for 700 million adults becoming account holders, leading to a 20 per cent decrease in the unbanked. This has happened especially in sub-Saharan Africa, where the use of mobile money is the greatest (Demirguc-Kunt et al., 2015).

Mobile money started with international remittances through Smart Communication's Smart Money in the Philippines in 2001. The mobile network operator (MNO) Smart Communications partnered with Banco de Oro (BDO), plus a number of retail merchants who acted as their agents overseas. Globe's GCash followed in November 2004. The MNO, Globe Telecom began alone, although in 2009 it became part of a new mobile savings bank called BPI Globe BanKO.

These two services addressed the needs of persons from the Philippines working overseas to provide better opportunities for their children. Pawnshops were among the important intermediaries, for they had traditionally acted as informal money transfer services. Pawnshops still have great reach in the Philippines for financial inclusion. At the end of 2001, there were 9,397 regulated pawnshops with quasi-banking functions compared with 7,587 bank branches (Lamberte, 1991; Lirio, nd). The Philippines provided a favourable environment because mobile phones were common in the Philippines in the early 2000s. People texted avidly. Cards were widely accepted. There was an enabling regulatory environment and the two MNOs were well established and trusted (Singh, 2013a).

Although the Philippines was the starting point for mobile money, the country has remained behind in the mobile money stakes and financial inclusion. Part of the problem has been that the agents were not paid enough. There were problems with liquidity and reach. Moreover, initially the Central Bank had required agents to go for training, thus losing money at work. The relaxation of training guidelines by the Central Bank has helped, as has the partnership with rural banks and the government's direct benefit transfers (Singh, 2013a). But, at present, these direct benefit transfers go to the mobile money agent rather than straight to the customer (Alampay and Cabotaje, 2013).

The stellar success story is of M-PESA, which, as mentioned, began in 2007 in Kenya for urban-rural remittances. Although transfers and payments remain the most prominent part of mobile money, the industry has expanded to include a variety of financial services, such as savings, credit and insurance in partnership with banks.

In 2014, mobile financial services were available in 61 per cent of developing markets. There were 255 mobile money services, across 89 countries, with 300 million registered accounts. In December 2014, active mobile money accounts numbered 103 million. The trend is towards greater interoperability between MNOs. Together with regulatory approval, this is enabling international remittances in parts of West Africa and sub-Saharan Africa (Scharwatt and Williamson, 2015).

Text Box 15.1   Case Study: M-PESA

M-PESA began in Kenya in 2007, building on the use of airtime as currency. It started with the idea that the mobile phone will make repayment of microcredit more efficient. To that end, it partnered with a microfinance organization. But the partnership did not work because it was difficult to get the back ends of the operation to talk to each other. Instead, they found in the trials that people were most interested in 'sending money home'. This was a need as people working in the urban areas needed to send money to their families in the rural areas. You either had to take the money personally, send it with friends who were going to your village, or send it with a 'mutatu' bus driver.

M-PESA was a payments mechanism and so came under the purview of the Central Bank, that is, the Bank of Kenya. The Bank of Kenya recognized that this could be a way of moving people from informal to formal payments as a first step towards financial inclusion. The Central Bank gave M-PESA a letter of no objection. This was after it was satisfied that the customers' money would be put in a trust in a commercial bank or banks which are regulated by the Central Bank, and M-PESA was unable even to use the interest.

Safaricom had asked for a bank to partner it, but banks in 2007 did not see the poor as an important market. This attitude changed as M-PESA was adopted quickly. It succeeded because Safaricom, the Vodafone subsidiary that was launching M-PESA, was the largest MNO in Kenya. It was the market leader in mobile phones with a large, trusted network of agents who used to sell air time. These agents gained a greater

(Continued)

(Continued)

commission from mobile money than air time. What also pushed people to try this new way of sending money was that violence broke out after the elections in 2007. It was impossible to send money by the regular route. So, people tried M-PESA and found that it worked (Singh, 2013a).

That was the beginning of a new way of sending money to family and friends in Kenya and in the global South. The instantaneous transfer of money accompanied by communication made mobile money a relational tool for keeping relationship with family and friends.

Mobile money enables e-money transactions such as paying bills, school fees, buying goods and services. However, the vast majority of transactions still begin and end with cash. The primary activity remains to 'send money home', that is to send money to family and friends. Mobile money expanded into mobile financial services as M-PESA partnered with the Commercial Bank of Africa to offer saving deposits, short-term immediate loans through M-Shwari (Omwansa and Sullivan, 2012; Singh, 2013a).

M-PESA is now used by the majority of adult Kenyans, including the poor. It was found that 78 per cent of poor men and women at the bottom of the pyramid have used the mobile phone to send and receive money (Crandall et al., 2012). This is partly because mobile phones became cheaper in 2009, when the Kenyan government removed VAT from them.

Women use M-PESA to receive money from their children and friends and also from a range of matrikin. In a patrilineal kinship system, where men control the land and most of the household resources, M-PESA augments a woman's ability to manage a separate pool of money (Kusimba et al., 2015).

As mobile money was a new concept in sub-Saharan Africa in 2007, M-PESA was able to get permission to operate without ensuring that people on mobile networks other than Safaricom could also use M-PESA. A person needs to have a Safaricom SIM to use M-PESA. This situation is slowly changing as a result of competition reviews and court cases challenging Safaricom's practices (Mumo, 2014; Mwenesi, 2014). However, in July 2015, Safaricom accounted for 67.4 per cent of mobile money subscriptions in Kenya (Mohammed, 2015).

TRANSLATING M-PESA ACROSS BORDERS AND CULTURES

M-PESA's success has not been easy to translate. By March 2014, M-PESA had been introduced by Vodafone in slightly different versions of its name in Tanzania, Fiji, South Africa, DRC, India, Mozambique, Egypt, Lesotho and Romania (Vodafone, 2015). In no country has M-PESA achieved the market dominance that it has in Kenya. Fear of a monopoly presence has meant that countries like Tanzania have mandatory inter-operability. In West Africa, mobile money has gone further than M-PESA, in that partnerships between MNOs and banks together with enabling regulation has made mobile international remittances possible in parts of Africa (Scharwatt and Williamson, 2015). Kenya has followed that initiative by introducing mobile international remittances via M-PESA in six other countries in Africa (Mark, 2015).

India is a case in point. Vodafone is the second largest mobile operator in India. It piloted M-PESA in India in 2010, and launched it in 2013 as a semi-open mobile wallet in partnership with ICICI bank. By November 2014, only 1.5 million of Vodafone's 170 million subscribers were enrolled with M-PESA. Less than a third of the enrolled subscribers were active users (Sen, 2014).

India's regulatory structure held up the expansion in the early years as India did not allow an MNO to offer mobile money without partnership with a bank. However, in 2015, Vodafone m-pesa Ltd received one of the 11 in-principle payment bank licences. These banks offer remittances, payments and deposits but are not allowed to offer credit.

The cultural aspects of payments are even more difficult. India is second only to Indonesia in its reliance on cash. Cash accounts for 98 per cent of the volume of consumer payments and 68 per cent of the value. Cash is familiar and easy to use. It allows for avoidance of tax. The customer does not bear part of the INR210 billion (US$3.1 billion as on 9 August 2016) direct annual costs of administering cash. Moreover, electronic alternatives have been patchy with difficult access. Even e-commerce at times offers the cash on delivery alternative. So, moving from cash to electronic money is a major challenge (Internet and Mobile Association of India and Payments Council of India and PwC, 2015).

Cash also does not need complex documentation. This is why even people with access to bank accounts often send money to family via informal means, that is, taking cash with them when they visit, via cash couriers or with friends and family. The majority (54.3 per cent) sent money by informal means (Bakshi et al., 2014).

The move towards digitizing payments has the potential to disrupt the Indian financial sector. But, for this to happen, Suresh Sethi, business head for m-pesa at Vodafone India, says that a behavioural change has to take place. Customers need to move from 'assisted behaviour' to 'self-service'. This will happen when people become more familiar with technology and doing the transactions themselves rather than relying on others (*Mint Asia*, 2015).

The prospects are encouraging. India has more than 933 million mobile connections. More than 117 million Indians use smart phones. Of those aged 21–35 years, 80 per cent use electronic channels to pay rent. By 2018, an estimated 70–80 per cent of Indians will use their mobiles to access Internet services (Internet and Mobile Association of India and Payments Council of India and PwC, 2015).

The domestic remittance market in India is large. In 2010–11, some 11.5 million households received domestic remittances amounting to an estimated INR0.5 trillion (US$7.4 billion as on 19 May 2016). Although two-thirds of the receiving households had bank accounts, 55 per cent of the households receiving remittances received them through informal channels (Bakshi et al., 2014). Suresh Sethi, speaking in 2015, says that about 50 per cent are sent informally, with the rest accounted for by bank transfers and postal money order. In this space, the value of mobile wallets has tripled over two years, to reach INR27 billion (US$402 million as on 19 May 2016) in the financial year 2015 (*Mint Asia*, 2015).

PRACTITIONER AND CUSTOMER-CENTRIC PERSPECTIVES IN THE GLOBAL SOUTH

The practitioner perspective is invaluable as innovations take different shapes in various cultural contexts. The development practitioner needs to adopt a customer-centric perspective to see how different financial activities and needs can be satisfied within the customer's social and cultural context. This is often the significant corrective when dealing with technologists, governments and international development organizations.

The practitioner needs to place the customer at the centre of financial inclusion. It is important first to discover the customers' needs and the current impediments. Are the services that are offered accessible? Are they appropriate? One of the criticisms of financial inclusion in India a few years ago was that banks were focusing on CASA – Current Account and Savings Account. The financial needs of customers were broader, however, including remittances, insurance and pensions. So, pushing CASA at customers meant that banks opened bank accounts and could therefore tick off one of their financial inclusion commitments, but the majority of the bank accounts then lay dormant.

Some of the changes to microcredit happened because it became clear that customers' needs were not being met. Customers needed flexible credit and not just credit for microenterprises. People needed to save regularly in small amounts at a readily accessible institution. General insurance was a great unmet need. Hence, the impact assessment of the broadening of microcredit into microfinance has been more favourable.

I illustrate this customer-centric approach by detailing some of the innovative steps that have contributed to the success of Kshetriya Gramin Financial Services (KGFS) that began in India in 2008. KGFS concentrates on rural people who have been ignored or only minimally served by other financial institutions. Analysing KGFS' success stories, two words appear often. It is a 'localized' branch within the village. The branches are simple, with wooden benches and open in design, but with the latest technology behind the desk to ensure the customer database is up to date. The branch staff seek to enroll all households within a five-kilometre radius. At the centre is understanding the customer and his or her aspirations for the household.

The staff are called 'wealth managers' and are evaluated according to how they have helped a household achieve its wealth management goals, rather than on the number of financial services sold. So, when members of the household come to KGFS, the first step is to record information about the household's financial situation. Also recorded are the household's aspirations. Staff members visit village households when they start the branch and then every six months to update their information. These are the starting points for advice about suitable products, services and strategies.

KGFS follows an aggregator model drawing on services and products from banks, insurance companies, mutual funds and other formal financial institutions. KGFS's wealth management approach backed by detailed customer information allows them to customize loans for crops, retail shops, livestock and education. They are able to give some of these loans within 10 to 15 minutes. Livestock and crop loans that require external expert verification can take a week (Singh, 2013a, 2013c).

The first set of branches became profitable within four years of its opening in India in 2008. It is increasing its reach, so that between 2008 and 2013, KGFS expanded to five independently managed KGFS institutions in five regions, covering 170 branches serving about 300,000 households (Ananth and George, 2013).

An evaluation of KGFS found that formal borrowing – that is, loans outstanding and repaid – in the KGFS areas is greater than in the control areas not served. KGFS has at the same time lowered the amount borrowed informally by its customers (Sadhu, 2014). This is transformative when seen from the customer perspective. When I visited KGFS in Pudhuaaru near Thanjavur in India in 2013, I met Sushila, 40 years old, who runs a successful village shop. Her husband fell ill 18 years ago and they had to borrow from money lenders. When the KGFS branch opened in 2008, she said, 'we moved from 10 paisa to 2 paisa'. This means that they moved from a 120 per cent interest rate to the money lender (10 paisa for every 100 paisa in a rupee every month) to 24 per cent. Her shop is now stocked, land has been bought, her eldest daughter is studying engineering. She has also bought 'moneyback' insurance for her daughters and has been putting INR1,000 (US$15 as on 9 August 2016) a year in a pension fund for the last four years (Singh, 2013b).

CONCLUSION: THE PRACTICE OF FINANCIAL INCLUSION

Financial inclusion is one of the most enabling aspects of personal and economic development. The economic indicators are valuable for governments and international development organizations to assess its impact and continue giving it priority. But, for the practitioner, it is the capability-enhancing aspect, particularly for women, which remains memorable in the field.

Nussbaum describes a case that encapsulates the empowering effect of financial inclusion. She tells the story of Vasanthi, 30, who left an abusive marriage in Ahmedabad, India, and went to live with her brothers and their families. She was fortunate that they welcomed her back. They gave her a loan to buy a sewing machine that rolls the edges of a saree to prevent it from unravelling. She began to repay them when she got a loan from the Self-Employed Women's Association (SEWA), one of India's first microcredit organizations. Several years later, she has repaid most of the loan. She has joined a friend to combat domestic violence in her community. She is also planning to learn to read and write (Nussbaum, 2011).

The successful practitioner needs to take the customer's perspective, connecting it to the need for enabling regulation, service design and provision that meets users' needs, and a sustainable business and technology model.

Questions for Discussion

1 What is money and what makes mobile money transformative?
2 In what ways do models of gender inhibit Bangladeshi women from taking advantage of all forms of financial opportunity? Is this pattern replicated across the global South?
3 Do people in developing societies really need microfinance?

📖 FURTHER READING

Chang, M.L. (2010) *Shortchanged: Why Women Have Less Wealth and What Can be Done About It*. Oxford: Oxford University Press.
Scharwatt, C. and Williamson, C. (2015). *Mobile Money Crosses Borders: New Remittance Models in West Africa*. London: GSMA Mobile Money for the Unbanked. Available

at: www.gsma.com/mobilefordevelopment/wp-content/uploads/2015/04/2015_MMU_ Mobile-money-crosses-borders_New-remittance-models-in-West-Africa.pdf (accessed 29 July 2016).

Singh, S. (2013a) *Globalization and Money: A Global South Perspective*. Lanham, MD: Rowman and Littlefield.

REFERENCES

Alampay, E.A. and Cabotaje, C.E. (2013) *Using Mobile Money as a Conditional Cash Transfer Conduit in the Philippines* (online). Irvine, CA: Institute for Money, Technology & Financial Inclusion. Available at: www.imtfi.uci.edu/files/docs/2014/Alampay%20 and%20Cabotaje_IMTFI%20Final%20Report.pdf (accessed 18 December 2016).

Ananth, B. and George, D. (2013) 'What's Next for KGFS?' 5 February. Available at: www.financialaccess.org/blog/2015/7/30/whats-next-for-kgfs (accessed 27 February 2017).

Bakshi, I., Sharma, A., Kakkar, P. and Sharma, A. (2014) *National Remote Payments Survey*. New Delhi: National Council of Applied Economic Research

Banerjee, A., Karlan, D. and Zinman, J. (2015) 'Six Randomized Evaluations of Microcredit: Introduction and Further Steps', *American Economic Journal: Applied Economics*, 7(1): 1–21.

Banerjee, A., Bardhan, P., Duflo, E., Field, E., Karlan, D., Khwaja, A. and Rajan, R. (2010) 'Help Microfinance, Don't Kill It'. *The Indian Express*. 26 November. Available at: www.indianexpress.com/news/help-microfinance-dont-kill-it/716105/0 (accessed 27 February 2017).

Cabraal, A. (2011) 'The Impact of Microfinance on the Capabilities of Participants'. PhD Thesis, RMIT University, Melbourne. Available at: http://researchbank.rmit.edu.au/ view/rmit:9730 (accessed 27 February 2017).

Chang, M.L. (2010) *Shortchanged: Why Women Have Less Wealth and What Can be Done About It*. Oxford: Oxford University Press.

Collins, D., Morduch, J., Rutherford, S. and Ruthven, O. (2009) *Portfolios of the Poor: How the World's Poor Live on $2 a Day*. Princeton, NJ: Princeton University Press.

Crandall, A., Otieno, A., Mutuku, L., Colaço, J., Grosskurth, J. and Otieno, P. (2012) *Mobile Phone Usage at the Kenyan Base of the Pyramid: Final Report*. Nairobi: iHub Research and Research Solutions Africa.

Cull, R., Ehrbeck, T. and Holle, N. (2014) 'Financial Inclusion and Development: Recent Impact Evidence'. *Focus Note*. April. Available at: https://www.cgap.org/sites/default/ files/FocusNote-Financial-Inclusion-and-Development-April-2014.pdf (accessed 27 February 2017).

Demirguc-Kunt, A. and Klapper, L. (2012) *Measuring Financial Inclusion: The Global Findex Database*. Washington, DC: World Bank.

Demirguc-Kunt, A., Klapper, L., Singer, D. and Oudheusden, P.V. (2015) *The Global Findex Database 2014: Measuring Financial Inclusion around the World Policy Research Working Paper 7255*. Washington, DC: World Bank.

Ehrbeck, T. (2014) 'Microcredit Impact Revisited', Vol. 2015, CGAP. Available at: www. cgap.org/blog/microcredit-impact-revisited (accessed 29 July 2016).

Han, C. (2012) *Life in Debt: Times of Care and Violence in Neoliberal Chile*. Available at: http://RMIT.eblib.com.au/patron/FullRecord.aspx?p=896312 (accessed 27 February 2017).

Hart, K. (2007) 'Money is Always Personal and Impersonal', *Anthropology Today*, 23(5): 12–16.

Indian Express (2015) 'Hasten Slowly', 12 October.

Internet and Mobile Association of India and Payments Council of India and PwC (2015) 'Disrupting Cash: Accelerating Electronic Payments in India'. Internet and Mobile Association of India, Payments Council of India and PwC.

Johnson, S. (2004) 'Gender Norms in Financial Markets:Evidence from Kenya', *World Development*, 32(8): 1355–74, doi: 10.1016/j.worlddev.2004.03.003.

Khandker, S.R. and Samad, H.A. (2014) 'Dynamic Effects of Microcredit in Bangladesh', (D.R. Group, trans.). *Policy Research Working Paper*.

Kusimba, S.B., Yang, Y. and Chawla, N.V. (2015) 'Family Networks of Mobile Money in Kenya', *Information Technologies & International Development*, 11(3): 1–21.

Lamberte, M.B. (1991) 'An Analysis of the Role of Pawnshops in the Philippine Financial System', *Savings and Development*, 15(3): 229–245, doi: 10.2307/25830269.

Lirio, R.P. (nd) 'Central Bank's Regulatory Role Over Non-Bank Financial Institutions: The Philippine Experience'. Available at: info.worldbank.org/etools/docs/library/157239/nbfi-thailand/pdf/.../lirio04b.pdf (accessed 17 May 2016).

Mark, O. (2015) 'M-Pesa customers get access to seven African countries', *The East African*, 23 April.

Microfinance Barometer 2014 (2014) 'Microfinance Key Figures', 12 September. Available at: www.citigroup.com/citi/microfinance/data/lebarometre.pdf (accessed 29 July 2016).

Mint Asia (2015) 'The Last Mile', 9 October.

Mohammed, O. (2015) 'Kenya's Safaricom Might Have to Spin off M-Pesa, the World's Largest Mobile Money Business', *Quartz Africa*, 6 July. Available at: http://qz.com/445114/dominating-mobile-money-could-lead-to-the-break-up-of-kenyas-biggest-mobile-network/ (accessed 27 February 2017).

Mumo, M. (2014) 'Equity Bank Seeks Share of Telco Business', *Daily Nation*, 25 February.

Mwenesi, S. (2014) 'Airtel Wins Case Against Safaricom to Open up M-Pesa', 28 July. Available at: www.humanipo.com/news/46322/airtel-wins-case-against-safaricom-to-open-up-m-pesa/ (accessed 3 September 2014).

Nussbaum, M.C. (2011) *Creating Capabilities: The Human Development Approach*. Cambridge, MA: Belknap Press of Harvard University Press.

Omwansa, T.K. and Sullivan, N.P. (2012) *Money, Real Quick: The Story of M-PESA*, (Kindle edn). London: Guardian Books.

Rajan, R. (2010) *Fault Lines: How Hidden Fractures Still Threaten the World Economy*. Princeton, NJ and Oxford: Princeton University Press.

Sadhu, S. (2014) 'The Impact of KGFS in Rural Tamil Nadu: Early Evidence from a Randomised Control Trial', Vol. 2015. IFMR Finance Foundation.

Sanyal, P. (2009) 'From Credit to Collective Action: The Role of Microfinance in Promoting Women's Social Capital and Normative Influence', *American Sociological Review*, 74: 529–50.

Scharwatt, C. and Williamson, C. (2015). *Mobile Money Crosses Borders: New Remittance Models in West Africa*. London: GSMA Mobile Money for the Unbanked. Available at: www.gsma.com/mobilefordevelopment/wp-content/uploads/2015/04/2015_MMU_Mobile-money-crosses-borders_New-remittance-models-in-West-Africa.pdf (accessed 29 July 2016).

Sen, A. (1999) *Development as Freedom*. Oxford: Oxford University Press.

Sen, S. (2014) 'Inclusion by Mobile', *Business Today*, 23 November.

Singh, S. (1996) 'The Cultural Distinctiveness of Money', *Sociological Bulletin*, 45(1): 61–85.

Singh, S. (1997) *Marriage Money: The Social Shaping of Money in Marriage and Banking*. St. Leonards: Allen & Unwin.

Singh, S. (2013a) *Globalization and Money: A Global South Perspective*. Lanham, MD: Rowman and Littlefield.

Singh, S. (2013b) 'In the Field with KGFS, Part I', 18 September. Available at: https://moneydataprivacy.wordpress.com/2013/09/18/in-the-field-with-kgfs-part-i/ (accessed 27 February 2017).

Singh, S. (2013c) 'In the Field with KGFS, Part II', 15 September. Available at: https://moneydataprivacy.wordpress.com/2013/09/25/in-the-field-with-kgfs-part-ii/ (accessed 27 February 2017).

Singh, S. (Forthcoming) 'Money and Family Relationships: The Biography of Transnational Money', in N. Bandelj, F.F. Wherry and V. Zelizer (eds), *Money Talks*. Princeton, NJ: Princeton University Press.

The Economist (2013) 'Microfinance in India: Road to Redemption', 12 January, p. 62.

UN Women (2015) *Progress of the World's Women 2015–2016: Transforming Economies, Realizing Rights*. New York: UN Women.

United Nations Department of Economic and Social Affairs (2015a) *Sustainable Development Goals*. Available at: https://sustainabledevelopment.un.org/topics (accessed 13 October 2015).

United Nations Department of Economic and Social Affairs (2015b) *Transforming our World: The 2030 Agenda for Sustainable Development*. Available at: https://sustainabledevelopment.un.org/post2015/transformingourworld (accessed 13 October 2015).

Vodafone (2015) 'What is M-Pesa?' Available at: www.vodafone.com/content/index/about/about-us/money_transfer.html (accessed 15 October 2015).

Winn, J.K. (2016) 'Mobile Payments and Financial Inclusion: Kenya, Brazil and India as Case Studies', in J.A. Rothchild (ed.), *Research Handbook on Electronic Commerce Law*. Cheltenham: Edward Elgar, pp. 62–88.

Woetzel, J., Madgavkar, A., Ellingrud, K., Labaye, E., Devillard, S., Kutcher, E., Manyika, D. and Krishnan, M. (2015) 'The Power of Parity: How Advancing Women's Equality Can Add $12 Trillion to Global Growth', McKinsey Global Institute. Available at: www.mckinsey.com/global-themes/employment-and-growth/how-advancing-womens-equality-can-add-12-trillion-to-global-growth (accessed 29 July 2016).

Women's World Banking (2015) 'About Us'. Available at: www.womensworldbanking.org/about-us/what-we-do/ (accessed 21 October 2015).

Zelizer, V.A. (1994) *The Social Meaning of Money*. New York: Basic Books.

Zelizer, V.A. (2005) *The Purchase of Intimacy*. Princeton, NJ: Princeton University Press.

Zelizer, V.A. (2011) 'The Gender of Money'. *The Wall Street Journal*, 27 January. Available at: http://blogs.wsj.com/ideas-market/2011/01/27/the-gender-of-money/ (accessed 26 July 2016).

16

WHEN ADAPTATION FAILS: PLANNED RELOCATION AS A RIGHTS-BASED RESPONSE TO CLIMATE DISPLACEMENT

SCOTT LECKIE

INTRODUCTION

After languishing on the peripheries of global climate change discussions for decades, the issue of climate displacement has stormed to the forefront of policy debates in recent years. With the effects of climate change becoming increasingly evident along the world's coastlines and other vulnerable areas, so, too, are the very real displacement consequences of these dramatic environmental changes. People and organizations concerned with these developments are increasingly able to identify and understand the unique qualities of the actual territorial locations where climate displacement will likely take place (or has taken place) in most of the heavily affected countries, how many people will be affected (or are being affected) and the general time-frame during which this is most likely to occur (or is occurring). The nature and mandates of the institutions – both domestic and international – that will be required to provide the assistance needed to protect the rights of climate-displaced persons and communities are increasingly clear. So, too, are the legal frameworks that can be drawn upon to support the rights of climate-displaced persons when climate change adaptation measures fail to protect them, as well as their homes, lands and properties.[1] This chapter will provide a brief comparative overview of what will occur and what is already occurring when adaptation fails, and when people are forced to leave their homes to new settlements. It will examine the experiences in several countries where planned relocation measures by climate-affected communities are already underway and explore some of the policy challenges facing decision-makers in the years to come as the effects of climate change worsen.

THE EXODUS BEGINS

While many small island states face extremely worrying prospects that will almost inevitably involve flight from their island homes,[2] it is largely agreed that in terms of the numbers of people and communities affected, most climate displacement throughout the world will lead to measures involving internal resilience by people and communities including spontaneous/unorganized migration, voluntary planned relocation and climate-sensitive planning processes that guide threatened communities to safer residential options within the borders of their own countries. This chapter provides evidence that domestic land-based solutions to climate displacement may be more feasible than generally thought, recalling at the same time, of course, that they are clearly of limited utility in some of the more heavily affected small island nations without any elevated land to flee to. This reality is of tremendous importance in determining how best to formulate solutions to climate displacement, for those with least access to financial resources and generally those with lower levels of political power or participation, are, in fact, the ones most in need of assistance; assistance which is far more likely to occur within the borders of countries than within new countries receiving these victims of climate change.

For governments and others to take these rights seriously will require concerted, planned and targeted responses grounded in good faith and practices of due diligence that aim to secure these rights for everyone, at all times – attempting to prevent displacement, during displacement and, if prevention fails, ultimately in helping to facilitate the end of displacement through the provision of durable rights-based solutions. In practice, this means that states should, individually or collectively, provide climate change mitigation and adaptation assistance and support so that persons can remain in their homes for as long as possible or can move within their state or across borders in a planned manner over time that does not

---

[1]See, 'The Peninsula Principles on Climate Displacement Within States' 18 August 2013, available in many languages at: www.displacementsolutions.org. See also, Oliver-Smith et al., who support this contention:

> Unfortunately, to date, neither the concept of social vulnerability or social resilience has yet led to policies or practices that have significantly reduced losses or damages related to climatic stressors in much of the world. This is in part because of a continuing scientific and policy emphasis on the biophysical processes, rather than how these processes interact with human society. There is a bias in the pervading neoliberal economic regime that privileges economic growth over sustainable development. (2012: 17)

[2]See, for instance, the constantly updated and latest estimates of sea-level rise from NASA, available at: http://climate.nasa.gov/vital-signs/sea-level/(accessed 29 February 2017).

in any way result in homelessness or landlessness. Sometimes this works, however increasingly it does not. Preventing climate displacement is far preferable to resolving it once it has occurred. But, when it has occurred, states should provide climate-displaced persons under their jurisdiction with a practicable level of age- and gender-sensitive assistance including, without limitation, emergency services, evacuation and relocation, medical assistance, housing, food, clean water, measures necessary for social and economic inclusion, and the facilitation of family reunion. They should provide all necessary legal, economic, social and other forms of protection and assistance to those climate change-displaced persons displaced within their borders and to those likely to be displaced.

Appropriate laws and policies on compensation for material losses and damages incurred by climate change-displaced persons need to be developed. Targeted land reform, land acquisition, land allocation and land set-aside initiatives should be developed by all governments that are serious about protecting the rights of climate-displaced people and communities. States should, in particular, afford protection against displacement due to climate change to those such as indigenous peoples, minorities and other groups who are particularly dependent on and attached to their land. Adequately resourced and clearly mandated institutional mechanisms at all levels – local, state, national and international – need to be in place in all countries, in particular those with coastal areas and other portions of territory likely to be negatively affected by the consequences of a changing climate. Above all, people and communities forced to flee their homes and lands due to climate change, must be treated as rights-holders, with all of the corresponding state obligations and international support measures implemented in full to ensure these rights guarantees. Within this space there is thus a need, and a great many opportunities, for non-state entities, from non-governmental agencies to civic groups, to influence the normative structures of national and international climate change adaptation.

Laws, normative frameworks and international standards are one thing, but moving words on paper to deeds on the ground remains the key challenge for everyone who cares about the human consequences and human rights implications of climate displacement.

It is beyond contention that everyone who faces the spectre of climate displacement is, in the first instance, a rights-holder who should be afforded the full protection of all internationally recognized human rights and fundamental freedoms. This applies to Bangladeshis as much as to i-Kiribati, and to Guna Indians in Panama as much as to Maldivians, Solomon Islanders, native Alaskans and everyone else. Indeed, just as anyone anywhere can potentially become a refugee or a displaced person, so too can all of us potentially become a climate-displaced person. The rights that must be afforded climate-displaced people, therefore, include all human rights found within the body of international human rights law, as well as those human rights provisions found within the domestic laws of the country concerned.[3] As with all persons, climate-displaced people must be protected against discrimination of any kind, such as race, colour, sex, language, religion or belief, political or other opinion, national, ethnic or social origin, legal or social status, age, disability, property, birth, or on any other similar grounds. Rights such as the right to life, the right to water, the right to freedom of expression,

---

[3]See, for instance, Displacement Solutions, *The Rights of Climate Displaced Persons: A Quick Guide* (2015).

the right to health, the right to food, the right to an adequate standard of living, the right to political participation, the right to information, the right to be free from discrimination, the right to equal treatment, the right to security of the person, the right to privacy and a host of other rights should have a direct bearing on a wide cross section of climate change decisions made by governments and, thus influence, how the consequences of these decisions and the impact of climate change will be experienced by individual rights-holders. In addition, they must also be afforded the protections granted under both the *UN Guiding Principles on Internal Displacement* and the *UN Principles on Housing and Property Restitution* both of which are directly relevant to climate-displaced people and communities.[4] Climate displacement can impact the enjoyment of all human rights, particularly those linked to or dependent upon one's HLP rights and tenure status. People must have rights to stay in their homes and lands as long as possible, and simultaneously the right to leave should they wish to exercise it. Climate change has caused and will continue to cause mass displacement that can result in unspeakable hardship, as well as the erosion of the rights of those affected and the loss of financial and other assets, in particular losses relating to housing, land and property, and all of these losses will need to be appropriately addressed by governments the world over.

But, this must not merely be treated with dismay and despair, for a series of people-driven initiatives are underway in several of the most heavily affected countries that may lead the way in revealing that pro-active planning and targeted land policies hold out by far the best prospects for those displaced due to climate change.[5] The remainder of this chapter looks at several of these and outlines key lessons for the future.

Text Box 16.1   Case Study: Papua New Guinea (The Carteret Islands)[6]

The well-publicized planned relocation process currently underway from the Carteret Islands in Papua New Guinea to the much larger neighbouring island of Bougainville (also in PNG) is widely held to be one of the first organized resettlement movements of climate change-displaced persons, although the idea of resettling the islanders

[4]While the global scale of displacement caused by the effects of climate change will be massive, it is important to note that the vast majority of those to be displaced will remain, and will wish to remain, within their country of origin. Consequently, everyone affected is already entitled to the human rights protections (including the *Guiding Principles on Internal Displacement*) that will be required to ensure them a full and dignified life, including many of the rights that collectively make up the body of housing, land and property rights law.

[5]A 2012 report by the Asian Development Bank (ADB) (2012: 48–9) rightly recognizes the importance of land rights within countries (and across borders) affected by climate change, and thus by inference, the need for secure HLP rights for everyone *now* in countries likely to generate climate displacement.

[6]See: http://displacementsolutions.org/ds-initiatives/climate-change-and-displacement-initiative/papua-new-guinea-climate-displacement/ (accessed 27 February 2017).

to Bougainville stretches back several decades.[7] In 2007, the national government of PNG and the Autonomous Bougainville government (ABG) agreed to resettle the inhabitants of the Carterets and three other atolls to Bougainville. More than 3,000 Carteret Islanders and another 2,500 island dwellers from three other nearby atolls (the Mortlock, Tasman and Nuguria Islands) will need to relocate because of increasing land loss, salt-water inundation and growing food insecurity. When the national PNG government and the ABG decided to relocate those from the Carterets and other atolls to Bougainville, many expected the relevant governmental bodies to promptly manage this process by identifying and allocating sufficient land on Bougainville to resettle those fleeing their atolls. But, after a frustrating period of governmental inaction, the community-driven initiative *Tulele Peisa* was established to find concrete and accessible land solutions for those to be displaced from the neighbouring atolls.[8]

Tulele Peisa ('Riding the Waves on Our Own') is led by the dynamic Ursula Rakova, who has set out to find permanent housing, land and property solutions for the population of the Carterets on Bougainville.[9] The *Integrated Carterets Relocation Programme* of Tulele Peisa offers unique policy and planning lessons for planned relocation measures in other countries. Working against the odds and with very limited financial resources, as depicted in the Academy Award-nominated film *Sun Come Up*, Tulele Peisa thus far has been able to amass some 120 ha of land on Bougainville, most of which has been donated by the Catholic Church for the purposes of relocating a small portion of the Carteret Islanders.[10] Much more land is obviously needed, but an important start has been made in developing the methods required to provide sustainable land solutions to the atoll dwellers. Demand for relocation has increased as the impact of climate change on the Carterets has become ever more apparent.

The logistics of the relocation process developed by Tulele Peisa first involves a number of steps on the atoll itself. Initially, the Council of Elders was mobilized and the relocation plans discussed and approved. The plan was then put before the ABG and endorsed. The group then set out to raise awareness of the issues throughout the islands comprising the atoll and developed a Task Force Committee that became the lead body responsible for elements of the relocation process. Ceremonial preparations were then carried out, followed by the mobilization of public and private resources. In terms of activities on Bougainville, the *Carterets Integrated Relocation Plan* involves a detailed and complex 20-step process, including: scoping out available land; identifying traditional land owners; negotiating with land title holders; engaging with landowners; exchange programmes; entering into land negotiations; carrying out social and resource mapping; planting gardens; identifying families using objective selection criteria; preparing families for relocation; preparing host families for relocatee arrivals; building homes; and moving families to the new settlements. According to preliminary

(Continued)

---

[7]See, for instance, M. Loughry, 'The Case of the Carterets', Presentation at Conference on Climate Change and Migration in Asia-Pacific, Gilbert + Tobin Centre of Public Law, University of New South Wales, 10-11 November 2011, available at: tv.unsw.edu.au/video/climate-change-and-migration-session-2 (accessed 26 April 2012).

[8]See an overview of the work of Tulele Peisa in: Ursula Rakova, 'The Sinking Carterets Islands: Leading Change in Climate Change Adaptation and Resilience in Bougainville, Papua New Guinea', in Scott Leckie (ed.), *Land Solutions for Climate Displacement* Routledge/Earthscan, 2014.

[9]See: www.tulelepeisa.org (accessed 27 February 2017).

[10]See: www.suncomeup.com/film/Home.html (accessed 27 February 2017).

(Continued)

estimates by Tulele Peisa, some 14 million Kina (US$ 5.3m) will be required until 2019 to relocate all of those who wish to move to Bougainville, a figure which is well within the capacity of the PNG national government to provide.

Several years into the process, the identification of land for the relocation process remains the key challenge. In terms of the relocation criteria developed by the Carteret community, some 1,500 ha of land would ideally be required to accommodate all 300 families, with an additional 1,500 ha of land required for the full relocation of the other three affected atolls. Tulele Peisa has developed a land goal for each family that proposes that each relocated family receive land use rights of over 5 ha of land; 1 ha would be allocated for housing and personal gardens, 3 ha for livelihood purposes, including the growing of cocoa and copra, and the remaining 1 ha set aside for purposes of reforestation. Based on the experience of an earlier relocation process that failed, the islanders feel it is important that sufficient land be allocated to each family to enable them to earn a livelihood to ensure that any relocation is sustainable. This led to their conclusion that 5 ha per family would be required, in order to provide sufficient land for farming cash crops. As noted, to date, a total of 120 ha of land in several locations has been identified on Bougainville for use by those to be relocated. This is clearly a good start, but still leaves a considerable land shortfall. Because more than 96 per cent of Bougainville is governed by customary land rules and allotted using traditional land arrangements, which do not always facilitate the transfer of land to those not part of the customary group with rights to the land in question, an emphasis thus far has been placed on securing portions of the remaining 4 per cent of the land which is divided between private owners and State land. There are also a number of obstacles to obtaining clear legal title to land in Bougainville, coupled with extensive unresolved land disputes that will make the additional acquisition of new land for relocation a continuing challenge.

The relocation experience thus far concerning the Carteret Islanders, even at this very early stage, presents a number of lessons for similar exercises in other areas where climate-induced displacement will manifest, including: (a) *The importance of land identification* – the identification and allocation of sufficient land for relocation purposes is central to resolving climate displacement. While the Catholic Church has provided roughly 120 ha of land for relocation, this will cover only a small portion of the land reserves needed to resettle the entire population from the Carterets. This and other climate change-related relocation exercises will need to take a pro-active approach towards land allocation as a prerequisite for successful resettlement; (b) *The central role of the affected communities* – government efforts in support of relocation have been stalled by the unclear political situation in Bougainville, as well as limited political will to devote the resources required to ensure successful relocation. This, in turn, necessitated the emergence of Tulele Peisa, which again shows the vital role to be played by affected communities themselves in orchestrating land-based solutions to their climate displacement; and (c) *The need for sustainable and comprehensive relocation planning* – earlier relocation programmes to Bougainville (and elsewhere) justified by reasons not related to climate change, failed due to the lack of livelihood opportunities for those relocated. Because the mere provision of a new house and garden is never sufficient to restore the lives and livelihoods lost as a result of displacement of all types, the comprehensive needs of those to be relocated have been structurally built into the plans of Tulele Peisa. Those relocating still do not, however, have clear title to the land on which relocation is beginning to take place. The importance of establishing clear title to ensure security of tenure for all those who relocate is vital to its success.

Text Box 16.2   Case Study: Kiribati[11]

Few nations are as deeply and dramatically affected by the consequences of climate change as the Pacific atoll nation of Kiribati. While the situation facing the Carteret Islands in PNG is certainly tragic, most of PNG will not experience massive climate displacement in the coming decades. For Kiribati and other similarly threatened island and atoll nations, however, the territorial existence of *the country as a whole* is under threat. The country's looming fate has both the government and the citizenry of this nation ever more on edge as the once distant predictions of climate change come increasingly to pass. The very real and palpable sense of unease and often outright fear that is apparent is testimony to the human and displacement tragedy slowly unfolding in Kiribati. The more than 100,000 people of Kiribati now worry openly that their tiny land mass of only 719 km² is slowly but surely being eaten away by seas that have for an eternity provided a source of sustenance, beauty and tranquillity. After years of tirelessly urging the world to do more on climate mitigation and adaptation, former President Anote Tong and his government increasingly prioritized a sophisticated, well-thought out strategy of long-term *dignified migration*.[12] With requests to countries such as Australia to provide it with new territory in order to allow Kiribati to re-establish itself elsewhere falling (not surprisingly, given Australia's widely criticized climate change policies, particularly under the Abbott government) on deaf ears, with only minute amounts of adaptation funding having been provided thus far, in an era when corporate representatives show up in the capital South Tarawa selling manmade floating islands for a staggering US$1 billion, and when the developmental challenges facing the impoverished nation continue to worsen, dignified migration is clearly the next best, and most logical, policy outcome. The policy emphasizes, through a merit-based system, specialized educational opportunities in professional skills that are in short supply in the region, such as nursing and automotive engineering, based on the rationale that this will significantly increase the employment prospects of individual i-Kiribati citizens who eventually do migrate to countries such as Australia and New Zealand. This policy is seen effectively as a win-win proposition, because, even if those receiving the new educational opportunities choose to remain in or return to Kiribati, the nation as a whole will benefit from their newfound skills. It is recognized that dignified migration is most likely to result in mutually beneficial outcomes for both the migrants and host countries if a number of preparatory measures are pursued.

At the same time, as the practical limits of dignified migration and other measures of internal relocation within Kiribati (including to the highest territory in the country, the island of Kiritimati) become ever clearer, the government is looking well beyond its borders for solutions. This has again centred on the critical question of land; not land in Kiribati, however, but rather a 6,000 acre plot of land called Naviavia on the island of Vanua Levu in Fiji, purchased in 2012 by the government. Even though there is a long history of i-Kiribati people moving among their own islands and between islands across the Pacific in search of a better life, the purchase of such a large land tract

(Continued)

---

[11]See: http://displacementsolutions.org/ds-initiatives/climate-change-and-displacement-initiative/kiribati-climate-displacement/ (accessed 27 February 2017).

[12]See the moving personal story of Linda Uan, at: www.climate.gov.ki/2013/02/12/i-kiribati-want-to-migrate-with-dignity/ (accessed 27 February 2017).

(Continued)

in a neighbouring country is clearly indicative of the rather dramatic policy directions in which the government is increasingly placing its hopes, even while the government officially denies that the land will be used for resettlement.[13] Inter-island relocation and inter-country resettlement are not new phenomena in the region, or to the people of Kiribati, but the new land acquisition is highly symbolic when viewed through the lens of climate change. The controversial resettlement of virtually the entire population of Banaba Island in Kiribati to Rabi Island in Fiji in 1945, as a consequence of resource depletion and associated phosphate mining, is perhaps a harbinger of what awaits Kiribati's population today, and lessons learned from this and other past resettlement experiences, such as when Tuvaluans from Vaitupu resettled to Kioa Island in Fiji in the 1940s, should inform the design of any possible relocation or facilitated migration programmes to Vanua Levu even at this very premature stage. As things now stand, suffice it to say that the Vanua Leva option could, if played out carefully and with the full political support of Fiji (where such issues are already a permanent part of political discourse), be pivotal in the multi-level efforts by Kiribati to simultaneously preserve the cultural identity of the people, protect their human rights and secure what would effectively amount to a safe haven for on-going governance of Kiribati should this be impossible within Kiribati itself. Done properly, an eventual exercise of this nature could in theory yield positive results for those choosing to move in this manner. Conversely, if done poorly and without adequate preparation, financing and planning, a mass relocation plan of this scale can all too easily have catastrophic consequences for everyone involved. All participants in the process – the people moving, the host community and both the government of Fiji and of Kiribati – need to be actively engaged in developing plans and processes that will prevent any relocation site from suffering the fate of so many other attempts at relocation – impoverishment, health crises, instability and insecurity.

It is still not too late to prevent worst case scenarios from taking place, and a new, vigorous and harmonized strategy of both 'fight' and 'flight' could positively transform Kiribati both in socio-economic and human rights terms, but also in terms of long-term viability as a nation in their fight against climate change. Many Pacific Island nations, including Kiribati, have always been vulnerable to an array of environmental threats including droughts, storm surges and occasional king tides and have shown considerable resilience in this regard. Today, however, the continued physical existence of Kiribati is far from secure, and the country could disappear entirely during the lifetimes of children who are alive today.

The pursuit of a coordinated strategy that focuses simultaneously on improving the human rights and development prospects of all i-Kiribati people today (*fight*), combined with an approach that guarantees the right to new land in safe locations, whether within the country or elsewhere, for everyone forced to flee the country as sea levels rise to unsustainable levels (*flight*) will hold out the best hope for the people of Kiribati. Although Kiribati has made repeated and valiant efforts advocating for climate change mitigation since joining the UN in 1999, as well as testing the region's political waters with proposals for mass migration and even the establishment of a new territorial configuration for the country, these pleas have largely gone unheeded. As a result, an understandable (but, nonetheless, worrisome for the implications this decision generates) consensus appears to be emerging within the country that neither mitigation nor adaptation will be substantial or rapid enough to save Kiribati in the long run. With

---

[13]See, for instance: www.theglobalmail.org/feature/kiribati-a-nation-going-under/590/ (accessed 20 June 2013).

hopes of adaptation diminishing, therefore, debate has centred on whether Kiribati should prioritize a flight strategy involving mass migration and relocation, or whether a series of major adaptation projects might yet yield the results needed to preserve Kiribati's place among the family of nations. Because of the seeming inevitability of i-Kiribati migration to safe third countries, most notably Fiji, New Zealand and Australia, some decision-makers have taken the view that adaptation measures are effectively a waste of both precious time and resources, in effect asking: 'Why spend money on adapting to climate change and improving the social and economic prospects of the country if the population is just going to leave anyway?' Indeed, a simultaneous focus on both adaptation and migration requires a careful, yet precarious balancing act, and often this policy tightrope confounds both Kiribati supporters and donors as to which position to pursue; fight or flight? It is becoming increasingly clear, however, that an exclusive focus on either solution in isolation will not be sufficient, and that only a joint fight *and* flight solution will adequately protect the citizens of Kiribati and their culture.

A sole focus on adaptation might seem *prima facie* desirable, given the desire of many i-Kiribati to remain in their country of birth, the reluctance of either Australia, Fiji or New Zealand thus far to significantly loosen their immigration policies to allow larger-scale migration from Kiribati, and also the brain drain dangers that such mass migration could pose for the economy, i-Kiribati culture, society and sovereignty. However, even though climate change scenarios are inevitably uncertain, the risk that climate change will make Kiribati uninhabitable despite the best adaptation efforts is growing with each passing year. At the same time, however, with sufficient technical assistance, regional and global political backing and, above all, financial support, a meaningful portion of the physical territory of Kiribati can be preserved and improved in the coming decades, thus ensuring long-term human habitation, and hopefully, ever-growing prosperity. To achieve this, though, will be an extremely daunting task. The government has estimated, for instance, that it would cost some US$1 billion to construct a seawall around the capital South Tarawa alone. In a country with an annual GDP of less than US$175 million and which to date has accessed less than US$20 million in global adaptation funding, adaptation as a long-term strategy for national survival is clearly not without its practical limitations. As the main adaptation element in the government's overall strategy, the Kiribati Adaptation Programme is carrying out important work protecting key infrastructure and the freshwater supply, but these laudable efforts are no alternative for either a rights-based social and economic development policy designed to raise the entire population out of poverty or comprehensive adaptation measures that will secure the land mass of the nation as a whole.

Given all other possible policy options open to the government at the moment, the dignified migration approach is grounded in reasonable assumptions and the practical truth of looming climate displacement in the country already even at this early stage. On the other hand, however, an overall climate change policy skewed too much in the direction of migration at the expense of development or adaptation financing stands a good chance of transforming what *could* be a possible future scenario for the people into what *will* actually occur; in effect creating a self-fulfilling prophecy. As the population becomes increasingly aware that political decision-makers are placing ever more faith and resources into dignified migration, and possibly less resources into specific adaptation measures and general socio-economic development (both of which are seriously under-funded at the moment), it is possible that on-going crises in the key areas of health care, access to potable water, overcrowding, domestic violence and numerous other developmental challenges will go increasingly unaddressed, and worsen further.

(Continued)

(Continued)

To truly succeed, the government of Kiribati may best serve its people through a more balanced fight *and* flight approach which significantly expands attention to the many dramatic social requirements of the country today, while simultaneously exercising great caution in not overplaying its hand in the direction of dignified migration. Upholding and expanding the enjoyment of human rights and preserving and expanding dignity should be the mutual yardsticks used to measure any success in grappling with the immense and unprecedented challenges facing the people of Kiribati.

Text Box 16.3   Case Study: Bangladesh[14]

Although small island nations continue to receive the bulk of attention by the media and in broader discussions on climate displacement, in pure numbers of people affected by climate displacement perhaps no country will actually be more affected than Bangladesh; a very densely populated country with a population of no less than 160 million. Already severely struggling against land scarcity, overcrowding and slums that grow by two million dwellers each year, with half of Bangladesh's population living in areas less than five metres above sea level, the country has begun to witness climate-induced displacement across much of its coastline. According to one analysis:

In the severe climate change scenario, sea level rise poses an existential threat that would inundate 18 percent of Bangladesh's total land, directly impacting 11 percent of the country's population. Salt water intrusion from sea level rise in low-lying agricultural plains, along with other hazards, could lead to a 40 percent decrease in food grain production and will increase forced migration to the urban slum areas.[15]

Estimates show that just a 1–2 degree increase in temperature would force physical dislocation of 20–35 million people in Bangladesh.[16] The results of modelling longer-term changes in coastlines as a result of rising sea levels suggest that the government may be required to support mass movements of coastal population, with perhaps one in every seven Bangladeshis displaced by climate change by the year 2050.

While the government of Bangladesh has clearly recognized the immensity of the problem, it has yet to proffer any comprehensive plans, programmes, policies or institutional frameworks by which the climate displacement crisis can be prevented and resolved in a sustainable and rights-based manner.[17] The scale of this challenge is

[14]See: http://displacementsolutions.org/ds-initiatives/climate-change-and-displacement-initiative/bangladesh-climate-displacement/ (accessed 27 February 2017).

[15]Shamsuddoha and Chowdhury (2009).

[16]These are commonly cited figures, although a recent report gives substantially higher estimates of 95 million displaced persons by 2040. See: www.defence.pk/forums/bangladesh-defence/221847-95-72-million-may-climate-displaced-2040-a.html (accessed 27 February 2017).

[17]See, for instance, Dulal Chandra Roy, *Vulnerability and Population Displacements Due to Climate-Induced Disasters in Coastal Bangladesh,* Centre for Geoinformatics (Z_GIS), University of Salzburg, Austria.

understood by many within the government; however, neither the political will nor the financial or technical resources required to implement the rights-based adaptation responses needed to resolve this crisis are at all apparent in today's Bangladesh. Indeed, rather than designing and implementing rights-based national solutions, the government is increasingly claiming that these environmental 'refugees' require international solutions and should be received by other states as part of international migration programmes. This has meant that, to date, most of those displaced by natural hazards and the effects of climate change have received little or no formal support. There are currently no government programmes that provide targeted assistance to these climate-displaced persons to find new homes and new lands for their lost homes and lost lands. Many climate-displaced persons have been forced to make the difficult decision to relocate to other parts of the country, often to the slums of Dhaka or the hills of Chittagong, or for the vast majority who have already been displaced, to hold out the very distant prospects of returning to their former lands while waiting in often highly precarious circumstances. National policies concerning climate change and environmental issues such as the National Environment Policy (1992), the Coastal Zone Policy (2005), the National Adaptation Programme of Action (NAPA, 2005) and the Bangladesh Climate Change Strategy and Action Plan (2009) recognize climate change problems, but there are no clear indications how population displacement problems will be addressed in these policies (Akter, 2009).

CONCLUSION

These examples of real, on-going and permanent climate displacement and the responses and policy options available to address these are, of course, just some of the far larger number of places where these processes are already well underway. The monumental planned relocation of the 321 coastal dwelling villagers of Newtok Village on the western coast of Alaska in the USA to nearby Nelson Island is the start of what is likely to be a far larger relocation process of indigenous Alaskans as their long-inhabited coastlines become increasingly unviable.[18] In Panama, Guna (also referred to as 'Kuna') Yala, a narrow strip of land 400 km long and an archipelago of 365 islands off the Caribbean coast, inhabited by some 50,000 indigenous Guna people, is already engaged in planned relocations of residents.[19] A total of 36,000 people will be rehoused to the mainland to dwellings to be built by the government, along the road between the island of Carti Sugdup and the Pan American Highway. The project also includes roads and facilities, and will take years to complete. Many of Fiji's 900,000 people are already suffering the effects of climate change.[20] The government has, therefore, already determined that

---

[18]For an excellent and detailed overview of this process, see, Bronen (2011).

[19]See also (in German), 'Die Heimat der Kuna geht unter', *Neue Zurcher Zeitung* (19 July 2011) ('The Kuna Homeland is Going Under'). See also, Lohuizen (2012).

[20]See, for instance, Rawalai (2014) and Piazza (2014).

more than 676 villages will be affected by climate change and that many of these will need to be relocated in the coming years because of rising sea levels, with as many as 42 villages to be potentially relocated during the next decade. Several villages have already been relocated, including the villager-initiated relocation of Vunidogoloa. The government's Climate Change Department of the Ministry of Foreign Affairs is currently preparing a national climate relocation policy, and in many respects has led the world in finding land-based solutions to climate displacement. Nearly 300,000 coastal properties along the Australian coast are recognized by the government as under threat from climate change.

Sadly, the list goes on and all indications are that it will continue to grow in the coming decades. In all corners of the planet, therefore, people are beginning to leave or contemplate their eventual departure from their homes and lands because of climate change. It is now certain that these numbers will continue to grow in the coming years and decades. Many of those engaged in the climate-displacement field now know with increasing accuracy where climate displacement will occur, how many people will be affected and to which locations the displaced are most likely to seek refuge. Many gaps in knowledge remain, of course, and much more research is required, but our collective understanding of the scale, scope and location of climate displacement is clearly and measurably evolving. What remains, then – beyond the inevitable political will and economic resources that will be required to address this crisis – is to identify the policy options available to people and those governing them that will secure land-based solutions to climate-displaced communities the world over.

Questions for Discussion

1 What is the purpose of defining specific rights for persons displaced by climate change?
2 How does this rights-based approach to climate displacement complement the UN HRBA (discussed in Chapter 7)?
3 What obstacles are there to the creation of a specific protocol or convention on climate-displaced persons?

📖 FURTHER READING

Displacement Solutions (2013) *The Peninsula Principles on Climate Displacement within States*. Available at: http://displacementsolutions.org/wp-content/uploads/2014/12/Peninsula-Principles.pdf (accessed 1 July 2016).

Milman, O. (2015) 'UN Drops Plan to Create Group to Relocate Climate Change Affected People', *Guardian*, 7 October. Available at: https://www.theguardian.com/environment/2015/oct/07/un-drops-plan-to-create-group-to-relocate-climate-change-affected-people (accessed 1 July 2016).

Stevenson, H. and Dryzek, J.S. (2014) *Democratizing Global Climate Governance*. Cambridge: Cambridge University Press.

REFERENCES

Akter, T. (2009) *Climate Change and Flow of Environmental Displacement in Bangladesh.* Dhaka: Unnayan Anneshan –The innovators. Available at: www.unnayan.org/documents/Climatechange/climate_change_flow_environmental_displacement.pdf (accessed 1 July 2016).

Asian Development Bank (ADB) (2012) *Addressing Climate Change and Migration in the Asia and the Pacific*, Final Report. Available at: www.adb.org/publications/addressing-climate-change-and-migration-asia-and-pacific (accessed 1 July 2016).

Bronen, R. (2011) 'Climate-Induced Community Relocations: Creating an Adaptive Governance Framework Based in Human Rights Doctrine', *NYU Review of Law and Social Change*, 35(2): 101–48.

Leckie, S. (2013) 'A Challenge Like Few Others: Finding Land Solutions for Climate Displacement', Displacement Solutions. Available at: http://displacementsolutions.org/wp-content/uploads/2014/12/DS-Report-Finding-Land-Solutions-to-Climate-Displacement.pdf (accessed 1 July 2016).

Leckie, S. (ed.) (2014) *Land Solutions for Climate Displacement.* London: Routledge/Earthscan.

Lohuizen, K. (2012) 'On the Run from the Water, Kuna Yala, Panama', NOOR. Available at: http://noorimages.com/feature/on-the-run-from-the-water-kuna-yala/ (accessed 1 July 2016).

Oliver-Smith, A., Cutter, S.L., Warner, K., Corendea, C. and Yuzva, K. (2012) *Addressing Loss and Damage in the Context of Social Vulnerability and Resilience.* UNU-EHS Publication Series: Policy Brief, No. 7.

Piazza, B. (2014) 'Rising Sea Levels Prompt Relocations in Fiji', *World News Australia Radio*, 31 January. Available at: www.sbs.com.au/news/article/2014/01/31/rising-sea-levels-prompt-relocations-fiji (accessed 1 July 2016).

Rakova, U. (2014) 'The Sinking Carterets Islands: Leading Change in Climate Change Adaptation and Resilience in Bougainville, Papua New Guinea', in S. Leckie (ed.), *Land Solutions for Climate Displacement.* London: Routledge/Earthscan, pp. 268–90.

Rawalai, L. (2014) 'Climate Change Impacts Villages', *Fiji Times Online*, 17 January. Available at: www.fijitimes.com/story.aspx?id=257164 (accessed 1 July 2016).

Roy, D.C. (nd) *Vulnerability and Population Displacements Due to Climate-Induced Disasters in Coastal Bangladesh.* Salzburg: Centre for Geoinformatics (Z_GIS), University of Salzburg.

Shamsuddoha, M. and Chowdhury, R.K. (2009) *Climate Refugee: Requires Dignified Recognition under a New Protocol.* Equity and Justice Working Group Bangladesh, pp. 3–4. Available at: www.mediaterre.org/docactu,Q0RJLUwtMy9kb2NzL2N-saW1hdGUtbWlncmFudC1wcmludGVkLXBvc2l0aW9uLWRlYy0wOQ==,1.pdf (accessed 1 July 2016).

17

GLOBAL HEALTH AND DEVELOPMENT PRACTICE

DEBBI LONG, PAUL KOMESAROFF AND ELIZABETH KATH

INTRODUCTION

The term 'Global Health' encompasses a range of concepts and activities, including concerns and practices relating to health that cross national borders and are implemented in multiple settings across the world (Brown et al., 2006; Koplan et al., 2009). The Executive Board of the Consortium of Universities for Global Health has argued for a 'unified definition', as follows:

> Global Health is an area for study, research, and practice that places a priority on improving health and achieving equity in health for all people worldwide. Global Health emphasizes transnational health issues, determinants and solutions; involves many disciplines within and beyond the health sciences and promotes interdisciplinary collaboration; and is a synthesis of population-based prevention with individual-level clinical care. (Koplan et al., 2009: 1995)

This definition entails a radical reformulation of previous ways of understanding the nature of health issues across international borders, especially in its call for multidisciplinary input into health solutions. The approach overcomes many of the criticisms to which the erstwhile concept of 'international health' was subjected, and it has been linked to progressive social and political movements and causes.

While recognizing the value of the shift from 'International Health' to 'Global Health', it is crucial also to explore the limitations and pitfalls associated with it. This chapter provides a critical overview of Global Health as an academic discipline and practice and the key developments that have taken place within Global Health discourse over the decades since the term emerged. It discusses both the strengths and limitations of current Global

Health approaches and goes on to critically examine developments over recent decades, such as the concept of the 'social determinants of health'. Finally, the chapter proposes that a way forward in response to these limitations is to mobilize the achievements of Global Health discourses in the service of novel and fecund practices based simultaneously on a global commitment to social and political change, respect for local cultures and knowledge, and respect for those who work within them.

STRENGTHS OF A GLOBAL HEALTH APPROACH

The concepts of 'development health' and 'global health' are often used interchangeably. This can obscure the interconnections between the health statuses of the different groups that make up the overall global health population. However, it should also be recognized that, if defined broadly, the consideration of health in a global context can provide access to valuable insights that were not previously possible.

The Global Health perspective presents an opportunity to explore interrelationships between the health conditions of populations in different parts of the world. For example, Schrecker and Bambra (2015) demonstrate that many of the factors associated directly or indirectly with malnutrition, or under-eating, can be linked also to nutrition problems associated with over-eating. Another example is the appropriation of land for industrial monoculture, which affects the health of local communities by limiting local access to prime horticultural and agricultural land, as well as that of multiple end users around the world through the provision of cheap but highly processed diets. Western hunger for cheap sugar and tobacco (dating to the colonization of the Americas) has adversely affected both British and Caribbean health, and has contributed to loss of both quality of life and years of life. As Thomas and Bean have pointed out, the only beneficiaries of the British transatlantic slave trade were the European consumers of tobacco, sugar and other products from the slavery sustained plantations, and here the 'gains' ultimately turned against them, in the form of 'dental decay and lung cancer at somewhat lower prices than would have been the case without the slave trade' (Thomas and Bean, 1974: 914, in Austen and Smith, 1990: 95).

In a similar vein, Sidney Mintz's work (1985) on sugar and other 'drug foods' produced under slavery elaborates the role of these products in fueling European industrialization through the sating and drugging of farm and factory workers. Here, too, the balance sheet was negative on both sides. The poor living conditions of the nascent European proletariat have been well-documented, while under the same global system of production the average working life expectancy of slaves in Caribbean sugar mills and plantations was around seven years, with many slaves dying in the first year of arrival from burns, injuries, violence and exhaustion (CLACS, 2016). The broad perspective that the Global Health approach potentially makes possible allows us to perceive interconnected health implications for geographically separated populations involved in the same global production systems.

A Global Health approach is useful if we are to properly understand local health issues in a globalized world. Used critically, framing health in a global perspective can allow us to examine and acknowledge the impacts on health systems and population health resulting from international development interventions, such as in the case of Haiti and Jamaica, where the IMF-led structural adjustment programmes have badly damaged the health of local populations (Handa and King, 2003; Pfeiffer and Chapman, 2010).

LIMITATIONS OF GLOBAL HEALTH

Against these strengths, the concept of Global Health and the mental models associated with it suffer from a variety of weaknesses. In what follows, we draw attention specifically to issues relating to the homogenization of culture, cultural biases, macro-economic and macro-political variables, the overestimation of Western contributions, the over-reliance on statistical markers of disease, medical dominance, and prevailing approaches to understanding cultural difference.

Inappropriate Homogenization of Culture

Global Health supports a tendency towards the homogenization of cultural knowledge and expertise. The very assumption that conditions of health can be described and addressed at a global level of generality stimulates theoretical formulations and practices that systematically ignore local cultural differences.

It cannot be taken for granted that somebody from an urban, wealthy, educated background in India, Sri Lanka, Australia or Brazil can understand the daily lived realities of – let alone communicate effectively with – rural people or impoverished, socially excluded people of their own nationality, although this is frequently assumed. In many countries around the world, entry to medical, nursing and/or allied health training is limited to those with educational and financial privileges not available to people born into poorer communities. This can create situations wherein health professionals do not readily understand the lived realities of their patients, causing communication barriers that make it even more difficult for the poorest and most disadvantaged populations to receive adequate and appropriate health care. For example, Nanko Van Buuren, Director of the Brazilian Institute for Innovations in Social Health, an NGO that provides pioneering health services in Rio de Janeiro's *favelas* (informal shantytown communities in urban areas), in a 2012 interview, listed common communication problems that arise in hospitals and other health facilities between patients from *favelas* and the Brazilian doctors treating them, most of whom are from wealthy backgrounds and unlikely to have entered any of their city's *favelas* during their lifetimes. Van Buuren explained that *favela* communities sometimes have their own vocabulary for diseases and health conditions and do not always recognize the language used by health practitioners. He described having witnessed many misunderstandings about diagnoses, and prescription of treatments that were confusing to patients and cases of patients being sent home with home treatment plans that would be entirely appropriate for a house in a wealthy suburb, but impossible to follow in a hut with a dirt floor and no running water or electricity (Kath/Van Buuren interview, 2012; see also Kath and Van Buuren, 2014). Similar communication barriers exist in innumerable other settings.

The assumption of a single worldwide system, according to which the meanings associated with health and illness and the causal relationships between 'society' and health outcomes can be conceptualized, fails to recognize the often critical importance of local systems of symbolization by which meanings and values are formed and developed. Fadiman's (1997) documentation of differences in understandings of health between the American medical team and the Hmong family of Lia Lee shows that even when a child is surrounded by a team of dedicated and caring health professionals, family and community in a relatively well-resourced environment, failure to explore foundational differences in understandings of health can result in avoidable tragedy. Kleinman argued that an essential part of every health practitioner's role is to be active in understanding the health belief systems of both themselves and their patients (1978). These are not insights that have yet fully permeated all Global Health practice.

Cultural Biases

The concept of Global Health incorporates key assumptions about the nature of health and wellbeing, and the meaning-construction processes around them. Despite formal acknowledgement of the importance of culture in relation to health practices and outcomes, much development health theory and practice continues to operate within a particular culturally constructed set of values and methods of analysis that is largely unquestioned. Despite its supposed democratic intentions, the implementation of health policies and services often intensifies the very relationships associated with colonialism and hierarchy that it claims to oppose. For all their radical-sounding language, Global Health discourses remain embedded in a hierarchical and imperialist framework that upholds Western medical systems as templates for ideal health systems in non-Western countries.

The framework that emerges from these assumptions provides a structural impediment to much development health practice. The cultural biases associated with the underlying concepts are never far from the surface, as the mere use of the word 'global' shows. While this is generally taken to imply an acceptance of – and respect for – 'non-Western' perspectives, the reality is that, in both theory and practice, populations are regularly classified in accordance with Western socio-economic, class and educational categories, the financial contributions and positive impact of donor countries are overestimated, and the unilinear direction of influence, policy, knowledge and practice is disguised.

Macro-Economic and Macro-Political Factors

One of the ways in which Global Health discourses differ from the erstwhile International Health approaches is in their – albeit limited and often inchoate – acknowledgement of the damage caused by neoliberalism and of the negative impact on health caused by the 'structural adjustment' and austerity programmes that have been associated with it.

Although critiques of neoliberalism are far from new, they have only recently been meaningfully incorporated into discussions about development health and they remain peripheral and underdeveloped. Economist Susan George's insightful early critiques of the health costs of neoliberal economics and structural adjustment programmes (1974, 1988)

were not taken up widely in public health discourse. Similarly, Paul Farmer's (2004) articulation of 'structural violence' (that is, institutionalized disadvantage that prevents certain
groups of people from meeting their fundamental needs), using Haiti as an illustration
of the harm caused by International Monetary Fund (IMF) policies, is recognized as a
major contribution in critical medical anthropology (Baer et al., 2013: 63–6), but has not
yet penetrated deeply into international and Global Health theory. Global Health discourses pay superficial attention to these critiques, but rarely enter into serious analyses
of how macro-economic and macro-political factors and associated inequities in resource
distribution are connected with health outcomes. For example, the roles of transnational
corporations in global systems of production have far reaching impacts on the health of
individuals and communities across the world, and yet these connections still do not feature prominently in Global Health discussions.

Furthermore, while reference to the 'social determinants of health' – discussed in more
detail below – has been widely popular in discussions about international public health
(Wilkinson and Marmot, 2003; Marmot, 2015), this has not generated a critical reflection on the need to address large-scale economic factors in determining WHO policy
(Schrecker and Bambra, 2015). The uncritical adoption of a social determinants approach
is embedded in the SDGs and the preceding MDGs. The MDGs contained eight goals
and a total of 21 targets and were informed by health and education agendas as drivers of
development, supported by economist Jeffrey Sach's argument that improving a nation's
health is an investment rather than a cost, and inevitably has flow-on effects measurable
by an increase in economic growth (Brown, 2015).

The MDGs were widely regarded as a qualified success. Some of their targets were
achieved, making a significant impact in several areas, although results in other areas
were disappointing (Murray, 2015). The SDGs saw new players enter the arena and were
associated with a longer, more extensive and more inclusive consultation process (ibid.;
Fukuda-Parr, 2016). The increased breadth and depth is reflected in the number of goals
(17) and targets (169). One goal, containing 13 targets, is specifically health related, while
another 10 health-related targets arise from other goals (see Brown, 2015: 1392).

Sach's argument has been widely accepted, and was one of the central principles driving the MDGs (Murray, 2015). The reverse idea – that economic growth as measured
by GDP is a necessary driver for both development and improved Global Health – has
been incorporated firmly into the SDGs in Goal 8: 'Promote sustained and inclusive
economic growth, full and productive employment and decent work for all.' Economic
growth is, in other words, enshrined as a stimulant for development and assumed to be
able to underpin the pathway to environmental sustainability, which is central to seven of
the goals. These assumptions have been the subject of widespread criticism. For example,
in a piece scathingly titled 'The Oxymoron of Sustainable Development', Brown (2015)
roundly rejects the idea that environmental sustainability can be achieved through neoliberal capitalist economic growth model. Similarly, Constanza et al. argue that the 'single
minded focus on GDP growth has exacerbated inequity and environmental damage in
many countries' (2016: 59). As a result, Brown suggests that we 'need aggregate metrics of
human and ecosystem well-being to replace growth in Gross Domestic Product (GDP)
as the primary development goal for nations' (2015: 1027; see also, e.g., Hawkes and
Popkin, 2015; Wanner, 2015; Constanza et al., 2016).

In spite of extensive evidence of the flaws in the proposition that economic growth models are pathways to environmental sustainability, the SDGs incorporate the assumption that economic growth within global markets leads to improvements in individual and community health. This exposes the neoliberal paradigms embedded within global policy instruments, which remain unchanged despite decades of research demonstrating the damage of this model.

Development practitioners become agents of economic globalization, particularly when they implement programmes involving biomedically oriented clinics and hospitals, health technology, equipment, pharmaceuticals and Western-trained practitioners, all of which require on-going relationships with global markets in order for health infrastructure to be maintained.

When it is conflated with the concept of 'development health' – that is, the development of health infrastructure and resources – the expression 'global health' becomes a misnomer. The focus of development health is unequivocally on one section of the world's population: the poorer section. Global Health debates frequently give only passing reference to health in wealthy industrialized countries, and then this is usually only by way of drawing comparisons to disease burdens in relatively disadvantaged contexts. University courses in Global Health frequently start with statistics about how people in the Euro-American countries are more likely to die of cardiovascular disease or cancer than those in poorer countries (WHO, 2015), and continue with a discussion about how the inhabitants of sub-Saharan Africa are more likely to die of infectious diseases, malnutrition and respiratory illnesses (ibid.). Although lip service is paid to the fact that the USA spends the largest amount on health care per capita in the world and, yet, still significantly underperforms in most, if not all, indicators of equity and effectiveness of health delivery (Mintzberg, 2012: 4), this is not seen as an impediment to US agencies being granted a major voice in Global Health policy. Critical evaluation of Western-style health systems (see, e.g., Lock and Nguyen, 2010; Baer et al., 2013), increasingly a core component of Health Science curricula, is not generally included in the training of health development practitioners.

Overestimation of Western Influence

The popularity of Global Health as a subject of study and public comment, and the dominance of Western practitioners among its key advocates, has created an exaggerated sense of the importance of the West in directing or controlling health outcomes around the world. As mentioned above, the IMF commitment to neoliberal reforms has greatly damaged the health systems of many poorer countries. However, this should not obscure the fact that the contribution of Western aid to health budgets in poorer countries is generally very limited. There are few instances where donor money supports a significant proportion of health needs. In a few isolated cases, external donations support up to a half of national health budgets (WHO, 2016); however, on average, the impact is far more modest. On average, less than 10 per cent of African nations' health budgets came from external sources in 2014 (ibid.). The – largely self-serving – overemphasis of donor input and the undervaluing of local health systems and traditional health practices undoubtedly results in loss of opportunities for meaningful, sustainable health system improvement. Indeed, it is likely that a greater focus on support for existing, culturally appropriate, local health systems would enable development health programmes to achieve significantly greater impact.

Over-Reliance on Statistical Markers of Disease

The current philosophy and ideology of Global Health place excessive emphasis on quantitative measures of health. This leads – among other things – to distortions in health programmes and to the deskilling of health development workers.

The establishment of an integrated system of concepts supported by an extensive body of 'factual data' generated by a well-supported academic industry leaves little room for immersed cultural learning. Working from a deficiency model, statistics are collected, 'causes' are identified and interventions are designed and evaluated, usually with the aim of improving standardized quantitative measures. Health statistics can reveal important features of population health needs and outcomes. However, quantitative measurements always rely on qualitative assumptions about what is worth measuring and how those constructs are interpreted and conceptualized (Bowen, 1996), and these constructs can be subject to political manipulation (Kath, 2010). By their very nature, quantitative measures reflect averages across selected populations and can often obscure local discrepancies or inequities. Accurate quantitative variables only represent measurable phenomena and in themselves can provide at best limited information about causal relationships. Further, the ease of measuring quantitative markers has led to a focus on their use to guide not only Global Health theory but also the allocation of material resources, even where their limited utility in relation to assessment of desirable health outcomes is recognized. Such important deficiencies are rarely acknowledged.

The Cuban health system provides an interesting example of the limitations of a reliance on quantitative health measures. Celebrated over many years for its positive key health statistics, including high life expectancies and low infant and under-five mortality outcomes, the goal of improving health statistics became transformed into a political as well as a humanitarian goal. Over decades, the Castro regime pursued the improvement of key health statistics, not only as ends in themselves, but also as powerful symbols in the context of a 'health battlefield' with the USA (Kath, 2010: 74–6; see also Brotherton, 2005: 348; Diaz-Briquets, 1986: 39–40; Feinsilver, 1989). This strategy undoubtedly contributed to significant public health improvements in Cuba. However, it also led to situations wherein the production of positive statistics became prioritized at the expense of pressing health needs of the local population, often via paternalistic processes that seriously compromise other important aspects of health care quality, including patients' lived experiences (Kath, 2010; Hirschfeld, 2007; Brotherton, 2012).

The health situation of Australian Indigenous populations provides another example. The same key statistical outcomes that are most celebrated in Cuba, including life expectancy, infant mortality and under-five mortality are often cited as demonstrating the abject failure of longstanding government and social policies in Australian Indigenous communities (Anderson et al., 2006; Holland, 2016). While the figures undoubtedly highlight genuine disadvantage, the narrow focus on quantitative measures obscures distinctive positive aspects of the organization of health care among Australian

Indigenous communities. These include the crucial, pioneering role of 'community controlled' health services and Indigenous health workers (Kelaher et al., 2014; Panaretto et al., 2014) that provide culturally appropriate care and support in a wide range of settings, many of which are invisible to Western health care experts. Indeed, the richness of this experience could potentially carry lessons for mainstream Australian health services, and indeed even countries such as Cuba.

Medical Dominance

The conceptual hegemony of medical models of health care has also limited the development of Global Health discourses. In development theory and practice, Western concepts of medicine and 'health' itself are widely conflated (Clark, 2014: 1). Critiques of 'medical dominance' have a decades-long history (Friedson, 1970; Willis, 1983) in social science research of health systems in Western contexts (e.g. Willis, 2006; Long et al., 2006; Latimer, 2013). However, the cultural biases associated with narrowly conceived concepts of health, health care and 'biomedical' science are rarely articulated in development health discourse. Indeed, when questions are raised about the application of Western medical models to non-Western cultures they often portray the host culture as a problem to be overcome to allow the implementation of valid, 'scientific' or 'evidence-based' medical care. Rarely is there a genuine questioning of the appropriateness or effectiveness of the particular medical model itself.

Western professional training does not necessarily prepare health care workers, especially doctors, to be culturally aware, responsive or adaptable. Doctors, nurses and allied health workers may be encouraged to reflect on their personal practices, but they also operate within a system where critical reflection on the deeper assumptions underlying their discipline is stigmatized and actively discouraged (Lock and Nguyen, 2010). As Lakshmi et al. point out: 'A hierarchy of systems of medicine, often unacknowledged, is exercised in most societies, with allopathy at the top, certain traditional, complementary and alternative systems of medicine systems next and local healing traditions last' (2015: 1067). Even where some value is attributed to such systems and local healing approaches, these remain on the periphery. In spite of extensively researched and well-articulated work pointing out the limitations of 'evidenced-based medicine' as defined within the conventional Western biomedical paradigm (Feinstein and Horwitz, 1997; Greenhalgh, 2014; Kirmayer, 2012), this ideological construct remains sacrosanct (Lock and Nguyen, 2010). As a result, approaches to health and wellbeing that are not based on Western biomedical science are frequently either dismissed or actively suppressed.

Cultural Competency

Rather than working with a goal of shared understanding with existing local health systems, and adopting a role of collaborator, the role of development health workers is often assumed to be a superior cultural position that has the beneficent goal of intervening to improve behaviour and practice.

The ability to adapt Western trained technical skills and expertise to culturally local circumstances is often referred to as an important attribute of health workers in general

(Purnell, 2013). To this end, many nursing and medical courses now include components on 'cultural competency' (Kleinman and Benson, 2006). However, in practice, the supposed conceptual openness of Western medical science is strictly limited. In addition, the concept of cultural competency, which was originally devised for the purpose of supporting critiques of standards of care offered to diverse, non-dominant populations in Western medical systems, has not been effectively transferred into development contexts. The assumption of a generic 'competency' or skill that can be applied across all cultures is in reality merely another version of the Western bias towards universalistic, instrumental characterisation of culture and cultural practices (ibid.). Rather than generating openness, it can (and often does) serve as a barrier to authentic dialogues across systems of difference, according to which no theoretical assumptions can be excluded from critical scrutiny.

Underlying conceptions of Global Health is a confidence in the assumptions that technocratic, instrumentally based modes of thought and action provide benevolent alternatives to the harshness of neoliberal market-based policies. This is expressed through the familiar preoccupations with large-scale public health campaigns – for example, mass vaccination campaigns – which can make an important contribution but can come to be seen as all encompassing solutions that distract from the importance of incorporating local knowledge. It is expressed through the emphasis on pharmacotherapy and 'educational' programmes to control HIV/AIDS, in absence of consideration for the importance of the cooperative fostering of community capacity. It is expressed through military-style operations to control and quarantine populations to limit the spread of Ebola virus and other epidemic diseases. It is manifested in campaigns to control obesity and diabetes that depend on paternalistic strategies to direct dietary and lifestyle change, rather than addressing the deep cultural, economic and political roots of unhealthy diets. And it is evident in the reliance on instrumental, positivistic notions of causality in tracing the 'social determinants' of ill health and proposing monocausal remedies that often compound the problems rather than ameliorating them.

We note in passing that the regime of 'foreign aid' in general is based on the same pathology: that is, the implicit dependence on epistemological and ontological assumptions linked to constructions of Western culture, science and medicine. Like cultural competency itself, rather than promoting mutual learning and teaching through fluid and open dialogues across cultures and belief systems, it imposes a systematic and impenetrable barrier.

SOCIAL DETERMINANTS OF HEALTH

The concept of the 'social determinants of health' has become an important element of some versions of Global Health theory and is today widely accepted as providing a solution to many of the deficiencies described above. Notwithstanding its undoubted positive contributions, however, this approach has itself contributed to the further limitation of both understanding and practice in this field.

The introduction of the idea of social determinants was an important step forward because it led to a mainstream acknowledgement that the health of individuals is influenced not only by individual circumstances but also by the broader social context in which they live. The awareness of the impact of social factors on health has a long history in public health (Cook et al., 2013). As John Frank and Fraser Mustard (1994: 1) observe:

> At certain times socioeconomic factors have figured predominantly in policy making; at other times the emphasis has been largely on identifying the causes of disease and treating the sick. Theories about the determinants of health ... necessarily affect how illness is defined, what public policies are initiated, and how resources are allocated.

The idea of the social determinants of health has been widely accepted as providing the basis for an analytical framework that is now central to the current World Health Organization and United Nations approach to Global Health (CSDH, 2008; Marmot, 2015). The resulting theory has served as an important reminder that improvements in health can often not be separated from programmes to address underlying social and economic variables, which often relate to conditions of inequity and injustice. However, it is important to recognize that the radicalism of the theory has often been over-stated and, in particular, that it does not challenge the basic conceptual foundations of 'Global Health' – a fact that may, indeed, partly explain its popularity with establishment institutions, including governments.

A major limitation of social determinants theory arises from the reductionism underpinning it and its radical isolation from the dynamic and fluid conditions of social action. It depends on narrowly instrumental concepts of causality in the fields of society and culture, which largely replicate the positivistic foundations of Western biomedical epistemologies. In this manner, it fails to provide a viable critique of the fundamental categories of Global Health or to offer a conceptual framework for the development of alternative strategies in theory and practice.

The variables identified as 'social' refer to high-level, abstract concepts (just like those of international health) and ignore local cultural forms and processes. The WHO launched the Commission on the Social Determinants of Health in 2005. According to the Commissioner, Michael Marmot, a 'major thrust of the Commission is turning public-health knowledge into political action' (2005: 1099). The report, released in 2008 as *Closing the Gap in a Generation* (CSDH, 2008), had a significant influence on the 2015 Sustainable Development Goals. The Commission on the Social Determinants of Health was convened to 'review evidence on the social determinants of health that are relevant to Global Health: inequalities among countries and within' (Marmot, 2005: 1102), following from the 'evidence on the social determinants of health' (ibid.; Wilkinson and Marmot, 2003). This publication 'reviewed evidence from Europe, aimed mainly at reducing inequalities between countries' (Marmot, 2005: 1102), concluding that the 'solid facts' of social determinants of health fell into ten categories: 'the social gradient, stress, early life, social exclusion, work, unemployment, social support, addiction, food and transport' (ibid.). These social determinants, derived from a Western European context, appear to have been applied to 'Global Health' with very little adaptation to non-European societal realities. From there, they seem to have slipped into Global Health discourse with remarkably little scrutiny or critique.

Where a focus on employment and unemployment, work conditions and job security may, indeed, be significant health stressors in Western Europe, to have applied those directly to global contexts without considering non-Western forms of existential security is problematic. The uncritical stretching of social determinants from one continent to apply them globally risks overlooking aspects of existential security that may be of crucial importance to health in other contexts, such as land tenure (CSDH, 2008: 69–70), extended family structures and community governance (ibid.: 84–91).

Social determinants discourse reproduces Cartesian mind-body dichotomies that are inherent in Western constructs of self and biomedical constructs of health. 'Belief' is classified in terms of 'mental health', with the absence of any place for discussions of spirituality in Global Health discourse. The Western separation of spirituality and health is not echoed in all cultures, and the disenfranchisement of spirituality in development health contexts is a major hurdle to culturally appropriate care. Similarly, the importance of 'community' in health is trivialized and marginalized to a 'sense of belonging', which individualizes the role that community plays in health, rather than understanding 'community' and collective experiences of identity and how they impact on health. Community is thereby reduced to how individuals experience their identities in relation to those around them (i.e., their sense of 'belonging'), ignoring aspects of community such as intergenerational transfer of knowledge and competency (Saravanan, 2008) or community nurture mechanisms (McCoy, 2008).

The assumptions underlying social determinants theory both circumscribe its outcomes and provide an indication of the possible conditions for alternative, more rigorous approaches. The characterization of individuals as ontologically separate from community or sociality lies at the heart of much Western theorizing and becomes operationalized in Western health systems in a wide variety of forms – including in ethical ideas about individual 'consent' and 'rights' – which may be inapplicable or inappropriate in many non-Western settings. The processes by which health is 'determined' are set by this philosophical framework, which is in turn directly linked to narrowly defined notions of causality and meaning. It is not the place of this chapter to propose alternative strategies to the closed and limited paradigm of Global Health. However, these considerations suggest that, rigorously pursued, such strategies may seek to incorporate a formal deconstruction of the modes of social theorizing identified with colonial thinking and to respond to the greater complexity arising out of local cultural forms expressed in world views, mythological systems, artistic and religious expressions, and processes of communication embedded in communities.

CONCLUSION

Despite its strengths, Global Health theory and practice is subject to many limitations and deficiencies, including assumptions about the homogenization of culture, cultural biases, exaggeration of Western influence on health in the developing world, and over-reliance on broad statistical measures of health and disease and other culturally biased concepts and tools of analysis. There is a need for the further development of the ideas underlying the 'social determinants of health' that would acknowledge the diversity of social variables across different global contexts.

An effective and ethically secure Global Health approach needs to achieve more than the acknowledgement of the existence of non-Western health approaches while navigating around these to implement 'legitimate' (Western 'evidenced-based' biomedical) systems. Rather, such an approach should take integration seriously, precisely for the purpose of avoiding the annulment of local knowledge and the tokenistic incorporation of traditional products or decontextualized practices. Instead, it should seek to support genuinely interactive dialogues between systems of knowledge production themselves. The dialogues might include among their objectives the integration of different health modalities in ways that respect core epistemologies and the generation of novel healing practices. The challenges facing such an endeavour are admittedly considerable (Adamu, 2013; Lakshmi et al., 2015).

There is a need for 'Global Health' – as a broad collection of practices as well as an academic discipline – to be complemented with 'local health' and reconciliatory engagements and dialogues around health and health care. The separation of health and politics, at both the large-scale level of the organization of social institutions and the distribution of power and the micro-level of community-based interactions, is no longer tenable. Attacks on hospitals in war zones, the manipulation of issues relating to refugees and asylum seekers for cynical political purposes, and the links between poverty, privilege and access to health care resources are only too familiar and the long-term, multidimensional impact of neoliberal economic policies on all aspects of health and wellbeing in many countries around the world have been well documented. The role of local forms of engagement through the fostering of and support for civil society dialogues may be less well appreciated. However, facilitation of community-based conversations about the conditions of daily life and the forces that threaten to destabilize and transform them are no less important a part of Global Health practice. The large-scale and the local processes, furthermore, are inter-dependent: the broad social and political variables set material circumstances and possibilities for health and wellbeing, while community dialogues provide the mechanisms for reshaping cultural systems and structures of understanding to adjust to the changed conditions.

The critique of International Health generated both new insights and enhanced forms of practice. The contemporary task is to mobilize the achievements of Global Health discourses in the service of novel and fecund practices based simultaneously on a global commitment to social and political change, respect for local cultures and knowledge, and respect for those who work within them.

Questions for Discussion

1   Why do the authors assert that Global Health is a flawed mental model?
2   How might Western conceptions of self and non-Western ideas of community and sociality be reconciled? Can they be reconciled?
3   Are there parallels to be drawn between the approach to health recommended here and models of governance proposed elsewhere in this volume?

FURTHER READING

Baer, H.A., Singer, M. and Susser, I. (2013) *Medical Anthropology and the World System: Critical Perspectives* (3rd edn). Santa Barbara, CA: Praeger.

Marmot, M. (2015) *The Health Gap: The Challenge of an Unequal World.* London: Bloomsbury.

Schrecker, T. and Bambra, C. (2015) *How Politics Makes Us Sick: Neoliberal Epidemics.* Basingstoke: Palgrave Macmillan.

REFERENCES

Adamu, U.F. (2013) *Modern and Traditional Medicine: Conflicts and Reconciliation.* Ibadan: Safari Books.

Anderson, I., Crengle, S., Kamaka, M.L., Chen, T.-H., Palafox, N. and Jackson-Pulver, L. (2006) 'Indigenous health in Australia, New Zealand, and the Pacific', *The Lancet*, 367(9524): 1775–85.

Austen, R.A. and Smith, W.D. (1990) 'Private Tooth Decay as Public Economic Virtue: The Slave–Sugar Triangle, Consumerism, and European Industrialization', *Social Science History*, 14(1): 95–115.

Baer, H.A., Singer, M. and Susser, I. (2013) *Medical Anthropology and the World System: Critical Perspectives* (3rd edn). Santa Barbara, CA: Praeger.

Bowen, K. (1996) 'The Sin of Omission – Punishable by Death to Internal Validity: An Argument for Integration of Qualitative and Quantitative Research Methods to Strengthen Internal Validity'. Available at: www.webcitation.org/5ZpE08ugR (accessed 7 April 2017).

Brotherton, P.S. (2005) 'Macroeconomic Change and the Biopolitics of Health in Cuba's Special Period', *Journal of Latin American Anthropology*, 10(2): 339–69.

Brotherton, P.S. (2012) *Revolutionary Medicine: Health and the Body Politic in Post-Soviet Cuba.* Durham, NC: Duke University Press.

Brown, J.H. (2015) 'The Oxymoron of Sustainable Development', *Bioscience*, 65(10): 1027–9.

Brown, T.M., Cueto, M. and Fee, E. (2006) 'The World Health Organization and the Transition from "International" to "Global" Public Health', *American Journal of Public Health*, 96(1): 62–72.

Centre for Latin American and Caribbean Studies (CLACS), New York University (2016) 'Sugar and the Link to Slavery in Latin America: Background'. New York: CLACS.

Clark, J. (2014) 'Do the Solutions for Global Health Lie in Healthcare?', *British Medical Journal*, 349, doi: http://dx.doi.org/10.1136/bmj.g5457.

Commission on Social Determinants of Health (CSDH) (2008) *Closing the Gap in a Generation: Health Equity through Action on the Social Determinants of Health.* Geneva: World Health Organization.

Cook, H.J., Bhattacharya, S. and Hardy, A. (eds) (2013) *History of the Social Determinants of Health.* Hyderabad: Orient Blackswan.

Costanza, R., Fioramonti, L. and Kubiszewski, I. (2016) 'The UN Sustainable Development Goals and the Dynamics of Well-Being', *Frontiers in Ecology and the Environment*, 14(2): 59.

Diaz-Briquets, S. (1986) 'How to Figure out Cuba: Development, Ideology and Mortality', *Caribbean Review*, 15(2): 8–42.

Fadiman, A. (1997) *The Spirit Catches You and You Fall Down: A Hmong Child, Her American Doctors, and the Collision of Two Cultures*. New York: Farrar, Straus and Giroux.

Farmer, P. (2004) 'An Anthropology of Structural Violence', *Current Anthropology*, 45: 305–26.

Farmer, P. (2005) *Pathologies of Power*. Berkeley, CA: University of California Press.

Feinsilver, J.M. (1989) 'Cuba as a "World Medical Power": The Politics of Symbolism', *Latin American Research Review*, 24(2): 1–37.

Feinstein, A.R. and Horwitz, R.I. (1997) 'Problems in the "Evidence" of Evidence-Based Medicine', *American Journal of Medicine*, 103(6): 529–35.

Frank, J.W., and Fraser Mustard, J. (1994) 'The Determinants of Health from a Historical Perspective', *Daedalus*, 123(4): 1–19. Available at: www.jstor.org.ezproxy.lib.rmit.edu.au/stable/20027264 (accessed 3 April 2017).

Friedson, E. (1970) *Professional Dominance: The Social Structure of Medical Care*. New York: Atherton Press.

Fukuda-Parr, S. (2016) 'From the Millennium Development Goals to the Sustainable Development Goals: Shifts in Purpose, Concept, and the Politics of Global Goal Setting for Development', *Gender & Development*, 4(1): 43–62.

Galtung, J. (1969) 'Violence, Peace, and Peace Research', *Journal of Peace Research*, 6(3): 167–91.

George, S. (1974) *How the Other Half Dies*. London: Penguin.

George, S. (1988) *A Fate Worse than Debt*. London: Penguin.

Greenhalgh, T. (2014) *How to Read a Paper: The Basics of Evidence-Based Medicine* (5th edn). Oxford: John Wiley & Sons.

Handa, S. and King, D. (2003) 'Adjustment with a Human Face? Evidence from Jamaica', *World Development*, 31(7): 1125–45.

Hawkes, C. and Popkin, B. (2015) 'Can the Sustainable Development Goals Reduce the Burden of Nutrition-Related Non-Communicable Diseases without Truly Addressing Major Food System Reforms?', *BMC Medicine*, 13(143), doi: 10.1186/s12916-015-0383-7.

Hirschfeld, K. (2007) *Health, Politics and Revolution in Cuba since 1898*. New Brunswick and London: Transaction.

Holland, C. (2016) *Close the Gap: Progress and Priorities Report 2016*. Canberra: Close the Gap Steering Committee.

Kath, E. (2010) *Social Relations and the Cuban Health Miracle*. New Brunswick and London: Transaction.

Kath/Van Buuren interview (2012) Interview by Elizabeth Kath with Nanko G. Van Buuren. Rio de Janeiro, Brazil, February.

Kath, E. and Van Buuren, N.G. (2014) 'Soldados Nunca Mais: Child Soldiers, Football and Social Change in Rio de Janeiro's Favelas', in N. Schulenkorf and D. Adair (eds), *Global Sport for Development: Critical Perspectives*. Basingstoke: Palgrave Macmillan, pp. 194–215.

Kelaher, M., Sabanovic, H., Le Brooy, C., Lock, M., Lusher, D. and Brown, L. (2014) 'Does More Equitable Governance Lead to More Equitable Health Care? A Case Study Based on the Implementation of Health Reform in Aboriginal Health Australia', *Social Science & Medicine*, 123: 278–85.

Kirmayer, L.J. (2012) 'Cultural Competence and Evidence-Based Practice in Mental Health: Epistemic Communities and the Politics of Pluralism', *Social Science & Medicine*, 75(2): 249–56.

Kleinman, A. (1978) 'Concepts and a Model for the Comparison of Medical Systems as Cultural Systems', *Social Science & Medicine*, 12: 85–93.

Kleinman, A. and Benson, P. (2006) 'Anthropology in the Clinic: The Problem of Cultural Competency and How to Fix It', *PLoS Medicine*, 3(10): e294.

Koplan, J.P., Bon, T.C., Merson, M.H., Reddy, K.S., Rodriguez, M.H., Sewankambo, N.K. and Wasserheit, J.N. (2009) 'Towards a Common Definition of Global Health', *Lancet*, 373: 1993–5.

Lakshmi, J.K, Nambiar, D., Narayan, V., Sathyanarayana, T.N., Porter, J. and Sheikh, K. (2015) 'Cultural Consonance, Constructions of Science and Co-existence: A Review of the Integration of Traditional, Complementary and Alternative Medicine in Low- and Middle-Income Countries', *Health, Policy and Planning*, 30(8): 1067–77.

Latimer, J. (2013) *The Gene, the Clinic, and the Family: Diagnosing Dysmorphology, Reviving Medical Dominance*. London: Routledge.

Lock, M. and Nguyen, V.-K. (2010) *An Anthropology of Biomedicine*. Oxford: Wiley-Blackwell.

Long, D., Forsyth, R., Iedema, R. and Carroll, K. (2006) 'The (Im)possibilities of Clinical Democracy', *Health Sociology Review*, 15(5): 506–19.

Marmot, M. (2005) 'Social Determinants of Health Inequalities', *The Lancet*, 365: 1099–104.

Marmot, M. (2015) *The Health Gap: The Challenge of an Unequal World*. London: Bloomsbury.

McCoy, B. (2008) *Holding Men: Kanyirninpa and the Health of Aboriginal Men*: Canberra: Aboriginal Studies Press.

Mintz, S. (1985) *Sweetness and Power: The Place of Sugar in Modern History*. New York: Viking-Penguin.

Mintzberg, H. (2012) 'Managing the Myths of Health Care', *World Hospitals and Health Services*, 48(3): 4–7.

Murray, C. (2015) 'Shifting to Sustainable Development Goals – Implications for Global Health', *New England Journal of Medicine*, 375(15): 1390–2.

Panaretto, K.S., Wenitong, M., Button, S. and Ring, I. (2014) 'Aboriginal Community Controlled Health Services: Leading the Way in Primary Care', *Medical Journal of Australia (MJA)*, 200(11): 649–52.

Pfeiffer, J. and Chapman, R. (2010) 'Anthropological Perspectives on Structural Adjustment and Public Health', *Annual Review of Anthropology*, 39: 149–65.

Purnell, L.D. (2013) *Transcultural Health Care: A Culturally Competent Approach*. Philadelphia, PA: F.A. Davis.

Saravanan, S. (2008) 'Training of Traditional Birth Attendants: An Examination of the Influence of Biomedical Frameworks of Knowledge on Local Birthing Practices in India'. PhD Thesis, University of Queensland.

Schrecker, T. and Bambra, C. (2015) *How Politics Makes Us Sick: Neoliberal Epidemics.* Basingstoke: Palgrave Macmillan.

Wanner, T. (2015) 'The New "Passive Revolution" of the Green Economy and Growth Discourse: Maintaining the "Sustainable Development" of Neoliberal Capitalism', *New Political Economy*, 20(1): 21–41.

Willis, E. (1983) *Medical Dominance: The Division of Labour in Australian Health Care.* Sydney: Allen & Unwin.

Willis, E. (2006) 'Taking Stock of Medical Dominance', *Health Sociology Review*, 15(5): 421–31.

Wilkinson, R. and Marmot, M. (eds) (2003) *Social Determinants of Health: The Solid Facts* (2nd edn). Geneva: WHO.

World Health Organization (WHO) (2015) *World Health Statistics 2015.* Geneva: WHO.

WHO (2016) *Health Expenditure Ratios 1995–2014.* Geneva: WHO.

CONCLUSION

CONCLUSION

18

DEVELOPMENT THEORY AND BEYOND

JONATHAN MAKUWIRA

INTRODUCTION

In bringing the various perspectives in this volume together, a quick recap of the notion of 'development' is necessary, but with a different emphasis to that of Richard P. Appelbaum in Chapter 3. Navigating through the chapters in this volume, one senses the intricacies of development theory and practice. Development, as an idea, has come a long way. So, too, has 'Development Theory' – essentially the thinking behind development itself. Contestation of the idea of development persists (see Nisbet, 1969; Seers, 1969; Crush, 1995; Escobar, 1995; Rist, 2008; Peet and Hartwick, 1999), as does the problematization of the notion of development as a 'solution'. Even in practice, the adoption of various theoretical perspectives has proven challenging, with the one-size-fits-all approach enjoying some success, but mostly failure (Chambers, 1997; Sachs, 1992; Willis, 2011; Makuwira, 2006, 2014). Here, I examine these issues by bringing a sub-Sahara African perspective to the debate. In doing so, I question the UN's post-2015 agenda and ask if global institutions have learned anything at all about the need to build global frameworks of governance from the ground up (see Chapter 4, in this volume).

An inclusive approach, I argue, must be organically initiated, with priorities defined by those most affected by divergent and convergent patterns of global social and economic change (see Chapter 11). Marxism, dependency, post-development and post-colonial theories (see Chapter 3), have influenced development practice in different ways and at different levels, and I briefly re-examine these impacts from a cultural perspective. I then focus on post-development modes of operation, examining post-colonial responses to the discursive practices of development. I reflect on Sector-Wide Approaches (SWAPs), decentralization and current aid modalities to donor funding of development in Africa. I conclude the chapter by making a call to reconceptualize research, teaching and learning within the global knowledge system.

THE ROAD TO 'POST-DEVELOPMENT' THEORY AND PRACTICE

'Development' is constantly in a state of flux. The various theoretical positions discussed in this volume, and the practical examples therein, attest to a longstanding argument that development is never static, rather it is a process of negotiating and renegotiating relationships through activities which we call 'projects' or, in a broader scheme of things, 'programmes'. However, these projects and/or programmes are informed by particular theoretical underpinnings. Since the mid-1940s, the world has witnessed a period of development which has necessitated the formation of such fields of scholarship as 'Development Studies' and 'International (Community) Development', just to name a few. Africa has been a major recipient of international development aid, yet, during this time, the net gains against over a nominal trillion dollars spent in the name of development, begs more questions than answers. The yawning chasm between the huge resources spent and the gains made must be understood from both historical and cultural as well as political perspectives.

The question of what development means is largely driven by how the concept 'Development' has been framed theoretically. Thus, a good starting point is to understand how, over the past decades, development is understood. Obviously, this is not an easy task because the definition of 'Development' theoretically, politically and practically, carries with it layers of meanings. The state of flux with which it has been known to be in, itself, very difficult to negotiate. However, *development* often refers to a series of activities required to bring about change or progress and is often linked with economic growth. In some instances, development has been understood to imply a standard against which different rates of progress may be compared and, that being the case, can take on a subjective, judgemental element in which societies, communities or even countries are sometimes compared and then placed at different stages of an evolutionary process. Development theorists such as Cowen and Shenton (1996) and Hettne (2008) point out that development, as perceived in the modern era, is sometimes understood as intentional social change as designed by societies but which is ultimately envisaged to improve something for the better. While such 'change' is subjective, this definition is broad enough to offer a simple understanding of such a complex concept.

MARXISM AND DEVELOPMENT

Marxist Theory (see Chapter 3) has had a major impact on our understanding of how capitalist societies operate, and hence how interventions to correct deficiencies are best orchestrated. Marx's notion of 'class struggle', also known as 'class conflict' and 'class warfare', evolved into 'conflict theory' – a critical theorizing of how, according to Marx, society in our world today is in a state of perpetual conflict as a result of competition for limited resources. Fundamentally, Marx and his associate, Friedrich Engel, posited in the *Communist Manifesto* what in summary is an issue about the fraught relationship between the 'powerful' and the 'powerless'. Under capitalism, a tension exists between those who sell their labour in return for wages and those who control the means of production, the masters, managers and employers who determine how much wage is tagged against a particular piece of work. Marxism, as a political theory, unpacks the political and economic contradictions inherent in capitalism, where people offer their labour in return for a meagre salary that does not meet the needs for their survival because the major focus of a capitalist means of production is about maximization of profit over people's welfare. By inference, therefore, conflict theory as a way of understanding class struggle, elucidates how power is maintained by domination rather than consensus and conformity. Thus, according to conflict theory, the wealthy and the powerful try to hold on to power by any means possible, often by suppressing and subordinating the poor and powerless.

The importance of this theory from a development perspective cannot be overemphasized. According to Homes et al. (2007) and Akard (2001), the elite in society, governments, organizations and those in the decision-making position, often make decisions that affect the lives of other people. Such critical decisions are often in their favour, rather than those that are disadvantaged. Marx was deeply concerned with unseen structural power, which innocently dominates over others who, as a result of lack of knowledge, become subsumed into the global apparatus of power dynamics. Ultimately, the more the hegemonic power dynamics are at play, the more the chasm between the ruling elites and working class gets wider, thereby creating inequality, which, in today's society, is the major challenge of development. In the words of Krawford (2009: 4):

> The working class is disadvantaged by becoming attached to the external world of commodities and alienating themselves from their inner world also known as externalisation, the materialistic world of consumerism. This process advances the interests of capitalists who thereby hold a strong interest, with help from the media, in ensuring the working class are kept busy working by consuming the products of their labour.

Closer scrutiny of Marxism's exposure of capitalist operations through the exploitation of workers by elites leads us to the conclusion that global discontent, often highlighted by a growing global civil society advocating for social justice, accountability, transparency, good governance, human rights and the rule of law, is a consequence of class struggle – be it in nationalist, anti-colonial, anti-racist and feminist struggle (Makuwira, 2014; Bell, 1977).

MODERNIZATION THEORY AND AFRICA

In Africa, over the decades since modernization theory was first advanced, there has been a relentless critique of dominant theories of development (Makuwira, 2006; Matunhu, 2011; Njoh and Ayuk-Etang, 2012; Obeng-Odoom, 2013). In an African context, modernization was allegedly a matter of following in the footsteps of the former colonizers, which, by inference, was to follow a Eurocentric development model given that most of the former colonizers of the African continent were European countries. The view that the undeveloped areas of the so-called 'Third World', many of which are in Africa, is due to their being 'traditional societies', provided the impetus for the colonizers to intervene in what was seen as stagnation or lack of progress. To embrace the social, cultural and economic systems of the developed countries as a cure to such stagnation was to transform from tradition to modernity.

Africa, despite the predominance of agro-based economies, is rapidly urbanizing. The application of modernization theory in Africa, especially in the agricultural sector, has in many ways been detrimental to development. As Ellis and Biggs (2001) note, the introduction of modernist policies which were intended to raise the living standard of the poor often consisted of knowledge and information disseminating about effective and efficient techniques of agricultural production. This process of agricultural modernization has since emphasised innovation, that is, the introduction of *new techniques* of encouraging farmers to try new crops, new production methods and new marketing skills (Matunhu, 2011). It is through agricultural innovation that we have seen the introduction of hybrids, green technology, genetically modified (GMO) food, artificial fertilizers, insecticides, as well as industrial technologies like tractors to replace traditional agricultural means and practices. Reliance on these new technologies has had both positive as well as negative impacts on the economic development in many developing nations. While in some cases there have been improvements in economic outlook, overall the negatives outweigh the positives.

DEPENDENCY THEORY AND AFRICA

As outlined in Chapter 3 of this volume, dependency theory provided perhaps one of the earliest challenges to the myriad assumptions and effects of modernization thinking. As discussed, dependency theory was premised on the observation that economic growth in some of the rich countries has resulted in the impoverishment of the underdeveloped world through internationalization of capitalism, which progressively began to grow in influence and dominated world trade. There was a growing unease that modernization thinking was truly misleading, in that it failed to clarify the exact relationship between the developed world and the developing regions of the world (Frank, 1967). In other words, this distortion of the truth about the colonizer and the colonized needed to be made clear. Even the Brandt Commission of 1980 admitted that development based on the modernization approach had failed.

When applied to a continent like Africa, dependency theory, in all its manifestations, must be viewed from pessimistic and structural perspectives. To start with, from a structural perspective, dependency theory and the expansion of the Western European nations through industrial and mercantile capitalism on the one hand, and the colonization of the continent on the other, was not merely a system of exploitation but also one with the fundamental purpose to expropriate profits made in Africa back to Europe (Rodney, 1972). Matunhu (2011: 68) notes:

> From a dependency perspective repatriation of profits represents a systematic expatriation of the surplus values that was created by African labour using African resources. Hence the development of Europe can be viewed as part of the same dialectical processes that underdeveloped Africa. In other words, the domination of Europe over Africa retarded the economic development of the continent. For five running centuries, Europe capitalized on its encounter with Africa.

Matunhu's observation reflects those of earlier commentators such as Peet and Hartwick (1999), Burkey (1993) and Isbister (1991), who also note that European development was merely based on extraction through colonialism and resource control, ultimately leading to what Isbister called a 'Global Geography of European First World Centre' and 'non-European Third World Periphery', where the centre–periphery dichotomy has been used as a means of social, economic and cultural control. The unequal power relations between the developed and the underdeveloped nations have essentially led to the former being more developed and further underdeveloping the latter. The monopolistic tendencies of the developed nations today explain the rift between rich and poor countries. This state of affairs has therefore led to the current emergence of notions of 'Third World', 'developing world' and 'poor' countries, which largely depend on the developed countries for most of their development programmes.

While the modernization school saw the rich countries as having the potential to relieve the suffering of the poor nations, the dependency theorists viewed modernization as the major obstacle to the wellbeing of the poor. To date, the pro- and anti-capitalist sentiments from the two ideological standpoints also pose a significant challenge to the way in which they respond to alternative means of mitigating the challenge. One suggestion, according to Isbister (1991: 51), is to: 'fight fire with fire, to transform capitalism from the enemy of the Third World to its saviour'. In other words, the 'underdeveloped' nations should attempt to mobilize local resources in order to create local industries that challenge those from capitalist North. However, while there have been many attempts, through, for example, free trade, the skewed socio-economic status of the two worlds continues to widen. This resulted in a new wave of thinking from a development perspective.

ALTERNATIVE AND POST-DEVELOPMENT THEORIES

The mid-to-late 1990s saw a shift in development thinking with the emergence of two new development discourses and new additions to the development lexicon. 'Alternative Development' (Friedmann, 1992) and 'Alternatives to Development' (Escobar, 1995) from where 'post-development theory' emanates (see Ferguson, 1994; Rahnema and Bawtree, 1997; Crush, 1995), came to characterize the debate. Traced back to the 1960s, when one of the British economists, Dudley Seers, first posed three fundamental questions in relation to the linkage between poverty and development, 'Alternative' and 'Post-development' theories of development arose as a critique of classical development theories in the early 1990s, following the disillusionment over the perceived failure of modern development theories to bring about meaningful improvement in the conditions of living. The philosophical viewpoints of 'alternative development' and 'alternatives to development' as coined by the 'post-development' theorists have their locus in grassroots movements, urban and rural communities as well as the informal sector. These were efforts intended to address the failures of the mainstream development which, by their focus on economic growth, were at odds with people's aspirations. Alternative development theory, in particular, was concerned with the redefinition of the goals of development but not necessarily abandoning it. In addition, it was also concerned with introducing alternative practices such as empowerment, participatory and people-centred development (McGregor, 2007).

In a post-development theory from an Escobarian perspective, on the other hand, was a new wave of theoretical position against modernity (Escobar, 1995; Pieterse, 2000). It was a total rejection of development from the Western perspective. For Escobar, 'development was, and continues to be for the most part, a top-down, ethnocentric, and technocratic approach, which treated people and cultures as abstract concepts, statistical figures to be moved up and down in the charts of progress' (Escobar, 1995: 44). Therefore, for Escobar and other 'Alternative development' scholars such as Friedmann (1992), Brohman (1996) and Rahnema (1997a), post-development is a departure from the imposed development practice that disregards local knowledge. It was an ideology which, according to Rahnema (1997a: 391), 'should not be seen as an end to the search for new possibilities of change ... It should only mean that the binary, the mechanistic, the reductionist, the inhumane and the ultimately self-destructive approach to change is over.' In other words, post-development theory heralded a new era of inward-looking localization of knowledge, reflexivity, and space for grassroots engagement in search for alternatives to mainstream development practices which alienated and degraded people's knowledge and cultures. In a nutshell, these viewpoints were nested in the belief that the rural poor should actively participate in the decision-making of territorially organized communities.

Post-development thinking ensued amid frustrations by critics such as Ferguson (1990), Esteva (1992), Sachs (1992), Escobar (1995) and Apffel-Marglin (1996), who argued for a radical rethinking in ways to do development. Some even called for a complete rejection of the development paradigm. This group of theorists felt that the concept of development is obsolete and its implementation has resulted in more negative than positive consequences. McGregor (2007: 156) aptly and succinctly puts the argument into clear perspective:

> The 'post' refers to the theoretical conviction that the challenge is not so much to identify the most efficient and appropriate means to assist a country to develop but, instead, to question the very desirability and centrality of the notion of 'development' itself. In its skeletal form the common post-development argument claims that development has artificially naturalised an ideal state, modelled upon the 'developed' West, and promoted this state as universally desirable and achievable for all peoples and cultures. This vision has legitimised the rise of a development industry comprised of institutions, processes, practices, languages and knowledges which have systematically attempted to evolve 'deficient' underdeveloped nations into more desirable developed forms. ... Crucially post-development argues that it is not a matter of improving development theories or finding better technological fixes; instead it is a matter of dissolving the concept of development altogether so that alternative non-development futures can be imagined and pursued.

As a theoretical endeavour, seeking an 'alternative development' or 'alternatives to development' practice is a noble undertaking given the various theoretical perspectives canvassed in this chapter so far. To seek alternative development meant engaging in a kind of development free from market-oriented policies and a shift away from a centralized system to a more participatory and egalitarian form of approach embedded in cultural milieu. It meant a paradigm shift of development practice premised on reciprocity and social solidarity. However, this, by any definition, was, and still is, a political undertaking. Not surprisingly, the whole notion of post-development thinking came under intense criticism, not just for its focus on historical events but also for failing to contextualize the theory into practical lens. For example, critics like Ziai (2004) and Storey (2000) have noted, among other things, that the post-development school of thought failed to acknowledge the new and emerging development paradigm premised on the principles of participation, empowerment and bottom-up decision-making processes. Furthermore, not only did the theory fail to recognise the hybridization of knowledge but it also emphasized on the engagement of grassroots movement without considering on the on-going struggles experienced by these communities.

Other critics such as Pieterse (2000), Cornwall and Nyamu-Musembi (2004) and Jakimow (2008), warned that alternative development should not be romanticized or uto-pianized. They recount that, while alternative development can be created and sustained in small communities, it should not be in constant opposition to the state. In other words, while alternative development may focus on a local environment, it should not end there. There has to be continual collaboration with the state otherwise the poor may perpetually remain poor.

Another critique to post-development thinking comes from Chambers (1997), who, speaking from a poverty alleviation perspective, argues that practitioners who espouse alternative development thinking and seek to ameliorate poverty often lack proper under-standing of rural poverty because the majority of policy-makers and staff live in urban areas. He argues that, without proper knowledge, it is practically impossible to deliver alternative development interventions, except where local knowledge is tapped and inte-grated into the whole process by participation of the communities themselves. Meaningful change occurs where field experiences and theoretical knowledge are integrated to help the change agents (government or NGOs) and development workers to position their understanding of poverty and development appropriately. He warns, however, that alter-native development approaches, like participatory development, can easily be abused by development agencies. As Burkey once said, 'Without first protecting the poor people from different kinds of exploitation, everything poured in runs out' (1993: 205).

POST-COLONIAL THEORY AND DEVELOPMENT THINKING

It will be a remiss if this chapter did not engage in a brief analysis of post-colonial theory and how it has contributed to development thinking in the modern era. While post-development thinking emerged as a critical reflection on the colonizing practice – a devel-opment approach where the recipient is a passive player – alongside it emerged a new school of thought in the name of post-colonial theory. Spearheaded by such theorists as Edward Said (1978), Homi Bhabha (1994), Leela Gandhi (1998) and Frantz Fanon (1967), to name but a few, post-colonial theory has sought to inform us of the ways of deconstructing colonialism and its historical and cultural effects on its subjects – the colonized. Zein-Elabdin (2011) is of the opinion that post-colonial theory raises self-consciousness, which revolutionises the minds of the colonized and the colonizer to build a new society where liberty and equity prevail. Post-colonial theory engages both the colonizer and the colonized in the decolonization process. The post-colonial theory pro-vides a systematic way to examine how historically situated social relations have created oppression and continues to structure the social location of the oppressed people and to decide on the tangible conditions of their lives (Andreasson, 2007).

Post-colonial theory, like many other development theories and paradigms, is not immune to criticism. Of the many critics, I single out Ama Ata Aidoo (1991) whose critique of post-colonial theory I share for reasons that I will articulate later in the chapter. In one of her writings, Aidoo observes that: 'applied to Africa, India, and some other parts of the world, "postcolonial" is not only a fiction, but a most pernicious fiction, a cover-up of a dangerous period in our people's lives' (ibid.: 152). In reflecting on Aidoo's sentiments, Zein-Elabdin (2011: 215) interprets this to mean that by 'post-colonial' we seem to imply 'something finished'. But a closer scrutiny on a continent like Africa reveals that colonization has left indelible scars felt by such things as debt burden, poverty and now visible multinational piracy extractive to the core, yet those sitting on such resources continue to languish.

Looking beyond today's development practice, theoretical lenses such as post-colonial theory and others, we can only appreciate the usefulness of these ideas in helping us revisit the colonial archive where, in the words of Gandhi (1998), is a scene of 'intense discursive debate and conceptual activity, characterised by a profusion of colonised subjects'. This sentiment takes me into the second part of the chapter where I now canvass the practicalities of these theoretical positions.

LOCALISED RESPONSES TO DEVELOPMENT THEORY

In practice, development theories have been interpreted differently on the ground. Various approaches have been adopted and adapted to suit specific contexts. Some of them have worked in certain contexts while others have failed to deliver the desired effects. Not only does this attest to the fact that development is a game of trial and error, but it also affirms the fact that the application of certain theoretical propositions in different contexts may yield ambivalent results. This not only calls for a reconceptualization of new ways of looking at development, but it also calls for both development theorists and practitioners alike to rethink the popularized development practice where the so-called 'best practices' have to be carefully reconsidered.

The fundamental question that we ought to be asking is: how do we respond to the ills of poverty through development programming and practice that are often informed by Western theoretical thinking? The starting point is a reflection by the former President of South Africa, Thabo Mbeki, and one of South Africa's political activists, Steve Biko (n.d.). Mbeki echoes: 'Our society has been captured by a rapacious individualism which is corroding our social cohesion, which is repudiating the value and practice of human solidarity, and which totally rejects the fundamental precept of Ubuntu' (2007: 14). Although sharply contrasting their meaning is, however, complementary in principle, Biko (quoted in Mbeki, 2007: 16) believes that: 'In the long run, the special contribution to the world by Africa will be in the field of human relationships.'

The two sentiments from Mbeki and Biko lay the foundation for understanding the current state of development practice in an African context and beyond. While various approaches – such as assest-based community development (ABCD) (Mathie and Cunningham, 2003), basic needs (Hopkins and van der Hoeven, 1983; Farooq, 1988), rights-based approach (Hamm, 2001), freedom-based approach (Sen, 1999), people-centred (Pieterse, 1998), to name just a few – have been, and continue to be, adopted, the overarching approach to development has been from a Western-style growth and mass consumption perspective. There are two contrasting approaches that I want to tease out in order to bring the arguments above to the fore. These are 'Sector-Wide Approaches' and 'Decentralization' approaches to development.

FROM A PROJECT-BASED TO A SECTOR-WIDE APPROACH TO DEVELOPMENT

Whereas for a long time a project-based development approach was dominant in the early 1970s and 1980s, using NGOs as conduits of donor funding (Fowler, 1997; Bebbington et al., 2008), Sector-Wide Approaches (SWAPs) have become a preferred mode of development practice (Garner et al., 2000). In SWAPs, funds are pooled towards the same objectives through a consolidated investment plan. This is only done when there is a robust national development framework. The fact that SWAPs allow development stakeholders to contribute to a national development programme, instead of piecemeal project-specific development, means that the approach improves donor coordination and reduces the likelihood of overlapping and duplication of initiatives. SWAPs also enhance government uniform practices by reducing the administrative burden of dealing with a number of donors, who often apply different policies and administrative practices in the financial management. It also allows the participation of NGOs, who can be sub-contracted to implement projects under the wider programmatic arrangement (Makuwira, 2014).

While the SWAP has now been widely acknowledged as one of the best strategies for development, evidence suggests that, in most cases, it is used as an end rather than a process. Campbell (2011) observes that, while SWAPs give governments overall control, in countries like Uganda, Malawi, Tanzania, Ghana, Kenya and Cambodia, there still remain issues of: poor management of information; lack of capacity to coordinate development activities and projects; low donor buy-in; lack of gender mainstreaming; and poor timing and continuity. Where NGOs have been used as conduits of donor or government sub-contracting, the practice, to date, is marred by issues of poor coordination and often times duplication of efforts in an attempt to make themselves known. In addition, NGOs' encroachment onto the centre stage of development practice is not only an acknowledgement of their desire to contribute to the public good, but also an indication that there exists an environment in which other development actors can operate and add value to communities where governments may not be able to reach.

Text Box 18.1   Case Study: Capacity Building and Women's Empowerment: Income-Generating Initiatives

In 1999, I worked with an NGO funded by one of the major donors. The purpose was to empower women, who were perceived to be powerless, to develop skills to enable them to run small-scale businesses so that they could fend for themselves. The funding was substantial. The funding was channelled through an international NGO which, in turn,

(Continued)

(Continued)

channelled its support through an emerging NGO, whose staff had not been theoretically grounded in development issues. The approach used was, first, to extract women from their families (husbands) and train them in how to run businesses. Trained, indeed, they were. Missing from this approach was that, from an African perspective, a woman's voice is often suppressed by men. The women were given a substantial amount of money as capital for their businesses. After a while, the truth started to emerge from the trained women. Every time the women came back from the market, their husbands demanded money immediately. The empowered women, in an attempt to show their empowerment, refused to hand over the money. Families started to shake, some to the point where these ended in divorce. What was the problem? A lack of understanding the culture within which households operate. In this case, both men and women would have been the beneficiaries of such an intervention and empowerment. Not only that, the NGO failed to understand the power dynamics in a family unit, not to mention other factors such as religious beliefs where 'the two will become one', hence the extraction of 'half' of one leaves the other 'half' wondering what is going one. Power kicks in and the project failed miserably.

Decentralized Development Practice

One of the major criticisms of post-development theory, as alluded to earlier, was that it failed to consider the main agent of development – government. While there are other legitimate institutions whose legitimacy is through things, governments are the only legitimate entities whose legal contract with their citizenry is through the ballot box and, therefore, have a legal obligation to provide basic social services. Governments can be held accountable, at least in theory, if they fail to provide basic social services. For African states, especially those in the sub-Saharan region, the introduction of structural adjustment programmes in the 1980s, and their subsequent devastating effects on the African economy (see Davies and Sanders, 1988; Bond, 1998; Jones, 2011), heralded a new era of thinking on alternative measures to enhance development.

Decentralized development governance came into play, with many countries in sub-Sahara Africa adopting models under World Bank and IMF sponsorship. Premised on improving efficiency, decentralization as a model of development practice is the transfer of public authority, resources and personnel from the national to sub-national level in order to improve service delivery (Ndegwa, 2002). This model assumed a democratic development process, which was believed to organically evolve to allow ordinary people to decide what kind of development they want. However, stories emerging in countries such as Zimbabwe (Bond, 1998; Makuwira, 2014), Malawi (Chisukwa et al., 2013), South Africa (Elhiraika, 2007), Ghana (Crawford, 2009), Kenya (Boex and Kelly, 2011), Rwanda (Mukamunana and Brynard, 2005) and Uganda (Bashaasha et al., 2011; Gore and Muwanga, 2013), show that while there have been significant success stories, there remain serious issues of: weak capacity; poor accountability; limited consultation; political interference; continued central government control; fear of local people to hold the 'giants' to account; and ethnic cleavages encroaching on resources control and disparities in resources mobilization. Perhaps the only viable way to rectify this state of affairs is to build capacity from below.

CONCLUSION: RE-THEORISING DEVELOPMENT PRACTICE

Since the Second World War, the world has witnessed a tremendous enrichment in the field of development. We have seen new waves of thinking through scholarly contributions from the academy. Time and again, a critique of the ways in which development is understood now as compared to six decades ago is no secret in the Social Sciences. I want to offer my agreement with Pieterse (2001: 158), who observed: 'In a brief time span there have been profound changes in the Gestalt of development.' Not least, is the way in which globalization is shifting the development boundaries and redefining global development thinking and aid architecture (Steger, 2009). As we grapple with 'globality' and new discourses of security, so we, too, should rethink development theory. Development ideas and practices, as Obeng-Odoom (2013: 170) concurs, 'evolve and are often contested. It [development] means different things at different times'. Taking this into consideration, it is time not only to redefine development theory but also to reshape mental models of development practice. But where is the starting point?

For a long time, institutions of higher learning have remained a breeding ground for development theorists and practitioners. In the development lexicon, the emergence of development studies as a field of scholarship has been on the increase and knowledge in this field has obviously been that of Western thought. If you take it and argue how this knowledge is created and disseminated, it is not difficult to note that, in the case of a continent like Africa, Western knowledge and academy has been dominant. Yet, Africa as a continent, offers rich resources for a regeneration and reshaping the development discourse. It is my argument and conclusion that there has to be a new era of teaching, researching and learning in the academy. First, institutions of higher learning need to be 'learning institutions'. How? There should be more emphasis now for 'action-research', rather than the traditional 'extractive' research (see Chapter 12). Institutions of higher learning must promote research that 'solves' problems in communities and 'document' the lessons so that we can challenge the old theories of development. Second, our teaching needs to be informed by empirical evidence. Research and teaching are inseparable bedfellows. Case studies that challenge our students can provide a new way of teaching in institutions of higher learning. The traditional university is under strain.

In the context of Africa, there is a renewed thinking to 'humanise pedagogy' by using the '*ubunthu*' philosophy (Abdi, 2013). The humanist education is viewed as a vehicle through which Africa's renaissance into the modern world order can only be enhanced if, at the centre of (development studies) teaching and learning, lies the human; a theme to which both Biko and Mbeki have alluded to earlier. This means redefining development studies curricula to accommodate contemporary issues such as globalization, climate change, global migration, disability-inclusive development, ICT and other forms of new technologies. It requires a complete overhaul of learning in order to unlearn the way in which the traditional university has been doing things. But, like the former Vice Chancellor of Cape Peninsula University of Technology in South Africa once said, attaining change in universities is like trying to relocate a cemetery, as the 'inmates' do not cooperate.

To re-theorize development theory is to ensure that there is a link between scholarship (knowledge), practice and application of theory into practice. The international community engaged in support development interventions in places like Africa need to come down to earth and learn what takes place on the ground. This may help widen their scope of understanding of the intricacies of local contexts so that they can shape their aid policies according to the realities on the ground. This is not an easy thing to do but, in the context of this chapter, this is how we go beyond the traditional theories of development.

Questions for Discussion

1   What is meant by the term 'post-development'?
2   How might post-development critiques reshape global development agendas and practices in the twenty-first century?
3   What are the most practical ways to unlock human potential across the global South?

FURTHER READING

Friedmann, J. (1992) *Empowerment: The Politics of Alternative Development*. Cambridge: Blackwell.

Makuwira, J.J. (2006) 'Development? Freedom? Whose development and freedom?', *Development in Practice*, 16(2): 193–200.

Tanya, J. (2008) 'Answering the Critics: The Potential and Limitations of the Knowledge Agenda as a Practical Response to Post-Development Critiques', *Progress in Development Studies*, 8(4): 311–23.

REFERENCES

Abdi, A.A. (2013) 'In the Spirit of Ubuntu: Stories of Teaching and Research', *Alberta Journal of Educational Research*, 58(4): 714–716.

Aidoo, A.A. (1991) *Changes: A Love Story*. New York: The Feminist Press.

Akard, P. (2001) 'Social and Political Elites', in E.F. Borgatta and R.J.V. Montgomery (eds), *Encyclopaedia of Sociology*, Vol 4 (2nd edn). New York: Macmillan Reference USA.

Andreasson, S. (2007) 'Thinking Beyond Development: The Future of Post-Development Theory in South Africa'. Draft Paper Prepared for the British International Studies Association Annual Conference University of Cambridge, 17–19 December. Available at: www.open.ac.uk/socialsciences/bisa-africa/confpapers/Andreasson_BISA_2007.pdf (accessed 1 December 2015).

Apffel-Marglin, F. (1996) 'Introduction: Rationality and the World', in F. Apffel-Marglin and S. Apffel-Marglin (eds), *Decolonising Knowledge: From Development to Dialogue*. Oxford: Clarendon, pp. 1–39.

Bashaasha, B., Mangheni, M. and Ephraim, N. (2011) 'Decentralization and Rural Service Delivery in Uganda'. IFPRI Discussion Paper. Available at: www.ifpri.org/sites/default/files/publications/ifpridp01063.pdf (accessed 7 December 2015).

Bebbington, A.J., Hickey, S. and Mitlin, D. (2008) 'Introduction: Can NGOs Make a Difference? The Challenge of Development Alternatives', in: A.J. Bebbington, S. Hickey and D.C. Mitlin (eds), *Can NGOs Make a Difference? The Challenge of Development Alternatives*. London: Zed Books, pp. 3–37.

Bell, P.F. (1977) 'Marxist Theory, Class Struggle and the Crisis of Capitalism', in J. Schwartz (ed.), *The Subtle Anatomy of Capitalism*. Santa Monica, CA: Goodyear.

Bhabha, H. (1994) *The Location of Culture*. London: Routledge.

Boex, J. and Kelly, R. (2011) *Fiscal Decentralization in Kenya: A Small Step or Giant Leap?* Available at: www.urban.org/uploadedpdf/412332-fiscal-decentralization.pdf (accessed 10 December 2015).

Bond, P. (1998) *Uneven Zimbabwe: A Study of Finance, Development and Underdevelopment*. Trenton: Africa World Press Inc.

Brohman, J. (1996) *Popular Development: Rethinking the Theory and Practice of Development*. Oxford: Blackwell.

Burkey, S. (1993) *People First: A Guide to Self-Reliant, Participatory Rural Development*. London: Zed Books.

Campbell, J. (2011) *Sector-wide Approaches: Lessons from West Africa's Agricultural Sector*. Exeter, UK: The Innovation Centre.

Chambers, R. (1997) *Whose Reality Counts? Putting the First Last*. London: Intermediate Technology Publications.

Chisukwa, M., Chiweza, A.L. and Chikapa-Jamali, M. (2013) 'Public Participation in Local Council in Malawi in the Absence of Local Elected Representatives – Politics of Elitisms or Pluralism?', *Journal of Asian and African Studies*, 49(6): 705–20.

Cornwall, A. and Nyamu-Musembi, C. (2004) 'Putting the "Rights-Based Approach" to Development into Perspective', *Third World Quarterly*, 25(8): 1415–37.

Cowen, M. and Shenton, R. (1996) *Doctrines of Development*. London: Routledge.

Crawford, G. (2009) '"Making Democracy a Reality?" The Politics of Decentralisation and the Limits to Local Democracy in Ghana', *Journal of Contemporary African Studies*, 27(1): 57–83.

Crush, J. (1995) *Power of Development*. London: Routledge.

Davies, R. and Sanders, D. (1988) 'Adjustment Policies and the Welfare of Children: Zimbabwe, 1980–1985', in G.A. Cornia, R. Jolly and F. Stewart (eds), *Adjustment with a Human Face: Ten Country Case Studies*. Oxford: Clarendon Press, pp. 272–300.

Elhiraika, A. (2007) 'Fiscal Decentralization and Public Service Delivery in South Africa'. Available at: www.uneca.org/sites/default/files/publications/58.pdf (accessed 29 November 2015).

Ellis, F. and Biggs, S. (2001) 'Evolving Themes in Rural Development, 1950s–2000s', *Development Policy Review*, 19(4): 437–48.

Escobar, A. (1995) *Encountering Development: The Making and Unmaking of the Third World*. Princeton, NJ: Princeton University Press.

Esteva, G. (1992) 'Development', in W. Sachs (ed.), *The Development Dictionary: A Guide to Knowledge as Power.* London: Zed Books Ltd, pp. 6–25.

Fanon, F. (1967) *The Wretched of the Earth.* New York: Grove Press.

Farooq, M.O. (1988) 'Basic Needs Approach: Appropriate Technology and Institutionalism', *Journal of Economic Issues*, 22(2): 363–70.

Ferguson, J. (1990) *The Anti-Politics Machine: 'Development', Depoliticisation and Bureaucratic Power in Lesotho.* Cambridge: Cambridge University Press.

Ferguson, J. (1994) 'The Anti-Politics Machine: Development, Depoliticization, and Bureacratic Power in Lesotho', *The Ecologist*, 24(5): 176–81.

Fowler, A. (1997) *Striking a Balance: A Guide to Enhancing the Effectiveness of Non-Governmental Organisations in the International Development.* London: Earthscan Publications.

Frank, A.G. (1967) *Crisis in the Third World.* New York: Holmes and Meier.

Friedmann, J. (1992) *Empowerment: The Politics of Alternative Development.* Cambridge: Blackwell.

Gandhi, L. (1998) *Postcolonial Theory: A Critical Introduction.* Frenchs Forrest, NSW Allen and Unwin.

Garner, P., Flores, W. and Tang, S. (2000) 'Sector-Wide Approaches in Developing Countries: The Aid Given Must Make the Most Impact', *BMJ*, 321: 129–30.

Gore, C.D. and Muwanga, N.K. (2013) 'Decentralization is Dead, Long Live Decentralization! Capital City Reform and Political Rights in Kampala, Uganda', *International Journal of Urban and Regional Research*, 23(6): 2201–16.

Hamm, B. (2001) 'A Human Rights Approach to Development', *Human Rights Quarterly*, 23(4): 1005–31.

Hettne, B. (2008) *Thinking about Development.* London: Zed Books.

Homes, D., Hughes, K. and Julian, R. (2007) *Australian Sociology: A Changing Society* (2nd edn). Frenchs Forrest, NSW: Pearson Education Australia.

Hopkins, M. and van der Hoeven, R. (1983) *Basic Needs in Development Planning.* Aldershot: Gower.

Isbister, J. (1991) *Promises Never Kept: The Betrayal of Social Change in the Third World.* West Hartford: Kumarian Press.

Jakimow, T. (2008) 'Answering the Critics: The Potential and Limitations of the Knowledge Agenda as a Practical Response to Post-Development Critiques', *Progress in Development Studies*, 8(4): 311–23.

Jones, T. (2011) *Uncovering Zimbabwe's Debt: The Case for a Democratic Solution to the Unjust Debt Burden.* London: Zimbabwe Debt Network, Eurodad and Jubille Debt Campaign. Available at: www.jubileedebtcampaign.org.uk/zimbabwereport (accessed 1 December 2015).

Krawford, K. (2009) *Power in Society – Marx Conflict Perspective and Elite Theory Social Analysis.* Available at: www.academia.edu/2365041/Marx_and_Conflict_Theory_-_Analysis_of_Power_in_Society (accessed 29 November 2015).

Leys, C. (1996) *The Rise and Fall of Development Theory.* EAEP-Bloomington, IN: Indiana University Press.

Makuwira, J.J. (2006) 'Development? Freedom? Whose development and freedom?', *Development in Practice*, 16(2): 193–200.

Makuwira, J.J. (2014) 'People-Centred Development', in M. Steger, P. Battersby and J. Siracusa (eds), *The SAGE Handbook of Globalization, Vol. 1.* Thousand Oaks, CA: Sage, pp. 902–18.

Marx, K. and Engels, F. (1965/1848) *The Communist Manifesto* (S. Moore, trans. and J. Katz, ed.). New York: Washington Square Press (original work published 1848).

Mathie, A. and Cunningham, G. (2003) 'From Clients to Citizens: Asset-Based Community Development as a Strategy for Community-Driven Development', *Development in Practice*, 13(5): 474–86.

Matunhu, J. (2011) 'A Critique of Modernisation and Dependency Theories in Africa: A Critical Assessment', *African Journal of History and Culture*, 3(5): 65–72.

Mbeki, T. (2007) 'Steve Biko Memorial Lecture', Cape Town, 12 September. Available at: www.polity.org.za/attachment.php?aa_id=7218 (accessed 4 December 2015).

McGregor, A. (2007) 'Development, Foreign Aid and Post-Development in Timor-Leste', *Third World Quarterly*, 28(1): 55–170.

Mukamunana, R. and Brynard, P.A.P. (2005) *The Role of Civil Society Organisations in Policy Making Process in Rwanda.* Available at: http://repository.up.ac.za/handle/2263/3911) (accessed 9 December 2015).

Ndegwa, S. (2002) *Decentralization in Africa: A Stocktaking Survey.* Available at: www.worldbank.org/afr/wps/wp40.pdf (accessed 3 December 2015).

Nisbet, R.A. (1969) *Social Change and History: Aspects of the Western Theory of Development.* London and New York: Oxford University Press.

Njoh, A.J. and Ayuk-Etang, E.N.M. (2012) 'Combating Forced Labour and Human Trafficking in Africa: The Role of Endogenous and Exogenous Forces', *African Review of Economics and Finance*, 4(1): 30–52.

Obeng-Odoom, F. (2013) 'Africa's Failed Development Trajectory: A Critique', *African Review of Economics and Finance*, 4(2): 151–75.

Peet, R. and Hartwick, E. (1999) *Theories of Development.* New York: The Guilford Press.

Pieterse, J.N. (1998) 'My Paradigm or Yours? Alternative Development, Post-Development, Reflexive Development', *Development and Change*, 29: 343–73.

Pieterse, J.N. (2000) 'After Post-Development', *Third World Quarterly*, 21(2): 175–91.

Pieterse, J.N. (2001) 'Hybridity, So What?: The Anti-Hybridity Backlash and the Riddles of Recognition', *Theory, Culture and Society*, 18(2–3): 219–45.

Rahnema, M. (1997a) 'Introduction', in M. Rahnema and V. Bawtree (eds), *The Post-Development Reader.* London: Zed Books, pp. ix–xix.

Rahnema, M. (1997b) 'Development and the People's Immune System: The Story of another Variety of AIDS', in M. Rahnema and V. Bawtree (eds), *The Post-Development Reader.* London: Zed Books, pp. 111–129.

Rahnema, M. and Bawtree, V. (eds) (1997) *The Post-Development Reader.* London: Zed Books.

Rist, G. (2008) *The History of Development: From Western Origins to Global Faith* (3rd edn; trans. Patrick Camiller). London: Zed Books.

Rodney, W. (1972) *How Europe Underdeveloped Africa.* Dar es Salaam: Tanzanian Publishing House.

Sachs, W. (ed.) (1992) *The Development Dictionary: A Guide to Knowledge as Power.* London: Zed Books.

Said, E.W. (1978) *Orientalism.* New York: Random House.

Seers, D. (1969) 'The Meaning of Development', *IDS Communication* No. 44. Available at: https://www.ids.ac.uk/files/dmfile/themeaningofdevelopment.pdf (accessed 4 December 2015).

Sen, A. (1999) *Development as Freedom.* Oxford: Oxford University Press.

Steger, M.B. (2009) 'Globalisation and Social Imaginaries: The Changing Ideological Landscape of the Twenty-First Century', *Journal of Critical Globalisation Studies*, 1(1): 9–30.

Storey, A. (2000) 'Post-Development Theory: Romanticism and Pontius Pilate Politics', *Development*, 43(4): 40–6.

Willis, K. (2011) *Theories and Practices of Development*, 2nd edn. New York: Routledge.

Zein-Elabdin, E.O. (2011) 'Postcoloniality and Development: Development as a Colonial Discourse', in L. Keita (ed.), *Philosophy and African Development: Theory and Practice.* Dakar: Codesria, pp. 215–30.

Ziai, A. (2004) 'The Ambivalence of Post-Development: Between Reactionary Populism and Radical Democracy', *Third World Quarterly*, 25(6): 1045–160.

INDEX